Behavior Modification

An Introductory Textbook

Behavior Modification
An Introductory Textbook

Alan S. Bellack, Ph.D.
Department of Psychology
University of Pittsburgh

Michel Hersen, Ph.D.
Western Psychiatric Institute
  & Clinic
University of Pittsburgh
School of Medicine

The Williams & Wilkins Company
Baltimore

Library of Congress Cataloging in Publication Data

Bellack, Alan S
  Behavior modification.

    Bibliography: p.
    Includes index.
    1. Behavior modification. I. Hersen, Michel, joint author. II. Title.
BF637.B4B47   153.8'5   76-48942
ISBN 0-683-00513-8

Composed and printed at the
Waverly Press, Inc.
Mt. Royal and Guilford Aves.
Baltimore, Md. 21202, U.S.A.

DEDICATION

To

Barbara and Jonathan
and
Lynn and Jonathan

Preface

One of the most gratifying aspects of working on this book was the knowledge that there were both undergraduate and graduate courses for which it would be applicable. When we were in graduate school (early to mid 1960s through 1970), only a limited number of informal seminars represented our exposure to behavior modification. Our behavioral education came primarily from reading scholarly journals and several professional-level books and by simple trial-and-error of practice. However, the development of behavior modification in the last few years has been meteoric and has been accompanied by a parallel increase in popularity. Presently, formalized training, even at the undergraduate level, is now widely available. As the number of interested students and courses have increased, the need for a comprehensive introductory text has become manifest. We hope that the present volume will fulfill this need.

Our focus throughout the book has been two-fold. *First,* we have attempted to provide an up-to-date survey of behavior modification. Although coverage is not exhaustive, we have attempted to present a review of the current state of the field that is balanced in breadth, depth, and clarity. *Second,* we have tried to provide a picture of the way behavior modifiers conceptualize what they do. Thus, the emphasis is on a critical presentation, amplified by the empirical approach synonomous with behavior modification. It is our expectation that by describing clinical techniques in the context of specific research, the student will develop an appreciation for how and why behavior modification developed such an effective technology in such a relatively brief period of time, as well as the directions it might take in the future.

The book is organized around intervention strategies, rather than around specific disorders. This approach should offer the student a clear grasp of the theoretical and empirical issues pertinent to each of the techniques. While each chapter contains a description of how the various techniques are applied, this is not intended to be a "how-to-do-it" manual. Numerous such manuals are currently available to the student with specific interests. On the other hand, we have given considerable attention to the ethical and legal issues which must be considered when employing each of the techniques.

We have assumed that courses in abnormal psychology and learning would be prerequisites for students using this text. Some background in experimental psychology and statistics might also be helpful, but not necessary. With respect to format, we have employed an incremental learning strategy in organizing material within and across chapters. Chapter 1 presents basic concepts and definitions as well as a description of behavioral assessment strategies and single subject research methodology. These issues are essential for adequate understanding of clinical and research data presented in subsequent chapters. The remaining chapters may be read in one of two sequences. We recommend that Chapters 2–5 and Chapters 6–10, respectively, be read in order, as the later chapters in each section frequently refer back to earlier chapters for amplification of basic concepts.

In terms of the writing, at times we have attempted to avoid a sexist orientation by using "his/her." In other places, for the sake of readability we have succumbed to the sexist "his." Also, throughout the book we have used the terms "client" and "patient" interchangeably.

Finally, we would like to express our appreciation to a number of individuals for their contributions to our work. First and foremost are our accommodating wives. Second, we thank Joseph Matarazzo for his illuminating commentary. Third, we appreciate Mary Newell's secretarial skill and efforts and good humor throughout this project. Fourth, we thank our past and present students, whose probing questions forced us to clarify our thinking. And last but hardly least of all, we extend our appreciation to Leonard Pace and his colleagues at Williams & Wilkins who so cooperatively smoothed the way.

We also wish to thank the following for permitting us to reprint tables and figures from their publications: *American Journal of Psychiatry, Archives of General Psychiatry, Behavior Therapy, Behaviour Research and Therapy, British Journal of Psychiatry, Journal of Abnormal Psychology, Journal of Applied Behavior Analysis, Journal of Behavior Therapy and Experimental Psychiatry, Journal of Consulting and Clinical Psychology, Journal of the Experiimental Analysis of Behavior, Journal of Nervous and Mental Disease, Journal of Personality and Social Psychology, Psychological Record, Psychological Reports, and Psychotherapy: Theory, Research and Practice.*

Alan S. Bellack   *Pittsburgh, Pennsylvania*
Michel Hersen

Contents

6 Operant Approaches with Children

7 Aversive Techniques

8 Token Economic Techniques for Psychiatric Patients

9 Other Operant Techniques

10 Comprehensive Approaches

1

Basic concepts in behavior modification

Introduction*

Behavior modification or behavior therapy represents both a specific model of behavior and a group of behavior change (treatment) techniques. The behavior therapist not only applies different treatment techniques than his non-behavioral colleagues, but views his clients from a different perspective (the "behavioral" model). The "behavioral" model involves an explanation of how and why clients behave the way they do. In addition, it presents a specific view on the focus of treatment (i.e., what should be treated) and a determination of how treatment should be carried out. The rationale for the development and application of specific treatment techniques is intimately related to the behavior therapist's conception of human behavior. Therefore, behavioral treatment cannot be properly understood without a preliminary grasp of the underlying behavioral model. The purpose of this chapter, then, is to introduce the major concepts that characterize the behavioral point of view.

First, we will briefly discuss what the terms behavior modification and behavior therapy mean. Then, we will describe the behavioral model and contrast it to the traditional psychodynamic or personality

---

* Throughout this book the terms client and patient will be used interchangeably.

model. The final two sections of the chapter will be devoted to two issues that are central to the behavioral model: data collection and research methodology.

What is Behavior Modification?

The terms behavior modification and behavior therapy have become fairly common additions to the English language, appearing frequently in the popular media as well as in behavioral science and mental health circles. Despite their relatively frequent appearance, there is a considerable amount of popular confusion about what the terms actually refer to, and their use is often accompanied by a negative emotional reaction. While there is less confusion and emotionality among adherents of the behavioral viewpoint, there still is some disagreement about what the terms should represent. Some writers (e.g., Hersen, Eisler, & Miller, 1975) have pointed out that all mental health workers who attempt to alter behavior are, in essence, behavior modifiers (i.e., do behavior modification). In this context, the term *behavior therapy* is reserved for those behavior modifiers whose theoretical orientation is "behavioral" and who use a specific set of treatment techniques based on a behavioral model. However, the broad usage of "behavior modification" is frequently rejected by non-behaviorists, who generally believe the word "behavior" has a narrow meaning and "undervalues" their efforts. As a result, behavior modification and behavior therapy are generally used synonomously to refer to the model and the techniques. For example, there is one behavioral journal entitled *Behavior Therapy* and still another entitled *Behavior Modification*.

There are several related terms (e.g., applied behavior analysis, contingency management, behavioral engineering, and stimulus control) that frequently are used by behavior modifiers. While there are some (subtle) differences in the meaning of these terms, they all refer to behavior modification techniques which emphasize operant conditioning principles. Thus, they are more specific and can be subsumed under the synonomous terms behavior modification and behavior therapy.

What exactly is "behavioral modification?" Before answering this question we must briefly consider the history of the approach (the interested student is referred to Franks, 1969; Hersen et al., 1975; and Yates, 1970, for more extended discussion of the historical development of behavior modification). The elements of behavioral strategies (e.g., reinforcement, punishment) have been known and practiced throughout the recorded history of man. However, it was only in the twentieth century that modern behaviorism began to systematically examine human behavior in this context. It is clear that work of Pavlov, Watson, Hull, and Skinner began to demarcate the nature and importance of learning principles. Despite periodic demonstrations of the relevance of this work to human behavior and its modification (e.g., Watson & Rayner, 1920), such principles were relatively ignored outside of the laboratory until the late 1950s and early 1960s. Throughout that period the predominant conception of human behavior (especially maladaptive behavior) was psychoanalytic. Supported more by religious fervor than empirical evidence, the analytic position was not easily challenged by data. Therefore, the "early" behavior modifiers adopted a somewhat extreme philosophical-political position in order to challenge the predominant psychoanalytic establishment. The basis for this position was "presumed" scientifically-based learning theory. Behavior modification was promoted as a "hard-headed" scientific approach to behavior change, based on and supported by an empirically validated theory of human learning.

Early definitions reflected this position. Eysenck (1960) published one of the first and most influential books on behavior therapy in which he referred to it as, " . . . a large group of methods of treatment, all of which owe their existence and their theoretical justification to modern learning theory: they thus derive from Pavlov, Watson, and Hull, rather than from Freud, Jung, and Adler. It will be argued that behavior therapy is an *alternative* type of treatment to psychotherapy; that it is a superior type of treatment, both from the point of view of theoretical background and practical effectiveness; and that, in so far as psychotherapy is at all effective, it is so in virtue of certain principles which can be derived from learning theory" (p. ix). As can be seen, the primary identifying features of behavior therapy were its explicit theoretical basis and its conflict with psychodynamic theory. One of the implications subsumed under this definition was a repudiation of the "medical model" and its presumption of underlying, mentalistic causes of behavior. (This will be discussed further below.) In fact, all reference to mental or cognitive activity was initially rejected.

During the following decade, as more experience and data were gathered with the behavioral approach, it became apparent that this early perspective was somewhat simplistic and overly restrictive. The laboratory-based learning theories of the 1940s could not be directly translated to human behavior (in fact, they are no longer presumed to adequately account for animal behavior). The need to account for cognitive activity also became apparent. Franks (1969) offered the following definition: " . . . the beneficial modification of behavior in accordance with experimentally validated principles based upon S-R concepts of learning and the biophysical properties of the organism" (p. 2). However, Franks qualified this definition with a set of corollaries which took into account much of the broadened perspective. He emphasized that no *particular* learning theory was specified and that not all behavior therapists limited themselves to S-R theories. He also pointed out that much of our current knowledge of learning is based simply on a few principles that lead to accurate predictions and that there is no current inclusive *theory* that has been validated. (The term "theory" has special meaning for science, presuming a degree of order and validation well beyond what is available to psychology or the study of behavior.) This means that we must remain somewhat cautious in the claims we make for the basis of our activities (especially in regard to critiques of other viewpoints). He included cognitions in his definition of behavior. Next, he recognized that while most behavior is learned, we must take genetic and biochemical factors into account. Finally, he stressed the importance of empiricism in the development of treatment techniques, stating: " . . . for most behavior therapists, the preferred sequence of events is from experimental observation to clinical practice" (p. 2).

The practice of behavior therapy was seen as a scientific endeavor rather than as an art or subtle interpersonal process (which is the predominant characterization of verbal psychotherapy). An overriding feature of Franks' position, therefore, is the importance of having a theoretical basis (specifically a learning theory) for behavior modification. " . . . it would seem to be highly desirable for the therapist to aspire to be a scientist even if this were difficult to realize. To function as a scientist it is necessary to espouse some theoretical framework" (Franks, 1969, p. 21).

The above viewpoint is not shared by all behavior modifiers. Lazarus (1971) and London (1972) have argued that behavior modification is (or should be) primarily a technological rather than a scientific discipline. The behavior modifier is viewed as being more like an engineer than a physicist, or like a physician rather than a biochemist (i.e., a practitioner rather than a theoretician). Lazarus and London argue that development of an allegiance to *any* theoretical system is secondary to the development and application of effective clinical techniques. Lazarus (1971) suggests that behavior modifiers should adopt any effective treatment from any source, even if it is not specifically "behavioral." He refers to this position as "technical eclecticism," which " . . . does not imply a random mélange of techniques taken haphazardly out of the air. It is an approach which urges therapists to experiment with empirically useful methods instead of using their theories as a priori predictors of what will and will not succeed in therapy" (p. xii). Thus, Franks (1969) suggests that we proceed from the laboratory (and our theoretical system) to the clinic, while Lazarus (1971) suggests that we can experiment with clinical techniques first. If they are effective, they should be returned to the laboratory for critical analysis to see why they work.

The difference between these two orientations (scientist versus technician) is more than semantic. Adoption of either view has implications for how behavior modifiers view their activity (theoretical-experimental versus clinical-practical), how and why they select treatment techniques (based on theoretical principles versus strictly pragmatic), and how they are trained (with emphasis on research skills or clinical skills). However, rather than posing a critical correct-incorrect choice, these two positions represent the growth of behavior modification in terms of effectiveness, numbers of adherents, and sophistication. One would not consider developing a technology if there were not an array of effective techniques and sufficient individuals to apply them. London (1972) has suggested that behavior modification used learning theory as a "battle flag" in pursuing a war with psychoanalysis. Now that the war has essentially been won, behavior modifiers can "drop the flag." However, the learning theory position that was adopted involved a model of behavior and how it should be studied in addition to being a theory of learning. It is this model (which will be discussed further below) rather than the theory which is central to a behavioral position. Both the science and technology models of behavior modification can be subsumed under a single broader framework: behavior modification as a viewpoint or a perspective for conceptualizing behavior and behavior change (Kanfer & Phillips, 1970; Yates, 1975). This orientation is well represented by the definition currently accepted (tentatively) by the Association for Advancement of Behavior Therapy (Franks & Wilson, 1975):

> "Behavior therapy involves primarily the application of principles derived from research in experimental and social psychology for the alleviation of human suffering and the enhancement of human functioning. Behavior therapy emphasizes a systematic evaluation of the effectiveness of these applications. Behavior therapy involves environmental change and social interaction rather than the direct alteration of bodily processes by biological procedures. The aim is primarily educational. The techniques facilitate improved self-control. In the conduct of behavior therapy, a contractual agreement is usually negotiated in which mutually agreeable goals and procedures are specified. Responsible practitioners using behavioral approaches are guided by generally accepted ethical principles." (pp. 1–2)

This definition emphasizes the applied focus of behavior therapy, but implies that it is more than a technology. It makes no reference to any specific (e.g., S-R) learning theory. There are a number of assumptions common to most behavior therapists, several of which are included in this definition (e.g., behavior therapy is empirical, ethical, and educational). We will consider those assumptions in the next section.

The Behavioral Model

As stated previously, it is our contention that the distinguishing feature of behavior modification is a particular conception of human functioning and how it should be studied and modified. We refer to this general conception simply as a behavioral model. Although there are some specific variants such as an operant model (e.g., Baer, Wolf, & Risley, 1968; Skinner, 1972), or a social learning model (e.g., Bandura, 1969; Mischel, 1973) in which particular theoretical positions are emphasized, there are atheoretical aspects of the general model that are relatively universal. The currently most accepted model in the mental health field is in rather sharp contrast to the behavioral model. The discussion below will, therefore, emphasize fundamental differences between these viewpoints while highlighting the basic premises of the behavioral model.

What Is Behavior?

Before considering models, it is necessary to specify the subject matter: behavior. Surprisingly, there is not much agreement between behavioral and non-behavioral views about what are the critical issues for study. The behavioral model identifies behavior in terms of responses or what the organism does (Franks, 1969). There are three categories or modalities in which responses occur: motoric, physiological, and cognitive. *Motoric* responses consist of the motor acts to which the word "behavior" usually applies: walking, eating, writing, hitting, etc. The *physiological* responses of most interest are changes in the autonomic nervous system such as heart rate, respiration rate, blood pressure and flow, and electrical activity of the skin such as GSR. (See Chapter 2, for more detailed discussion.) Recent interest has also been devoted to muscle tension (especially forehead muscles, which are involved in headaches) which is under central nervous system control. The most difficult responses to describe are *cognitive* (i.e., those events that occur privately inside the individual's head). The major form of cognitive response involves imagery: the visual, auditory, and olfactory products we form when thinking (or dreaming).

Non-behavioral theorists (e.g., Wachtel, 1973) have generally criticized this conception of behavior as being too narrow and thereby missing "more important" aspects of functioning such as emotion, self-actualization, and unconscious processes. This difference in the definition of behavior represents a basic contrast between models. The behavioral position, based on the learning theory tradition, has emphasized two methodological criteria: (1) objectivity of observations; and (2) operational definitions of concepts (definition in terms of the measurement device; for example temperature is the height of a column of mercury). The objectivity criterion implies that no observation can be presumed valid unless it can be verified independently by two (or more) observers. This is easy to see in terms of motor acts, in which two observers might independently agree about whether or not an individual walked. Physiological responses cannot be observed directly, but they can be operationally defined in terms of the deflection of a polygraph pen, which two observers can score independently. The issue is much more complicated in the case of cognitions, where there can only be one observer: the individual making the response. However, the existence of cognitive responses cannot be denied or ignored simply because they are difficult to measure. Frequently, they can be identified semi-operationally in terms of their consequences. For example, if a male subject is instructed to imagine himself engaging in sexual activity and a polygraph record indicates a significant increase in penile blood flow (as occurs during erection), it can be assumed that the subject's report of having a clear image is accurate.

Most non-behavioral approaches have not required either objectivity or operationalism in specifying and assessing major concepts. The emphasis has been on self-report (introspection) and therapist (or assessor) inference about *hypothetical constructs*. These are variables which are presumed to affect or account for behavior. For the most part they are not responses, but processes which are not directly visible or measurable. Consequently, their existence and operation are characteristically postulated on a theoretical basis rather than by direct observation. Examples include feelings, self-concept, needs, and the unconscious. An extended discussion of this issue is beyond the scope of this volume; the interested reader is referred to Cronbach and Meehl (1955) and Skinner (1972). Nevertheless, it can be specified that behaviorists have generally -avoided the use of such hypothetical variables for two primary reasons: (1) They are viewed as circular pseudoexplanations (i.e., descriptions) which are offered retrospectively. For example, after observing a child who gets into numerous fights, one might hypothesize that he fights because he is *aggressive* or has an aggressive drive. How do you know he is aggressive? Because he fights a lot! When does he fight? When he feels aggressive. As can be seen in this example, the circularity and post-hoc nature of the explanation makes it impossible to disprove or invalidate such a construct. (2) Hypothetical constructs have not had heuristic value (i.e., utility). That is, they have not allowed for either the prediction or control of behavior (two hallmarks of an acceptable theoretical position).

Behaviorists have occasionally attempted to redefine some of these constructs in objective, operational terms. For example, feelings can be broken down into self-report statements and autonomic changes. Self-concept can be defined in terms of a score on a self-report inventory or the rate of positive self-statements during an interview. However, such translations are rarely satisfactory. If the hypothetical variable is not useful, there is little rationale for redefining it, even if the new definition is objective. For example, it will rarely be important to alter a person's responses to a self-report inventory, and if his rate of positive self-statements is a problem, calling it self-concept will not make behavior change easier. In addition, non-behaviorists characteristically argue that the "meaning" of their concepts is lost in the process of objectification. It seems premature to reject any possible role for hypothetical constructs. However, until the utility of such concepts is demonstrated it seems advisable to avoid such inferential processes. (See Chapter 4 for further discussion of this issue.)

What Are the Determinants of Behavior?

In observing the behavior of other people there are two *apparent* factors which quickly become obvious: (1) People can be differentiated from one another on the basis of their behavior; some people seem to be outgoing and pleasant; others, reticent and cool; some, aggressive; and still others, meek, etc. This is interindividual variability. (2) People appear to behave in a fairly recognizable manner over time; they appear to be consistent (ergo labeling statements such as, "He is shy. She is aggressive."). This is intraindividual consistency. In an attempt to explain these two (apparent) factors, the most superficially logical and most frequently reached conclusion has been that each individual possesses a unique, stable internal system: the personality.

This *personality model* of behavior has taken many forms: psychodynamic theory, trait and need theories, humanistic and growth theories, etc. These approaches differ in their conception of how the personality is formed, what elements it contains, and the directions in which it steers behavior. However, they are all similar in that they presume that behavior is an external manifestation of inner processes; behavior is caused or determined by the personality structure or system. In psychoanalytic theory, the primary determinants are unconscious conflicts and the drive for tension reduction. For humanistic theorists, the major factors are the self-system and the drive for self-actualization. Major conceptual interest (e.g., theory construction), efforts to understand behavior (e.g., assessment), and attempts to change behavior (e.g., therapy) are all directed to these stable internal processes rather than behavior itself.

Despite the fact that the personality model has predominated, it has not been validated (in any of its variants) and has had limited heuristic value (see Mischel, 1973). It should be specified first that the "personality" is not considered to be an actual physical structure (or homunculus), even by personality theorists. Rather, it is a hypothetical construct and suffers from the difficulties of all such concepts. Personality systems are much more effective at describing behavior and explaining responses after their occurrence than they are in predicting behavior or controlling it (by leading to the development of effective treatment techniques). As with all hypothetical constructs, it has been argued that the concept is valid but that current variants, assessment devices, research methodology, etc. have not provided an adequate test. However, it is incumbent upon scientists to demonstrate the validity of their constructs, not for the scientific community to demonstrate their invalidity.

The primary failing of the personality model does not stem from its hypothetical basis, but from the fundamental premises on which it is based: intraindividual consistency and internal causality or control of behavior. *First,* behavior is simply not highly consistent over time and across situations (Mischel, 1968, 1973). People behave in very different ways as a function of situational factors such as where they are, whom they are with, and what people around them are doing. For example, Eisler, Hersen, Miller, and Blanchard (1975) found psychiatric patients to be differentially assertive in positive and negative contexts, with males and females, and with familiar people versus strangers. Walker, Hops, and Johnson (1975) reported that children exhibiting maladaptive behavior in school did not necessarily exhibit such behavior problems at home and vice versa. (Numerous other examples will be reported throughout the book.) Much of the presumed consistency is the result of overgeneralization based on two major factors: (1) stability of physical attributes: we look the same, use the same voice inflection, etc.; and (2) the use of broad descriptive labels such as: aggressive, assertive, neurotic, phobic, etc.

Labeling is a common phenomenon as it simplifies communication and analysis by allowing for gross categorization. However, this process is dangerous because labeling facilitates generalization and reduces the likelihood of accurate perception and discrimination. This was clearly demonstrated in a study by Langer and Abelson (1974). They recruited groups of behaviorally oriented and psychodynamically oriented clinicians and showed them a videotape of a job interview. One-half of each group was told that the individual being interviewed was a "job applicant," and one-half was told that he was a "patient." After viewing the interview, the clinicians were requested to evaluate the level of adjustment of the person who was interviewed. The results are portrayed in Table 1.1. The data represent the mean of the adjustment ratings reported by each group. Adjustment was rated on a 10-point scale (1 = very disturbed; 10 = very well-adjusted). The labels had a clear effect on the psychodynamic clinicians, for whom labeling is a characteristic approach. They rated the interviewee as less well-adjusted when the "patient" label was applied. In contrast, there was little difference in the two ratings made by the behavioral clinicians, for whom assessment emphasizes description of behavior rather than labeling.

This argument should not be taken to mean that there is *no* consistency of behavior, simply that the amount of consistency has been vastly overestimated. The next issue, then, pertains to the reasons for the consistency that does occur, and identification of the determinants of behavior in general: whether consistent or not. One major factor men-

TABLE 1.1

Mean Adjustment Rating by Interviewee Label and Clinician Group[a]

Clinical Group	Interviewee Label	
	Job applicant	Patient
Behavior therapist		
Stony Brook	6.26	5.98
n	10	11
Traditional		
Yale	6.52	4.80
n	5	4
NYU	5.88	2.40
n	5	5

[a] From: Langer and Abelson (1974) (Table 1).

tioned previously is the physical stability of the organism. We have certain physical attributes, skills, and skill deficits which restrict the range of our behavior. If someone can only speak English today, he will not be speaking Russian tomorrow. This linguistic consistency does not result from an unconscious "drive" to speak English, but from a skill limitation. Similarly, if the only manner in which an individual knows how to express annoyance is physical aggression, he will have numerous fights; this does not imply an unconscious aggressive drive.

By far the most common cause of behavioral consistency is consistency of the stimulus situation; people are likely to behave in a similar manner in similar situations. This conclusion follows from perhaps the most fundamental behavioral concept: *behavior is under stimulus control*. This principle specifies that the primary determinant of behavior is the stimulus configuration in which it occurs, rather than any internal psychological process. This includes the controlling effects of both antecedent stimuli (those which precede a response) and consequent stimuli (those which follow a response). The primary forms of antecedent controlling stimuli consist of the UCS (unconditioned stimulus) and CS (conditioned stimulus) in the classical conditioning paradigm:

$$UCS \dashrightarrow UCR$$

$$CS \dashrightarrow UCS \dashrightarrow UCR$$
$$\searrow CR$$

and the discriminative stimulus (S^D) in the operant conditioning paradigm:

$$S^D \dashrightarrow R \dashrightarrow S^R$$

(the discriminative stimulus leads to a response [R] which is followed by reinforcement [S^R]). The primary consequent stimuli are reinforcers (S^R)

in the operant paradigm. This aspect of stimulus control is characteristically referred to as the *Law of Effect*: a response followed by a positive consequence will tend to recur with increased frequency, and a response followed by no consequence or an aversive consequence will tend to recur with decreased frequency.

The emphasis on stimulus control does not eliminate the contribution of the individual in affecting the course of behavior. Proprioceptive cues (e.g., feedback from physiological systems such as occurs with muscle fatigue) and cognitions (thoughts, imagery) serve as powerful stimuli to control behavior. The adequacy of performance is partially evaluated on the basis of internalized criteria (e.g., is a grade of B satisfactory for a particular course?), and such self-evaluations serve as filters for external stimuli and affect their impact; the same B grade can result in jubilation for one student while another experiences distress over failure to achieve an A (Bandura, 1976; Kanfer, 1976). Problem solving skills reduce the complexity of conflicting or ambiguous stimuli and maximize the likelihood of reinforcement (Goldfried & Goldfried, 1975). Similarly, we can structure the environment so as to alter the stimuli which impinge upon us, as when a dieter avoids purchasing candy (see the discussion of self-control in Chapter 4). "Contrary to the mechanistic metaphors – in which reinforcers supposedly alter conduct automatically and unconsciously – people are not much affected by response consequences if they are unaware of what is being reinforced. When they know what they are being reinforced for, they may respond in accommodating or oppositional ways depending upon how they value the incentives, the influencers, and the behavior itself, and how others respond. Thus, reinforcers serve mainly as incentive motivators rather than as mechanical or insidious controllers of conduct. Consequences alter behavior through the intervening influence of thoughts and valuations" (Bandura, 1974). Despite the acknowledged role of the individual in influencing the course of his behavior, this conceptualization of internal input is quite different from the abstract, dynamic forces postulated by the personality model. The behavioral model emphasizes explicit operations and observable effects with a minimum of hypothetical elaboration.

The stimulus control model represents a major departure from traditional psychological theorizing. As will be discussed below, it has important implications for the manner in which maladaptive behavior is conceptualized as well as for how assessment and treatment are conducted. Validity of the model can be determined by examination of the two major predictions to which it leads: (1) behavior can be *predicted* more accurately by knowledge of the context or situation and the individual's response repertoire (what he is capable of doing) than by knowledge or inference about any internal psychological processes (e.g., personality); and (2) behavior can be *modified* more effectively by altering antecedent and consequent stimuli than by focusing on internal processes. Most of the material in the remaining chapters in this book (i.e., most of the behavior modification literature) provides validational support for these two predictons and, therefore, for the stimulus control model.

Presentation of this approach to behavior generally elicits several questions:

1. Does this mean there is no such thing as personality?
   Yes. Personality is not a real thing, but a hypothetical concept which involves inference and overgeneralization. While it facilitates communication by avoiding details, it is not necessarily a scientifically heuristic (i.e., helpful, useful) variable and can result in distorted perceptions (e.g., Langer & Abelson, 1974).
2. What about the unconscious?
   We are not aware of all cognitive activity, and in that sense there are unconscious processes. However, like "personality," conceptualizing an active system or critical effect from such activity is an as yet unverified inference.
3. What about self-control?
   Conceptions of independent self-systems, including self-determination and self-actualization, are similarly unvalidated inferences. We *do* have the capacity for self-observation, which provides the illusion of self-determination. However, as discussed in Chapter 4, we control our own behavior indirectly by structuring the stimulus situation (e.g., by self-reinforcement), not by an unspecified "free will."

Conception of Psychopathology

The traditional (i.e., personality model) approach to psychopathology has been the "medical model," or more specifically the "disease model" (London, 1972). Maladaptive functioning is likened to an infectious disease process in which there is an internal disruption (e.g., a viral infection) which is manifested externally by a symptom (e.g., coughing, a fever). Maladaptive behavior, such as intense fear or passivity, is thereby presumed to be merely a symptom or sign of some underlying disturbance or disease process in the personality. For psychoanalytic theory the disease consists of unconscious conflicts based on fixations; in client-centered theory it is incongruence and lack of self-acceptance. The external manifestations are considered to be of secondary importance to the underlying disturbance (the implications of this model for assessment and treatment will be discussed below).

As a function of this model, the major approach to classification or diagnosis has been the etiological (causative) model developed by Kraepelin. This system is based on, " . . . the assumption that common etiological factors lead to similar symptoms and respond to similar treatment" (Kanfer & Saslow, 1969, p. 422). Thus, if a patient exhibiting hallucinations and bizarre gestures is diagnosed as a schizophrenic, it is implied that the underlying disease process *causing* those behaviors has been identified.

The "disease model" is an extension of the personality model and is an as yet unvalidated hypothetical approach. The purpose of diagnosis is to identify appropriate treatment techniques and predict the course of the disease (and its response to treatment). The medical model has not been especially useful in this capacity and, in addition, the labeling process has frequently led to abuse: "Once a person has been designated as being of a certain category, all the features of a person belonging to that category are ascribed to him. A person no longer is said to manifest those specific behaviors which led to his being placed in a category, for example, inappropriate affect or anxiety; he is called a schizophrenic or a neurotic and is responded to as such. He is treated as an abstraction rather than an individual" (Ullmann, 1969, p. 498).

Behavior modification has characteristically avoided classification in favor of identification and description of maladaptive behaviors. Just as there is presumed to be no underlying personality system, there is presumed to be no disease process underlying most behavior. Maladaptive behavior is different from adaptive behavior only insomuch that it has undesirable consequences for the individual or his environment. Hallucinations are maladaptive as they distract the individual and reduce his ability to work, relate to others, and problem solve. Exhibitionism is distasteful to others and leads to arrest. These behaviors are presumed to be learned and maintained in essentially the same manner as adaptive counterpart behaviors such as daydreaming and heterosexual intercourse. Rather than reflecting some internal pathology, they represent a restricted or unfortunate learning history.

The term "symptom" is not customarily appropriate in behavioral analysis, as it means "sign" and implies some internal cause (the concept of "symptom substitution" will be discussed in the section on treatment). However, there are responses which do involve underlying physical or physiological factors. Tremors can represent an epileptic seizure or the delirium tremens (DT's) of alcoholism. The reading problems (and consequent noise making and out-of-seat behavior) of a child might reflect a perceptual dysfunction. The critical issue is not whether or not there ever are organic processes which affect behavior. Rather, it pertains to the relative importance of organic and environmental factors and the nature of their effects. Some disturbances, such as manic-depressive illness or epilepsy, may be more properly considered to be biochemical and physical rather than psychological disorders. However, in most cases in which there is a significant behavioral disturbance, even when there is some organic factor, the specific behavior manifested is not necessarily caused by the disorder. That is, the disorder might limit the responses that can be made and distort perception, but the particular responses that are emitted are frequently under environmental control. In the case of the child mentioned above, his out-of-seat behavior is maintained by the anxiety reduction and negative attention derived from that activity. Those reinforcers are relevant due to the anxiety and lack of reinforcement attendant upon efforts at reading. This is far different from the contention that his out-of-seat behavior is a specific response to (i.e., is *caused* by) his perceptual problem or an unconscious conflict which results from his feelings of inadequacy.

This distinction has important pragmatic as well as theoretical implications. Modification of the child's behavior requires alteration of the stimuli (reinforcement) surrounding his behavior *as well as* remedial reading work and treatment for his perceptual dysfunction. Similarly, the asocial schizophrenic requires *both* social skills training *and* antipsychotic medication. In both cases, treatment format and prognosis must be based on a careful evaluation of the specific behavior pattern, not on a category label.

Assessment

The two models of behavior have led to discretely different strategies for assessment. The personality model has emphasized an *indirect* approach to assessment in which test responses are considered to be *signs* of underlying processes (Goldfried & Kent, 1972; Mischel, 1972). "It is usually assumed that the person's underlying dispositions are relatively generalized and will manifest themselves pervasively in diverse aspects of his behavior, especially when the situation is unstructured and ambiguous and the examiner's purpose is disguised, as in projective testing . . . . The overt behavior itself is 'superficial' and even misleading; the psychologist's attention is directed at inferences concerning the underlying hypothesized dispositions that motivate the observable events" (Mischel, 1972, p. 319). Humanistic theorists have characteristically placed greater emphasis on self-report inventories than on projective tests, thus reducing the level of inference in test interpretation. However, specific responses on self-report inventories have been submerged in favor of overall summary scores which are presumed to represent general (underlying) dispositions.

In contrast to this indirect-sign approach, behavior modifiers have emphasized a *direct* approach in which the assessor attempts to secure a *sample* of the subject's behavior. Rather than making inferences about in vivo behavior based upon highly indirect test responses, an effort is made to secure a direct observation or demonstration of the target behavior. The purpose of any "test" is to determine the overall status of some variable (e.g., ability, knowledge) in an economical, convenient manner. A college professor administers a final examination which *samples* what students have learned because he cannot spend 3 hours interviewing each student to determine *everything* they have learned. Everyone has taken at least one exam in which the specific questions failed to represent how much had been learned. In general, the longer the exam (i.e., the larger the sample) and the closer the questions are to the material presented in lectures and the text (i.e., the more direct the observation), the more representative the test results will be. This principle extends to clinical behavior assessment, in which the more behavior that is observed, and the more naturalisitic the observation, the more the target behavior will be understood (see Hersen & Bellack, 1976, and Mischel, 1968, for more extensive discussion of this issue).

The most desirable approach to assessment is direct in vivo observation, in which trained observers enter the subject's natural environment and examine what he actually does. This has been the characteristic format for assessment of children (see Chapter 6). Observers can sit in the rear of a classroom for several days and keep a careful record of what a child does, when he does and does not make some response (e.g., fighting), and with whom he does it (see below). In the case of parent-child interactions, the observer can either go to the family home or observe the family interacting in a clinic playroom. The target behaviors for which children are assessed are usually confined to either classroom or home settings, which simplifies the observation process. Similarly, institutionalized adults operate in circumscribed environments in which they can be easily followed. In contrast, the target behaviors reported by adult outpatients occur over a much wider range of settings, making it extremely difficult to conduct such observations.

When the target behaviors involve interpersonal behavior, an alternative that has been frequently employed involves observation of role-played or staged interactions. Clients are requested to interact with live or videotaped role models as if they were actually conversing in the natural environment. Arkowitz, Lichtenstein, McGovern, and Hines (1975) employed this approach for the assessment of heterosexual interpersonal skills of college males (see Chapter 5). Male subjects interacted with female experimental aides in a variety of scenarios that represented potentially real situations, including a phone conversation in which each subject attempted to arrange a date with an aide.

A third assessment strategy involves the use of self-report. The indirect-sign approach to self-report data has not been very effective. However, self-report can provide valid data if the individual is regarded as an observer of his own behavior, rather than as a passive participant in the assessment process (Bellack & Hersen, 1977). Self-observation can be retrospective as when the individual is asked to recall specific responses such as: How many dates did you have last month? How many hours did you sleep last night? Have you ever had sexual intercourse? The only limitations to the validity of such data are the individual's desire to cooperate and his recollection of the response in question. A second strategy is self-monitoring (Kazdin, 1974), in which the individual makes *ongoing* observations of his behavior such as: number of calories consumed, number of positive thoughts about himself, number of dates (see Chapter 4). These observations are characteristically recorded in a diary to insure accurate recall. Self-report data are often the only source of information that can be secured. When the target behavior is invisible to outside observers (e.g., thoughts, sexual behavior) or when it occurs at high frequency and at inconsistent times (e.g., cigarette smoking, eating), the cooperation of the client himself is essential.

In addition to differences in techniques and strategy for assessment, the personality and behavioral models differ in the goals of assessment and the role assessment plays in treatment. The goal of personality assessment is a description of the internal processes that determine behavior: psychodynamics, conflicts, needs, self-concept, etc. Attention is sometimes paid to environmental factors and the problem behaviors themselves, but only in a secondary fashion. The primary goal of behavioral assessment is the *functional analysis of behavior* (Ferster, 1965; Kanfer & Saslow, 1969). This term has emanated from the operant laboratory and in its simplest form involves three components. The first involves the identification of the primary problem behavior or *target*. For example, "depression" is an abstract label for a class of behaviors, and different individuals do not all use the term to refer to the same set of responses. In any individual case, "depression" might include: excessive crying, low activity level, sleep and eating difficulties (too much or too little), agitation and anxiety, and ruminative concerns about physical illness.

Once the target behavior is identified, the *second* step is to analyze its topography or form. In the case of a person with sleep problems: How many hours does the individual sleep? Is the sleep in one period or through the day? Does he sleep deeply or fitfully? (This analysis is often combined with target definition.) This degree of specificity is necessary if treatment is to be applied to the appropriate response in the most effective manner. The *third* phase involves analysis of the environment or stimulus situation in which the target occurs: what are the antecedents and consequences that structure and maintain the response? In the case of our sleepless individual: Where does he attempt to sleep? Is it quiet? Does he frequently become anxious or fight with his wife late in the evening? Does he get into bed only when he is sleepy or does he read or watch television in bed? Does he miss work after sleepless nights? Does his wife provide a great deal of attention when he has had a sleepless night? Given the critical role of the environment in controlling behavior, an analysis of the stimulus configuration surrounding the behavior is essential.

With the goal of functional analysis as a basis, Kanfer and Saslow

(1969) have provided a more extensive schema for behavioral assessment. Clients often come to treatment with multifaceted complaints such as: "I don't know what's wrong. I can't relate to people anymore and I'm always tense. I seem to get into a lot of arguments, especially with my boss. I can't get excited about things." The behavior modifier must somehow sift through this type of report to select appropriate target behaviors. As a guideline, Kanfer and Saslow (1969) suggest that the individual's complaints be analyzed in terms of *behavioral excesses* and *behavioral deficits*. Excesses are those behaviors which occur with too much frequency, intensity, or duration, or which occur when they are not socially sanctioned (e.g., exhibitionism). Examples include compulsions, tics, and addictions (alcoholism, obesity, etc.). Behavioral deficits include responses that occur with insufficient frequency or intensity or with inadequate form, or fail to occur at appropriate times. Examples include unassertiveness, sexual inhibition, low activity level (as in depression), and insufficient food consumption (as in anorexia nervosa).

In addition to the analysis of target behaviors and stimulus control, Kanfer and Saslow suggest assessment of a number of collateral factors which often have an impact on the client and his response to treatment. These include:

1. *Behavioral assets.* What strengths or skills does the individual have which might be utilized in treatment? These include self-control skills, hobbies, interpersonal skills, work skills, etc. For example, does a depressed middle-aged housewife have the skills to find a job or do volunteer work?
2. *Behavioral limitations.* Examples include physical debilities which limit the individual's activities or ability to follow the treatment plan.
3. *Environmental supports and restrictions.* This category refers to both physical aspects of the environment (e.g., funds available for reinforcing a child) and significant other individuals in the environment. For example: Will parents or spouse cooperate by reinforcing appropriate behavior? Will a change in the client's behavior, such as increased assertiveness, have a negative impact on the spouse?
4. *Motivational analysis.* This primarily involves two issues: (a) What are the relevant reinforcers in the individual's environment which might be incorporated into treatment? and (b) Are there potential consequences to any behavior change which would make the individual less likely to alter current behavior? For example, an alcoholic might lack the social skills sufficient to secure a job and deal with his wife, thereby, making sobriety aversive.

The focus of all of these assessment issues has been on current (or future) functioning. Behavioral assessment characteristically places slight emphasis on life history or history of the problem (Kanfer &

Phillips, 1970; Rimm & Masters, 1974). There are two major factors that account for this ahistorical approach. *First,* the individual can rarely give an accurate account of the circumstances in which the problem developed or its exact course. Few behavior problems develop dramatically based on one or two traumatic experiences. Most dysfunctions develop in a subtle manner over long periods of time based on modeling and large numbers of conditioning trials (Bandura, 1969). Even with problems of more recent onset, the specific contingencies applicable at the time of onset are obscure. Therefore, the individual can rarely provide accurate historical data.

The *second* factor is probably of greater importance. The purpose of assessment is to plan effective treatment. This requires identification of the *current maintaining factors*, not the factors present at the time the behavior was acquired. Bandura (1965) has shown how the conditions affecting *learning* (response acquisition) are different from those affecting *performance* (response emission). Behavior can be maintained by factors substantially different from those that led to its initiation. Heroin addicts often begin using the drug as a function of peer pressure and the feelings of euphoria associated with use of the drug. One of the most critical maintaining factors, however, is the physiological addiction and the aversiveness of withdrawal. This issue is especially manifest in the case of behavioral deficits: *why* the individual failed to learn a response is less important than the fact that he has not learned it.

The de-emphasis on historical factors does not mean that they are totally irrelevant. Behaviors with long histories are frequently more resistant to treatment than those of recent onset. An individual who becomes depressed after the death of a parent or spouse has a different prognosis than one who recently became depressed without such an intercurrent life event, or someone who has been depressed for an extended period of time. A homosexual male who has had satisfactory heterosexual experiences at some point in his life has a better prognosis than an individual who has never had such experience (presuming he wishes to function heterosexually) (Feldman & MacCulloch, 1971). However, historical factors are generally less significant in treatment planning than current factors. They can occasionally serve to modify the *form* of treatment, but treatment must be directed toward modification of current factors if it is to be effective.

With the exception of some psychotropic drug regimens, assessment and treatment are not intimately related in non-behavioral approaches. Verbal psychotherapies are characteristically initiated and planned in a uniform manner, independent of the personality description. For behavior modification, on the other hand, "Assessment and treatment are inseparable" (Ullmann & Krasner, 1965, p. 361). As will be discussed in the following section, behavioral treatments are highly specific. All of the elements essential for planning treatment are identified via intensive assessment: the behavior modifier would, quite literally, not know what to treat or how to treat without first conducting an assessment. Similarly, the empirical orientation to treatment requires that assessment continue throughout the course of treatment. The therapist cannot know whether or not treatment is working and when treatment goals are reached without ongoing assessment. This reliance on objective, detailed assessment both before and during treatment is one of the major distinguishing characteristics of behavior modification.

Treatment

The personality and behavioral models differ in their approach to treatment in a manner parallel to other differences between the two orientations. The personality model emphasizes the (disease) medical model. As the source of disturbance is presumed to lie within the psyche, the focus of treatment is intrapsychic modification. The traditional technique employed for this purpose is verbal psychotherapy. While the specific format and goals vary somewhat across theoretical orientations, this approach generally involves exploration of the psyche with a goal of insight and increased self-acceptance. Biological psychiatry with its emphasis upon psychotropic medication does not have such "psychological" change as a goal; however, the focus is still on modification of an internal disease process.

One of the most fundamental implications of this model is that treatment must be directed toward the underlying disturbance. Treatment focused only upon the external manifestations (i.e., symptoms) of the disease process will result in "symptom substitution": a new symptom will develop in response to the continued internal dysfunction. According to this argument, directing treatment to overt behavior is like treating tuberculosis with cough syrup.

In the 1960s the possibility of symptom substitution was a major controversy between behavior modifiers and other clinicians. The focus of behavioral treatment is on discrete, essentially observable target behaviors (which include cognitive responses) and maintaining factors in the environment. Behavioral treatment " . . . is not an effort aimed at removal of intrapsychic conflicts, nor at change in the personality structure by therapeutic interactions of intense nonverbal nature (e.g., transference, self-actualization). Instead, we adopt the assumption that the job of "psychological" treatment involves the utilization of a variety of methods to devise a program which controls the patient's environment, or enables him to control his behavior and the consequences of his behavior in such a way that the presenting problem is resolved" (Kanfer & Saslow, 1969, pp. 427–428). Once again, the behavioral model presumes that there are no internal maintaining factors and that problematic behaviors can be attacked directly without danger. New behavior problems can arise or the treated behavior can reappear if the individual has a new series of conditioning trials. However, such an occurrence would not imply an unresolved core conflict. Current evidence indicates that symptom substitution does not occur (e.g., Cahoon, 1968; Sloane, Staples, Cristol, Yorkston, & Whipple, 1975), and this is no longer a controversial issue.

Behavioral treatment techniques take a wide variety of forms. The subsequent chapters in this book will describe and evaluate the major behavioral strategies. Aside from the emphasis on direct intervention, there are several aspects of the behavioral approach to treatment that are common to almost all specific techniques. *First*, treatment is generally viewed as an *educational process*. Rather than being acted upon, the client is taught adaptive ways in which to alter his environment and maximize reinforcement. The learning process is not limited to cognitive input or understanding, but involves extended practice to insure mastery of new skills. *Second*, there is an emphasis on in vivo performance as well as change in the clinic. In what has become a behavioral maxim, Baer, Wolf, and Risley (1968) stated, "In general, generalization should be programmed, rather than expected or lamented" (p. 97). This can only be accomplished if treatment is oriented toward the client's natural environment. In addition to in-session practice and rehearsal, it is customary to require clients to systematically practice new skills in vivo, between sessions.

Third, treatment is specific to the client and his particular situation. The topography of target behaviors and the specific maintaining factors are unique to each individual. If treatment is to be effective, it must be structured according to a functional analysis of the target behavior. There are standard behavioral treatment techniques such as systematic densensitization. However, even their application must be structured to meet the unique parameters of each individual case. This orientation to treatment demands that treatment and assessment be intimately intertwined. *Fourth*, whenever possible, the goals of treatment and probable outcomes are made explicit. In contrast to the ambiguity of a goal such as "insight," behavioral goals take a concrete form, such as: losing 25 lbs. in 3 months, sleeping for at least 7 hours per night, or reducing the frequency of thoughts about death to three per week. These goals are established cooperatively by both the therapist and the client. In addition, the specific procedures entailed in reaching the goals and the anticipated duration of treatment are also made explicit in advance. These plans are often formalized in a contract, which is actually formally typed and signed by both therapist and client. These agreements are not meant to be legally binding. However, they explicitly clarify what treatment involves and specify the responsibilities of the client (e.g., to do homework) as well as the therapist.

A *fifth* aspect of the behavioral approach is essentially subsumed under the other elements, but deserves special emphasis. Target behaviors can be defined in terms of motoric, physiological, and cognitive channels. Behavioral treatment is directed towards whichever of those response modalities is relevant, not solely toward the cognitive channel. Non-behavioral treatments have characteristically emphasized cognitive change, presuming that it was most important and that change in other response systems would follow naturally. Conversely, until recently, behavior modification has emphasized change of motoric responses for the same reasons. As will be discussed in subsequent chapters (see especially Chapters 2 and 5), neither of these biases has been empirically supported. The exact relationship between the three response systems is still unclear. Changes in any one system are frequently not highly correlated with changes in either of the other systems (e.g., Lang, 1971; Leitenberg, Agras, Butz, & Wincze, 1971; Paul, 1966). Therefore, treatment must be directed toward *all* aspects of dysfunction. Generalization across response modalities cannot be automatically presumed any more than generalization across situations (e.g., Baer et al., 1968).

Humanistic Values and Ethics

Behavior modification has been subjected to a tremendous amount of criticism from a variety of sources including the public media, the legal profession, the United States Congress, and various humanist groups, as well as from within the mental health field. Most of this criticism stems less from empirical arguments about treatment effectiveness than from subjective attitudes about behavioral methods and goals. Behavior modification has been accused of being manipulative, authoritarian, communistic, and mechanistic. It has been avowed that unless it is controlled, behavior modification will lead to an Orwellian 1984. Behavior modifiers are accused of being callous and insensitive with patients and having little regard for human dignity and freedom of choice.

This emotional reaction has, apparently, evolved for several reasons other than what behavior modification is and can do. Much of the behavioral terminology is austere and mechanistic in comparison to the rich, personal, humanistic language: compare stimulus, contingency, and operant with self-concept, ego-ideal, and self-actualization. The emphasis on the terms "conditioning" and "control" are especially value-laden and imply manipulation. These impressions were reinforced by the overoptimistic claims of many early behavior modifiers and the well-intentioned but misinterpreted popular works of B. F. Skinner: *Walden Two* (1948) and *Beyond Freedom and Dignity* (1971). The use of aversive conditioning procedures has also generated critical attitudes.

In general, these negative reactions are both unfounded and misguided. Behavior modification is an applied discipline with the goal of alleviating human distress and modifying behavior for the benefit of the individual *and* society (Bandura, 1969). The emphasis of intervention is on *education* rather than manipulation. Rather than exerting control *over* the client, behavior modification expects him to be an active participant in treatment, helping to select goals, plan treatment techniques, and learn to control his own behavior and environment. In situations where the client cannot take such an active role (e.g., children, out-of-touch schizophrenics), planning is conducted with responsible agents of the client such as parents or legal guardians. Whenever possible, clients are provided with complete, accurate information about the (behavioral) rationale for treatment as well as its course, cost, and the prognosis *before* entering into any *voluntary* agreement to accept treatment.

Despite their emphasis on objective and explicit techniques, behavior modifiers are not cold and insensitive people. Clients are treated warmly and with respect. Sloane et al. (1975), for example, found that clients rated behavior therapists at least as high on interpersonal factors such as warmth and empathy as non-behavioral therapists. Application of specific training procedures and insistence on practice trials and assessment should not be confused with a callous or impersonal attitude. Behavior modifiers do not believe that the client-therapist relationship is the *source* of change. However, they do agree that a positive relationship is desirable in therapy, and that it is often a *necessary but not sufficient* factor in generating change (Morganstern, 1976).

Despite early claims to the contrary, behavior modification is not nearly as powerful as critics believe. We have not developed a technology of mind and behavior control that could easily lead to totalitarianism. There are too many uncontrollable factors, many of which reside within the organism, to allow for such control (Bandura, 1974). In addition, the effects of behavioral programs are not permanent. Behavior occurs as a function of the environment, and when the environment is altered, behavior can be altered. This is clearly demonstrated by the failure of token economies to effect generalized changes (see Chapter 8).

There are concerns about values and ethics which are common to all forms of intervention, behavioral and non-behavioral. Among the most salient of these is a concern about the actual amount of free choice a client has in *any* system. Therapists of all persuasions come to therapy with personal value systems which evolve from their cultural experience (Ullmann, 1969). These values influence the type of clients the therapist will agree to treat and the types of behavior he defines as maladaptive. The therapist is, thus, an agent of society as well as of the client. For example, few therapists will help a father reduce anxiety that he experiences after beating his children. However, some therapists will actively recommend that married clients have extramarital sexual experiences, and others will avoid influencing the client's decision in this regard. Similarly, society influences clients by applying social sanctions to various behaviors and restricting choices. An individual exposed to such pressure and subtle therapist influence is not entirely free to determine which behaviors he wishes to alter.

Current concern about both forms of influence is best represented in regard to treatment of homosexual behavior. Several behavior modifiers have argued that homosexuals reporting a desire to change sexual orientation are not free to choose an orientation. Rather, they are reacting to the aversive consequences applied by society for homosexual behavior (Begelman, 1975; Davison, 1976). Therefore, they recommend that these individuals not be treated, because to apply treatment implies agreement with society's conclusion that homosexuality is bad. Therapists are advised to direct their efforts in attempts to change society, or at the least, to teach the client to deal with society's pressure. There are several counter-arguments to this position. *First,* therapists are expected to maintain a humanistic ethical code which overrides any negative societal influence. In addition, they are expected to refrain from imposing their personal values on clients. *Second,* it is (thought to be) appropriate to alter behavior in a manner which increases the client's options so that he *can* freely choose a course of action. For example, it is only when the "homosexual" is able to experience heterosexual gratification that he can decide which orientation he prefers. *Third,* the client (outpatient) is in treatment voluntarily. He can withdraw at any time and must take some responsibility for his behavior.

Concerns about restricted choices are of greatest concern in situations in which the individual cannot be presumed to have entered treatment on a voluntary basis. This includes children, hospitalized psychiatric patients, and prison inmates. Society's goals are very often different from the goals of the individuals in these groups. A critical question then becomes: Whose agent is the therapist, society's or the client's? If he is society's agent, does the client have the right to refuse treatment (e.g., refuse to participate in a token economy or "therapeutic" hospital work program)? Winett and Winkler (1972) have criticized behavior modifiers for making children passive and compliant in school, rather than modifying regressive, repressive school systems. Holland (1974) has similarly been critical of token economy programs in prisons. He complains that these programs are repressive, deny inmates of basic human rights, and serve only the prison administration. Recent court decisions have supported this argument (with psychiatric patients), and the Law Enforcement Assistance Administration has ceased to fund token economy programs in federal prisons for similar reasons.

These issues are highly complex and have defied quick resolution. Skinner (1971) has argued that behavior modification techniques are "valueless" in that they are simply empirical strategies. However, as long as they are administered by human therapists, ethics and values will be at issue. Most behavior modifiers adhere to the codes of ethics of their professional associations (e.g., American Psychological Association). Major ethical violations are rare, and most clients appear to be satisfied with the way they are treated and the outcome of treatment. Nevertheless, a continued open dialogue about ethics and potential sources of conflict is necessary to prevent even unintentional abuses and to guarantee that ethical codes are adequate for current issues.

This section has presented an overview of issues pertaining to values and ethics. There are specific concerns that are relevant to several individual behavioral treatments such as aversion therapy. These issues will be discussed in subsequent chapters in the context of a description of the techniques themselves.

Research Methodology

A commitment to empiricism is one of the overriding values and distinguishing characteristics of behavior modification. There has been some disagreement about whether clinical techniques should be *derived from* empirical study or should be studied empirically *after* clinical derivation (e.g., Franks, 1969; London, 1972). However, there is no disagreement that empirical evaluation is a critical factor for continued application of treatment techniques. Behavior modifiers do not simply employ empirically validated techniques, but they approach clinical practice with an empirical, data-oriented framework. Validation of a clinical technique implies that it is *generally* effective for a specific form of behavior change. Each clinical case must be approached as an experiment, in which it is hypothesized that a specific intervention will be effective for that particular client (Yates, 1975). Data must be gathered (i.e., assessment must be conducted) throughout the experiment (i.e., treatment) in order to test the hypothesis. This approach to clinical practice customarily takes the form of controlled single-subject experimental methodology (Baer et al., 1968; Hersen & Barlow, 1976). Such research, which involves the intensive study of the individual organism rather than comparison of groups of subjects, will be described below.

As will be seen in subsequent chapters, both single-subject and group comparison designs have been used extensively in the development, analysis, and validation of treatment techniques. There has been considerable controversy about the relative merits of the two forms of research for this purpose. Paul (1969) has suggested that single-subject research is useful primarily for hypothesis development, as it allows for systematic observation of clinical applications. He believes that group comparison designs are appropriate for hypothesis validation, analysis of complex techniques to determine critical components, and comparison of different treatment techniques (e.g., is treatment A better than treatment B). His primary argument about single-subject research pertains to the limited extent to which results from any one subject can be generalized to others. Conversely, Hersen and Barlow (1976) have argued that the researcher can make a certain degree of generalization by conducting a series of single-subject studies with similar subjects. They also point out some major limitations of group comparison designs, the most important of which are: (1) There is an overemphasis on statistically significant differences between groups, which fails to specify the clinical significance of behavior changes (e.g., whether or not they are large enough to be important even if they *are* statistically significant): and (2) The data of individual subjects are submerged, thus losing potentially valuable data such as the *course* of behavior change. A full elaboration of this debate is beyond the scope of this book. The reader is referred to the sources cited above, as well as to any introductory statistics text for a description of group comparison research designs.

Data Collection

As a function of its empirical orientation, behavior modification places a premium on measurement and the collection of data. In previous sections we have specified the major categories in which behavior is measured (motoric, physiological, and cognitive) and specified that the most preferred collection strategy is direct sampling (observation). However, we have not specified what an observer actually looks at: the specific kinds of data that can be collected during observations. Prior to describing single-subject research methodology, we will present an overview of the most frequently employed forms of data collection. Because clinical application is regarded as an experiment, assessment and data collection are almost synonymous. With the possible exception of some paper-and-pencil inventories that are used for screening or subject selection (as in group comparison research), these procedures are used in both the laboratory and the clinic.

There are four common strategies for data collection: permanent products, event recording, duration recording, and interval recording (Mann, 1976).

Permanent Products. In contrast to the other three procedures, measurement of permanent products does not involve direct observation of behavior. Rather, this approach entails the observation of the effects or products of a response. The presence of the product *infers* that a specific response occurred. For example, results on an examination are an indication of the degree to which a student learned certain material. Washed and stacked dinner dishes indicate that someone (e.g., a child for whom such clean-up was a target behavior) cleaned up after dinner. The printed output of a polygraph indicates the nature of physiological responses. Self-report inventories are permanent product records of an individual's subjective impressions or attitudes about something. In each of these cases, the assessor is recording the presence of a product of a response instead of observing the response directly. In the case of the polygraph record, direct observation of physiological activity is not physically possible. In other cases, such as the school examination, observation might be possible, but would be exceedingly inconvenient or expensive. The use of such products ordinarily involves both inference about what responses actually occurred and a loss of data about the specific nature of the responses. Examination grades, for example, do not specify how well or how long a student studies. However, such measurement is easy to accomplish and is often employed when the sacrificed data are unimportant or too uneconomical to secure.

Event Recording. This is a method of measurement in which an observer records each occurrence of a target behavior during some specified period of time in order to establish its frequency. This form of assessment involves direct observation and recording of discrete responses. Examples include: cigarettes smoked, fights, head-banging, sexual experiences, and tics. Data derived from this type of measurement are usually converted into *frequencies* or *rates,* such as: cigarettes smoked per day, puffs taken per cigarette, sexual experiences per week, and tics per minute. The nature of the denominator (e.g., time interval) employed varies with the behavior and depends on how it can best be represented. For example, cigarettes per day conveys more commonly understood and meaningful information than cigarettes per minute or per month. Generally, the higher the frequency of the behavior, the shorter the time interval employed (e.g., heart beats per minute versus sexual experiences per week or month). Event recording is an effective and relatively simple procedure to employ.

Duration Recording. This procedure involves measurement of the length of time over which a response occurs. In contrast to event recording, in which the occurrence of a response is critical in and of itself, duration recording is employed when the duration of the response conveys important information. For a child suspected of having a short attention span, duration of time on task is more relevant than the number of times he is distracted. In evaluation of a man reporting premature ejaculation, the duration for which he can maintain an erection prior to ejaculation is critical. Amount of time spent studying is important in assessing a student who receives failing grades. An important form of duration data is latency: how long before a response occurs, such as time required to fall asleep. Durations for specific episodes can be summed over a fixed period to provide a percentage (such as percentage of time spent studying each day), or can be considered independently (e.g., average duration of each period of studying). Once again, choice of a scale or of a particular conversion depends upon utility: how much information does the measure convey and how accurately does it reflect the effects of treatment?

Interval Recording (Time Sampling). When conducting any form of recording, specific observation periods must be selected: e.g., from 10:00–10:30 A.M., 2:00–2:30 P.M., and 6:00–6:30 P.M. With event and duration recording, all target responses occurring within those periods are measured. This can be accomplished only if the target responses have clearly discernable beginning and end points. If these points are not clear, the event recorder cannot determine whether a new response has occurred or the previously scored response has continued, and the duration recorder cannot determine when to begin and cease timing. Examples of such responses are hallucinations and interpersonal interactions. Interval recording provides an alternative strategy for measuring such responses. In this technique, each observation period is subdivided into brief intervals (15–30 sec. is common), and the observer simply records whether or not the target response occurs during that interval. A common variation involves recording whether or not the response is occurring at the end of each interval. In either case, the observer need only be sure when the response has occurred, not exactly when it begins or ends.

Since interval recording does not require constant observation, it allows the observer to easily record up to five or six different target responses simultaneously in addition to the antecedents and consequences of the responses. When observation becomes this complex, observers are customarily trained to employ a coding system, in which varying responses and stimulus events can be quickly entered on a prepared data-recording sheet. An example of a coding system and target response definitions employed by Bijou, Peterson, Harris, Allen, and Johnston (1969) are presented in Table 1.2. Either all or a portion of this system might be employed. It could be supplemented to indicate responses directed *toward* a child subject by adding special symbols (e.g., initials) to represent other children or teachers.

The length of observation sessions and duration of recording intervals are determined by the nature of the target responses. Interval recording has the disadvantage of missing or losing data. The unit of measurement is simply whether or not the response occurred at all. A response is scored as an occurrence whether it lasted for the entire interval, occurred just before the interval ended, or occurred 12 times for brief duration during the interval. The specific pattern would not be recorded and would thus be lost to the therapist. This data loss can be reduced by selecting appropriate intervals. Generally, short duration or high frequency behaviors such as making noises in the classroom or tics should be measured in brief intervals: e.g., 5–10 sec. With briefer intervals there are fewer opportunities for unrecorded responses to occur. Responses occurring with long duration or low frequency, such as fighting, are best measured in longer intervals: e.g., 15-min. to 1-day blocks. Use of brief intervals with infrequent behaviors will simply result in a data record with numerous empty intervals.

TABLE 1.2

General Response Code for Studying Children in a Classroom[a]

Symbols	Classes	Class Definitions
X	Gross motor behaviors	Getting out of seat; standing up; running; hopping; skipping; jumping; walking around; rocking in chair; disruptive movement without noise; moves chair to neighbor; knees on chair.
N	Disruptive noise	Tapping pencil or other objects; clapping; tapping feet; rattling or tearing paper; throwing book on desk, slamming desk. (Be conservative, only rate if could hear noise when eyes closed. Do not include accidental dropping of objects or if noise made while performing X above.)
∧	Disturbing others directly	Grabbing objects or work; knocking neighbor's books off desk; destroying another's property; pushing with desk.
→	Aggression (contact)	Hitting, kicking; shoving; pinching; slapping; striking with object; throwing object at another person; poking with object; biting; pulling hair.
⌒→	Orienting responses	Turning head or head and body to look at another person, showing objects to another child, orienting toward another child. (Must be of 4 sec. duration, not rated unless seated; or more than 90° using the desk as a reference.)
V	Verbalizations	Carrying on conversations with other children when it is not permitted. Answers teacher without raising hand or without being called on; making comments or calling out remarks when no question has been asked; calling teacher's name to get her attention; crying; screaming; singing; whistling; laughing loudly; coughing or blowing loudly. (May be directed to teacher or children.)
//	Other tasks	Ignores teacher's question or command; does something different from that directed to do, includes minor motor behavior such as playing with pencil eraser when supposed to be writing; coloring while the record is on; doing spelling during arithmetic lesson; playing with objects; eating; chewing gum. *The child involves himself in a task that is not appropriate.*
—	Relevant behavior	Time on task; e.g., answers question, looking at teacher when she is talking; raises hand; writing assignment. (Must include whole 20-sec interval except for orienting responses of less than 4-sec duration.)

[a] From: Bijou et al. (1969) (Table 4).

Reliability. In an earlier section it has been stated that objective measurement requires two independent observations. That is, two observers watching independently must agree that a response occurred. When the target response is most explicit (e.g., a tantrum) and only one instance is at issue, finding interobserver agreement is relatively easy. However, when several responses are rated over several days or weeks, it is unlikely that independent observers would agree on all measurement points. The more they disagree, the less faith one can have in the ratings. Statistically, the validity (accuracy) of the overall ratings for that period are limited by the reliability of the ratings, or the extent of agreement between the raters. Simply put, if two raters disagree at least one must be incorrect. The more frequent the disagreement, the more incorrect ratings there must be, and the less one can draw valid conclusions about what the subject actually did or did not do. Therefore, it is necessary to evaluate the reliability or interrater agreement whenever one secures observational data. (Reliabilities are calculated on a scale from 0.00 to 1.00; ratings above 0.7 are considered satisfactory.) Whether or not satisfactory reliability is attained is not entirely a function of chance. Reliability generally can be increased if: (1) response definitions are highly explicit so that raters do not have to use subjective judgment (see, for example, definitions in Table 1.2); and (2) raters are carefully trained so that they become expert at observing and measuring behavior.

Single-Subject Research Designs

Single-case or single-subject research methodology evolved from the operant laboratory, where the emphasis has been on the intensive study of the single organism. Only by intensive study of one individual at a time can the researcher be sure he has isolated the specific variables that control behavior (rather than a variable which has an *averaged* effect on the behavior of a group). A basic feature of all research is an untreated (or differently) treated *control*, with which to compare the experimental treatment. The single-subject designs employ the individual as his own control, by measuring his behavior over time and comparing his response during different periods (when he has received different treatments).

Characteristically, single-subject research does not employ statistics for evaluation of results. Rather, results are portrayed graphically and analyzed by visual inspection. It is presumed that if a behavior change is clinically significant, it will be large enough to be clearly visible on a graph (figure). Conversely, a change that appears to be minimal graphically is assumed to be clinically unimportant. There has been some suggestion that graphic representation is not adequate, and that it can provide ambiguous and misleading information (see Kazdin, 1976, for a discussion of alternative views about this issue). Nevertheless, statistics are commonly viewed as more misleading than helpful by most re-searchers employing this strategy.

Establishing a Baseline. The first stage in any single-subject design is to determine the pre-treatment status of the subject on the dependent variable (i.e., the target response): the *baseline*. This is a reference point from which to judge any subsequent change. The minimal crite-rion for an adequate baseline is three data points; that is, the response must be measured on three separate occasions. This is to ensure either that the target response occurs stably over time, or that it is getting worse clinically. If the target behavior is changing in the desired direc-tion before treatment, any positive effects of treatment would be masked. If a stable (or declining) baseline is not attained after three measurements, further observations must be made; if the baseline continues to "improve," treatment might not be necessary.

A-B-A Designs. The simplest form of single-subject design involves two phases: baseline (A phase) and treatment (B phase). This design is referred to as an A-B design. It is typified by the uncontrolled clinical case study, in which treatment follows initial assessment and termi-nates after some criterion of change is reached (clinical case studies often do not involve development of a stable baseline). Because this design includes pre- and post-treatment assessment, it is adequate for demonstrating that behavior change occurred. However, it cannot pro-vide clear evidence that the change was under the control of the treat-ment. Any number of factors other than the treatment could have affected the behavior. Consider a child who is disruptive in school (e.g., out-of-seat behavior, hitting) and for whom treatment consisted of posi-tive social reinforcement for desired behaviors (see Chapter 6). A de-crease in the target responses could occur as a function of any number of uncontrolled changes which occur simultaneously with treatment in-cluding: parents threaten the child, child breaks his leg and is less mobile, a new teacher is placed in the classroom, or another child who stimulated the target responses moves across town.

There is no clear evidence that those factors were at work, but there is an unacceptably high probability that such factors might have been involved *at any one time*. There would be less likelihood that such factors controlled the change if it could be demonstrated that the change occurs *whenever* treatment is applied. That is, behavior changes in the desired direction when treatment is applied, ceases to change or changes in the undesired direction when treatment is removed, and changes in the desired direction again when treatment is reinstated. This concept of demonstrating control by repeated application of treatment is the basis for the A-B-A design and its variations.

The simplest and most common form of the A-B-A design is the *withdrawal* strategy. A baseline is established first (A), treatment is then applied (B), followed by a return to baseline (A). If the target behavior is under the control of the treatment, it should return to baseline level after treatment is removed. In most clinical cases, it is neither ethical nor desirable to leave the target behavior at baseline levels. Therefore, a second treatment phase is usually added, making the design an A-B-A-B. This extra phase also provides stronger demonstration that treatment was effective.

As an example, consider again the disruptive child. If the target behavior is out-of-seat behavior, a simple treatment would entail positive social reinforcement by the teacher whenever she observes the child in his seat. The results of a hypothetical withdrawal design to test this treatment are portrayed graphically in Fig. 1.1. Each phase contains three measurement (data) points. An essentially stable baseline is established in phase A, and treatment in phase B results in a substantial decrease in percentage of time out-of-seat. When treatment is withdrawn in the second A phase, the behavior returns to baseline levels. Finally, when treatment is reinstituted, out-of-seat behavior again decreases. This figure portrays one of the major advantages of single-subject methodology. Because data are collected throughout the intervention and are displayed in this manner, it becomes quickly apparent whether or not treatment is effective and when a criterion (goal) is reached. Treatment can thus be modified or terminated with a minimum of wasted time or effort.

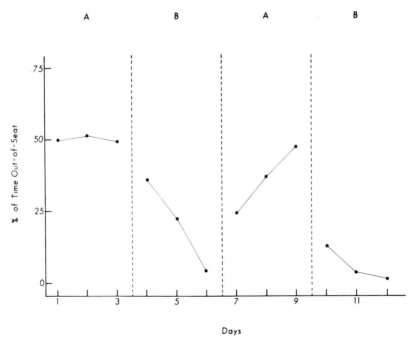

Fig. 1.1 A hypothetical example of an A-B-A-B withdrawal design for treatment of a child exhibiting excessive out-of-seat behavior.

The A-B-A design can be varied and expanded in a number of ways to answer different experimental questions. For example, the out-of-seat behavior of many children is maintained by teacher attention for getting out of seat. The child described above might, therefore, be treated with positive reinforcement for in seat behavior and extinction for out-of-seat behavior (i.e., teacher ignores him when he is out of his seat). The question of whether or not *both* extinction and positive reinforcement are necessary can be answered with an A-BC-B-BC design: A again represents baseline, B represents extinction, and C is positive reinforcement. The BC phases represent periods when *both* procedures are applied. If out-of-seat behavior decreases in BC, increases in B, and decreases again when BC is restored, it suggests that the behavior was under the control of positive reinforcement and that extinction was unnecessary. If the behavior does *not* increase during the B phase, it suggests that positive reinforcement alone is not sufficient to control the response and that some other factor is involved. (The reader is referred to Hersen & Barlow, 1976, for a detailed discussion of single-subject methodology including other variants of A-B-A designs).

Multiple Baseline Designs. The designs described above require that an effective treatment be withdrawn for some period and that the effects of that treatment are reversible. These requirements cannot always be met. An effective treatment cannot be ethically withdrawn if the target behavior can result in immediate or sustained harm to the client such as with self-injurious behavior (e.g., head banging). In other cases, the behavior change, once established, is relatively stable or control is taken over by naturally occurring reinforcers in the environment and, thus, cannot be reversed. The multiple baseline design does not employ withdrawal and, therefore, avoids those limitations. Rather than comparing the status of *one* target response at different points in time, the multiple baseline design compares *two or more* target responses with each other at successive points in time. Most commonly, three or four target behaviors are identified and a single treatment procedure is selected. Treatment is then applied to each behavior *sequentially* (rather than simultaneously). Control is demonstrated if each behavior changes when, and only when, treatment is applied to it. If the second or third behavior changes when treatment is applied to the first behavior, it cannot be presumed that an uncontrolled factor was not involved.

Let us again consider our disruptive child. It is not unusual for such a child to exhibit several undesirable behaviors. Three targets might be: out-of-seat behavior, hitting, and disruptive noise. All three of these responses are potentially modifiable by positive reinforcement of alternative, desirable behavior (in seat, positive social contact, and absence of disruptive noise). Hypothetical results of a multiple baseline analysis of the effectiveness of positive reinforcement is portrayed in Fig. 1.2. Each row represents the data for one of the target responses. Within each row, the data points to the left of the vertical dotted line represent

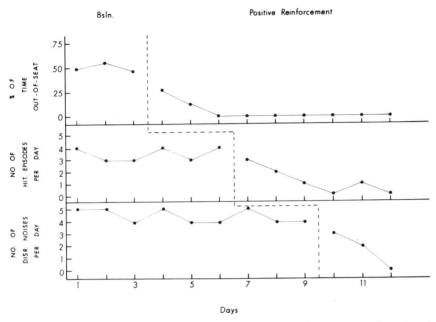

Fig. 1.2 A hypothetical example of a multiple baseline design across three target behaviors.

baseline (i.e., pre-treatment) assessment for that target response; treatment for each response begins to the right of the vertical dotted lines. Stable baselines are established for each response during days 1–3. Positive reinforcement is applied to sitting behavior beginning on day 4, while the other two responses remain untreated. Reinforcement continues for sitting and is *applied* to hitting beginning on day 7. Reinforcement continues for hitting and sitting and is applied to noise making beginning on day 10. As can be seen, each response decreases *when and only when* treatment is applied specifically to it. Therefore, there is an acceptably low probability that some uncontrolled factor affected *all three* responses at the *same time* treatment was applied.

This application of a multiple baseline design involved treatment of three different target behaviors. The baselines could also refer to a single target response across three different subjects. For example, positive reinforcement for interpersonal activity could be applied sequentially to three withdrawn schizophrenics in an institution. If they each then engaged in higher rates of social activity when, and only when, reinforcement was applied, the control of reinforcement would be demonstrated. Another variation, labeled the multiple baseline design across settings, involves sequential treatment of a single target response in different settings: e.g., a child who makes disruptive noises in three different classrooms could be positively reinforced for not making noises in each classroom in sequential fashion.

The major limitations of withdrawal designs pertain to either ethical restraints or physical inability to withdraw treatment. The primary difficulty in applying a multiple baseline is the identification of *several* target responses which are related, but which are not so closely interrelated that treatment of one automatically generalizes to the others. For example, if the target behaviors are dropping pens on the floor and dropping pencils on the floor, it is very likely that treatment for pen dropping will result in modification of pencil dropping as well (unless there is an emphasis on discrimination training). Nevertheless, the limitations with both designs are relatively minor compared with their advantages. Single-subject methodology has become an integral part of behavior modification practice and will likely have an increasing impact on its growth and development in the future.

Summary

This chapter has presented an introduction to behavior modification. A definition of the term was discussed which emphasized that behavior modification is a point of view. While learning theory had an historic role in its development, the current emphasis is on the empirical development and application of effective treatment techniques. The major assumptions underlying the behavioral viewpoint were described and contrasted with the assumptions of the personality model of behavior. Major issues that were discussed include:

1. Conceptions of What Constitutes Behavior and How It Is Determined. The behavioral model employs objective definition rather than hypothetical inferences and emphasizes the importance of the environment in controlling behavior.

2. Models of Maladaptive Behavior. Rather than the etiological viewpoint of the medical model, behaviorists emphasize functional determinism and maladaptive learning experiences.

3. Role of Assessment and How It Is Conducted. Behavior modification emphasizes a direct, sampling approach to assessment rather than an indirect, sign approach. A premium is placed on observation, on measurement of motoric, physiological, and cognitive response modalities, and on evaluation of the role of the environment.

4. Nature of Treatment. Behavioral treatment is direct and is designed for each client on the basis of a careful assessment. Goals are determined jointly with the client, and plans and expectations are clearly communicated in the form of a contract.

The role of humanistic values in behavior modification was then discussed along with the current concerns about the ethics of behavior modifiers. The last section dealt with research methodology. Major strategies for data collection were described followed by a brief overview of single-subject research methodology.

References

Arkowitz, H., Lichenstein, E., McGovern, K., & Hines, P. The behavioral assessment of social competence in males. *Behavior Therapy*, 1975, *6*, 3–13.

Baer, D. M., Wolf, M. M., & Risley, T. R. Some current dimensions of applied behavior analysis. *Journal of Applied Behavior Analysis*, 1968, *1*, 91–97.

Bandura, A. Influence of models' reinforcement contingencies on the acquisition of imitative responses. *Journal of Personality and Social Psychology*, 1965, *1*, 589–595.

Bandura, A. *Principles of behavior modification*. New York: Holt, Rinehart and Winston, 1969.

Bandura, A. *The ethics and social purposes of behavior modification*. Paper presented at the Eighth Annual Meeting of the Association for Advancement of Behavior Therapy, Chicago, Illinois: November 1974.

Bandura, A. Self-reinforcement: Theoretical and methodological considerations. *Behaviorism*, 1976, in press.

Begelman, D. A. Ethical and legal issues of behavior modification. In M. Hersen, R. M. Eisler, & P. M. Miller (Eds.), *Progress in behavior modification: Vol. 1*. New York: Academic Press, 1975.

Bellack, A. S., & Hersen, M. The use of self-report inventories in behavioral assessment. In J. D. Cone & R. P. Hawkins (Eds.), *Behavioral assessment: New directions in clinical psychology*. New York: Brunner/Mazel, 1977.

Bijou, S. W., Peterson, R. F., Harris, F. R., Allen, K. E., & Johnston, M. S. Methodology for experimental studies of young children in natural settings. *Psychological Record*, 1969, *19*, 177–210.

Cahoon, D. D. Symptom substitution and the behavior therapies: A reappraisal. *Psychological Bulletin*, 1968, *69*, 149–156.

Cronbach, L., & Meehl, P. E. Construct validity in psychological tests. *Psychological Bulletin*, 1955, *52*, 281–302.

Davison, G. C. Homosexuality: The ethical challenge. *Journal of Consulting and Clinical Psychology*, 1976, *44*, 157–162.

Eisler, R. M., Hersen, M., Miller, P. M., & Blanchard, E. B. Situational determinants of assertive behaviors. *Journal of Consulting and Clinical Psychology*, 1975, *43*, 330–340.

Eysenck, H. J. (Ed.). *Behaviour therapy and the neuroses*. London: Pergamon Press, 1960.

Feldman, M. P., & MacCulloch, M. J. *Homosexual behavior: Therapy and assessment*. Oxford: Pergamon Press, 1971.

Ferster, C. B. Classification of behavioral pathology. In L. Krasner & L. P. Ullmann (Eds.), *Research in behavior modification*. New York: Holt, Rinehart and Winston, 1965.

Franks, C. M. Introduction: Behavior therapy and its Pavlovian origins: Review and perspectives. In C. M. Franks (Ed.), *Behavior therapy: Appraisal and status*. New York: McGraw-Hill, 1969.

Franks, C. M., & Wilson, G. T. (Eds.), *Annual review of behavior therapy: Theory and practice: Volume 3*. New York: Brunner/Mazel, 1975.

Goldfried, M. R., & Goldfried, A. P. Cognitive change methods. In F. H. Kanfer & A. P. Goldstein (Eds.), *Helping people change: A textbook of methods*. New York: Pergamon Press, 1975.

Goldfried, M. R., & Kent, R. N. Traditional versus behavioral personality assessment: A comparison of methodological and theoretical assumptions. *Psychological Bulletin*, 1972, *77*, 409–420.

Hersen, M., & Barlow, D. H. *Single-case experimental designs: Strategies for studying behavior change*. New York: Pergamon Press, 1976.

Hersen, M., & Bellack, A. S. (Eds.). *Behavioral assessment: A practical handbook*. New York: Pergamon Press, 1976.

Hersen, M., Eisler, R. M., & Miller, P. M. Historical perspectives in behavior modification: Introductory comments. In M. Hersen, R. M. Eisler, & P. M. Miller (Eds.), *Progress in behavior modification: Vol. 1*. New York: Academic Press, 1975.

Holland, J. G. *Behavior modification for prisoners, patients, and other people as a prescription for the planned society*. Paper presented at meeting of the Eastern Psychological Association, Philadelphia, Pennsylvania: April 1974.

Kanfer, F. H. *The many faces of self-control, or behavior modification changes its focus.*

Paper presented at Eighth International Banff Conference, Banff, Alberta, Canada: March 1976.

Kanfer, F. H., & Phillips, J. S. *Learning foundations of behavior therapy*. New York: John Wiley & Sons, 1970.

Kanfer, F. H., & Saslow, G. Behavioral diagnosis. In C. M. Franks (Ed.), *Behavior therapy: Appraisal and status*. New York: McGraw-Hill, 1969.

Kazdin, A. E. Self-monitoring and behavior change. In M. J. Mahoney & C. E. Thoresen (Eds.), *Self-control: Power to the person*. Monterey, Calif.: Brooks/Cole, 1974.

Kazdin, A. E. Statistical analyses for single-case experimental design. In M. Hersen & D. H. Barlow, *Single-case experimental designs: Strategies for studying behavior change*. New York: Pergamon Press, 1976.

Lang, P. J. The application of psychological methods to the study of psychotherapy and behavior modification. In A. E. Bergin & S. L. Garfield (Eds.), *Handbook of psychotherapy and behavior change*. New York: John Wiley & Sons, 1971.

Langer, E., & Abelson, R. A patient by any other name . . . Clinician group difference in labeling bias. *Journal of Consulting and Clinical Psychology*, 1974, *42*, 4–9.

Lazarus, A. A. *Behavior therapy and beyond*. New York: McGraw-Hill, 1971.

Leitenberg, H., Agras, W. S., Butz, R., & Wincze, J. Relationship between heart rate and behavioral change during the treatment of phobias. *Journal of Abnormal Psychology*, 1971, *78*, 59–68.

London, P. The end of ideology in behavior modification. *American Psychologist*, 1972, *27*, 913–920.

Mann, R. A. Behavioral excesses in children. In M. Hersen & A. S. Bellack (Eds.), *Behavioral assessment: A practical handbook*. New York: Pergamon Press, 1976.

Mischel, W. *Personality and assessment*. New York: John Wiley & Sons, 1968.

Mischel, W. Direct versus indirect personality assessment: Evidence and implications. *Journal of Consulting and Clinical Psychology*, 1972, *38*, 319–324.

Mischel, W. Toward a cognitive social learning reconceptualization of personality. *Psychological Review*, 1973, *80*, 252–283.

Morganstern, K. P. Behavioral interviewing: The initial stages of assessment. In M. Hersen & A. S. Bellack (Eds.), *Behavioral assessment: A practical handbook*. New York: Pergamon Press, 1976.

Paul, G. L. *Insight versus desensitization in psychotherapy: An experiment in anxiety reduction*. Stanford, Calif.: Stanford University Press, 1966.

Paul, G. Behavior modification research: Design and tactics. In C. M. Franks (Ed.), *Behavior therapy: Appraisal and status*. New York: McGraw-Hill, 1969.

Rimm, D. C., & Masters, J. C. *Behavior therapy: Techniques and empirical findings*. New York: Academic Press, 1974.

Skinner, B. F. *Walden two*. New York: Macmillan, 1948.

Skinner, B. F. *Beyond freedom and dignity*. New York: Knopf, 1971.

Skinner, B. F. (Ed.). *Cumulative record: A selection of papers* (3rd ed.) New York: Appleton-Century-Crofts, 1972.

Sloane, R. B., Staples, F. R., Cristol, A. H., Yorkston, J. J., & Whipple, K. *Psychotherapy versus behavior therapy*. Cambridge, Mass.: Harvard University Press, 1975.

Ullmann, L. P. Behavior therapy as social movement. In C. M. Franks (Ed.), *Behavior therapy: Appraisal and status*. New York: McGraw-Hill, 1969.

Ullmann, L. P., & Krasner, L. (Eds.). *Case studies in behavior modification*. New York: Holt, Rinehart & Winston, 1965.

Wachtel, P. Psychodynamics, behavior therapy, and the implacable experimenter: An inquiry into the consistency of personality. *Journal of Abnormal Psychology*, 1973, *82*, 324–334.

Walker, H. M., Hops, H., & Johnson, S. M. Generalization and maintenance of classroom treatment effects. *Behavior Therapy*, 1975, *6*, 188–200.

Watson, J. B., & Rayner, R. Conditioned emotional reactions. *Journal of Experimental Psychology*, 1920, *3*, 1–14.

Winett, R. A., & Winkler, R. C. Current behavior modification in the classroom: Be still, be quiet, be docile. *Journal of Applied Behavior Analysis*, 1972, *5*, 499–504.

Yates, A. J. *Behavior therapy*. New York: John Wiley & Sons, 1970.

Yates, A. J. *Theory and practice in behavior therapy*. New York: John Wiley & Sons, 1975.

2

Fear reduction I

Introduction

Systematic desensitization is the primary behavioral technique for the treatment of fears and phobias. Developed by Wolpe (1958), this procedure has tremendous historic significance in the growth of behavior modification, as well as being an important clinical tool. Desensitization is one of two approaches (the other is the token economy) that are most responsible for bringing notoriety and then general acceptance of behavior modification. For many non-behaviorists, desensitization is synonomous with behavior therapy. Moreover, there probably has been more research conducted to evaluate systematic desensitization than any other behavioral approach.

It would be difficult to develop an appropriate perspective of the procedures involved, and of the empirical evaluation of the procedures, without first understanding the theoretical model on which desensitization is based. We will begin with a discussion of the traditional behavioral view of the development and maintenance of fears. With this as a context, we will describe the procedure, the rationale on which it was developed, and Wolpe's view of the process of fear reduction. At the present time, there is little doubt that desensitization is a highly effective procedure. However, the manner in which it works and the restrictions on how it must be conducted are not at all certain. We will, therefore, present a critical review of the research conducted and arguments offered in regard to the procedure as a whole, the specific components of the procedure, and its theoretical basis. Our discussion in this chapter will be limited to an evaluation of systematic desensitization. Chapter 3 will be devoted to a review and evaluation of other forms of fear reduction techniques. We have divided the material into two chapters as it is our view that the mechanics and rationale of desensitization are not subject to criticism simply on the basis of the effectiveness of alternative procedures. That is, there can be more than one method to reduce fear or fearful behavior.

Fear and Anxiety

Fear and anxiety are among the most commonly experienced forms of psychological distress. Both terms refer to aversive emotional reactions, which typically involve both subjective discomfort and physiological arousal. Some writers use the two terms synonomously (e.g., Borkovec, Weerts, & Bernstein, 1977). However, the term fear is usually reserved for those reactions that have a specific focus or stimulus referent, and anxiety refers to reactions for which no specific context, focus, or stimulus can be identified. For example, an individual might be *afraid* of dogs, snakes, heights, or crowds. In contrast, one might feel *anxious* but not know precisely why when thinking about the future, or when an instructor says he wishes to see you after class, or while sitting in a hospital waiting room.

Most of us frequently experience mild fears and anxieties. They are either realistic, in the sense that there are real dangers present, or they are mild and do not result in much distress or restriction of activity. Occasionally, fears reach extreme levels and are accompanied by major behavioral handicaps or limitations. These intense reactions may be in response to situations that are not inherently dangerous, such as fears of social situations and examinations. More frequently, they have some basis in reality, but are extreme beyond justification. In either case, these reactions are referred to as *phobias*. It should be recognized that the term phobia, as used here, refers to a *degree* of distress, not a *type* of distress. As we shall see in the following sections, both phobic level and non-phobic level fears come about, can be maintained, and can be modified in the same manner. Furthermore, the term does not imply a specific diagnostic category, as is the case with the medical model use of the term phobia as a type of psychiatric condition.

The Development of Fears

The traditional behavioral conception of how fears develop is well represented in a classic experiment conducted by Miller (1948). The subjects were laboratory rats. The experimental manipulations were conducted in a box containing two compartments joined by an open doorway. One compartment was painted white and on its floor contained gridwork through which an electric shock could be administered. The other compartment was black and contained no grid. Miller first placed the rat in one compartment and then in the other in order to demonstrate that the rats did not react negatively to the box. The rat was then placed in the *white* compartment and the shock was turned on. The animal responded by jumping, quivering, defecating, and running. During the course of such feverish activity, the rat would eventually (by chance) pass through the doorway into the black compartment, thus escaping from the shock. The rat was then returned to the white compartment with the electric shock, and it again, eventually, ran into the black section. This sequence was repeated many times, and each time the rat escaped after progressively less time. Eventually, it began running directly to the black compartment as soon as it was placed in the box. This was not unexpected; the rat had learned to *escape* an aversive situation. The learning sequence can be represented schematically as follows:

$$\text{Shock} \longrightarrow \text{Pain}$$
$$\text{(UCS)} \qquad \text{(UCR)}$$
$$\qquad \qquad \text{Pain} \longrightarrow \text{Running} \longrightarrow \text{Pain Reduction}$$
$$\qquad \qquad (S^D) \qquad \quad (R) \qquad \qquad \quad (S^R)$$

The above schematic indicates that shock is an unconditioned stimulus that elicits pain. Pain serves as a discriminative stimulus for a number of behaviors, including running (through the doorway), which is reinforced by pain reduction. This is a basic two-stage learning process.

Once the escape response is firmly established, the second stage of the experiment begins. The rat is again placed in the white compartment, but the shock is no longer turned on. However, the rat continues to run directly to the black compartment. It is no longer escaping the painful shock; it is *avoiding* the shock. (Technically, since the shock is turned off there is nothing to avoid, but the rat behaves *as if* it were avoiding an impending shock.) In the case of escape, pain serves as the stimulus for running. What serves as the stimulus in the avoidance situation? – a classically conditioned fear response. The schematic is as follows:

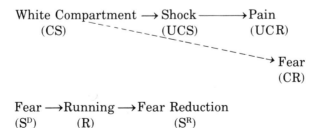

$$\text{Fear} \longrightarrow \text{Running} \longrightarrow \text{Fear Reduction}$$
$$(S^D) \qquad \quad (R) \qquad \qquad \quad (S^R)$$

The white compartment is a stimulus that is contiguous with shock.

With repetition, it becomes a conditioned stimulus capable of eliciting a conditioned response—fear. It should be noted that a CR is similar to, but not an exact duplicate of the associated UCR. Fear, like pain, is an aversive state, typically involving physiological arousal, behavioral disorganization, and motor responding. (In humans, there is also an associated cognitive response component.) In this situation, fear serves as a discriminative stimulus for running, which is reinforced by *fear reduction* rather than *pain reduction*. At this point, it would be logical to ask why the rat does not delay the running response in an effort to determine whether or not the shock is still present. If the rat did delay, the fear and avoidance responses would quickly extinguish. However, the avoidance response begins as soon as the rat is placed in the white compartment; it is repeatedly reinforced (by fear reduction) and there is no alternative reinforcer to be obtained in the white compartment. Therefore, the animal continues to avoid, never pausing long enough to discover the change in the environment.

This pattern is presumed to be prototypic of human fear and avoidance behavior (i.e., classically conditioned fear responses accompanied by operantly reinforced avoidance behavior). However, such extrapolation from animal to human behavior is not directly testable because of the ethical constraint on experimentation with humans. There have been numerous demonstrations of the development of such fear and avoidance behavior in the laboratory through the use of mild electric shock (e.g., Bellack, 1973), but this type of laboratory demonstration is merely suggestive. There has been one often quoted exception—the classic case of Little Albert. Watson and Rayner (1920) generated a conditioned fear in a 5-year-old child by systematically creating a loud noise behind him while simultaneously introducing a white rabbit into the room. Very shortly the child developed a fear of white rabbits. Furthermore, the child's fear response generalized to other white furry objects including different animals, rugs, and Santa Claus whiskers. While there is no indication as to how long the fear persisted, this experiment provides support for the model of learned fear. In natural situations, it is unlikely that aversive experiences would occur in such a systematic fashion. The specific factors necessary and sufficient to generate fears are still unknown. Some of the factors that are probably relevant are: severity of aversive experiences, frequency of experiences, and the pattern of experiences (e.g., several in quick succession).

Bandura (1969) suggests that modeling or vicarious conditioning (see Chapter 3) plays an even greater role in the development of fears than direct experience. For example, a child regularly observing his mother responding fearfully to and avoiding dogs is learning by observation that "dogs are dangerous," even if he is never chased or bitten. Similarly, being repeatedly *told* that dogs are dangerous and that they should be avoided (another form of vicarious learning) could also lead to a pattern of fear and avoidance. Whether by direct experience or vicarious learning, the specific circumstances (e.g., learning history) through which fears are acquired are almost always unknown. However, these historical circumstances are typically of secondary importance to the maintaining factors (i.e., distress and avoidance) that can be identified.

A Theory of Fear Reduction

The conception of fear development presented above places major emphasis on the effects of avoidance behavior. The initial distress-response cannot extinguish as the individual avoids the fear-producing stimulus. Therefore, a logical approach to treatment involves engineering extinction by exposing the individual to the feared stimulus under non-noxious circumstances. Numerous procedures for generating such exposure have been developed, including modeling (Bandura, Blanchard, & Ritter, 1969), flooding (Boulougouris, Marks, & Marset, 1971), implosion (Stampfl, 1967), and anxiety management training (Suinn & Richardson, 1971). (See Chapter 3 for a discussion of these procedures.) Systematic desensitization also emphasizes exposure, but is based on a physiological model of fear that leads to a distinctive strategy.

Some basic knowledge of the operation of the human nervous system is necessary if Wolpe's model is to be understood. The nervous system has two subdivisions. The central nervous system (CNS) controls primarily voluntary, skeletal muscle activity: movement of arms, legs, neck, fingers, etc. The autonomic nervous system (ANS) controls primarily involuntary, striate muscle activity: digestive functions, cardiovascular processes, sexual arousal, etc. The ANS has two sub-systems which operate in an antagonistic manner. The sympathetic nervous system (SNS) operates to increase arousal or activation of the organism. SNS discharge (activity) increases heart and respiration rate, results in constriction of peripheral blood vessels and dilation of central vessels, and decreases skin temperature and skin resistance (GSR). It also inhibits digestive and sexual processes. The parasympathetic nervous system (PNS) performs essentially the exact opposite functions. The PNS tends to stimulate decreases in all functions that the SNS increases, and it stimulates increases in all functions that the SNS decreases. While the systems ordinarily function in a dynamic balance or equilibrium, heightened activity of either system serves to inhibit or suppress the effects of the other system.

The SNS is often referred to as the "fight or flight" system, as one of its primary functions is to gear the organism for survival in the presence of danger. As such, a major stimulus for SNS activation is fear (Ax, 1953; Sternbach, 1966). The PNS, on the other hand, controls the organism in such low danger and low activity situations as deep relaxation (e.g., sleep) and sexual arousal, and while eating. Thus, both subjectively and physiologically, one cannot be both fearful and relaxed simultaneously. This principle is central to desensitization. Graduated nonaversive exposure to feared stimuli is managed by simultaneously creating a positive affective and physiological state (relaxation) and presenting the feared stimuli. Relaxation serves to *reciprocally inhibit* the fear, thus resulting in its counterconditioning or extinction.

As we shall see later, there is considerable controversy over the manner in which desensitization works and, therefore, in the specific manner in which it should be administered. Much of the controversy centers around differences in the use of the terms reciprocal inhibition, counterconditioning, extinction, and habituation — all of which have been used to explain the effects of desensitization. All four terms refer to response reduction processes. According to van Egeren (1971), reciprocal inhibition and habituation refer to short-term neurological processes, while counterconditioning and extinction refer to long-term changes that are more apparent at more global levels of functioning. Furthermore, reciprocal inhibition and counterconditioning refer to response reduction based on some antagonistic response that has an inhibiting effect, while habituation and extinction involve no antagonistic inhibition. Reliance on one or another of these four processes would lead to considerably different treatment strategies. For example, Wolpe emphasizes reciprocal inhibition and counterconditioning. His procedure involves repeated exposure of phobic stimuli under SNS inhibition, while relaxation is incorporated as a counterconditioning response that prevents the experience of anxiety. (This will be discussed in more detail in subsequent sections.) In contrast, Marks (1975) emphasizes extinction and has made extensive use of *flooding,* in which the individual is exposed to highly feared stimuli for extended periods of time.

Systematic Desensitization Procedure

There are any number of ways in which the fear response can be reciprocally inhibited. Wolpe suggested that drugs, sexual activity, assertive responses, muscle relaxation, and eating could all be incompatible to fear. However, he ultimately selected a muscle relaxation technique known as Deep Muscle Relaxation (DMR). Developed by Jacobson (1938) as a treatment procedure for anxiety and tension, DMR involves the focused relaxation of most of the major voluntary muscle groups in the body. The client undergoing training in DMR is seated in a comfortable chair (usually a recliner is used). Room lights are dimmed and the client is requested to close his eyes and relax as much as possible. The therapist then instructs the individual to first tense and then relax a series of muscle groups. The initial tension serves to focus attention on one specific muscle and to help sensitize the individual to feelings of tension. A typical sequence of muscle groups that might be involved in this procedure is as follows: right hand, right arm, left hand, left arm, forehead, eyelids, nose and cheeks, mouth and jaw, neck, shoulders, right side of chest, left side of chest, stomach, lower back, right thigh, right calf and foot, left thigh, left calf and foot. Throughout the sequence, the therapist directs the client's focus to relevant sensations, and promotes general relaxation with a soothing, hypnotic voice. A portion of a typical narrative is as follows:

> "You are becoming calm and relaxed. Feel yourself sinking deeper and deeper into the chair as your muscles relax. Breathe deeply and slowly and continue to relax. Now make a fist with your right hand. That's it. Pull it tighter; feel the tension across your fingers and up through your wrist. O.K., now let your hand relax; let the muscles relax as your hand falls into the chair. Feel them relaxing; feel the warmth as the blood flows back into your fingers. Concentrate on the feeling, how different it is from the tension. Feel the relaxation spreading up through your hand and wrist into your forearm. Now make a fist with that hand again and feel the difference . . ."

Each muscle group is tensed and relaxed two or three times. Training is usually conducted for five or six sessions, and clients are instructed to practice at home between sessions. After a few weeks of training the procedure can be abbreviated, and most clients can become deeply relaxed with deep breathing and focused tension-relaxation of the hands alone. In contrast to such additional fear-inhibiting activities as assertion, sex, and eating, DMR is portable, can be systematically generated and controlled, and has relatively universal applicability. These characteristics make it highly attractive for use in treatment.

One possible disadvantage of the muscle relaxation state as described above is that it requires the client to remain immobile in a semi-prone position in a darkened, quiet room. Direct exposure to most feared stimuli is, thus, precluded. Such commonly feared stimuli as swimming pools and lakes, airplanes, heterosexual interactions, and public speaking engagements cannot be duplicated in a clinic room under such restrictive conditions. This difficulty led to what perhaps is Wolpe's (1958) major contribution—the exposure to feared stimuli in imagination. It had long been recognized that fear could be aroused by thoughts or images of feared stimuli (e.g., Dollard & Miller, 1950). Wolpe reasoned, therefore, that fear could be eliminated if feared stimuli were imagined when the fear was reciprocally inhibited. Reciprocal inhibition could be accomplished by instructing the client to imagine phobic stimuli while in a deeply relaxed state, such as could be produced by

DMR. If the SNS arousal (of fear) could be inhibited, then the PNS activity (as produced by relaxation) would be dominant. However, most clinically significant fears result in such extreme arousal that the relaxation response is not sufficient to suppress this arousal. This problem led to the third key element of desensitization—the presentation of feared stimuli in hierarchical order.

As with most other response patterns, fears are subject to stimulus generalization. Most fears are not aroused solely by one or two focal stimuli, but by numerous stimuli that have some relationship with or similarity to the focal stimuli. For example, individuals who experience fear of flying are frequently not only afraid of flying per se, but of being near airplanes, of airports, of movies about airplanes, of newspaper stories and advertisements about airplanes, of the sound of an airplane in the sky, etc. The generalization pattern is idiosyncratic for each individual as a function of his learning history. However, most patterns can be conceptualized in the form of a gradient such as that shown below in Fig. 2.1.

The abscissa represents the degree of similarity to or distance from the focal stimulus. There are three common stimulus parameters that frequently might be found along the abscissa (i.e., common types of generalization patterns). One of these is time (e.g., length of time before an event such as an examination). A second concerns *spatial* characteristics (e.g., physical distance between the individual and a rat or snake; number of people in a crowd for an individual with fear of crowds). The third parameter is *thematic;* this refers to such content themes as those described above for fear of flying. The ordinate of the graph in Fig. 2.1

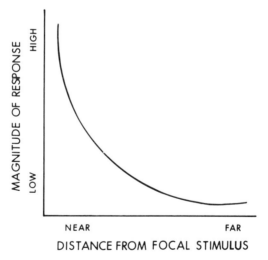

Fig. 2.1 A stimulus-generalization gradient.

represents the magnitude of the fear response. As can be seen, the magnitude of response decreases as dissimilarity or distance increases. For example, a student with examination anxiety is likely to become increasingly anxious as the time of an examination approaches and the closer he approaches the classroom in which the examination is to be conducted on the day of the examination. The generalization phenomenon is utilized in two ways in systematic desensitization. *First,* the client's general fear pattern (e.g., fear of flying) is analyzed or dissected so that the particular generalization pattern can be identified. A hierarchy of feared stimuli is then constructed, ranging in small steps from low to highly feared items (see discussion of Table 2.1 below). Treatment begins by exposing items from the low end of the hierarchy simultaneous with relaxation. The DMR response is powerful enough to inhibit arousal to these low feared stimuli. *Second,* as fear to these stimuli is counterconditioned (through repetition), the relaxation response generalizes up the hierarchy, reducing the fearfulness of items initially eliciting considerable fear. In this manner, items that at first resulted in extreme fear gradually elicit decreasing arousal. Finally, all items can be inhibited by DMR. An analogy to this procedure is the dismantling of a tower of children's blocks by slightly lifting the tower and removing blocks from the base one at a time; the top block is slowly lowered without its being touched directly.

Given this model of fear reduction, the construction of a fear hierarchy is a delicate and critical process. The client is typically asked to analyze his actual or anticipated fearfulness across a number of imagined life events put together by him and the therapist, identifying specific components or experiences that result in differing degrees of fear. As a guide, the client is often instructed to rate experiences on a 100-point scale of Subjective Units of Discomfort (SUDS). A score of 100 SUDS represents the client's maximal fear, 50 SUDS is moderate, and 0 SUDS represents no fear. A characteristic hierarchy contains 10–20 items ranging in distress level from a low of 5 or 10 to a high of 100 SUDS. The items are separated by small and relatively even increments. Table 2.1 contains examples of a temporal hierarchy for examination fear and a thematic hierarchy for heterosexual dating anxiety.

When it is determined that desensitization is the treatment of choice, the client is given a complete and truthful explanation of the procedure and its rationale. The next few sessions of treatment are devoted to training in DMR and in the construction of a hierarchy. Treatment proper then begins. The client is asked to relax and he is instructed to imagine the least fear-provoking item on the hierarchy he has helped construct. The therapist describes the scenario in detail and the client signals (by raising an index finger) when the image is clear. The client continues to imagine the scene for about 30 sec., or until he begins to

TABLE 2.1
Examples of Temporal and Thematic Hierarchies

Item	SUDS
Temporal Hierarchy (Examination Anxiety)	
Teacher passes out exams	100
Sit down in exam room	90
Enter exam room	80
Standing in hall, waiting to enter the exam room	70
Walking to school on day of exam	60
At home on the morning of an exam	50
Studying on the night before an exam	40
1 week before an exam	30
Teacher announces that an exam will be upcoming in 2 weeks	20
Teacher announces he will give a midterm and a final	10
Thematic Hierarchy (Heterosexual Dating Anxiety)	
Ringing a date's doorbell	100
Calling a prospective date on the telephone	90
Asking a girl to dance	80
Asking a girl for her phone number	70
Leaving to pick up a date	60
Asking a girl for a date	50
Dressing for a date	40
Talking to a girl in class	30
Being introduced to an attractive girl	20
Thinking about next Saturday night	10

experience some anxiety, which he immediately signals to the therapist by, again, raising his index finger. In either case (anxiety or 30 sec.), the client is instructed to terminate the image and focus again on relaxation. It is presumed to be critical that the imagery be curtailed *as soon as* any anxiety is experienced. (This presumption has been the subject of some controversy. We will discuss it further in subsequent sections of this chapter.) After 60–90 sec. of relaxation, the therapist again presents the first hierarchy item. This sequence (relaxation, imagery, relaxation, imagery) continues until the client can imagine the scene with no anxiety on three or four successive presentations. The next item in the hierarchy is then presented in similar fashion, with a similar criterion. If the criterion of three non-anxious repetitions cannot be met, the item is presumed to be too anxiety-provoking to be handled at this stage of treatment. Further practice is then provided on the preceding item, or a new item which is less anxiety provoking is constructed. This procedure continues, at the rate of three or four items per session, until the most feared item on the hierarchy (often the presenting symptom) can be imagined with no distress. Treatment is then concluded. Occasionally, the client will be instructed to expose himself to previously feared stimuli to both assess and facilitate generalization from imagination to the natural environment. However, the procedure as devised by Wolpe is presumed to be effective without such in vivo practice.

Treatment is rarely this simple in actual clinical practice. Clients frequently present themselves for therapy describing a number of general difficulties, rather than specific fears. Complaints such as the following are common: "I can't seem to relate to people," "I always seem to be anxious or tense. I don't know what is happening," or "My life is just a mess. I can't study or relate to people. I don't know what I want to do with my life." The therapist must first determine what specific behavioral targets need to be treated. That is, what are the behavioral excesses or deficits and what are the associated cognitions, feelings, and environmental factors that are involved? If it can be determined that any or all of the difficulties are based on fear, desensitization may then be applied. If there are multiple fears that do not appear to be related, treatment might involve the sequential desensitization of a series of hierarchies. If there are additional target behaviors other than fears, the therapist might simultaneously or sequentially apply desensitization and any other appropriate treatment techniques (e.g., social skills training, thought stopping, or a weight control program).

Empirical Evaluation of Systematic Desensitization

As stated earlier, systematic desensitization is probably the most widely researched behavioral technique. At this point, after almost 20 years of critical evaluation, there is little question that the treatment package is effective in the amelioration of both single and multiple fears. Early support came from the clinical work of Wolpe and his colleagues (e.g., Arnold Lazarus). Summarizing the results of their clinical work, Paul (1969a) reported that Wolpe reported a success rate of 92% (for 85 cases) and Lazarus reported a success rate of 86% (for 220 cases). Eysenck (1960) has concluded that verbal psychotherapy has a success rate similar to that which could be expected from natural remission—about 60–70%. (This conclusion has been subjected to considerable criticism, especially from Bergin [1971]. He has pointed out that some psychotherapists tend to make clients better, while others make them worse. The resultant average improvement rates, therefore, do not reflect what psychotherapy might do under optimal circumstances. Furthermore, the Eysenck data on natural remission rates are also suspect and might be gross overestimates.) In comparison, the Wolpe-Lazarus results were excellent. However, their reports of success were based on a series of uncontrolled case studies; the results are, therefore, suggestive but not conclusive. Most of the cases were treated in the late 1950s and early 1960s, and the success stimulated the interest of several researchers who provided extensive empirical support for the initial clinical claims.

Two of the earliest and most significant studies were conducted by Peter Lang and his colleagues (Lang & Lazovik, 1963; Lang, Lazovik, & Reynolds, 1965). Both studies compared desensitization with pseudotherapy and no treatment control conditions. These studies provided a clear demonstration that desensitization was effective in reducing fear. By including appropriate experimental controls, they also provided evidence to indicate that treatment effects were a function of the desensitization procedure, and not to the non-specific (placebo) effects of being in a treatment program or to mere suggestion. Furthermore, the studies introduced a number of experimental procedures that have had a significant impact on behavioral research. An initial difficulty in conducting large group (parametric) experimentation to evaluate a procedure such as desensitization is the identification of a large number of individuals with equivalent problems. There are few settings in which a sizeable population (25–50) of individuals with homogeneous fears can be easily recruited. Lang and Lazovik solved this problem by identifying a sub-clinical or analogue population (i.e., college students with fear of snakes). The small animal fears of college students are not typically sufficiently severe for them to seek out treatment, but on most college campuses there are many students with such common fears who can be recruited for experimental treatment. While they are less severe, the development and maintenance of these fears parallel actual clinical problems in many respects. (Whether or not the parallels extend to remediation has recently been a subject of controversy. We will discuss this point in a later section.)

A second major difficulty in conducting this form of research is securing objective data on which to evaluate outcome. While the customary subjective reports from the client and therapist are important data, they are not sufficient for drawing clear conclusions for two reasons. *First,* self-reports are subjective and are highly susceptible to expectancy effects, demand characteristics, and bias. That is, clients will often tell a therapist what they believe he would like to hear and not really how effective they (the clients) believe the therapy to have been. *Second,* such reports do *not* correlate highly with motoric and physiological changes (Bellack & Hersen, 1977). That is, self-report of decreased fear does not necessarily imply that there was an increase in approach behavior or decrease in SNS arousal to the feared stimulus. In response to this difficulty, Lang and Lazovik developed an objective technique for assessing avoidance behavior — the Behavioral Avoidance Test (BAT). They placed a harmless snake (snake-phobic college students were subjects) in a glass cage at one end of a long narrow room. Individually, the subjects entered the room and were asked to approach as close to the snake as they could, touching it if possible. The floor of the room was marked at fixed intervals. Degree of fear could be rated objectively by noting the closest point to which the subject approached (i.e., how many feet away or how much contact with the snake); decreasing fear was mainfested by decreasing distance (i.e., increased approach). The BAT is adaptable to a wide variety of fears. It is characteristically accompanied by a self-report measure (the Fear Thermometer [FT]), in which the subject is asked to evaluate his discomfort at the point of closest approach on a 10-point scale (10 equals maximal distress).

The single most persuasive and influential investigation of desensitization was conducted by Gordon Paul (1966). Paul selected public speaking anxiety as the focus of treatment and he used rigorous selection procedures to insure that his subjects were highly fearful. His study included five groups; systematic desensitization, insight-oriented psychotherapy, attention-placebo, waiting list control, and a no contact control. The therapists were skilled, practicing psychotherapists who were not behaviorally oriented or trained. Paul taught them how to conduct systematic desensitization therapy for the study. Dependent variables included a stress test (giving a speech before an audience) with observer ratings of performance and anxiety, physiological measures, and self-report measures. Following treatment, subjects in the desensitization group evidenced significantly greater improvements on pre-post measures than all other groups. These effects persisted at 6-week and 2-year post-treatment follow-ups (Paul, 1967). Furthermore, there were no indications of symptom substitution. The psychotherapy and attention-placebo groups did not differ from one another, despite the fact that therapists for these groups had predicted that psychotherapy would be effective and conducted treatment in accordance with their own preferences and style. This investigation clearly demonstrated the short- and long-term effectiveness of systematic desensitization.

These positive findings were amplified in a large scale study of actual clinic cases conducted by Sloane, Staples, Cristol, Yorkston, and Whipple (1975). They compared groups receiving behavior therapy, dynamic psychotherapy, or minimal contact. As they employed a general clinic population rather than college student volunteers, subjects in the three groups were matched on severity of disturbance, but could not be matched on specific symptoms. All treatment was conducted by experienced therapists. The behavior therapy group received desensitization and other behavioral treatments (e.g., assertion training) as necessary (this lack of control was also necessitated by the nature of the population). The results for the behavior therapy group were generally better than the control group and better than or equal to the psychotherapy group on all dependent measures. Eighty percent of the behavior therapy subjects improved on target behaviors compared to only 48% of control subjects, and 93% improved on overall adjustment compared to only 77% of control and psychotherapy subjects. These results were maintained over a 1-year follow-up. In addition, behavior therapy was effective for most patients treated, while psychotherapy was effective for only certain types of individuals. While this study is an excellent example of non-analogue treatment research, it did not (could not) include objective behavioral measures of change due to the variability of presenting problems.

When conducting treatment research, it is not sufficient to demonstrate that a specific treatment group changes more than a non-treatment group (e.g., that a specific treatment procedure is effective). The researcher must also show that the changes were related in a cause and effect manner to the (presumed) critical elements of treatment. There are a number of non-specific factors that commonly result in some, often temporary, behavior changes. These include expectation of success, exposure to a "helpful" therapist, simply being involved in a discussion about one's problems, and being exposed to phobic stimuli in pre- and post-treatment assessment. The control groups in the Paul study effectively controlled for these common factors. The results, therefore, provide a strong indication that changes in the desensitization group were a function of the *desensitization package*. (These data do not demonstrate that all of the elements of the package are critical and must be administered in the standard manner. Research that examines this issue will be discussed in the following sections.)

Subsequent research has tended to support and expand on the clinical and empirical results described above. Thus, desensitization appears to be an effective procedure. Several interesting and economical variations have also proved to be effective. Meichenbaum, Gilmore, and Fedoravicius (1971) and Paul and Shannon (1966) reported that desensitization could be conducted effectively in a group format. In this approach, either a hierarchy common to all group members or individual hierarchies are constructed. The procedure is analogous to that used in individual treatment except that fear images are terminated at the first signal of anxiety by *any* group member, and progress through the hierarchy is geared to the slowest (most fearful) member of the group. Di Loreto (1971) conducted a study of group desensitization that is in many respects as notable as the Paul (1966) study. He recruited 100 volunteer subjects (college students) who were suffering from interpersonal anxiety and assigned them at random to one of five groups: (1) rational-emotive therapy (see Chapter 3); (2) client-centered therapy; (3) systematic desensitization; (4) no-treatment control (these subjects were seen for several brief, non-therapeutic meetings); and (5) no-contact control. Treatment was conducted for nine group sessions by advanced graduate student therapists. Several dependent measures were employed to evaluate treatment including self-report measures of anxiety, therapist ratings of anxiety during treatment sessions, and objective ratings of anxiety behavior during sessions (e.g., stuttering, hand-wringing) made by trained observers. The desensitization, rational-emotive therapy, and client-centered therapy conditions were significantly more effective in reducing anxiety than both control conditions. However, the systematic desensitization group was significantly more effective than both of the other treatment groups on most dependent measures. These differences persisted through a 3-month follow-up period. Desensitization was not only more effective than the other treatments on the average, but was more consistently effective. That is, the other two procedures were highly effective for some subjects and not at all effective for others, but the results for desensitization were consistent across subjects.

Peter Lang (1969) has developed a device for administering desensitization automatically, thus eliminating the need for a therapist (after assessment has been completed and desensitization is identified as the treatment of choice). This device, labeled the Device for Automated Desensitization (DAD), is a computer-like apparatus that contains a tape-recorded hierarchy and relaxation instructions, and makes physiological recordings of the client's responses during item presentations. Progress is controlled by predetermined criteria (e.g., number of non-anxious repetitions) combined with assessment of the client's physiological activity. Less elaborate devices have been developed in other laboratories and clinics in which clients control progress by advancing or resetting automatically operated tape recorders. Krapfl and Nawas (1969) and Lang (1969) found automated desensitization to be as effective as desensitization with a live therapist. Both group and automated desensitization are useful procedures for clinical facilities which typically see numerous clients suffering from similar fears. This is often the case with university counseling centers, where many students are seen experiencing test anxiety, speech (public speaking) anxiety, and heterosexual (dating) anxiety.

Our presentation of desensitization thus far has described a "traditional" view of how it is to be applied and how if functions to alter behavior. While the overall efficacy of desensitization seems clear, the Wolpean view of theory, rationale, and procedure has been the subject of considerable controversy. The studies described above did not critically examine the specific contributions made by each element of the procedure (DMR, the use of imagery, hierarchies, etc.). Rather, they evaluated the package as a whole. Numerous researchers have questioned the use of each of those elements as well as the manner in which they are combined (e.g., whether imagery should be terminated as soon as anxiety is experienced). Similarly, there have been questions about how each element operates and how fear is actually reduced. The answers to these questions have considerable significance. If it could be demonstrated that any of the existing treatment elements were not necessary, treatment might be simplified and/or improved, and the theory supporting current procedure severely challenged. In subsequent sections, we will present a critical review of these issues, focusing first on the components and then on the theory.

Muscle Relaxation

Three major questions have been raised about muscle relaxation: (1) Does the DMR procedure suggested by Wolpe actually result in SNS inhibition? (2) Is DMR a necessary component of desensitization? (3) Can the DMR procedure be modified or circumvented?

As originally practiced by Jacobson (1938), DMR training required up to 100 sessions and involved a much more extensive series of muscle groups than suggested by Wolpe. Wolpe recommended that five to six training sessions be conducted, Paul (1966) provided two sessions, and many researchers have successfully conducted training in one session. There is no clear indication of how much training is needed, how many muscle groups must be involved, and how many tension-relaxation sequences are necessary. Paul (1969b) investigated the physiological concomitants of DMR based on two sessions of training. He found that DMR resulted in substantial decreases in several measures of SNS activity and that it was more effective (e.g., resulted in greater SNS decreases) than hypnotically induced relaxation and self-generated attempts by subjects to relax. While DMR does apparently result in SNS suppression, it is unlikely that it is singularly effective or a non-alterable procedure. Muscle relaxation is a CNS response, not an ANS response. Any ANS (e.g., SNS) suppression resulting from relaxation of voluntary muscles would have to be indirect. That is, muscle relaxation would result in an intermediary response (e.g., cognitive quiescence, calming thoughts, or proprioceptive feedback) which has a direct impact on SNS activity. Therefore, other procedures which have a direct impact on ANS functioning should be equally or more effective than DMR.

Some indirect evidence for an alternative was reported by Bellack (1973). The experimental subjects were college students. Bellack first developed a conditioned fear to a red light by contingently applying a mild electric shock when the light was flashed. One-half of the subjects were then taught DMR while one-half were taught a cognitive relaxation procedure which involved concentrated focus on highly positive and calming imagery. This procedure paralleled DMR except that no tension-relaxation sequences were included. Also, the focus was on imagery and not the muscles. An example of the cognitive procedure is as follows: "Imagine you are lying on a quiet beach. Feel the sun warming your face. You can hear the gentle lapping of the waves. Feel yourself becoming warm and relaxed. . . . " The effectiveness of the two procedures in counterconditioning the fear was then compared. Both procedures were equally effective in reducing SNS arousal to the conditioned stimulus. Another alternative to DMR is the use of biofeedback (Schwartz, 1973). This is a shaping procedure in which individuals are trained to control their physiological activity by observing actual ongoing recordings of that activity. Several recent studies suggest that biofeedback can supplement or supplant the effects of DMR by providing more specific and systematic information about the actual level of physiological activity (Budzynski & Stoyva, 1969).

Presuming that muscle relaxation (DMR or otherwise) results in reduction of SNS activity, the next question is whether or not such relaxation is a necessary component of treatment. Davison (1968) conducted an experiment that has often been cited in support of the counterconditioning explanation of desensitization, in addition to providing evidence for the use of relaxation. His experiment is also important as it provides an excellent example of a research strategy referred to as "systematic dismantling." This approach involves the critical evaluation of a treatment package by comparing experimental groups that contain all of the treatment elements with other groups that parallel the entire procedure with the exception of some specific components. For example, if the full treatment consists of three sub-procedures (A, B, and C), a dismantling design might involve four groups as follows: (1) A, B, C; (2) A, B; (3) A; and (4) no treatment control. If the full treatment package is necessary, Group 1 should be better than Groups 2 and 3, as well as Group 4. The Davison (1968) study included four conditions with snake phobic subjects: (1) standard systematic desensitization, (2) relaxation (DMR) with a hierarchy irrelevant to snake phobia, (3) exposure to a snake-relevant hierarchy without relaxation, and (4) no treatment control. Group 1, receiving the complete desensitization procedure, improved significantly more than all of the other groups. The partial treatment groups (2 and 3) did not differ from the no treatment group. Thus, relaxation alone and graded exposure alone were not effective, but relaxation with graded exposure was effective, as would be predicted by desensitization theory.

Despite this seemingly effective demonstration, the role of relaxation is still not entirely resolved. For example, Nawas, Mealiea, and Fishman (1971) failed to replicate the Davison results, and Lomont and Edwards (1967) found no difference between a muscle relaxation group and a group that tensed their muscles whenever relaxation would ordinarily be applied. While both of those studies suffer from methodological flaws, their findings (and those of other related experiments) cannot be entirely discounted. There is also considerable evidence for the effectiveness of procedures that definitively preclude muscle relaxation such as flooding (Marks, 1975) and in vivo desensitization (in which real life phobic stimuli are presented rather than imaginary stimuli) (Sherman, 1972). At this point no definitive conclusions about relaxation can be reached. However, it is probably safe to argue that: (1) relaxation *can* be an effective adjunct to exposure as occurs in desensitization, and (2) DMR is a viable, quick training procedure which is effective for many individuals. It can be substituted for or supplemented by other techniques such as cognitive relaxation and biofeedback.

Imaginal Hierarchies

Wolpe (1958) considered hierarchy construction as one of the most delicate and critical aspects of treatment. First, items had to be selected so as to accurately represent the specific elements of the client's idiosyncratic phobic pattern. Faulty description could decrease the effectiveness of treatment and reduce generalization to the natural environment. Second, the sequence of items and gaps between them had to be fairly exact. If the increase in anxiety arousal from one item to the next were too large, the client could become more fearful or, at a minimum, treatment could be needlessly delayed. As with relaxation, these presumptions about hierarchies and images have been subjected to critical review and empirical evaluation. Two fundamental questions revolve around the effects of imagining hierarchy items: (1) Do they result in anxiety? and (2) Do items high in the hierarchy result in more anxiety than those low in the hierarchy? There is little doubt that visual images and self-talk are capable of generating emotional reactions such as fear and anxiety. One need only think back to a personal tragedy or a terrifying experience to demonstrate this phenomenon. Controlled laboratory research has supported the fact that different images can stimulate differential physiological arousal (e.g., Lacey, Smith, & Green, 1955; Lang, 1969). Support for the use of hierarchical presentation is provided in the Lang and Lazovik (1963) and Lang et al. (1965) studies discussed above. In both studies, degree of fear reduction was highly related to progress through the hierarchy. Using a time-limited treatment, these researchers found that the greater the number of hierarchy items desensitized, the greater the resulting fear reduction. All subjects in the desensitization groups had a similar number of trials (repetitions of images), suggesting that it was the range of items covered and not simple exposure that was important.

While the data described above provide support for the use of imaginal hierarchies, there are two other kinds of data that are somewhat contradictory. *First,* the vividness of the images does not appear to be related to degree of anxiety experienced (Rehm, 1973) or to outcome of desensitization (McLemore, 1972). Vividness refers to the clarity or depth of the

image. A *second* and more critical finding is that standardized hierarchies as used in automated or group desensitization are no less effective
than individualized hierarchies (McGlynn, 1971). While these data do
not contraindicate the use of hierarchies, they do suggest that item
selection and placement and the magnitude of anxiety increments between items are not absolutely critical. Similarly, it is uncertain at this
point whether or not there is any consistent difference between massed
versus spaced practice, long versus short exposure durations, or few
versus many repetitions of each scene. (However, numerous repetitions
with long exposures should be desirable as these involve more practice.)

These findings have a bearing on the theory of desensitization as well
as on the way in which it is conducted. Reciprocal inhibition as con-
ceived by Wolpe is a rather delicate neurological process, with little
leeway for error. The success of standardized, group, and automated
desensitization procedures indicates a robustness to the technique which
would not be predicted or easily explained by the reciprocal inhibition
model. That is, these procedures are likely to result in variable degrees
of relaxation, vividness of imagery, and without immediate termination
of imagery upon experience of anxiety.

Therapist Effects

The effect of the particular therapist conducting treatment on the
success of that treatment has long been recognized as a danger in the
evaluation of therapeutic procedures. Apparently, some therapists are
better than others, and most are more effective with some types of
clients than with others (Bergin, 1971). This variability is probably of
greater concern in relationship therapies (such as client-centered therapy) than in most behavioral treatments. The reason for this is that the
focus in behavioral treatment is on education and implementation of
discrete techniques, rather than on the relationship between therapist
and client. The literature on desensitization certainly substantiates this
viewpoint. Paul (1966) clearly controlled for therapist effects and found
desensitization to be effective above and beyond what could be expected
from therapist factors alone. The research on automated desensitization
suggests that a therapist need not even be present for the treatment to
be effective.

This is not to say that a warm, friendly, positive therapist-client
relationship is not desirable. These relationship factors have been
shown to relate positively to outcome in some non-behavioral therapies
(Garfield & Bergin, 1971; Truax & Mitchell, 1971). Sloane et al. (1975)
showed that behavioral therapists maintained therapeutic relationships
that were at least as high in warmth, empathy, and positive regard as
did non-behavioral therapists. While there are no data to suggest that

such positive relationships are critical in behavioral interventions, it seems likely that such a relationship could have a positive effect on the course of treatment, even if it is not sufficient to generate change. The client is more likely to comply with instructions and carry out assignments if he has favorable attitudes about therapy and the therapist. Conversely, non-compliance and/or premature termination are apt to result from a negative interaction. Interestingly, Morris and Suckerman (1974) found that taped desensitization was more effective when the taped voice was warm and friendly than when it was cold and impersonal.

Cognitive Factors

When used in the context of behavior modification, the terms "cognitive" or "cognition" refer to internal, symbolic processes such as language, thought, imagery, and self-observation. The determination of what role these processes play in the stream of behavior has frequently been a source of difficulty and confusion for both behavioral and non-behavioral theorists. Behaviorists have traditionally viewed cognition as behavior, different only in form from other behaviors such as motor responses. Cognitions or cognitive responses are thus presumed to follow the basic laws to which all behavior is subject. This view is typified by desensitization as conceptualized by Wolpe. Cognition is involved in the process of desensitization at all points from problem definition and assessment through treatment and outcome evaluation. Self-report of fear is a cognitive process, as is hierarchy construction, imagery, and perception and report of anxiety. Nevertheless, the procedure is viewed as a conditioning process involving an application of the laws of learning.

As with other aspects of Wolpe's construction, the role of cognition in desensitization has been the subject of evaluative research and controversy. Several writers have challenged Wolpe's entire theoretical model, reconceptualizing desensitization as a cognitive process, rather than as a conditioning or learning process (Marcia, Rubin, & Efran, 1969; Valins & Ray, 1967; Wilkins, 1971). This alternative model of desensitization presumes that fear can be modified by changing the client's *attributions* about his behavior. That is, he initially engages in fearful behavior because he perceives or identifies himself as fearful. Behavior change simply requires that the client learn to re-label his experience or perceive himself differently (e.g., as non-fearful).

The above model is clearly demonstrated by the research designs that have been employed by its proponents. The Valins and Ray (1967) study is something of a standard in this regard. They exposed college student subjects to a series of slides, some of which depicted snakes and some containing only the word SHOCK. The SHOCK slides were accompanied by an uncomfortable electric shock. Along with the slide presentations, subjects heard an audiotape of heartbeats, which remained at a steady and moderate rate between slides and during snake slides, but which quickened noticeably when SHOCK slides were presented. One group of subjects was informed that the sound was an amplified measure of their own heart, while another group was informed that it was "irrelevant background noise." Subjects in the group given the "own heart" instruction were expected to re-evaluate their reaction to the stimuli, believing that they were afraid of shock, but not of snakes. In a subsequent Behavioral Avoidance Test these subjects did, in fact, show more approach behavior than the control group (irrelevant noise). The authors concluded that desensitization works in a similar manner, not by counterconditioning fear but by changing the client's attribution about his behavior via relaxation.

This particular study, despite its renown has several methodological deficiencies which vitiate the authors' conclusions. No measures of actual physiological activity were made (there might have been actual physiological changes), the results of several subjects were discarded, and no pre-treatment assessment was conducted. Furthermore, there have been several attempts to replicate the results, all of which have been unsuccessful (e.g., Gaupp, Stern, & Galbraith, 1972; Sushinsky & Bootzin, 1970). The results of other studies which purport to demonstrate cognitive sources of behavior change have also suffered from poor methodology and/or have also been non-replicable. These data, therefore, do not support a cognitive explanation of desensitization.

It should be mentioned here that behavior theory, while incorporating cognition, does not accept such hypothetical constructs as attributions. This term refers to a cognitive process in which the individual actively scans the environment, makes an interpretation of what he perceives, and operates on the basis of his interpretation. Rather than positing an attributional process, the role of cognition can be more parsimoniously viewed as part of the stimulus input and processing stages of behavior in which past history and stored information interact with current input and output to maximize effective responding (e.g., increasing the probability of reinforcement). This information processing conception avoids reference to intentional, personalistic, hypothetical processes. Such terms as attribution and expectancy are useful *descriptively* as an aid in communicating about behavior. For example, one might say "the client behaved *as if* he had an expectancy about treatment" or "*as if* he had made an attribution about the source of his fear." However, such "as if" statements are quite different from *explanatory* statements such as "He responded to treatment *because* he had an expectancy of success," or "He developed a fear *because* he attributed his reaction to the stimulus."

Such explanatory statements are unjustified and problematic in that they ascribe real, causal status to invisible, hypothetical, and as yet still unverifiable processes.

The role played by cognitive factors in desensitization has also been questioned by a number of investigators who are in fundamental agreement with a behavioral conditioning model. The primary question posed by these researchers concerns the importance of a group of related factors including expectancy of success and therapeutic instructions. It was mentioned earlier that the experiments of Lang and Lazovik (1963), Lang et al. (1965), and Paul (1966) demonstrated that expectancy or placebo effects *alone* were not sufficient to account for the results of desensitization. The issue of concern here, however, is whether or not desensitization can work without positive expectancy. If so, would positive expectancy make it more effective?

A number of authors have found that positive expectancy and therapeutic instructions increased the effectiveness of desensitization (McGlynn, Reynolds, & Linder, 1971; Oliveau, Agras, Leitenberg, Moore, & Wright, 1969; Rosen, 1974; Woy & Efran, 1972). The Rosen (1974) experiment is in many ways prototypic of the research that has been conducted in this area. Subjects were undergraduate volunteers who were snake-fearful. They were recruited under the false pretense that the study was designed to examine the physiological reactions of snake-fearful individuals to imagined scenes of snakes. All subjects, in fact, received a somewhat disguised version of desensitization. Half of the subjects were given a highly positive therapeutic set; they were told that the experimental procedure had therapeutic benefit for snake-fearful individuals. The other subjects were given no therapeutic expectancy instructions; they presumably believed that the procedure was a simple experimental operation. If expectancy were not a factor in the desensitization process, both groups would be expected to manifest similar reductions in phobic behavior. In contrast, the results supported the hypothesis that expectancy *does* contribute to treatment outcome. The group receiving the therapeutic set manifested significantly greater changes on both behavioral and self-report measures than the experimental-set group. These and related findings have much appeal. As in our discussion about therapist effects, it is typical therapeutic procedure to instill positive expectations for the outcome of therapy. It is logical to presume that such expectancy can have a positive impact. However, despite the results reported above, this issue remains unresolved.

Reviews of the literature indicate that there are at least as many studies that have failed to find expectancy effects as studies that have found such effects (Borkovec, 1973; Davison & Wilson, 1973). There are a number of factors that might explain the differences between these two groups of studies. *First,* it cannot be safely concluded that subjects hold an expectancy simply because instructions have been designed to provide a set or expectancy. For example, Rosen (1974) found (on a post-treatment questionnaire) that five of 18 therapeutically oriented subjects did *not* believe that the procedure would be helpful, and six of 18 non-therapeutically oriented subjects *did* believe the procedure would be therapeutic. These data demonstrate the difficulty inherent in positing the existence of an internal process, whether from a behavioral or non-behavioral perspective. Retrospective self-reports are not sufficient to demonstrate what, if any, expectancy the subject held. These reports are affected by demand and social compliance, and represent the subject's post hoc interpretation of his behavior and what he believes the experimenter is asking (or looking for). The results of all such studies are suspect, as it can always be argued (inconclusively) that the appropriate expectancy was or was not developed.

A *second* difficulty is related to the manner of assessing change. It has long been known that self-report measures are especially subject to distortion and bias (e.g., expectancy) (Bellack & Hersen, 1977). Demonstration of the potency of cognitive factors has therefore emphasized changes in approach behavior. Bernstein (in press), in a series of studies, has now demonstrated that the Behavioral Avoidance Test can be similarly affected. For example, approach scores can be increased by providing information about the handling of snakes (e.g., they are not slimy) and by placing explicit demands on the subject to approach despite discomfort. Multiple exposures (as in pre- and post-treatment assessments) can also result in increased approach. The results of many studies are not clearly interpretable, based on their failure to adequately control for these factors.

The *final* issue pertains to the subject population employed in this research. Based on the model developed by Lang and Lazovik (1963), most desensitization studies have recruited volunteers with small animal phobias from introductory psychology courses. Typically, a paper-and-pencil fear inventory (the Fear Survey Schedule) is administered to a large number of individuals. Those reporting fear of snakes (or other targets) are then telephoned and asked to volunteer for an experiment. Those accepting then report in for a BAT, and a subgroup of those doing poorly on the BAT are again asked to volunteer for a second experiment. They may or may not be told that this second experiment involves a treatment procedure. Depending on the type of BAT employed (e.g., low or high demand) and the minimal BAT cutoff score used (e.g., no closer than 3 feet to the snake), it is quite possible to select a relatively low fear sample. One can, for instance, employ a low demand BAT and accept subjects who will do everything but pick up the snake. This, in fact, probably occurs more often than not. Reviewing the literature on expectancy studies, Borkovec (1973) reported that most studies finding an expectancy effect used less fearful subjects than studies finding no expectancy effects. He concluded that the behavior of high fear individuals was much less modifiable by such extra-therapeutic factors as expectancy and demand.

The use of analogue procedures with college undergraduates as subjects has broad implications for our understanding of desensitization. A large majority of studies have used such subjects, presuming that they differed only in degree of fear from clinical patients. However, this belief has been open to question. Marks (1975), in a recent review, considered the results of all such studies independently of the results of research conducted on actual patients. The two groups of subjects differ in a number of ways other than degree of fear. Most notably, the fears of patients typically have a longer history, have much more effect on their daily lives than do the mild fears of college students (e.g., most college students in urban settings have probably never seen a snake outside of zoos), and patients initiate treatment at their own volition (rather than being recruited). Patients are much less likely to profit from minimal interventions such as standardized taped desensitization (McGlynn, Williamson, & Davis, 1973) or expectancy manipulations (Borkovec, 1973). Bernstein and Paul (1971) argued persuasively that the results of research on analogue populations can be generalized to patient populations if appropriate controls are employed (e.g., careful subject selection, high demand BAT). We concur with that view, but urge caution in the evaluation of such research.

Theoretical Basis of Desensitization

In the preceding sections we have presented a critical evaluation of desensitization technique and procedure. Given that the technique is intimately related to Wolpe's theoretical model, criticism of the procedure is indirectly a critique of the model. Failure to support Wolpe's hypotheses about such central issues as relaxation and hierarchies, therefore, places his entire construction in doubt. The relative leeway apparently allowed in relaxation training, hierarchy construction and presentation, and the experience of anxiety does not coincide with the subtle neurological process of reciprocal inhibition. The latter factor is especially telling. The magnitude of arousal (anxiety) and duration of the experience necessary for an individual client to signal anxiety is highly variable. It is unlikely that many clients can proceed through a hierarchy without experiencing "too much" or "too little" anxiety.

Perhaps the major failing of reciprocal inhibition theory is that it is based on an overly simplistic model of the nervous system. A basic aspect of the theory is that avoidance behavior is a response to SNS arousal. Wynne and Solomon (1955) surgically ablated (severed) the

SNS connections in dogs that had previously learned an avoidance response. This procedure precluded the occurrence of SNS arousal to the conditioned stimulus. Nevertheless, the dogs continued to make avoidance responses (e.g., something other than SNS activity had served as a stimulus). While such a surgical procedure could obviously not be attempted with human subjects, other forms of research have similarly demonstrated the relative independence of autonomic and motoric manifestations of fear (Lang, 1971). For example, Leitenberg, Agras, Butz, and Wincze (1971) examined changes in heart rate (HR) and avoidance behavior after desensitization. They found a highly variable relationship. While some subjects had HR increases as avoidance decreased, others had no HR change, and still others had HR decreases. These data contradict reciprocal inhibition theory (as it pertains to desensitization), in which physiological inhibition is presumed to be a necessary precursor of behavior change.

Similar inconsistencies between response modalities have been found for the relationships of self-report with physiological and motoric responses (Bellack & Hersen, 1977; Hersen, 1973). Becker and Costello (1975) and Kennedy and Kimura (1974) demonstrated that avoidance behavior could be decreased despite a lack of change in self-report of fear. Paul (1966) found that subjects in control groups reported less distress in a public speaking situation after placebo or no treatment control conditions despite a lack of change in motoric or physiological responses.

It appears now that the term "fear" refers to a behavioral complex involving motoric, autonomic, and cognitive (self-report) elements. These three response factors can interact in an infinite variety of combinations. Some individuals can have an essentially motoric (avoidance) problem with little or no autonomic and cognitive distress. Other individuals might be primarily physiological responders, while still others might suffer from what is essentially a cognitive disturbance. Modification of one response component can sometimes have profound effects on other components, while the changes can also be independent. Given this pattern, the consistent, clear effectiveness of desensitization across response modalities is both startling and difficult to explain. It is quite possible that the procedure is broad-based enough that it can have a variety of effects which vary with the particular therapist and client. The relaxation element might reduce autonomic responding. Rehearsal of approach and repeated exposure (albeit in imagination) could affect avoidance behavior. Finally, cognitive elements, including expectancy, self-observation of successful approach, and the learning of a coping response (DMR) might affect cognitive responses. If this were the case, no single theory or explanation would account for all of the potential effects of the procedure.

Summary

Behavior therapists conceptualize fears and phobias as conditioned emotional responses involving classically and operantly conditioned components. The primary behavioral treatment strategy for these disorders is systematic desensitization. Developed by Wolpe (1958), desensitization involves the construction of a graded series of phobic stimuli (the hierarchy) which are presented in imagination while the client is in a state of deep muscle relaxation. Wolpe theorizes that the fear response is reciprocally inhibited by relaxation, and through repetition it is counterconditioned.

The effectiveness of desensitization as well as the component techniques and Wolpe's theory were critically examined. The research literature suggests that desensitization is a highly effective technique. However, the specific manner in which it must be conducted and the actual processes of fear reduction are uncertain. Muscle relaxation appears to be effective in reducing sympathetic nervous system arousal, but can be supplemented or supplanted by other techniques. Imaginal presentation of phobic stimuli is effective, but a moderate degree of leeway is allowable in hierarchy construction. The effectiveness of desensitization does not require an intensive therapist-client relationship. Attempts to explain desensitization as a cognitive reattribution process have not been supported by research. Positive expectancy for success contributes to the effectiveness of desensitization with low fearful, analogue populations, but not with high fearful, clinical populations. Finally, the literature does not support Wolpe's conceptualization of fears or of the manner in which desensitization operates. Fear appears to be a behavioral complex that involves semi-independent motoric, physiological, and cognitive elements.

References

Ax, A. F. The physiological differentiation between fear and anger in humans. *Psychosomatic Medicine*, 1953, *15*, 433–442.

Bandura, A. *Principles of behavior modification*. New York: Holt, Rinehart & Winston, 1969.

Bandura, A., Blanchard, E. B., & Ritter, R. The relative efficacy of desensitization and modeling approaches for inducing behavioral, affective and attitudinal changes. *Journal of Personality and Social Psychology*, 1969, *13*, 173–199.

Becker, H. G., & Costello, C. G. Effects of graduated exposure with feedback of exposure times on snake phobias. *Journal of Consulting and Clinical Psychology*, 1975, *43*, 478–484.

Bellack, A. S. Reciprocal inhibition of a laboratory conditioned fear. *Behaviour Research and Therapy*, 1973, *11*, 11–18.

Bellack, A. S., & Hersen, M. The use of self-report inventories in behavioral assessment. In J. D. Cone & R. P. Hawkins (Eds.), *Behavioral assessment: New directions in clinical psychology*. New York: Brunner/Mazel, 1977, in press.

Bergin, A. E. The evaluation of therapeutic outcomes. In A. E. Bergin & S. L. Garfield (Eds.), *Handbook of psychotherapy and behavior change: An empirical analysis*. New York: John Wiley, 1971.

Bernstein, D. A. Situational factors in behavioral fear arousal: A progress report. *Behavior Therapy*, in press.

Bernstein, D. A., & Paul, G. L. Some comments on therapy analogue research with small animal phobias. *Journal of Behavior Therapy and Experimental Psychiatry*, 1971, *2*, 225–237.

Borkovec, T. D. The role of expectancy and physiological feedback in fear research: A review with special reference to subject characteristics. *Behavior Therapy*, 1973, *4*, 491–505.

Borkovec, T. D., Weerts, T. C., & Bernstein, D. A. Behavioral assessment of anxiety. In A. R. Ciminero, K. S. Calhoun, & H. E. Adams (Eds.), *Handbook of behavioral assessment*. New York: John Wiley & Sons, 1977.

Boulougouris, J. C., Marks, I. M., & Marset, P. Superiority of flooding to desensitization as a fear reducer. *Behaviour Research and Therapy*, 1971, *9*, 7–16.

Budzynski, T. H., & Stoyva, J. An instrument for producing deep muscle relaxation by means of analog information feedback. *Journal of Applied Behavior Analysis*, 1969, *2*, 231–237.

Davison, G. C. Systematic desensitization as a counterconditioning process. *Journal of Abnormal Psychology*, 1968, *73*, 91–99.

Davison, G. C., & Wilson, G. T. Processes of fear-reduction in systematic desensitization: Cognitive and social reinforcement factors in humans. *Behavior Therapy*, 1973, *4*, 1–21.

Di Loreto, A. *Comparative psychotherapy*. New York: Aldine-Atherton, 1971.

Dollard, J., & Miller, N. E. *Personality and psychotherapy: An analysis in terms of learning, thinking, and culture*. New York: McGraw-Hill, 1950.

Eysenck, H. J. The effects of psychotherapy. In H. J. Eysenck (Ed.), *Handbook of abnormal psychology*. London: Pittman Medical Publishers, 1960.

Garfield, S. L., & Bergin, A. E. Therapeutic conditions and outcome. *Journal of Abnormal Psychology*, 1971, *77*, 108–114.

Gaupp, L. A., Stern, R. M., & Galbraith, G. C. False heart-rate feedback and reciprocal inhibition by aversion relief in the treatment of snake avoidance behavior. *Behavior Therapy*, 1972, *3*, 7–20.

Hersen, M. Self-assessment of fear. *Behavior Therapy*, 1973, *4*, 241–257.

Jacobson, E. *Progressive relaxation*. Chicago: University of Chicago Press, 1938.

Kennedy, T. D., & Kimura, H. K. Transfer, behavioral improvement, and anxiety reduction in systematic desensitization. *Journal of Consulting and Clinical Psychology*, 1974, *42*, 720–728.

Krapfl, J. E., & Nawas, M. M. Client-therapist relationship factors in systematic desensitization. *Journal of Consulting and Clinical Psychology*, 1969, *33*, 435–439.

Lacey, J. I., Smith, R. L., & Green, B. A. Use of conditioned autonomic responses in the study of anxiety. *Psychosomatic Medicine*, 1955, *17*, 208–217.

Lang, P. J. The mechanics of desensitization and the laboratory study of human fear. In C. M. Franks (Ed.), *Behavior therapy: Appraisal and status*. New York: McGraw-Hill, 1969.

Lang, P. J. The application of psychological methods to the study of psychotherapy and behavior modification. In A. E. Bergin & S. L. Garfield (Eds.), *Handbook of psychotherapy and behavior change*. New York: John Wiley & Sons, 1971.

Lang, P. J., & Lazovik, A. D. Experimental desensitization of a phobia. *Journal of Abnormal and Social Psychology*, 1963, *66*, 519–525.

Lang, P. J., Lazovik, A. D., & Reynolds, D. J. Desensitization, suggestibility, and pseudo-therapy. *Journal of Abnormal Psychology*, 1965, *70*, 395–402.

Leitenberg, H., Agras, S., Butz, R., & Wincze, J. Relationship between heart rate and behavioral change during the treatment of phobias. *Journal of Abnormal Psychology*, 1971, *78*, 58–68.

Lomont, J. F., & Edwards, J. E. The role of relaxation in systematic desensitization. *Behaviour Research and Therapy*, 1967, *5*, 11–25.

Marcia, J. E., Rubin, B. M., & Efran, J. S. Systematic desensitization: Expectancy change or counterconditioning? *Journal of Abnormal Psychology*, 1969, *74*, 382–387.

Marks, I. Behavioral treatments of phobic and obsessive-compulsive disorders: A critical appraisal. In M. Hersen, R. M. Eisler, & P. M. Miller (Eds.), *Progress in behavior modification* (Vol. 1.) New York: Academic Press, 1975.

McGlynn, F. D. Individual versus standardized hierarchies in the systematic desensitization of snake avoidance. *Behaviour Research and Therapy,* 1971, *9,* 1–5.

McGlynn, F. D., Reynolds, E. J., & Linder, L. H. Systematic desensitization with pretherapeutic and intra-treatment therapeutic instructions. *Behaviour Research and Therapy,* 1971, *9,* 57–63.

McGlynn, F. D., Williamson, M., & Davis, D. Semi-automated desensitization as a treatment for genuinely fearful subjects. *Behaviour Research and Therapy,* 1973, *11,* 313–316.

McLemore, C. W. Imagery in desensitization. *Behaviour Research and Therapy,* 1972, *10,* 51–57.

Meichenbaum, D. H., Gilmore, J. B., & Fedoravicius, A. Group insight versus group desensitization in treating speech anxiety. *Journal of Consulting and Clinical Psychology,* 1971, *36,* 410–421.

Miller, N. E. Studies of fear as an acquired drive: I. Fear as motivation and fear reduction as reinforcement in the learning of new responses. *Journal of Experimental Psychology,* 1948, *38,* 89–101.

Morris, R. J., & Suckerman, K. Therapist warmth as a factor in automated systematic desensitization. *Journal of Consulting and Clinical Psychology,* 1974, *42,* 244–250.

Nawas, M. M., Mealiea, W. L., & Fishman, S. T. Systematic desensitization as counterconditioning: A retest with adequate controls. *Behavior Therapy,* 1971, *2,* 345–356.

Oliveau, D. C., Agras, W. S., Leitenberg, H., Moore, R. C., & Wright, D. E. Systematic desensitization, therapeutically oriented instructions and selective positive reinforcement. *Behaviour Research and Therapy,* 1969, *7,* 27–33.

Paul, G. L. *Insight versus desensitization in psychotherapy: An experiment in anxiety reduction.* Stanford, Calif.: Stanford University Press, 1966.

Paul, G. L. Insight versus desensitization in psychotherapy two years after termination. *Journal of Consulting and Clinical Psychology,* 1967, *31,* 333–348.

Paul, G. L. Outcome of systematic desensitization: I. Background procedures and uncontrolled reports of individual treatment. In C. M. Franks (Ed.), *Behavior therapy: Appraisal and status.* New York: McGraw-Hill, 1969. (a)

Paul, G. L. Physiological effects of relaxation training and hypnotic suggestion. *Journal of Abnormal Psychology,* 1969, *74,* 425–437. (b)

Paul, G. L., & Shannon, D. T. Treatment of anxiety through systematic desensitization in therapy groups. *Journal of Abnormal Psychology,* 1966, *71,* 124–135.

Rehm, L. P. Relationships among measures of visual imagery. *Behaviour Research and Therapy,* 1973, *11,* 265–270.

Rosen, G. M. Therapy set: Its effects on subjects' involvement in systematic desensitization and treatment outcome. *Journal of Abnormal Psychology,* 1974, *83,* 291–300.

Schwartz, G. E. Biofeedback as therapy: Some theoretical and practical issues. *American Psychologist.* 1973, *28,* 666–673.

Sherman, A. R. Real-life exposure as a primary therapeutic factor in the desensitization treatment of fear. *Journal of Abnormal Psychology,* 1972, *79,* 19–28.

Sloane, R. B., Staples, F. R., Cristol, A. H., Yorkston, N. J., & Whipple, K. *Psychotherapy versus behavior therapy.* Cambridge, Mass.: Harvard University Press, 1975.

Stampfl, T. G. Implosive therapy: The theory, the subhuman analogue, the strategy, and the technique: Part 1. The theory. In S. G. Armitage (Ed.), *Behavior modification techniques in the treatment of emotional disorders.* Battle Creek, Mich.: V. A. Publication, 1967.

Sternbach, R. A. *Principles of psychophysiology.* New York: Academic Press, 1966.

Suinn, R., & Richardson, F. Anxiety management training: A nonspecific behavior therapy program for anxiety control. *Behavior Therapy,* 1971, *2,* 498–510.

Sushinsky, L. W., & Bootzin, R. R. Cognitive desensitization as a model of systematic desensitization. *Behaviour Research and Therapy,* 1970, *8,* 29–33.

Truax, C. B., & Mitchell, K. M. Research on certain therapist interpersonal skills in relation to process and outcome. In A. E. Bergin & S. L. Garfield (Eds.), *Handbook of psychotherapy and behavior change: An empirical analysis.* New York: John Wiley, 1971.

Valins, S., & Ray, A. A. Effects of cognitive desensitization on avoidance behavior. *Journal of Personality and Social Psychology,* 1967, *7,* 345–350.

van Egeren, L. F. Psychophysiological aspects of systematic desensitization: Some outstanding issues. *Behaviour Research and Therapy*, 1971, *9*, 65–77.

Watson, J. B., & Rayner, R. Conditioned emotional reactions. *Journal of Experimental Psychology*, 1920, *3*, 1–14.

Wilkins, W. Desensitization: Social and cognitive factors underlying the effectiveness of Wolpe's procedure. *Psychological Bulletin*, 1971, *5*, 311–317.

Wolpe, J. *Psychotherapy by reciprocal inhibition*. Stanford, Calif.: Stanford University Press, 1958.

Woy, J. R., & Efran, J. Systematic desensitization and expectancy in the treatment of speaking anxiety. *Behaviour Research and Therapy*, 1972, *10*, 43–49.

Wynne, L. C., & Solomon, R. L. Traumatic avoidance learning: Acquisition and extinction in dogs deprived of normal peripheral autonomic function. *Genetic Psychology Monographs*, 1955, *52*, 241–284.

3

Fear reduction II

Introduction

In the preceding chapter, we discussed the most frequently used and most empirically validated fear reduction treatment: systematic desensitization. Despite the effectiveness and popularity of desensitization, several alternative techniques have been developed for the elimination of fears and anxiety. In this chapter we will discuss the most notable of these alternative approaches including: implosion (Levis, 1967; Stampfl, 1967) and flooding (Boulougouris, Marks, & Marset, 1971; Stern & Marks, 1973), in vivo desensitization (Sherman, 1972), shaping (Barlow, Leitenberg, Agras, & Wincze, 1969; Leitenberg, Agras, Allen, Butz, & Edwards, 1975), modeling (Bandura, Blanchard, & Ritter, 1969; Blanchard, 1970), and self-control approaches (Goldfried, 1971; Suinn & Richardson, 1971).

These procedures are all clearly behavioral in that they involve fairly direct, learning theory-based approaches to behavior change. Nevertheless, they all emphasize specific theoretical and technique variations that make them quite different from one another and from desensitization. Implosion and flooding involve forced exposure to intensely feared stimuli in contrast to the hierarchical approach in desensitization. In vivo desensitization and shaping require exposure to real phobic stimuli rather than imaginal stimuli. The modeling approaches incorporate observational (vicarious) learning experiences with or without direct practice or exposure. Finally, the self-control approaches emphasize development of general anxiety management skills which can be applied by the client himself, rather than therapist-controlled deconditioning in the clinic.

In some cases (e.g., implosion) these techniques have been postulated as clear alternatives to each other or to desensitization. In such instances, a comparison of the techniques can be based on clear empirical considerations: which technique is more cost-effective? The term "cost-effective" refers to the interaction of clinical effectiveness per se, and the "cost" of the procedure in terms of such factors as pain experienced, duration of treatment, amount of therapist time involved, etc. For example, a treatment that requires 10 weeks and involves minimal duress for the client might be more desirable than a 5-week treatment that is highly stressful for the client. In other instances (e.g., shaping, self-control approaches), the various treatments can be considered as complimentary components of a comprehensive therapeutic armamentarium. In this context, the techniques are viewed as being applicable to different types of clients or at different points in treatment rather than as direct competitors for all fearful individuals. For example, while in vivo densensitization might be more cost effective than imaginal desensitization, some clients are too fearful to tolerate in vivo exposure, and might require the imaginal approach first.

The treatment procedures listed above will be described in subsequent sections of this chapter. As with desensitization, we will discuss the theoretical issues involved in the development of the technique, describe the clinical procedures, and review the empirical literature. Whenever possible, we will relate the material to systematic desensitization technique and research.

Implosive Therapy and Flooding

Implosive Therapy (IT)

One of the earliest alternatives to desensitization was Implosive Therapy (Levis, 1967; Stampfl, 1967), also referred to as implosion or IT. Developed primarily by Thomas Stampfl (1967), IT is based on an unusual amalgam of fundamental laboratory research with animals and psychoanalytic theory. *First,* Stampfl adopted the two-factor theory of fear development described in Chapter 2 and hypothesized, therefore, that the most effective procedure for eliminating fear is extinction. *Second,* after reviewing the animal learning literature, he determined that extinction occurs most rapidly and completely when the organism is exposed to highly anxiety-arousing stimuli that closely resemble the original stimuli to which the fear response was conditioned. He also equated extinction of emotional responses in humans with the psychoanalytic concept of "abreaction"—the experience and release of intense emotional feeling. The *third* premise underlying the approach relates to identification of the original or fundamental sources of fear in humans. Stampfl hypothesized that, consistent with psychoanalytic theory, fears are typically developed in early childhood based on the experience of pain and guilt around several characteristic issues or themes: orality, anality, sexuality, and aggression. The overt adult symptomatology (e.g., fear of heights, public speaking, etc.) simply represents content that is far out along the generalization gradient from the underlying psychodynamic issues. Stampfl argued that if the individual is exposed solely to those secondary stimuli, he will not experience sufficiently intense and relevant anxiety, and extinction will be incomplete. Given these three premises, elimination of adult fears is presumed to require exposure to intensely anxiety-producing stimuli (psychodynamic material) under conditions in which real pain or aversion is not experienced (e.g., in imagination).

While both IT and desensitization involve extinction (or counterconditioning) of fear by imaginal presentation of phobic stimuli, the procedures differ in many respects. In contrast to the use of muscle relaxation and non-anxiety-arousing exposure employed in desensitization, IT requires clients to experience intense anxiety for extended durations. In desensitization, a fear hierarchy is developed systematically based on the client's report and cooperation. In IT, "The fact of repression makes it impossible for the patient to reproduce the dangerous associations even if he wanted to. However, . . . it is not too difficult for the clinician to infer on the basis of interviews and diagnostic test material the general areas over which repression extends. For example, it is usually quite easy to infer stimulus situations which involve repressed hostile, aggressive, and sexual stimuli" (Stampfl, 1967, p. 18).

Treatment itself involves the presentation of phobic stimuli with sufficient elaboration of details to insure continuous, extended experience of heightened anxiety. Themes are organized in hierarchical fashion involving increased approach to psychodynamic material. When anxiety to any one content issue is finally reduced (by exhaustion or extinction), a new content theme is presented in a similar manner. Treatment continues until all hypothesized anxiety stimuli are no longer anxiety-arousing. An example of the imagery presented in IT is provided by Stampfl (1967) in the context of a compulsive handwasher: ". . . the patient is asked to imagine himself approaching a wastepaper basket. Now when he gets to the wastepaper basket, is he confronted with a clean wastepaper basket? No, that is not what he is afraid of. He is afraid of what might be in the wastepaper basket and it is not clean. So he reaches in with his hand and what does he come out with? His hand is dripping with a combination of mucous, saliva, vomit, and feces . . . the implosive therapist might well have the patient lick off this material into his mouth. And this also is just the beginning, for it is easy to speculate that when obsessive fears of dirt are present there might also be a distinctive set of repressed stimulus patterns involving anal material. Following this hypothesis, one might then pitch the patient into a septic tank. He lives there, he eats there, he sleeps there, he mushes around in there, he throws cocktail parties in there" (p. 14). As is apparent from this example, the images are extreme, fantasy-like productions in which the client imagines himself in aversive situations well beyond what he might ever experience in real life.

In contrast to many other behavioral treatments, IT has received relatively little empirical interest. This is probably a function of both the distasteful aspects of administration (e.g., the intense anxiety and unappealing imagery involved) and the psychoanalytic aspects of the theory. The literature evaluation of IT, therefore, does not provide a clear indication about its overall effectiveness, how it operates, or the circumstances in which it might be differentially applicable. Several initial reports (e.g., Hogan & Kirchner, 1967, 1968) suggested that IT is a highly effective treatment. Barrett (1969) compared IT with desensitization in the treatment of snake phobia. He found that both techniques were equally effective, but IT worked more quickly. Crowe, Marks, Agras, and Leitenberg (1972) found IT to be more effective than desensitization, but not as effective as a shaping procedure.

In contrast, several other studies have reported that IT is not effective. For example, Fazio (1970) and Mealiea and Nawas (1971) found no differences between IT groups and various control groups. Hekmat (1973) compared IT with several other treatment conditions and a control condition. The IT group exhibited significantly *more* avoidance behavior than the control group after treatment; the implosive procedure apparently increased fear!

Unfortunately, most of the research investigating IT has been marked by poor experimental design (Morganstern, 1973). Hogan and Kirchner (1968), for example, used the MMPI (a self-report inventory) as the sole dependent variable. Both Fazio (1970) and Mealiea and Nawas (1971) used audiotaped exposure of aversive imagery, and it is not certain that their IT subjects actually listened to the tapes and maintained high levels of anxiety throughout. Neither Barrett (1969) nor Crowe et al. (1972) controlled for time of exposure to phobic imagery. Subjects in IT and desensitization groups had the same number of sessions; therefore, as a function of the concentrated exposure in the IT procedure, such subjects would have actually imagined the phobic imagery for longer periods of time. The Hekmat (1973) study was well designed, but IT subjects were administered many scenes with brief exposure durations rather than the typical procedure in which extended exposure durations are incorporated. As a function of both design flaws and variations in administrative technique, the literature on implosion is difficult to interpret.

Several recent investigations have examined IT from a different perspective, focusing on the physiological changes associated with prolonged exposure to extreme phobic imagery. Borkovec (1972, 1974) reported that, as suggested by IT theory, implosion did result in gradual decreases in skin conductance and heart rate as exposure time to phobic imagery increased. Orenstein and Carr (1975) found a similar pattern. McCutcheon and Adams (1975) reported that duration of exposure is a critical factor in physiological change. They found that, parallel to the results reported by Hekmat (1973), a 20-min. period of IT *sensitized* subjects (resulted in increased SNS arousal to a real stressor), while 60 min. of IT resulted in decreased arousal. These studies suggest that IT may be effective and that further research is warranted. However, they also indicate that greater caution and clarity of procedures is necessary in conducting IT research or treatment. There is a possibility that fear can be increased rather than decreased with this procedure.

Flooding

As discussed above, one of the bases of IT is the inclusion of psycho-dynamic content themes. However, most reports describing or evaluating IT have eliminated this component of the procedure, simply emphasizing the use of highly aversive imagery. With this modification, IT is highly similar to *flooding*, which also requires the subject to experience extended exposure to highly anxiety-provoking stimuli (Marks, 1975). However, in contrast to the semi-hierarchical presentation of fantastic imagery (psychodynamic or otherwise) employed in IT, flooding involves the non-hierarchical exposure of stimuli that the client might actually encounter. For example, a height-phobic client in IT might imagine himself looking out over the Grand Canyon and falling, while in flooding he would imagine himself standing on a terrace in a tall building. Flooding has been used primarily in Europe for the treatment of agoraphobics (individuals with intense fear of crowds, open spaces, and the out-of-doors) and obsessive compulsives (see Marks, 1975, for a review). In contrast to the analogue research typical in the United States, most of these reports have involved clients (or experimental subjects) with extreme clinical problems, who have often been treated in inpatient settings, allowing for the administration of psychotropic medication and for extended treatment sessions (2 hours or more) several times per week.

Much of the research investigating flooding suffers from similar methodological weaknesses as does the literature on IT (Morganstern, 1973). This is partially a function of the difficulties involved in conducting treatment research with severely disturbed patients. It is usually impossible to recruit enough subjects to fill control groups. Moreover, there are major ethical difficulties involved in withholding treatment from highly distressed patients. Similarly, the necessity of offering maximal help to such individuals limits the possibility of administering partial treatments (as in a dismantling design) so as to identify the potent treatment elements. Nevertheless, several recent studies have included sufficient experimental controls to provide a considerable amount of suggestive (rather than conclusive) data about flooding procedures.

Boulougouris, Marks, and Marset (1971) divided their subjects into two groups. One group received six sessions of imaginal flooding followed by six sessions of systematic desensitization, and the second group received the two treatments in reversed order. Subjects also received two sessions of in vivo desensitization or flooding (exposure to real rather than imaginary phobic stimuli) at the end of each imaginal treatment. Flooding was found to be more effective on therapist and patient ratings and on physiological measures. The results were maintained during a 1-year follow-up. The absence of a control group and confounding of imaginal and in vivo treatments limit the conclusions that may be reached, but the clinical effectiveness of the combined flooding with severe phobics is clear. In a similar study, Gelder, Bancroft, Gath, Johnston, Mathews, and Shaw (1973) found flooding and desensitization to be equally effective. This study did employ a control group, but the results are again confounded as the two imaginal treatments were supplemented by real life exposure to phobic stimuli.

Several studies have investigated the use of in vivo flooding independent of imaginal exposure. In this procedure, the client is directed to actually enter the phobic situation for an extended period of time, rather than simply imagine himself in the situation. This variant can be conducted with or without the therapist's being present during exposure. For example, in a study by Emmelkamp and Wessels (1975), each agoraphobic subject, ". . . had to walk outside alone uninterruptedly for 90 min. and was not allowed to take with him anything which might reduce his anxiety, such as an umbrella, a bicycle, sunglasses, a dog, etc. Therapist and client had agreed upon a route through the town which was a difficult one and which ran in a straight line in a direction away from the home of the client" (pp. 8–9). (Graduated in vivo exposure techniques will be discussed in the next section.) The results of research on flooding are parallel to the findings of research on IT. In vivo flooding has generally been found to be more effective than audiotaped imaginal flooding (e.g., Emmelkamp, 1974; Emmelkamp & Wessels, 1975). In addition, moderate exposure durations (1/2 hour or less) are not as effective as extended exposures (e.g., 2 hours or more) (Stern & Marks, 1973).

Regardless of the effectiveness of these procedures, there are several aspects of their application that raise serious ethical questions about whether or not they should be employed. One concern stems from the subjective reactions of subjects to such concentrated exposure and high anxiety. For example, several subjects in both Emmelkamp studies had highly negative emotional reactions to the in vivo flooding procedure. "One client, for instance, hid in the cellar out of fear of being sent into the street for 90 minutes by the therapist" (Emmelkamp & Wessels,

1975, p. 14). A second factor is the apparent risk involved in conducting these treatments. The results reported by Hekmat (1973) and Mc-Cutcheon and Adams (1975) suggest that clients might be made *more fearful* under certain circumstances.

In the Introduction to this chapter we discussed the issue of cost effectiveness. This is a clear example of the considerations involved in selecting a treatment procedure from among a set of potential techniques. While the data are still unclear, flooding and IT might well be effective approaches for the elimination of fear. However, they both involve placing the client in a highly aversive state for extended periods of time and with a risk of countertherapeutic (i.e., negative) consequences. Without clear evidence that these procedures are either considerably more effective or quicker than desensitization (or the other procedures to be discussed below), there is little justification for their use. The clinician would be advised to select a less stressful technique of known effectiveness whenever possible. It should be pointed out that for many subjects in the flooding studies other forms of treatment had been ineffective, making the use (risk) of flooding more acceptable.

In Vivo Desensitization and Shaping

The term "extinction" has played a prominent role in our discussion of fear reduction in the preceding chapter and in earlier sections of this chapter. In the context of both desensitization and implosion-flooding, extinction refers to the elimination of the classically conditioned emotional (fear) reaction by exposure of the CS (phobic stimulus) in the absence of the UCS (aversive consequence). The operant avoidance behavior was presumed to drop out once the fear response that had maintained it was eliminated. In consequence, in vivo practice or actual exposure to the feared stimuli was not thought to be necessary be either Wolpe or Stampfl. However, this presumption of automatic transfer from imaginal extinction to approach behavior is based on an oversimplified model of phobic behavior.

Wynne and Solomon (1955), for example, demonstrated that conditioned avoidance responses could be developed in dogs in which sympathetic nervous system connections were surgically severed (i.e., when there was no preliminary emotional arousal). Black (1959) found that avoidance responses persisted after autonomic arousal was extinguished. Leitenberg, Agras, Butz, and Wincze (1971) studied adult human phobics and showed that approach behavior could be increased prior to and independent of "fear" reduction as measured by heart rate. As different individuals approached the phobic stimulus, heart rates either increased, decreased, or remained unchanged. Becker and Costello (1975) conducted an analogue study in which subjects were required to practice systematic exposure to phobic stimuli. At the conclusion of the treatment period, there were significant increases in approach behavior but no changes in self-report of anxiety. The behavioral changes were maintained at a 1-month follow-up and generalization session, and by that time there were also decreases in self-reported fear. These data suggest that avoidance responses were modified prior to conditioned emotional responses. The general independence of the three primary response modalities has been discussed in Chapter 2. The implications of this independence for fear reduction are two-fold. *First*, transfer from one modality to another cannot be presumed, but must be demonstrated in each case. *Second*, as demonstrated by Leitenberg et al. (1971) and Becker and Costello (1975), it is possible to modify phobic responses by focusing on approach (avoidance) behavior directly, rather than first eliminating the conditioned emotional response.

We have already described in vivo flooding, which has been applied both subsequent to and independent of imaginal flooding. The more frequently employed strategy for in vivo exposure, however, involves more gradual approach and low levels of anxiety arousal. Variously referred to as shaping, in vivo desensitization, reinforced practice, or graduated exposure, this strategy requires the client to practice increasingly difficult interaction with the actual phobic stimulus. Exposure duration or intensity (e.g., progressively increasing heights) is systematically increased, with or without the use of such response facilitation aids as praise and performance feedback. (A parallel procedure referred to as contact desensitization will be discussed later in this chapter in the section on Modeling.) Rate of progress can be determined by the client or by the therapist, based on a moderate and consistently increasing performance criterion. In some cases such as claustrophobia or knife phobia (Leitenberg, Agras, Thomson, & Wright, 1968), practice exposure can be conducted in the office or laboratory. However, for most fears, such as agoraphobia (Emmelkamp & Ultee, 1974), the client practices in the natural environment with or without the therapist's presence.

An early investigation of in vivo practice was conducted by Cooke (1966), who compared imaginal and in vivo desensitization in an analogue study. The in vivo group was actually exposed to the same stimuli the imaginal group faced in imagination. Both procedures were more effective than a control condition. In a similar study, Barlow, Leitenberg, Agras, and Wincze (1969) reported that an in vivo desensitization group had greater increases in approach behavior and decreases in sympathetic nervous system arousal to phobic stimuli than a parallel imaginal desensitization group. This study did not include a control group, a fact which tempers possible conclusions.

A well-controlled experiment that provides strong support for the value of in vivo desensitization was conducted by Sherman (1972). Subjects were aquaphobic college students who had to take a physical education course with a swimming requirement. Half of the subjects received in vivo desensitization which consisted of practice in 26 water activities. The activities were hierarchically arranged so that they varied in the degree of stress they aroused (e.g., depth of water in which an activity was performed). Progress was determined by subjects themselves based on performance of each activity with minimal anxiety. The other half of the sample had no in vivo exposure to water activities. Each of those two groups was divided into thirds. A third of the subjects received systematic desensitization involving an imaginal hierarchy of the same 26 water activities. Another third received a "predesensitization" procedure, which was a control for non-specific treatment factors involved in desensitization. The last third received no other treatment (these subjects thus received either in vivo desensitization or no treatment). This design allowed for a comparison of in vivo and imaginal desensitization alone and in combination. Dependent variables included both self-report and behavioral performance measures (performing the 26 activities). The results are presented in Fig. 3.1. In vivo exposure was superior to non-exposure conditions on all measures. While a combination of imaginal and in vivo desensitization was most effective, the combined group was not significantly better than exposure alone, and in vivo exposure alone was more effective than imaginal desensitization alone. The primary change agent, therefore, appears to have been the in vivo practice. Furthermore, the exposure procedure required approximately 1 hour compared to 7 hours for systematic desensitization.

A group of researchers at the University of Vermont conducted a series of studies to evaluate in vivo exposure procedures; they were interested in how such exposure could be accomplished as well as whether or not it was effective. Two initial investigations employed single-subject experimental methodology. Agras, Leitenberg, and Barlow (1968) found that social reinforcement for gradually increasing exposure was effective in increasing amount of time and distance away from home for three agoraphobics. Leitenberg, Agras, Thomson, and Wright (1968) provided their subjects with feedback as to time exposed to phobic stimuli. Feedback alone was sufficient to increase exposure time; the addition of praise for improved performance did not increase the effect.

The relationship of praise and feedback was further examined in a study by Leitenberg, Agras, Allen, Butz, and Edwards (1975). Leitenberg et al. (1968) administered praise after feedback, which had already been effective. It is possible that praise would have been effective if it had been administered first. In this study, five subjects were treated in single-subject designs in which a praise condition was followed by performance feedback, which was then withdrawn and readministered. The results for one of the subjects are presented in Fig. 3.2 and are representative of the other subjects. The subject, ". . . reported avoiding contact with any pointed object that she could use to hurt someone and

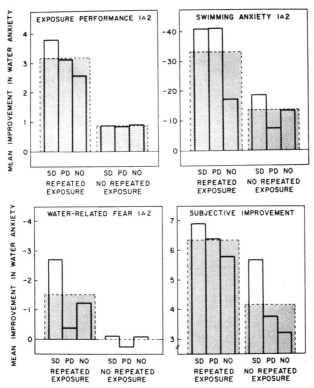

Fig. 3.1 Mean improvement in water anxiety from pre- to post-treatment for the six treatment groups and for the combined repeated exposure groups versus the combined no-repeated exposure groups, as reflected in the four basic water anxiety measures. (Note: SD = systematic desensitization; PD = pre-desensitization; NO = No office treatment.) (Reprinted with permission from: A. R. Sherman: *Journal of Abnormal Psychology,* 79: 19, 1972.)

of obsessive thoughts and urges to kill people, especially by knifing them" (Leitenberg et al., 1975, p. 396). Treatment consisted of the subject's opening a small box and looking at a knife for as long as she could without experiencing anxiety. During praise phases, the therapist provided social reinforcement and approval whenever the subject exceeded criteria of gradually increasing exposure time. During feedback phases she was told how long she had looked and if the criteria were surpassed. As can be seen in Fig. 3.2, praise was not sufficient to increase exposure time but feedback was effective. Progress continued when feedback was withdrawn, stabilized when both praise and feedback were absent, and increased again only when feedback was reinstituted. The authors concluded that, "Feedback was apparently more important than therapist praise in getting approach behavior underway, but once gains had been made, praise plus the repeated graduated practice procedure per se was able to sustain continuing improvement on its own" (p. 396). The effectiveness of feedback of exposure or practice

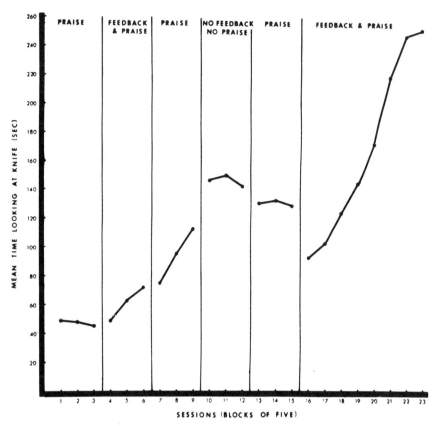

Fig. 3.2 Mean time spent looking at phobic stimulus as a function of praise and feedback-plus-praise conditions: Subject 1. (Reprinted with permission from: H. Leitenberg, W. S. Agras, R. Allen, R. Butz, and J. Edwards: *Journal of Consulting and Clinical Psychology*, 43: 396, 1975.)

time was also demonstrated in a group comparison study conducted by Rutner (1973).

The exact manner in which feedback affects phobic behavior is unclear. One possibility is that performance feedback has conditioned reinforcing properties. Feedback (information) of improved performance would be a conditioned positive reinforcer and feedback of nonimproved or worsened performance would be a conditioned punisher. A related hypothesis is that feedback is a discriminative stimulus for subsequent positive reinforcement or punishment. For a phobic patient, feedback would signal either improvement and stress reduction or nonimprovement and continued life stress. Further research is needed to determine how and under what circumstances feedback is effective. (The function of feedback will be discussed further in Chapter 9.)

While feedback is apparently a useful treatment technique, it is unlikely that a program of feedback alone will be sufficient for most phobic individuals. A more comprehensive package of techniques is often needed. Several studies have been conducted to examine multifaceted programs. Leitenberg and Callahan (1973) demonstrated that "reinforced practice" (a combination of graduated practice, social reinforcement, feedback, and positive expectancy instructions) was effective for treatment of a variety of fears with adults and children. Leitenberg, Agras, Barlow, and Oliveau (1969) compared three treatment conditions: (1) desensitization combined with positive reinforcement for progress through the hierarchy and for practice in vivo exposure; (2) standard imaginal desensitization; and (3) a control condition. The first condition was significantly more effective than the latter two, which did not differ from one another. Barlow, Agras, Leitenberg, and Wincze (1970) found that graduated exposure (shaping) with positive reinforcement for improvement was more effective than imaginal desensitization. Both Barlow et al. (1970) and Emmelkamp and Ultee (1974) reported that shaping procedures could be effective with or without the presence of the therapist. As stated previously, Crowe et al. (1972) found that shaping was more effective than implosion or desensitization.

This series of studies examining in vivo approach procedures suggests that the strategy can be used effectively either as an adjunct or an alternative to imaginal desensitization. Extinction of a conditioned emotional response is apparently not a necessary precursor to effective approach behavior. Furthermore, the success of graduated approach procedures provides an ethical, cost-effective alternative to flooding. However, the literature does not yet support the conclusion that the in vivo approach invariably is a desirable alternative to imaginal desensitization. Further research is needed to determine the client characteristics (e.g., degree of fear, relative significance of motoric, cognitive, and physiological response channels) which make either in vivo, imaginal, or combined programs the treatment of choice. It is also unlikely that all phobic individuals would be amenable to approaching the feared stimulus early in treatment. The factors which determine when, how, and with which clients such an early approach can best be accomplished must be determined.

Modeling

Most applications of traditional learning theory to models or conceptions of fear development and fear reduction have emphasized the role of direct, trial-and-error experience. Fears have been presumed to develop on the basis of a single traumatic experience or a series of moderately aversive conditioning trials. Fear reduction procedures have similarly involved repeated, non-reinforced exposure to the conditioned stimulus either in imagination or in vivo. This trial-and-error model has been questioned by Albert Bandura (1969; 1971a, 1971b), the major proponent of social learning theory. He has emphasized the role of modeling or observational learning in the development and modification of a significant portion of human behavior. He states: "It is evident from informal observation that human behavior is transmitted, whether deliberately or inadvertantly, largely through exposure to social models. . . It is difficult to imagine a culture in which language, mores, vocational activities, familial customs, and educational, religious, and political practices are gradually shaped in each new member by direct consequences of their trial-and-error performances without benefit of models who display the cultural patterns in their behavior. . . Under circumstances in which mistakes are costly or dangerous, skillful performances can be established without needless errors by providing competent models who demonstrate the required activities. Some complex behaviors can be produced solely through the influence of models. . . Even in instances where it is possible to establish new response patterns through other means, the process of acquisition can be considerably shortened by appropriate models" (Bandura, 1971a, pp. 1–3).

The terms modeling, observational learning, imitation, social learning, and vicarious conditioning have all been used semi-synonymously in the literature. While some definitional differentiation has been suggested (e.g., Rachman, 1972), the diverse terms all generally refer to learning by observation of other people or of symbols (as in reading) rather than learning by trial-and-error. For example, a child can learn how to hit a baseball more easily by first watching his father at bat, than by picking up a bat and making random attempts (i.e., trial-and-error) *without ever having observed* someone hitting a ball with a bat. Similarly, the child can learn that snakes, or dogs, or speeding automobiles are dangerous by observing his parents avoiding those objects, and becoming tense and gasping in their presence, as well as by being bitten by a dog or hit by the car. In an experimental analogue of this process, Berger (1962) demonstrated that a "conditioned" fear response (as manifested by GSR changes) could be developed by having subjects observe what they thought was another subject receiving a series of aversive conditioning trials. In fact, Bandura (1969, 1971a) has suggested that most fears are developed by such social transmission rather than by direct aversive experiences.

There are three major learning or behavior effects that can be produced by modeling (Bandura, 1971a, 1971b). The *first* is acquisition of new response patterns or skills. Learning to play baseball, to speak a language, to dance, and to interact in a socially approved manner are all examples of responses acquired by observation of appropriate models. The *second* effect is the inhibition or disinhibition of responses already in the individual's response repertoire. That is, the individual learns to avoid making (inhibit) a certain response by observing a model receiving a negative consequence for making a similar response. In the case of disinhibition, he learns to perform an inhibited response by observing a model receiving positive consequences (or not receiving negative consequences) after making a similar response. For example, the first successful looters in an urban disturbance often serve to disinhibit the behavior of otherwise law-abiding individuals. Thus, looting becomes widespread. The *third* effect is response facilitation, in which the behavior of a model serves as a discriminative stimulus for performance of a response that is already in the observer's repertoire, and which has not been inhibited. "People applaud when others clap; they look up when they see others gazing skyward; they adopt fads that others display; and in countless other situations their behavior is prompted and channeled by the actions of others" (Bandura, 1971a, p. 6).

An excellent example of both the response acquisition and inhibitory effects of modeling is provided in a study by Bandura (1965). Nursery school children were exposed to a videotape in which a model behaved in a highly aggressive and stylized manner to a Bobo doll (e.g., the modeled aggression contained unusual verbalizations and gestures). One group of children saw the model rewarded for the aggressive display, while a second group saw him punished. For a third group, the model received no consequence. The children were then placed, alone, in the room in which the model had performed and two observers rated the degree to which the child performed modeled aggressive responses. Immediately after the observation, an experimenter entered the room and offered the child reinforcement (juice, toys) to perform modeled responses.

During the initial observation phase, children who had seen the model reinforced or receive no consequence performed significantly more matching responses than children in the model-punished condition. However, these differences disappeared in the subsequent reinforcement phase, when children in each group performed a similar, high number of matching responses. Children in all three groups had learned the model's routine (i.e., response acquisition), but children who had seen the model punished for his behavior *inhibited* the response until they were offered a positive incentive. This experiment is also significant as it demonstrates the difference between learning and performance. Bandura (1965) concluded that observational learning takes place on a cognitive basis without the need for reinforcement. However, reinforcement is necessary if the individual is to perform learned responses. (An extensive presentation of Bandura's Social Learning Theory and alternative views is beyond the scope of this book. The interested student is referred to Bandura [1969, 1971a, 1971b].)

Of primary interest in our discussion of fear reduction are the disinhibitory effects of modeling. In this context, the phobic individual is viewed as having inhibited approach behavior. The approach response is in his repertoire (i.e., he knows how to walk in crowds, talk to women) but is inhibited by fear. The social learning conception hypothesizes that observation of a model interacting with the phobic stimulus and not experiencing any aversive consequences should disinhibit the approach response and result in extinction of the fear (these two processes could occur in either order). Bandura and Barab (1973) suggest that there are three factors that contribute to this process. *First,* the observer receives accurate information about the feared stimulus and the process of interacting with it. For example, observation of a model interacting with a dog would provide information about how to maintain control of the animal and what it would be likely to do. *Second,* there is an increased incentive to approach the feared stimulus, as the observer feels somewhat foolish being unable to perform a desired response which he has just observed someone else perform without great difficulty or any negative results. *Third,* and probably most critical, is vicarious extinction: elimination (extinction) of the fear as a function of observing a model approach the feared stimulus and experience no aversive conse- quence. Bandura and his colleagues have conducted a series of studies to evaluate the effects of vicarious extinction processes on fear behavior and to examine the factors which govern its operation.

The earliest studies were conducted with children who were very afraid of dogs. Bandura, Grusec, and Menlove (1967) divided their subjects into four groups. One group observed a fearless model interact with a dog while attending a party. A second group observed the same model, but under neutral conditions. In both cases, the modeled activity became increasingly more fear provoking over sessions, in a manner analogous to the graduated tasks which comprise in vivo desensitization hierarchies. The third group received exposure to the dog in the party context, but with no model. The fourth group attended a party but received neither exposure nor modeling. After treatment, children in both modeling groups displayed significantly more approach behavior to both the dog used in modeling sessions and a new (generalization) dog than did children in either of the other two groups. There was no difference between children in the exposure-only and party-only groups. The positive context of the party was expected to reduce anxiety and facilitate the effects of modeling. However, there was no difference between the two modeling groups; modeling was sufficiently potent so that the party condition did not further contribute to fear reduction.

In a second, related study, Bandura and Menlove (1968) examined the use of videotaped modeling (rather than use of a live model) in reducing fear of dogs in children. This study also compared the effects of observ- ing a single model versus observing several different models. One group of children saw a series of videotapes of a single model displaying the same sequence of dog-approach behaviors as the model in Bandura et al. (1967). A second group was shown videotapes of several male and female children interacting with several different dogs. A third group viewed dog-irrelevant movies. Both modeling procedures were more effective than the control condition, suggesting that videotaped modeling is an effective treatment technique with children. While there was no differ- ence between the two modeling conditions at the conclusion of treat- ment, the multiple model procedure was more effective by the time of a 1-month follow-up.

Similar results were reported by O'Connor (1969), who found that exposure to a videotape of multiple models reinforced for social interaction was effective in reducing the isolation of withdrawn nursery school children. Use of multiple models is generally more desirable than single models (Meichenbaum, 1971). Observation of multiple modeling displays should result in greater generalization of vicarious extinction effects, as multiple models provide a greater range of appropriate cues and it is more difficult for the observer to label the modeled performance as unique to one particular model or situation (e.g., "He can do it if he wants to, but he is crazy.").

In addition to the number of models presented, the characteristics of the models or modeled behaviors will also affect what is learned. Meichenbaum (1971) compared mastery models (MM) and coping models (CM) in the treatment of snake phobia. Mastery models walked calmly up to a snake, systematically and confidently proceeded through a hierarchy of snake-interactions, and manifested no hesitation in their performance. In contrast, coping models proceeded slowly, appeared to be somewhat cautious, and periodically hesitated and took slow, deep breaths. The CM models portrayed overcoming fear in contrast to the fearlessness of the MM models. In addition, for one-half of the subjects, models verbalized about their behavior while performing. Mastery models verbalized competence and coping models verbalized gradually decreasing apprehension. The study thus contained four groups: mastery-verbalization, mastery-no verbalization, coping-verbalization, and coping-no verbalization. Both coping groups exhibited significantly more approach behavior during treatment than both mastery groups. As shown in Table 3.1, coping groups performed many more high difficulty steps on the Behavior Avoidance Test (BAT) than mastery groups; 39% of the CM subjects performed the terminal step in contrast to 0% for MM groups. In addition to the BAT, therapist ratings and subject self-report

TABLE 3.1

Number of Subjects in Each Modeling Treatment Group Who Performed Terminal Approach Tasks on Post-test[a]

Item	Treatment Conditions			
	Behavior mastery	Behavior mastery plus verbalization	Behavior coping	Behavior coping plus verbalization
Total no. Ss	9	9	9	9
Approach tasks				
Hold snake barehanded in cage	2	2	6	7
Hold snake barehanded outside of cage for 5 sec.	0	1	4	5
Outside of cage for 30 sec.	0	0	3	4
Outside of cage for 60 sec.	0	0	3	4

[a] From: Meichenbaum (1971) (Table 2).

ratings of fear were secured during in vivo performance. Only the coping-verbalization group had significant reductions in fear on these two measures. The coping procedure appeared to be highly effective in facilitating behavioral approach, and the addition of coping verbalizations greatly increased fear reduction as represented by cognitive and motoric indices of anxiety.

Meichenbaum (1971) hypothesized that this pattern of results could have been a function of either of two factors: (1) coping models were seen as more similar to the fearful subjects than mastery models, thus increasing their imitative value; or (2) subjects learned coping skills from the coping models that facilitated their ability to deal with the snake and control their anxiety. The results of a study by Bandura and Barab (1973) suggest that while observer-model similarity is an important factor, the effects of such similarity are not uniform and are less critical than response consequences.

Bandura and Barab (1973) exposed their adult subjects to one of three modeling displays: adult models interacting with phobic stimuli, child models interacting with phobic stimuli, or irrelevant modeling. Both relevant model procedures resulted in significantly greater increases in approach behavior than the irrelevant model condition; the two relevant model groups did not differ from one another. However, the adult model group also had significant decreases in fear as measured by GSR, while the child model group did not. Apparently, the similar model (adult) condition resulted in vicarious extinction of fear, while the dissimilar model (child) resulted in increased incentive to perform the approach response (e.g., "If a child can do it, I can do it."). Commenting on this differential effect, Bandura and Barab state: "The differential correlation findings raise the interesting possibility that similar behavioral outcomes induced through variant forms of modeling are mediated by different mechanisms. . . Modeling influences, depending on their content and form, could operate to varying degrees through informative, motivational, and extinctive processes" (p. 8).

This conclusion was supported in a study by Kornhaber and Schroeder (1975). Snake fearful children were exposed to one of five conditions: adult-fearless model, adult-fearful (i.e., coping) model, child-fearless model, child-fearful model, or a control condition. As measured on a behavioral approach test, age similarity but not response similarity (i.e., level of fearfulness) was critical; both child model groups differed from the control group but the adult model groups did not. On attitude measures (self-report of fear), however, similarity on both dimensions was necessary; only the child-fearful group differed from the control group. The results of these studies suggest that model similarity, especially on the response dimension (i.e., coping versus mastery), is an important treatment factor. But the effects of similarity are not consistent across subjects or response modalities. Further research is necessary to determine how model similarity affects behavior and the circumstances under which different forms of similarity are most relevant.

The majority of studies exploring the use of modeling with adult phobics have employed a procedure called participant modeling or contact desensitization (Bandura, Blanchard, & Ritter, 1969; Ritter, 1969a, 1969b). Rather than passively watching a modeling display, the client undergoing participant modeling actually performs the modeled response after observing the model. This procedure, in effect, combines live modeling with in vivo desensitization or shaping (recall Sherman, 1972, for example). In contact desensitization, the client's efforts to perform modeled behaviors are assisted by supportive physical contact by the therapist. For example, the therapist might first model picking up and holding a snake. The client would then place his hands on top of the therapist's hands as the therapist picked up the snake. The therapist might then remove one of his hands and place the client's hand on the snake. He might then place the client's second hand on the snake, while holding the client's shoulder, until eventually all physical contact is withdrawn. The physical contact is presumed to provide support and reduce client anxiety. Both participant modeling and contact desensitization characteristically include graduated exposure, in which progress is controlled by the client based on the experience of minimal anxiety.

Contact desensitization was developed by Ritter (1969a, 1969b), who used it successfully in the treatment of acrophobia (fear of heights). Rimm and Mahoney (1969) demonstrated that participant modeling was effective in reducing snake avoidance in subjects who had initially been unable to approach snakes despite a monetary incentive. The first well-controlled experimental test of this approach was a study by Bandura, Blanchard, and Ritter (1969). Snake phobic subjects were recruited from the community (i.e., they were clinically phobic, not college students) and assigned to one of four groups: (1) live modeling with guided participation (contact desensitization); (2) symbolic (videotaped) modeling with relaxation training; (3) systematic desensitization; and (4) no treatment control. Subjects in the symbolic modeling group were first taught deep muscle relaxation and instructed to stop and reverse the modeling film and to relax whenever they experienced anxiety. All three treatment procedures were significantly more effective than the control condition. However, live modeling with participation was significantly more effective than either symbolic modeling or desensitization; 92% of the live modeling subjects were able to perform the terminal (highest) items on the behavior approach test after treatment (compared to 33% and 25%, respectively, for symbolic modeling and desensitization). The results of this study not only indicate that participant modeling is a very powerful treatment, but the results are impressive because it was highly effective for almost all subjects. In a similar study, Lewis (1974) reported that participant modeling was more effective than passive modeling with children (who were water phobic).

There are several possible factors which might have made the participation procedure employed by Bandura et al. (1969) more effective than modeling alone: in vivo practice, therapist reinforcement, transmission of additional information not available via the symbolic model, etc. Blanchard (1970) conducted a study in an effort to isolate the most important factors. He employed four groups in a systematic dismantling design (see Chapter 2). Group 1 received modeling, information about snakes, and guided participation. A second group received modeling and information. Group 3 recieved modeling alone, and Group 4 was an untreated control. All three treatment conditions were significantly more effective than the control on both behavioral approach and self-report measures. In comparing Groups 1, 2, and 3, Blanchard found that modeling with participation was more effective than modeling alone and that the addition of information did not contribute to either motoric or self-report changes. He concluded that modeling accounted for approximately 60% of the behavioral change and 80% of the change in affect and attitudes about snakes (i.e., self-report measures); participation thus accounted for 40% of the behavioral and 20% of the self-report changes.

While the results of the Blanchard (1970) study indicate that guided participation provides a significant increment over modeling alone, the specific critical elements of such participation were still not identified. Subjects in that condition not only had practice exposure, but therapist contact and reinforcement as well as other response facilitation aids. Bandura, Jeffery, and Wright (1974) conducted a study in which they attempted to analyze the guided participation procedure more completely. Highly snake-fearful subjects were recruited and treated with one of three participant modeling variations that differed in the number of "response induction" aids provided to facilitate practice exposure. All three groups received live modeling and graduated exposure. In addition, for the high induction aid group, "To facilitate the first contact responses, the experimenter held the snake securely by the head and tail, thus affording complete protection against any feared injury. Should subjects still resist touching the snake, they were asked to don either light or heavy-weight gloves and touch and hold the midsection. Similar performance aids, glove protectors, and assured control of the snake were used to foster more intimidating contact with the snake's head and entwining tail. For the severely incapacitated phobics who remained immobile even under secure conditions, the dreaded response was first performed with appropriate supports toward a baby king snake which had a much weaker threat value" (Bandura et al., 1974, p. 59). A moderate induction aid group received modeling, graduated practice and joint performance, but no physical protectors or baby snake. A low aid group had modeling and graduated practice only. Results indicated that while all three procedures resulted in significant changes in approach and self-report measures, the high and moderate induction aid conditions were significantly more effective than the low aid condition. In general, the high and moderate groups did not differ from one another. Fifty-eight percent of the subjects in each of those groups performed the terminal Behavior Avoidance Test item in contrast to only 17% of the low aid subjects.

The above mentioned results extend and clarify the findings of Blanchard (1970) and replicate the findings of Ritter (1969a, 1969b). They indicate that therapist contact and control play a significant part in the effectiveness of participant modeling; graduated practice exposure with such contact is significantly more effective than unsupported exposure. The additional induction aids (e.g., gloves, baby snake) are, apparently, unnecessary when therapist contact is provided. Bandura (1971b) suggests that modeling supplements such as the induction aids employed here or muscle relaxation are useful when subjects are highly fearful and when rapid treatment is needed; such supplements are not necessary with less fearful individuals or when gradual treatment can be employed.

This series of studies provides relatively unequivocal support for the effectiveness of participant modeling procedures. However, the results have not indicated the degree to which the effects generalize. It is possible that subjects learn to approach a single snake fearlessly in the laboratory, but isolate their behavioral and cognitive changes to that special situation. Bandura, Jeffery, and Gajdos (1975) examined this possibility and evaluated the utility of two supplemental self-mastery procedures for increasing generalization. Adult snake phobic subjects received either participant modeling alone, or participant modeling followed by self-directed performance with either a single familiar snake, or the familiar snake and a new snake. Immediately following conclusion of the participant modeling treatment, subjects in the self-directed-single snake group spent another hour with the snake. "They were instructed to perform, in the order of their own choosing, the activities they had previously executed with the therapist's assistance" (Bandura et al., 1975, p. 144). The therapist remained in the room for a short period, then withdrew. Subjects in the varied snake condition received a similar 1-hour exposure, but with the original snake and an unfamiliar snake. Post-treatment assessments included approach tests to a familiar and an unfamiliar (generalization) snake. In addition, 1- and 6-month follow-ups were conducted.

The results of the Behavior Avoidance Test are presented in Fig. 3.3. As can be seen, while all three treatments were highly effective, the two self-directed treatments eliminated avoidance behavior in almost all subjects. Differences between those groups and the non-mastery groups are especially apparent with the generalization snake. This pattern of results was also found on self-report measures of anticipatory fear before exposure to the snakes and experienced fear during exposure to the snakes. Differences between the single snake-mastery groups were maintained through the follow-up periods. These results indicate that scheduled mastery experiences can have a powerful effect on the generality and durability of behavior changes after treatment. Furthermore,

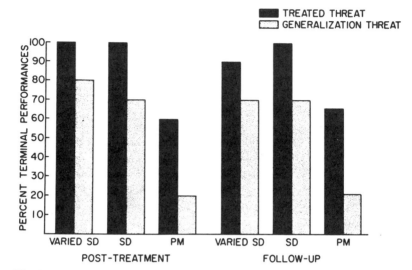

Fig. 3.3 Percent of subjects who achieved terminal performances with the treatment and generalization snakes depending upon whether they received participant modeling alone or supplemented with either uniform or varied self-directed performance. (Reprinted with permission from: A. Bandura, R. W. Jeffery, and E. Gajdos: *Behaviour Research and Therapy,* 13: 141, 1975.)

mastery subjects reported increased self-confidence and reduction of other, unrelated fears as well as an increase in behaviors such as hiking and camping which were previously avoided due to fear of snakes. Changes on self-report measures were not maintained as well by subjects in the varied-mastery condition. The investigators hypothesized that subjects in that group might have been forced into an experience that was too anxiety-arousing (i.e., a novel snake) before they had developed sufficient mastery with the familiar snake. This finding suggests the importance of planning carefully designed mastery experiences in treatment both to facilitate generalization and to circumvent or reduce the impact of unplanned aversive experiences outside of treatment.

Self-Control Techniques

The fear reduction techniques we have discussed thus far have emphasized the application of discrete conditioning procedures for the elimination of specific target behaviors. For example, desensitization attempts to countercondition one particular fear; if the client has several fears, desensitization (counterconditioning) is essentially readministered for each fear. Similarly, in vivo approaches attempt to extinguish specific avoidance and fear responses or shape in specific approach responses. A client with more than one avoidance pattern would be instructed to approach systematically and independently each phobic stimulus. There have been several anecdotal accounts of generalized behavior and attitudinal change after these treatments such as spontaneous reduction of other fears and increased self-confidence (Bandura et al., 1975; Paul, 1966; Sherman, 1972). However, such generalized change would not be predicted on the basis of theoretical rationales for these treatments. In fact, this form of change has not been demonstrated to occur on a systematic basis. Different fears are ordinarily presumed to be independent of one another and, therefore, to require separate treatment. In addition, there is nothing to prevent new fears from developing after treatment is terminated, in which case a new set of counterconditioning or extinction trials must be conducted.

With rare exceptions (e.g., Bandura et al., 1975), the emphasis in treatment has been on remediation (of current disturbance) rather than on prevention. Commenting on this approach, Cautela (1969) stated that, ". . . the behavior therapist has not, to any extent, attempted to make the individual less susceptible to the development of future maladaptive behaviors; neither has he provided means for the individual to eliminate any such maladaptive behavior without the aid of the therapist" (p. 323). In response to this criticism, several treatment strategies have recently been developed in which there is a focus on the development of general anxiety control or coping skills which have generalized and durable effects (Goldfried, 1971; Russell & Sipich, 1973; Suinn & Richardson, 1971). These procedures are generally classified as self-control techniques, as they involve training the client in skills which are to be self-applied in the natural environment, independent of the therapist's control or direction (the behavioral conception of self-control will be discussed at length in Chapter 4). This is in contrast to the therapist-directed conditioning trials applied in the approaches we have described previously. By mastering such skills, the client is expected to be better able to deal with all forms of current fear and stress as well as being less susceptible to the development of new fears in the future.

One of the initial stimuli for this alternative approach to fear reduction was criticism of Wolpe's conception of systematic desensitization. Goldfried (1971) and Wilkins (1971) independently hypothesized that cognitive mediational factors rather than counterconditioning were responsible for the effects of desensitization (see Chapter 2, for discussion of this issue). While their specific views differed to some extent, both writers suggested that there were several aspects of the desensitization procedure that contributed to the development of general coping skills. These factors included: (1) the development of positive expectancies about ability to approach and deal with feared stimuli, (2) information feedback about physiological and motoric changes in response to feared stimuli (e.g., level of arousal or extent of ability to approach), and (3) development of skills to control physiological arousal and terminate fearful cognitions (e.g., deep muscle relaxation). In general, Goldfried (1971) and Wilkins (1971) argue that clients in desensitization are provided with skills and expectancies that allow them to become more aware of their reactions to fear provoking stimuli and better able to exert a high level of control over their fear-relevant behavior (including motoric, cognitive, and physiological components). Consequently, they are able to either circumvent or reduce anxiety by applying these skills on an ongoing basis in the natural environment.

In addition to providing an alternative explanation for the operation of desensitization, Goldfried (1971) recommended a number of procedural modifications which were designed to amplify the self-control effects of the treatment. (1) The rationale for the treatment emphasizes that it provides training in coping skills which will permit the client to *deal* with his anxiety. This is in contrast to the customary rationale which emphasizes the fact that it is a counterconditioning procedure which operates *on* the client. (2) Deep muscle relaxation training is modified to emphasize increased sensitivity to proprioceptive (muscle feedback) tension cues so that the client is fully aware of the preliminary stages of anxiety arousal (when anxiety is more easily controlled). (3) Goldfried (1971) suggested two major changes in the construction and use of hierarchies. *First,* items are selected so as to represent a variety of different life stresses rather than a single content theme as in desensitization. *Second,* when the client reports anxiety during scene presentation, he is instructed to "relax it away" while maintaining the image, rather than to immediately terminate the image. (4) Finally, the client is instructed to practice the use of relaxation in the natural environment whenever he experiences anxiety or stress.

In a subsequent paper, Goldfried (1973) described an application of this procedure with a 17-year-old girl (Lynne) who was suffering from extreme, generalized anxiety. "Included among the long list of objects and situations which elicited anxiety were insects, elevators, high places, being along at night, traveling by herself, criticism by others, people, situations, or activities with which she was unfamiliar, speaking in public, examinations, and listening to her sister and parents argue. In addition to experiencing subjective discomfort when placed in these situations, Lynne would respond with uncontrollable crying" (p. 298). Treatment followed the recommendations offered by Goldfried (1971). Modified desensitization was conducted with the following multi-theme hierarchy:

1. With your boyfriend, sitting near a pond (pleasant scene)
2. Taking an English test, and not knowing exactly how to answer the question
3. Sitting next to father, who is driving the car
4. Sitting next to boyfriend, who is driving the car
5. Driving the car at night on highway, with boyfriend sitting in front seat
6. Driving car alone at night on highway
7. Standing on top of beginner's hill, about to ski down

8. Walking into a girlfriend's house for the first time
9. Sitting in bar with boyfriend and wondering if they will check proof of age
10. Teacher is about to distribute questions for history test
11. Babysitting at night by yourself, watching TV
12. Helping father at work, and don't know where to find something he asks for
13. Standing in a lobby, waiting for the elevator
14. Walking into an elevator alone and pressing the button
15. Girlfriend tells you she doesn't like your hairstyle
16. Standing in front of class, about to read a paper
17. At home along during the day, sitting in your room
18. With boyfriend at train station, and he leans over to see if train is coming
19. At beach during vacation, and walk over to a group of strangers your age to say hello
20. Boyfriend on top of hill, calling for you to climb up
21. Holding rail at skating rink, about to skate away from it
22. Sitting in large auditorium, taking state-wide exams
23. At home alone at night, sitting in room and thinking you hear noises
24. Sitting in room, and hearing your parents and sister have a loud argument
25. Sitting in living room with your father and sister, who are arguing

Each item was presented repeatedly until the criterion of two successive trials on which there was no report of anxiety was reached. When Lynne did report anxiety (which she did on all but four items), the image was maintained until she became relaxed: usually after about 30 to 40 sec. In addition, Lynne was directed to apply relaxation in vivo whenever she experienced tension. Treatment required 13 sessions and was highly successful. By the time of a 5-month follow-up, "a review of the items in the hierarchy revealed that Lynne had encountered virtually all of the illustrations in real life without feeling anxious. In one situation, where she was reluctant to climb to the top of a hill (item 20), a simple reminder from her boyfriend about what she had learned in therapy was sufficient in (sic) help her overcome the difficulty" (pp. 302–303).

Several other behavior modifiers have suggested similar types of programs. Suinn and Richardson (1971) described a technique referred to as Anxiety Management Training (AMT). While it is similar to Goldfried's approach in most respects, AMT does not include hierarchical scene presentation, and scenes are terminated after anxiety is experienced for a brief interval rather than being maintained until anxiety is reduced (or terminated *immediately* after anxiety is reported as in desensitization). Another related technique is cue-controlled relaxation (Russell & Sipich, 1973, 1974). Clients receiving this treatment are first trained in the use of deep muscle relaxation. They then receive a series of conditioning trials in which they practice relaxing to a sub-vocalized cue word such as "calm" or "relax." After the cue word becomes a conditioned stimulus for relaxation, clients are instructed to use the cue word to relax themselves in vivo whenever they experience anxiety.

This entire set of techniques has been somewhat difficult to evaluate empirically as they are not designed to modify discrete, specific target behaviors (e.g., fear of dogs, heights). For the most part, desired effects involve somewhat general changes in overall life experience and long-term immunity to future distress. These changes are not amenable to assessment by a stimulus specific behavior approach procedure like the Behavior Avoidance Test. The primary indication of change, therefore, is self-report of generally reduced levels of anxiety and increased ability to cope with stress. There have been several uncontrolled case studies which have described successful applications of these techniques. Gold-fried-type procedures have been used successfully in the treatment of heterosexual anxiety (D'Zurilla, 1969) and (as described above) for a case of pervasive or generalized anxiety (Goldfried, 1973). Russell and Sipich (1973, 1974) employed cue-controlled relaxation for the treatment of text anxiety, and Gurman (1973) found it effective for a client with public speaking anxiety.

Several empirical studies have been conducted in which self-report measures have been the sole dependent variables. Suinn and Richardson (1971) found AMT to be as effective as desensitization in the treatment of mathematics anxiety, and Russell, Miller, and June (1975) reported that cue-controlled relaxation was as effective as desensitization in the treatment of test anxiety. While these studies examined the use of the self-control approach for reducing specific fears, Sherman and Plummer (1973) evaluated the more broad-based impact of such techniques. They taught relaxation skills to relatively "normal" college students. Both at the end of training and after a 2-year follow-up (Sherman, 1975), subjects reported greater ability to deal with anxiety and stress. They also reported using relaxation as an aid in such situations as falling asleep, taking examinations, and for the alleviation of headaches. The uncertain reliability of self-report data as well as the danger in drawing conclusions based on data from only one response modality have been pointed out earlier in this chapter as well as in Chapter 2. Therefore, the results of these studies can only be considered as suggestive.

There have been relatively few controlled studies in which measures of actual behavior change have been employed as well as self-report. Zeisset (1968) compared a self-control relaxation procedure with desensitization and two control procedures for the treatment of interview anxiety. Both treatment conditions were more effective than the control procedures as measured by overt signs of anxiety during a staged interview. In contrast to the previously discussed studies, there were no differences on self-report measures. In the best controlled study of cue-controlled relaxation to date, Marchetti, McGlynn, and Patterson (1977) examined the effectiveness of the procedure for reducing test anxiety. In addition to self-report data, heart rate and skin resistance (GSR) were assessed during actual course examinations. Despite receiving six 30-min. training sessions, cue-controlled relaxation was no more effective than placebo or no-treatment conditions on either self-report or physiological measures.

A self-control application of relaxation training was compared with standard relaxation training and an attention-placebo control in a study by Goldfried and Trier (1974). Subjects were college students with public speaking anxiety. Both relaxation groups were given equivalent training in deep muscle relaxation. Subjects in the standard group were told that the training would generally lower their tension level while subjects in the self-control group, ". . . were told that the purpose of the training procedure was to provide them with a coping skill, which they could actively employ in relaxing away tension in a variety of anxiety-provoking situations, including those involving public speaking" (Goldfried & Trier, 1974, p. 350). In addition, self-control subjects were told to apply relaxation in vivo whenever they felt tense. The self-control procedure was more effective than either of the other two treatments on both a behavioral measure (anxiety signs in a speech situation) and several self-report measures. Differences between the groups were even greater after a follow-up period. This continued change after treatment would be expected if subjects were gradually mastering a self-control skill by practicing it in vivo. Finally, the standard relaxation and control groups rated their satisfaction in relation to their degree of improvement as only 19.4% and 12.5%, respectively, while the self-control group rated its satisfaction as 47.5%.

The overall effectiveness of the various self-control strategies is still uncertain. The results for cue-controlled relaxation have been mixed. Controlled and uncontrolled studies for the other procedures have generally had positive results and suggest that those approaches are as effective as desensitization in reducing a variety of specific fears. This is not surprising as the self-control procedures contain many of the same elements as desensitization. There is also some suggestion that the self-control approach is effective in reducing general tension levels and untreated as well as treated fears (e.g., Zemore, 1975). However, there have been few controlled studies that have employed dependent variables from several response modalities. This is especially true in regard to assessment of the generalized changes and stress immunization that these techniques are designed to promote. Greater attention must be paid to securing independent measures (e.g., other than self-report) of such changes before firm conclusions may be reached. Longer term follow-ups must also be conducted to determine if these techniques do, in fact, reduce the occurrence of new fears and anxiety after treatment has been concluded.

Summary

A number of fear reduction techniques have been developed as alternatives to desensitization. Implosive therapy incorporates a psychoanalytic conception of fear development with an extinction model of fear reduction. The procedure requires the client to experience intense levels of anxiety in contrast to the anxiety avoidance strategy of desensitization. The effectiveness of implosion is still uncertain. Flooding also involves the experience of heightened levels of anxiety, but without reference to any psychodynamic material. Clients are exposed to phobic stimuli for extended periods either in imagination or in vivo. The empirical literature suggests that flooding might be an effective technique, but it apparently involves a risk of increasing fear under certain circumstances.

An alternative to intensive in vivo exposure as employed in flooding is graduated exposure (used in shaping and in vivo desensitization). There have been several empirical demonstrations of the effectiveness of these techniques in reducing a variety of fears. In many cases, performance feedback is sufficient to stimulate increased exposure. These procedures appear to be a cost-effective alternative to flooding and may be used either in conjunction with or instead of desensitization.

Bandura (1969, 1971a) has emphasized the role of observational learning in both the development and the elimination of fears. Modeling has proven to be a highly effective procedure for the elimination of fears in both children and adults. Exposure to multiple models and similar models is generally more effective than exposure to single or dissimilar models. Contact desensitization is a modeling procedure which supplements observation of a model with graduated practice and therapist support. This procedure is generally more effective than modeling alone. Graduated practice is, apparently, a critical factor.

Most fear reduction techniques emphasize the explicit countercondi-tioning or extinction of specific fears. Little attention is paid to reduction of general life stresses or prevention of future fear conditioning. Consequently, several techniques have recently been developed that focus on the development of self-control coping skills. Most of the research evaluating these techniques has relied on self-report data to gauge effectiveness. Conclusions about this approach must, therefore, be reserved until research is conducted that assesses several response modalities and long-term preventative effects.

References

Agras, S., Leitenberg, H., & Barlow, D. Social reinforcement in the modification of agoraphobia. *Archives of General Psychiatry,* 1968, *19,* 423–427.

Bandura, A. Influence of model's reinforcement contingencies on the acquisition of imitative responses. *Journal of Personality and Social Psychology*, 1965, *1*, 589-595.

Bandura, A. *Principles of behavior modification*. New York: Holt, Rinehart, & Winston, 1969.

Bandura, A. Analysis of modeling processes. In A. Bandura (Ed.), *Psychological modeling: Conflicting theories*. New York: Aldine-Atherton, 1971. (a)

Bandura, A. Psychotherapy based upon modeling principles. In A. E. Bergin & S. L. Garfield (Eds.), *Handbook of psychotherapy and behavior change: An empirical analysis*. New York: John Wiley & Sons, 1971. (b)

Bandura, A., & Barab, P. Processes governing disinhibitory effects through symbolic modeling. *Journal of Abnormal Psychology*, 1973, *82*, 1-9.

Bandura, A., Blanchard, E. B., & Ritter, R. The relative efficacy of desensitization and modeling approaches for reducing behavioral, affective, and attitudinal changes. *Journal of Personality and Social Psychology*, 1969, *13*, 173-199.

Bandura, A., Grusec, J. D., & Menlove, F. L. Vicarious extinction of avoidance behavior. *Journal of Personality and Social Psychology*, 1967, *5*, 16-23.

Bandura, A., Jeffery, R. W., & Gajdos, E. Generalizing change through participant modeling with self-directed mastery. *Behaviour Research and Therapy*, 1975, *13*, 141-152.

Bandura, A., Jeffery, R. W., & Wright, C. L. Efficacy of participant modeling as a function of response induction aids. *Journal of Abnormal Psychology*, 1974, *76*, 55-61.

Bandura, A., & Menlove, F. L. Factors determining vicarious extinction of avoidance behavior through symbolic modeling. *Journal of Personality and Social Psychology*, 1968, *8*, 99-108.

Barlow, D. H., Agras, W. S., Leitenberg, H., & Wincze, J. P. An experimental analysis of the effectiveness of 'shaping' in reducing maladaptive avoidance behaviors: An analogue study. *Behaviour Research and Therapy*, 1970, *8*, 165-174.

Barlow, D. H., Leitenberg, H., Agras, W. S., & Wincze, J. P. The transfer gap in systematic desensitization: An analogue study. *Behaviour Research and Therapy*, 1969, 191-196.

Barrett, C. L. Systematic desensitization versus implosive therapy. *Journal of Abnormal Psychology*, 1969, *74*, 587-592.

Becker, H. G., & Costello, C. G. Effects of graduated exposure with feedback of exposure times on snake phobias. *Journal of Consulting and Clinical Psychology*, 1975, *43*, 478-484.

Berger, S. M. Conditioning through vicarious instigation. *Psychological Review*, 1962, *69*, 450-466.

Black, A. H. Heart rate changes during avoidance learning in dogs. *Canadian Journal of Psychology*, 1959, *13*, 229-242.

Blanchard, E. B. The relative contributions of modeling, informational influences and physical contact in the extinction of phobic behavior. *Journal of Abnormal Psychology*, 1970, *76*, 55-61.

Borkovec, T. D. Effects of expectancy on the outcome of systematic desensitization and implosive treatments for analogue anxiety. *Behavior Therapy*, 1972, *3*, 29-40.

Borkovec, T. D. Heart-rate process during systematic desensitization and implosive therapy for analog anxiety. *Behavior Therapy*, 1974, *5*, 636-641.

Boulougouris, J. C., Marks, I. M., & Marset, P. Superiority of flooding to desensitization as a fear reducer. *Behaviour Research and Therapy*, 1971, *9*, 7-16.

Cautela, J. R. Behavior therapy and self-control: Techniques and implications. In C. M. Franks (Ed.), *Behavior therapy: Appraisal and status*. New York: McGraw Hill, 1969.

Cook, G. The efficacy of two desensitization procedures: An analogue study. *Behaviour Research and Therapy*, 1966, *4*, 17-24.

Crowe, M. J., Marks, I. M., Agras, W. S., & Leitenberg, H. Time-limited desensitization, implosion and shaping for phobic patients: A cross-over study. *Behaviour Research and Therapy*, 1972, *10*, 319-328.

D'Zurilla, T. J. Reducing heterosexual anxiety. In J. D. Krumboltz & C. E. Thoresen (Eds.), *Behavioral counseling: Cases and techniques*. New York: Holt, Rinehart, & Winston, 1969.

Emmelkamp, P. M. G. Self-observation versus flooding in the treatment of agoraphobia. *Behaviour Research and Therapy*, 1974, *12*, 229-237.

Emmelkamp, P. M. G., & Ultee, K. A. A comparison of "successive approximation" and "self-observation" in the treatment of agoraphobia. *Behavior Therapy,* 1974, *5,* 606–613.

Emmelkamp, P. M. G., & Wessels, H. Flooding in imagination vs. flooding in vivo: A comparison with agoraphobics. *Behaviour Research and Therapy,* 1975, *13,* 7–15.

Fazio, A. Treatment components in implosive therapy. *Journal of Abnormal Psychology,* 1970, *76,* 211–219.

Gelder, M. G., Bancroft, J. H. J., Gath, D. H., Johnston, D. W., Mathews, A. M., & Shaw, P. M. Specific and non-specific factors in behavior therapy. *British Journal of Psychiatry,* 1973, *123,* 445–462.

Goldfried, M. R. Systematic desensitization as training in self-control. *Journal of Consulting and Clinical Psychology,* 1971, *37,* 228–234.

Goldfried, M. R. Reduction of generalized anxiety through a variant of systematic desensitization. In M. R. Goldfried & M. M. Merbaum (Eds.), *Behavior change through self-control.* New York: Holt, Rinehart, & Winston, 1973.

Goldfried, M. R., & Trier, C. Effectiveness of relaxation as an active coping skill. *Journal of Abnormal Psychology,* 1974, *83,* 348–355.

Gurman, A. S. Treatment of a case of public-speaking anxiety by in vivo desensitization and cue-controlled relaxation. *Journal of Behavior Therapy and Experimental Psychiatry,* 1973, *4,* 51–54.

Hekmat, H. Systematic versus semantic desensitization and implosive therapy: A comparative study. *Journal of Consulting and Clinical Psychology,* 1973, *40,* 202–209.

Hogan, R. A., & Kirchner, J. H. A preliminary report of the extinction of learned fears via short term implosive therapy. *Journal of Abnormal Psychology,* 1967, *72,* 106–111.

Hogan, R. A., & Kirchner, J. H. Implosive, eclectic verbal, and bibliotherapy in the treatment of fears of snakes. *Behaviour Research and Therapy,* 1968, *6,* 167 171.

Kornhaber, R. C., & Schroeder, H. E. Importance of model similarity on extinction of avoidance behavior in children. *Journal of Consulting and Clinical Psychology,* 1975, *5,* 601–607.

Leitenberg, H., Agras, W. S., Allen, R., Butz, R., & Edwards, J. Feedback and therapist praise during treatment of phobia. *Journal of Consulting and Clinical Psychology,* 1975, *43,* 396–404.

Leitenberg, H., Agras, W. S., Barlow, D. H. & Oliveau, D. C. Contribution of selective positive reinforcement and therapeutic instructions to systematic desensitization therapy. *Journal of Abnormal Psychology,* 1969, *74,* 113–118.

Leitenberg, H., Agras, S., Butz, R., & Wincze, J. Relationship between heart rate and behavioral change during the treatment of phobias. *Journal of Abnormal Psychology,* 1971, *78,* 59–68.

Leitenberg, H., Agras, S., Thomson, L. E., & Wright, D. E. Feedback in behavior modification: An experimental analysis in two phobic cases. *Journal of Applied Behavior Analysis,* 1968, *1,* 131–137.

Leitenberg, H., & Callahan, E. J. Reinforced practice and reduction of different kinds of fears in adults and children. *Behaviour Research and Therapy,* 1973, *11,* 19–30.

Levis, D. J. Implosive therapy: The theory, the subhuman analogue, the strategy, and the technique: Part II. In S. G. Armitage (Ed.), *Behavior modification techniques in the treatment of emotional disorders.* Battle Creek, Mich.: V. A. Publication, 1967.

Lewis, S. A comparison of behavior therapy techniques in the reduction of fearful avoidance behavior. *Behavior Therapy,* 1974, *5,* 648–655.

Marchetti, A., McGlynn, F. D., & Patterson, A. S. Effects of cue-controlled relaxation, a placebo treatment, and no treatment on changes in self-reported and psychophysiological indices of test anxiety among college students. *Behavior Modification,* 1977, *1,* in press.

Marks, I. Behavioral treatments of phobic and obsessive-compulsive disorders: A critical appraisal. In M. Hersen, R. M. Eisler, & P. M. Miller (Eds.), *Progress in behavior modification, Volume 1.* New York: Academic Press, 1975.

McCutcheon, B. A., & Adams, H. E. The physiological basis of implosive therapy. *Behaviour Research and Therapy,* 1975, *13,* 93–100.

Mealiea, W. L., & Nawas, M. M. The comparative effectiveness of systematic desensitization and implosive therapy in the treatment of snake phobia. *Journal of Behavior Therapy and Experimental Psychiatry,* 1971, *2,* 85–94.

Meichenbaum, D. Examination of model characteristics in reducing avoidance behavior. *Journal of Personality and Social Psychology,* 1971, *17,* 298–307.

Morganstern, K. P. Implosive therapy and flooding procedures: A critical review. *Psychological Bulletin*, 1973, *79*, 318–334.

O'Connor, R. D. Modification of social withdrawal through symbolic modeling. *Journal of Applied Behavior Analysis*, 1969, *2*, 15–22.

Orenstein, H., & Carr, J. Implosion therapy by tape-recording. *Behaviour Research and Therapy*, 1975, *13*, 177–182.

Paul, G. L. *Insight versus desensitization in psychotherapy: An experiment in anxiety reduction*. Stanford, Calif.: Stanford University Press, 1966.

Rachman, S. Clinical applications of observational learning, imitation and modeling. *Behavior Therapy*, 1972, *3*, 379–397.

Rimm, D. C., & Mahoney, M. J. The application of reinforcement and participant modeling procedures in the treatment of snake-phobic behavior. *Behaviour Research and Therapy*, 1969, *7*, 369–376.

Ritter, B. Treatment of acrophobia with contact desensitization. *Behaviour Research and Therapy*, 1969, *7*, 41–45. (a)

Ritter, B. The use of contact desensitization, demonstration, demonstration-plus-participation, and demonstration alone in the treatment of acrophobia. *Behaviour Research and Therapy*, 1969, *7*, 157–164. (b)

Russell, R. K., Miller, D. E., & June, L. N. A comparison between group systematic desensitization and cue-controlled relaxation in the treatment of test anxiety. *Behavior Therapy*, 1975, *6*, 172–177.

Russell, R. K., & Sipich, J. F. Cue-controlled relaxation in the treatment of text anxiety. *Journal of Behavior Therapy and Experimental Psychiatry*, 1973, *4*, 47–49.

Russell, R. K., & Sipich, J. F. Treatment of test anxiety by self-controlled relaxation. *Behavior Therapy*, 1974, *5*, 673–676.

Rutner, I. T. The effect of feedback and instructions on phobic behavior. *Behavior Therapy*, 1973, *4*, 338–348.

Sherman, A. R. Real-life exposure as a primary therapeutic factor in the desensitization treatment of fear. *Journal of Abnormal Psychology*, 1972, *79*, 19–28.

Sherman, A. R. Two year follow-up of training in relaxation as a behavioral self-management skill. *Behavior Therapy*, 1975, *6*, 419–420.

Sherman, A. R., & Plummer, I. L. Training in relaxation as a behavioral self-management skill: An exploratory investigation. *Behavior Therapy*, 1973, *4*, 543–550.

Stampfl, T. G. Implosive therapy: The theory, the subhuman analogue, the strategy, and the technique: Part 1. The theory. In S. G. Armitage (Ed.), *Behavior modification techniques in the treatment of emotional disorders*. Battle Creek, Mich. V. A. Publication, 1967.

Stern, R., & Marks, I. Brief and prolonged flooding: A comparison in agoraphobic patients. *Archives of General Psychiatry*, 1973, *28*, 270–276.

Suinn, R., & Richardson, F. Anxiety management training: A nonspecific behavior therapy program for anxiety control. *Behavior Therapy*, 1971, *2*, 498–510.

Wilkins, W. Desensitization: Social and cognitive factors underlying the effectiveness of Wolpe's procedure. *Psychological Bulletin*, 1971, *5*, 311–317.

Wynne, L. C. & Solomon, R. L. Traumatic avoidance learning: Acquisition and extinction in dogs deprived of normal peripheral autonomic function. *Genetic Psychology Monographs*. 1955, *52*, 241–284.

Zeisset, R. M. Desensitization and relaxation in the modification of psychiatric patients interview behavior. *Journal of Abnormal Psychology*, 1968, *73*, 18–24.

Zemore, R. Systematic desensitization as a method of teaching a general anxiety-reducing skill. *Journal of Consulting and Clinical Psychology*, 1975, *43*, 157–161.

4

Self-control and cognitive behavior modification

Introduction

Behavior modification has been stereotyped as a mechanistic approach which ignores or underestimates the role of the individual and of cognitive processes in the determination of behavior. This view has some historical justification and is understandable given the emphasis on Watsonian behaviorism and the earlier writings of Skinner. However, as discussed in Chapter 1, this stereotype is not an accurate portrayal of current behavior therapy. As experience and success with behavioral techniques have increased, behavior therapists have begun to critically evaluate their own work. In consequence, the initial rejection of the role of cognitive mediation has been questioned. More and more, it has become apparent that the black box S-R model, in which the individual is viewed as a passive responder to the environment, is not adequate to explain substantial portions of behavior (Bandura, 1976; Mahoney, 1974a).

The focus of this chapter will be the growing body of behavioral literature on self-control and cognitive oriented treatment techniques. The first section will specify what behavior therapists mean when they refer to these traditional-sounding terms. We will then describe the major behavioral models of self-control, with an emphasis on the work of Frederick H. Kanfer and of Albert Bandura. After considering some of the extensive analogue literature pertaining to these models, we will describe clinical applications of self-control procedures. The next two sections of the chapter will consider behavioral treatments that place a major emphasis on cognitive processes and cognitive change (covert conditioning and self-verbalization techniques). The final section will dscribe a technique for self-control of physiological activity: biofeedback.

Cognition and Behavior Therapy

If this text were being written in 1966 rather than 1976, the role of cognition in behavior therapy could have been described briefly (i.e., little to none). Behavior therapists (and behaviorists including Watson and Skinner) did not argue that there was no such thing as thought. Obviously, anyone writing about behavior therapy recognized that they were *thinking* about what to write. However, there was reason to believe that an effective technology of behavior could be developed without reference to a concept as elusive as cognition.

First of all, cognition could not be easily objectified. It was not observable by two independent observers and could not be reliably assessed or operationally defined. That is, if I ask you how you feel, I can reliably assess your answer, but am unable to specify what went on inside your head and stimulated your answer. I can only infer (or hypothesize) about it. Based on the methodological behaviorism of Watson and the empirical pragmatism of Skinner, it was deemed advisable to avoid reference to processes or concepts that must be *inferred* rather than observed. It was argued that reference to such inferential concepts as thought, belief, or feeling would impede the development of a science of behavior.

This viewpoint appeared to be justified by the failure of existing theoretical models (which all emphasized cognition) to adequately predict or permit the control of behavior. In that regard, the *second* factor which supported a non-cognitive model was the apparent power of conditioning procedures, which held out the promise of an essentially mechanistic behavior change technology. Initial demonstration of the dramatic effects of conditioning (see, for example, Ullmann & Krasner, 1965) suggested that the active participation of the patient and his cognitive processes was not necessary either for the development or modification of his behavior. In a classic example, Haughton and Ayllon (1965) taught a chronic schizophrenic patient to carry a broom around the hospital by reinforcing broom-holding with cigarettes. After two psychiatrists, uninformed about the conditioning, offered interpretations about the symbolic meaning of the broom for the patient, Haughton and Ayllon quickly eliminated the response by ceasing to reinforce it (i.e., extinction). Similarly, Wolpe's (1958) theoretical rationale for systematic desensitization emphasized the automatic nature of the development and deconditioning of fear.

As behavior therapy matured in the late 1960s and early 1970s, two things became apparent. *First,* conditioning procedures were not as "powerful" as was originally assumed. For example, as discussed in Chapters 7 and 9, many behaviors are not easily modified by simple operant interventions. In other cases, such as in token economies, changes were often quite temporary and did not easily generalize out of the token system. *Second,* initial theoretical rationales underlying several effective techniques have not been supported when subjected to empirical scrutiny. Systematic desensitization, as discussed in Chapter 2, is a prime example of an effective technique for which no satisfactory rationale is available. These two interrelated developments have led many behavior therapists to question the utility of ignoring or discounting the role of internal processes such as cognitive mediation between stimulus input and response output.

The influence of cognitive processes on response acquisition and performance has had innumerable empirical demonstrations. (See Mahoney, 1974a, for a comprehensive review.) "Awareness" of contingencies can result in immediate "conditioning" or extinction of responses. For example, driving speed can be controlled much more easily by announcing speed limits and the consequences of violation than by requiring every driver to learn the rule by first speeding and being caught and fined. Just as compliance with rules can be facilitated by awareness, individuals can decide to be non-compliant and defy or resist contingencies and exert what Davison (1973) has called "countercontrol." Another example of the effects of cognitive mediation is work on semantic conditioning or semantic generalization (e.g., Lacey, Smith, & Green, 1955). In the typical paradigm, a conditioned autonomic response (i.e., fear or anxiety) is established for a word or word class, such as barn and rooster. It can then be demonstrated that words with associated meanings (such as farm words) result in greater arousal than non-associated words. Much of Bandura's work on modeling and vicarious learning (see Chapter 3) similarly emphasizes the importance of cognitive mediation. Bandura (1971a, 1971b) provides an extensive amount of evidence demonstrating that learning can occur without performance of the response to be conditioned, as well as without the direct experience of reinforcement or the UCS-UCR pairing (in classical conditioning). Rather, observation and information processing are often sufficient for learning to take place.

Not only are mediational processes such as awareness sufficient to establish new response patterns, but beliefs about contingencies can sometimes supercede the actual contingencies that are in effect. Davison, Tsujimoto, and Glaros (1973) demonstrated the effect of beliefs in an experiment with individuals suffering from insomnia. All subjects were initially treated with a clinically appropriate dosage of a sleep-inducing medication and training in a muscle relaxation technique. After a 1-week treatment period the drug was discontinued, and one-half of the

TABLE 4.1

Mean Latency to Sleep in Minutes for Subjects Who Improved during Treatment[a]

| Perceived dosage | Treatment Weeks | | | | | |
| | Baseline | | Treatment | | Post-treatment | |
	X̄	SD	X̄	SD	X̄	SD
Optimal (n = 7)	54.6	.374	17.4	.133	62.4	.300
Minimal (n = 5)	43.8	.172	23.4	.133	36.6	.313

[a] From: Davison et al. (1973) (Table 2).

subjects were told that they had been receiving an optimal dosage while one-half were told they had been receiving a sub-clinical dosage. All subjects were urged to continue use of the relaxation procedure. The results are presented in Table 4.1. While both groups initially had a significant decrease in time to fall asleep, only the group given the "sub-clinical dosage" message maintained their gains. Subjects' *belief* about the source of their improvement (self-relaxation versus drug) had a significant impact on the effects of treatment. Subjects who attributed their improvement to the drug could not maintain their gains without it.

While it is clear that cognitive processes can have a powerful effect on behavior, the manner in which cognitive activity can best be incorporated into a science of behavior is still uncertain. However, there are several factors which favor some directions over others. In considering "in-the-head activity" we are making inferences about what is taking place. As such, there are important differences in the *manner* in which inferences are drawn and the *nature* of what is inferred.

We can draw inferences about cognitive activity in basically two ways: (1) retrospectively on the basis of observation of an individual's behavior (e.g., he carried an umbrella, therefore, he must have *expected* it to rain), or (2) by securing an individual's own report about his experience (e.g., "I *expect* it to rain"). We cannot determine exactly what the inferred concept (expectancy) is in either case (see below). Nevertheless, use of the second form of inference is somewhat more justifiable than the first form because it can have pragmatic utility. The retrospective inference does not allow us to predict behavior; expectation of rain yesterday does not foretell umbrella-carrying tomorrow. This form of inference simply provides a retrospective explanation which is frequently unverifiable and rarely useful. In contrast, subject reports can be prospective and, thereby, can increase our ability to predict and control behavior. If, for example, an individual reports that he expects rain, we can accurately predict that he will carry an umbrella. It would be counterproductive to ignore the mediational construct solely because it is inferential if it can aid our clinical efforts (Mahoney, 1974a).

Perhaps more important than the manner in which inferences are drawn is the issue of what is inferred. Characteristically, the term cognitive mediation refers to *processes* that are presumed to occur within the individual, such as thinking, feeling, attributing, expecting. The difficulty with such hypothesized processes is that they are poorly specified and their existence is currently unverified and often unverifiable. While terms such as expectancy and attribution appear to convey meaning, we do not know exactly what they are, or how and when they operate. Consider our umbrella-carrier above; how does this expectancy develop? How strong a conviction must he have for it to qualify as an expectancy? How strong must the expectancy be before it affects his behavior? How does it affect behavior? How can it be modified? Obviously these questions cannot be answered, but they point out the difficulty involved in employing such hypothetical processes. If as suggested above, such inferences have utility despite their unclarity, their use may be justified. However, reference to such mediational processes should be qualified with an *as if* label. That is, he behaved *as if* he expected it to rain, or *as if* he attributed his improvement to the medication. In this fashion, such concepts can provide pragmatic benefits without being reified (treated as if they were real) and impeding either theoretical or clinical progress.

An alternative to inferences about abstract processes is to consider cognitive activity as covert *responses*. For example, "thinking" can be conceptualized as the occurrence of semantic or visual images. "Expectancies" can be viewed as verbal statements which reflect learned probabilities about the environment. This approach is analogous to the specification involved in translating such general behavioral reports as "he is aggressive" to specific descriptions such as "he hits other children on an average of twice per hour." Analysis of cognitive activity in this manner allows for much greater specification and a lower level of inference than process conceptions. It can be described with the same language and measured with the same techniques as overt behavior. In addition, if cognitive activity is conceptualized as a series of responses rather than as a unique phenomenon, it can be presumed that the *same rules and laws governing overt responses apply to the covert, cognitive responses*. Thus, covert responses can be expected to develop, be maintained, and be modified through the same learning mechanisms as overt responses. Consider an abstraction such as expectancy. As we do not know what it is and how it operates, we cannot directly measure or modify it. In contrast, the occurrence of covert self-statements such as, "I expect to fall asleep, or I expect to be unable to fall asleep," can be assessed and systematically reinforced or punished. Thus, the covert response approach to cognition allows us to control (i.e., modify) behavior as well as predict it.

As stated above, behavior therapists have not agreed on the best way in which to incorporate cognitive phenomena. However, there are four major premises which in our view represent the most productive approach: (1) There is no doubt that cognitive mediation does affect learning and behavior. (2) Retrospective inferences about mediational *processes* are rarely justifiable or useful and should be avoided. (3) Prospective inferences can occasionally improve prediction and, as such, their use is justified. However, their *as if* quality should be emphasized. (4) Cognitive activity can best be conceptualized in terms of covert responses which are presumed to be governed by the same rules as overt responses.

Self-Control

In reviewing definitions of behavior modification in Chapter 1, we specified that a basic goal of behavioral interventions is to increase self-control. At first glance, this goal appears to be inconsistent with two basic behavioral premises: (1) behavior is under stimulus control, and (2) reference to hypothetical internal processes is unwarranted. However, as with other concepts (such as behavior), the terms self and control have special meanings for behavior therapy which allow "self-control" to be incorporated in a logically (and pragmatically) consistent manner. We have already discussed the probabilistic nature of stimulus control. Contingencies affect the likelihood of responses rather than autocratically managing behavior. In many instances, such as interpersonal interactions, the individual's responses alter the environment (and contingencies) which he encounters. There are also many situations in which no specific contingencies have been established, such as when we peruse a menu in a restaurant or choose which movie to see. Thus, there is ample opportunity for the individual to influence the course of his behavior.

In common parlance and traditional psychological theorizing, "self-control" has implied the existence of some abstract internal system such as "will" or "ego." Behavior therapists have approached self-control in the same manner in which they have approached cognitive processes in general: by concretizing the phenomenon in terms of specific responses. The individual exerting self-control is not presumed to be engaging in some metaphysical process, but rather affecting behavior by making specific responses such as covert verbalizations. Analogous to our discussion above about the similarity of covert and overt responses, self-control is presumed to follow the same laws as external control. The primary difference between the two forms of control is not in how they operate, but in the primary locus of the control: from within or from without (this issue will be discussed further in the section on self-reinforcement) (Bandura, 1976; Kanfer, 1976).

Self-control is generally viewed as a special case or sub-category of self-regulation or self-management. The latter two terms refer to any instances in which the primary determinant of the course of behavior is the individual. This includes non-conflictual behavior such as practicing a new skill or hobby and walking aimlessly through the woods (Kanfer, 1975). The term self-control is generally reserved for situations in which the individual experiences some conflict, such as in dieting or when attempting to quit smoking. This parallels common notions of situations requiring "willpower" or the ability to resist temptation. In attempting to define behavioral self-control, Thoresen and Mahoney (1974) have specified, "A person displays self-control when in the relative absence of immediate external constraints, he engages in behavior whose previous probability has been less than that of alternatively available behaviors (involving lesser or delayed reward, greater exertion or aversive properties, and so on)" (p. 12). For example, eating carrots (rather than candy) is a response made by a dieter which, prior to the diet, was less likely to occur. The individual is thus acting against an existing contingency (the reinforcing value of candy in the situation).

Self-control involves at least two responses: the high probability response *to be controlled* and a low probability *controlling* response. In addition, the controlling response must emanate from the individual rather than the environment (as when the party hostess serves only low calorie foods). The controlling response is not initiated via will power, but is itself subject to contingencies, which often come from the external environment. Thus, tight-fitting clothes and spouse or girlfriend criticism are forms of external control which might combine to stimulate dieting behavior (controlling responses). On a day-to-day basis, the dieter maintains the diet by making self-controlling responses, such as refusing to drink beer. (If the spouse follows the individual around, removing fattening foods and criticizing overeating, no self-control is involved.) If the prospective dieter buys a new wardrobe, or if his spouse ceases to "harp" on his weight, he might well stop dieting. Thus, *self-control is* based on external control. The two forms of control exist on a continuum, and we ordinarily evaluate responses in terms of the relative degree of self- and external control involved (Kanfer, 1976; Thoresen & Mahoney, 1974).

Behavioral Model of Self-Control

Our discussion thus far has involved a general description of what behavior therapists mean by the term self-control. We have not considered how and when individuals actually exert self-control. These specific aspects of self-control operation are best represented by a model developed by Frederick H. Kanfer (1975, 1976).

Kanfer has hypothesized that under ordinary circumstances the flow of behavior is smooth and uneventful and does not require self-regulatory responses. However, when the flow is interrupted or performed imperfectly, as in conflict situations or after an error, a three-stage self-regulatory process is initiated. The first stage is *self-monitoring*, in which the individual observes his performance and the context in which it is occurring. For example, a tennis player ordinarily pays little attention to his strokes, but after a few backhand errors, he might begin attending to his backhand in an effort to determine the reason for the difficulty. No self-regulatory responses are possible unless the individual first monitors his behavior.

The second stage in the sequence is *self-evaluation*. After monitoring his behavior, the individual then compares his performance with some standard or criterion, in order to determine its adequacy. The evaluative standards can be internalized, external, or both. In the case of our tennis player, he might have a history of an excellent backhand and determine that his stroke is no longer as effective as it was. Evaluation in reference to such a personalized history would involve an internalized standard. Conversely, a novice player might lack an internal criterion and evaluate his stroke in terms of his instructor's comments about his progress in learning to play. Evaluative standards are, thus, idiosyncratic with each individual: no two people evaluate a specific performance in exactly the same way. The standards are developed primarily via modeling or direct tuition, as when adults tell children that only A grades (or B or C) will be rewarded (Bandura, 1976). Regardless of the locus of the standard, the evaluation can have one of three outcomes: (1) insufficient data, which would stimulate further monitoring; (2) the response is judged as adequate, in which case no further action is required; or (3) the response is judged as above or below criterion, in which case the third stage of the self-regulatory sequence is initiated.

The final stage of the sequence is *self-reinforcement*, and involves the self-administration of positively reinforcing or punishing stimuli contingent upon good or poor performance, respectively. Self-reinforcement is presumed to operate in a manner identical with external reinforcement, the only difference being the source of the reinforcer. Self-reinforcement can take any of the forms of external reinforcement (e.g., activities, material) with the exception of social reinforcers. The self-reinforcement parallel to social reinforcers is highly valanced self-verbalizations such as, "I did really well," or "I blew it, that was lousy." These self-statements are presumed to have acquired reinforcing properties through their association with social reinforcers as well as by modeling (such as when a child observes his father verbally berate himself after making an error).

The actual regulatory control over behavior derives from self-reinforcement. By appropriately consequating his performance (i.e., administering a contingent consequence), the individual is able to alter the behavioral flow until it is once again smooth and up to criterion level. Self-monitoring and self-evaluation continue throughout the period when self-reinforcement is administered. Once criterion is reached or the conflict situation eliminated, self-control responses cease. Thus, the self-regulatory process is transitory and is not the sole maintaining factor for any long-term behavioral sequence.

Self-Reinforcement

Self-reinforcement is the most critical and most controversial element of the self-regulatory model. Speculations about whether we can or cannot control our own behavior hinge on whether or not we can withhold and present reinforcement to ourselves on a contingent basis. There are two basic issues which must be accounted for in validating the self-reinforcement conception.

The first issue pertains to what Bandura (1976) refers to as the *operation* of self-reinforcement. It is paradoxical that the individual must first deprive himself of a freely available reinforcer in order to apply it contingently when he surpasses criterion. It must be demonstrated that such self-deprivation can in fact occur when access to reinforcers is not restricted by others (i.e., when they are freely available). If self-denial in a free access situation is not possible, it must be presumed that when deprivation does occur it is under external control (such as threat of punishment for indulgence). The second issue pertains to the *process* of self-reinforcement. Does self-reinforcement actually affect the frequency of behavior independent of external reinforcement? That is, is "self-reinforcement" actually reinforcing?

There have been two widely used analogue research paradigms which have a direct bearing on the *operation* of self-reinforcement. Kanfer and his colleagues have employed a procedure referred to as a *directed learning paradigm*. In the typical experiment, subjects (usually college students) are first given external reinforcement for performance on a task in which they have little idea as to the quality of their efforts (such as time estimation and word association tests). They are then shifted to self-reinforcement, and either level of performance or the rate at which they administer reinforcement to themselves is compared to experimenter controlled conditions. These studies have demonstrated that self-reinforcement can maintain performance at a level similar to external reinforcement (Bellack, 1972; Kanfer & Marston, 1963), that subjects administer self-reinforcement at a rate similar to their experience with external reinforcement (Kanfer & Duerfeldt, 1967), and that rather than being freely administered, self-reinforcement rate is highly correlated with performance quality (Bellack, 1975b; Bellack & Tillman, 1974). These studies, taken together, suggest that individuals can deprive themselves of reinforcers and administer them contingently, and that self-reinforcement can affect the rate of behavior. However, studies employing this paradigm have used weak reinforcers (e.g., lights labeled correct or good) with an atypical subject population (Introductory

Psychology students). Therefore the results only confirm the *possibility* of a self-reinforcement effect.

Bandura and his colleagues have employed a *social learning* paradigm in a series of studies in which children served as subjects. In this paradigm subjects first observe adults or other children performing on a miniature bowling alley, using diverse scoring criteria to reward themselves with self-verbalizations and candy. The model might say, "Gee, that was a good one," and take candy after any score, or after moderate and high scores, or only after high scores. The subjects then perform, and their self-reinforcement patterns are observed. (The bowling apparatus is such that the experimenter determines the "score," so that actual skill is not a factor.) The results of this series of studies consistently demonstrate that children can be taught to adopt strict or lenient criteria for self-reinforcement by varying model characteristics (such as age and competence) and model self-reinforcement behavior (Bandura & Kupers, 1964; Bandura & Whalen, 1966; Mischel & Liebert, 1966). These results not only indicate that children can withhold available reinforcers from themselves, but that self-control behavior can be learned by observing models.

Analogue studies employing the two paradigms described above have provided only minimal support for the process of self-reinforcement. The effectiveness of self-reinforcement is best represented by two studies employing a different methodology. The first study was conducted by Bandura and Perloff (1967). The subjects were children 7–10 years of age. Upon reporting for the experiment, the child was seated before an apparatus containing a hand-operated crank and four lamps labeled 5, 10, 15, or 20. The crank was wired to the lamps so that 8, 16, 24, or 32 turns, respectively, were required for them to be illuminated. In addition, one token could be dispensed into a cup when one of the lamps was illuminated; tokens were exchangeable for prizes. Subjects were divided into four groups: (1) self-monitored reinforcement, (2) externally imposed reinforcement, (3) incentive-control, and (4) no token control.

Subjects in the self-reinforcement condition were instructed to *determine for themselves* how many cranks (i.e., how much effort) would be required per token. Subjects in the imposed reinforcement and incentive conditions were each yoked to one of the self-reinforcement subjects. Imposed reinforcement subjects worked under an imposed criterion which matched their partner's self-determined criterion. Incentive subjects received the total number of tokens earned by their partner before they began cranking (i.e., noncontingently). Finally, no token control subjects worked without reinforcement. The results are presented in Fig. 4.1. Subjects in the self- and imposed reinforcement groups turned the crank significantly more than subjects in the two control groups; differences between the two reinforcement groups were not significant. Thus, self-reinforcement was clearly as effective as external reinforce-

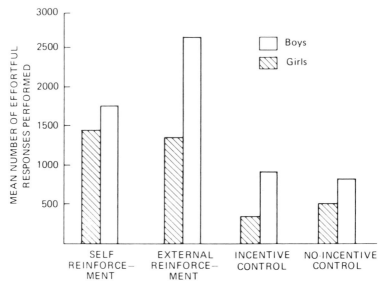

Fig. 4.1 Mean number of responses performed as a function of sex and type of reinforcement system. (Reprinted with permission from: A. Bandura and B. Perloff: *Journal of Personality and Social Psychology,* 7: 111, 1967.)

ment in maintaining effortful behavior. In addition, children were able to impose somewhat stringent demands on themselves for self-reinforcement; no child selected the most lenient criterion and almost one half chose the most stringent criterion.

Felixbrod and O'Leary (1973) conducted a parallel study which employed a more "natural" task: completing arithmetic problems. Subjects were children in the second grade. They were assigned to one of three groups and tested individually for six sessions. Children in a self-reinforcement group were told that they would receive points (redeemable for prizes) for correctly completing arithmetic problems. During each session, they were to determine how many correct problems they would require of themselves for each point. Children in an external reinforcement group were yoked to self-reinforcement subjects and had point criteria imposed on them. Children in a no reinforcement group worked with no incentive. Children in each group could work on an unlimited number of grade-appropriate problems for up to 20 min. in each session. Subjects in both reinforcement conditions worked significantly longer and completed significantly more problems than subjects in the no reinforcement condition. The self-control condition was as effective as the external control condition on both dependent variables. These results provide a replication and extension of the findings of Bandura and Perloff (1967) in that the ability of children to exert restrictive control over their own behavior was shown to be extended over time.

In both of these studies the children determined the standards for receiving reinforcement, but actually received reinforcers from an external source (the experimenter). This procedure appears to be more related to what Kanfer has called self-evaluation than to self-reinforcement. However, this differentiation of evaluation and reinforcement is often presumed to be more of a conceptual matter than a sequence of distinct responses that can be physically separated. Bandura (1976) subsumes a self-evaluative and criterion-setting process under the term self-reinforcement. The physical act of picking up a reinforcer (e.g., a toy) oneself or having it handed over by someone else appears to be secondary to the locus of control in determining whether or not the reinforcer is to be administered (Bandura, 1976). The children in these two studies did control administration by adopting somewhat restrictive criteria for reinforcement. They functionally told the experimenter how much reinforcement they should receive.

Related to this issue is the question of identifying the specific source of reinforcement in the behavior stream. For example, was the behavior of the children in the Bandura and Perloff (1967) study reinforced by reaching their criterion number of turns, or by the tokens they received, or by the prizes for which the tokens were redeemed? Some writers (e.g., Rachlin, 1974) have argued that "so-called" self-reinforcement is simply a discriminative stimulus that signals the future occurrence of external reinforcement. In that case, reaching criterion and tokens would have been discriminative for prizes. However, in the same way that conditioned or secondary reinforcers (e.g., money) achieve reinforcing value by their association with more primary reinforcers (e.g., food), these stimuli can attain reinforcing value. It should be pointed out that analogous to other conditioned reinforcers, self-reinforcers are maintained by periodic association with more primary reinforcers: in this case external reinforcement. When we refer to self-reinforcement, we do not imply total independence from the external environment. Rather, we are referring to a source of behavior influence which is ultimately maintained by external control, but which can have significant short-term impact on behavior (Bandura, 1976; Kanfer, 1976; Thoresen & Mahoney, 1974).

Clinical Applications of Self-Control Procedures

In the previous section we considered the possibility of exerting control over one's own behavior. This section will focus on the translation of that possibility for clinical practice. Despite the fact that the operations and processes of self-control (i.e., self-reinforcement) are still subjects of debate, self-control procedures have become a major part of the behavior therapist's armamentarium. Much of the support for the self-control model has come from successful clinical application of derived techniques. Two major clinical strategies have evolved: environmental planning and behavioral programming (Thoresen & Mahoney,

1974). While most clinical interventions combine both procedures, we will consider them in sequence.

Environmental Planning

A significant portion of our behavior unfolds rather automatically as a function of the stimuli (S^Ds) to which we are exposed. The driver's foot moves to the brake pedal when he sees a red light; notebooks are closed when the bell signals the end of class; we pick up the telephone when we hear it ring. While these behaviors are ultimately maintained by their consequences, on a moment-to-moment basis the antecedent stimuli have primary control. Frequently, these stimuli have such great control that the associated responses cannot be inhibited once the stimulus is presented. Consider, for example, a ringing telephone! As a function of this control, responses can be modified by preventing the occurrence or altering the nature of controlling stimuli, such as by taking the telephone off the hook before entering the shower. This form of control is represented by the old adage: "Out of sight, out of mind."

Environmental planning (often referred to as "stimulus control") involves the self-generated modification of the environment so as to maximize desired behavior and/or minimize undesired behavior. The specific nature of the modification varies, of course, with the nature of the controlling stimuli. In some cases, such as with smoking and overeating, the behavior is controlled by too many stimuli, and control must be narrowed. In other instances, such as with insomnia and studying deficits, appropriate stimuli (e.g., bed, desk) do not control the behavior and adequate control must be developed.

Some of the first reports of the use of environmental planning involved treatment for college students with studying problems (Fox, 1962; Goldiamond, 1965). There are many possible reasons for inadequate study behavior including inadequate incentives for studying and poor vision (which makes reading difficult). However, many of the students were observed to study at random intervals, in rooms with poor lighting, noise, and other distractions such as television or roommates. Environmental planning for stimulus-related study deficits typically focuses on the development of stimuli that are discriminative for studying and on the removal of distracting stimuli. Typical procedures include: (1) setting aside an appropriate study area (e.g., a desk) which is to be used for nothing other than studying, (2) establishing a studying routine (e.g., after English class, and after dinner), (3) removing inappropriate stimuli such as music and television, and (4) gradually increasing studying time from an initial low level (e.g., 5–10 min.) to periods of moderate length (e.g., 30–60 min.). Similar techniques have been employed in the treatment of insomnia. Treatment focuses on making the bed and bedtime discriminative for sleeping by: (1) avoiding such non-sleep responses as reading or television-watching in bed, and (2) by getting out of bed when not tired or unable to fall asleep. In the case of both studying and sleep deficits, the goal of treatment is to establish a strong relationship between the target behavior and one or two stimuli which are not discriminative for other, incompatible responses.

The most systematized application of environmental planning has been in behavioral treatment for obesity. The vast majority of obese individuals are overweight because they eat too much (Mayer, 1968). Schacter (1971) has hypothesized that a primary reason for this overindulgence is that the eating behavior of the obese is under the control of external stimuli rather than internal, hunger-produced stimuli. Thus, the overweight individual always feels "hungry," as he is constantly bombarded by such controlling stimuli as certain times of day, the sight of food or restaurants, parties, and such activities as watching television and reading. Several programs have been developed in which a primary component of treatment involves systematic attempts to reduce the number of situations in which eating occurs (Bellack, Rozensky, & Schwartz, 1974; Ferster, Nurnberger, & Levitt, 1962; Stuart & Davis, 1972). Rather than focusing treatment solely on the amount consumed or the amount of weight lost, a major emphasis is modification of eating style: how, when, and where people eat. By instructing clients in ways to avoid eating in response to inappropriate controlling stimuli, the controlling effect of those stimuli is expected to extinguish (as eating does not occur in their presence). The amount consumed would thus be reduced and the individual would lose weight. In addition, by developing new, appropriate, eating habits the individual should be better able to maintain his reduced weight.

Stimulus control techniques for weight reduction can be organized into three categories, which reflect the three primary eating dysfunctions of the obese: eating too much, too often, and eating highly fattening foods (Bellack, 1975a). A list of the most frequently employed techniques is presented in Table 4.2. In contrast to the techniques employed for study deficits and insomnia, application of these procedures requires a considerable degree of self-restraint and effort. Many of the directives, such as "eat in one place and do nothing else while eating," require the individual to consistently inhibit a high probability response. These guidelines are quite difficult to implement for extended periods of time. In contrast, establishing a study area conflicts with no strongly stimulated response. Consequently, weight reduction programs based solely on these procedures have had only limited success. However, programs that supplement the stimulus control approach with some form of consequation for compliance have proven to be the most effective treatments for weight reduction (Bellack, 1975a, 1977). For example, the client can administer self-reinforcement for emitting the

TABLE 4.2

Procedures to Reduce Stimulus Control of Eating [a]

Modification of Meal Quantity

1. Eat slowly: gradually increase minimal time allowed for each meal.
2. Take small bites.
3. Put eating utensil (or food item) down while chewing.
4. Take one helping at a time.
5. Leave table for a brief period between helpings.
6. Eat one food item at a time (e.g., finish meat, before taking vegetable).
7. Serve food from kitchen rather than placing platter on table.
8. Use small cups and plates.
9. Leave some food on plate at end of meal.

Modification of Meal Frequency

1. Do nothing else while eating.
2. Eat in only one place, sitting down (preferably not in kitchen and not where you engage in other activities).
3. Eat only at specified times.
4. Set the table with a complete place setting whenever eating.
5. Wait a fixed period after urge to eat before actually eating.
6. Engage in an activity incompatible with eating when urge to eat appears.
7. Plan a highly liked activity for periods when the urge to eat can be anticipated (e.g., read evening newspaper before bedtime).

Modification of Types of Food eaten

1. Do not buy prepared foods or snack foods.
2. Prepare lunch after eating breakfast and dinner after lunch (to avoid nibbling).
3. Do grocery shopping soon after eating.
4. Shop from a list.
5. Eat a low calorie meal before leaving for a party.
6. Do not eat while drinking coffee or alcohol.

[a] From: Bellack (1975a) (Table 1).

controlling response (e.g., doing nothing else while eating), which maintains its use and allows it to modify the response to be controlled (eating too often) (Bellack, 1976; Mahoney, 1974b). Compliance with program directions can also be facilitated by requiring the client to sign a contract specifying his responsibilities (Kanfer, 1975) (see also Chapter 1). Contract violation can be consequated by therapist and/or self-generated censure.

Cigarette smoking, like overeating, is presumed to be a behavior which is under the control of a large number of external stimuli. Smokers often smoke in response to many of the same kinds of cues which stimulate the obese to eat, such as when other people are observed smoking, when drinking coffee or alcohol, and when reading or watching television. Stimulus control programs for smoking have, thus, had structure and results similar to weight control programs. The primary focus has been stimulus narrowing: gradually reducing smoking rate by reducing the situations, places, or times at which smoking can occur. Powell and Azrin (1968) supplied subjects with a cigarette case that administered an electric shock when it was opened; subjects were to keep their cigarettes in the case and smoke only their own cigarettes. While the electric shock component of this procedure involves behavioral programming (see below), placing cigarettes in the case meets the criterion of environmental planning. In an analogous manner, cigarettes can be placed in a hard to reach place (e.g., in the garage, at the top of a closet), thereby increasing the response cost of smoking while removing the cigarette pack as a discriminative stimulus for smoking. Employing a parallel strategy, Nolan (1968) directed a subject to smoke only in a special "smoking chair." Her rate of smoking dropped from 30 per day to 12 per day within 9 days, and quickly dropped to zero when the chair was moved to the basement. Other procedures have also been employed, including gradually decreasing number of cigarettes allowed per day and smoking only in response to the ringing of a pocket timer, which is set to buzz at random and gradually increasing intervals.

The procedures described above involve what Kanfer (1976) has referred to as *protracted* self-control. The individual must continue to engage in self-deprivation or resist prolonged discomfort. At times, the altered behavior results in natural consequences which can maintain the behavior, such as weight loss in a diet. Ordinarily, however, these consequences are too much delayed (e.g., increased longevity due to lowered weight or not smoking) to be sufficient. The addition of self- or external-consequation for either the controlling or controlled response is frequently essential. An alternative strategy involves the use of *decisional* self-control. In this approach, the individual places control in the hands of a second party or otherwise removes the possibility of making the response to be controlled. For example, a student whose evening hours are under the control of the television set can have a friend keep the set during final exam period. Mann (1972) required subjects in a weight control study to deposit valuables with him; these were to be returned contingent on weight loss. In both cases, self-control was involved in making the initial decision (controlling response), but subsequent control rested with the environment. While this approach can be effective, it is generally considered to be less desirable than protracted self-control as it does not provide the individual with an enduring skill or resource.

Behavioral Programming

Thoresen and Mahoney (1974) reserve the term behavioral programming to refer to controlling responses that are made *after* the response to be controlled occurs (i.e., self-administered consequences). There are two major strategies for behavioral programming: self-monitoring and self-reinforcement. As self-reinforcement necessarily involves self-monitoring, we will consider monitoring first.

Self-Monitoring. This is one of the most frequently used techniques in behavioral intervention. As discussed in Chapter 1, monitoring has become an integral data collection tool in work with out-patient populations. Clients are routinely required to keep records, ranging from simple frequency counts to elaborate diaries, in which they detail their internal state and situational factors as well as target behaviors per se. As specified in Kanfer's model of self-regulation, self-monitoring is a necessary percurser to self-evaluation and self-reinforcement. Rather than leaving such self-observation to chance, systematic monitoring instructions are, therefore, almost invariably included as part of any self-control program. When employed in either of these contexts (data collection and cueing of self-reinforcement), self-monitoring has indirect therapeutic benefits for the individual. Monitoring has also been employed as a behavior change agent in and of itself.

The act of self-observation is more than a passive data-collection process. The information so gathered becomes a part of the ongoing behavior stream for the individual. As such, the information can affect behavior in the same manner as proprioceptive feedback and external input, including observational learning effects and imposed contingencies. Self-monitored data can allow for corrective responses, as when the artist steps away from the canvas to get a broader perspective of his work. It can serve as a discriminative stimulus for external reinforcement, such as when a student rereads homework or an examination paper before handing the work to a teacher. Finally, self-monitored information can be a conditioned stimulus for self-evaluation and self-reinforcement, such as when a dieter observes that he has eaten a high caloric meal (Bellack, 1976). Self-monitoring thus has *reactive* effects; behavior changes as a function of self-observation (Kazdin, 1974e; Nelson, Lipinski, & Black, 1975).

Reactivity is an undesired consequence when monitoring is used for data collection, as the naturally ocurring rate of the response is altered. The direction of the change is determined to a great extent by the valence of the behavior or its expected consequences (Kazdin, 1974d; Lipinski, Black, Nelson, & Ciminero, 1975). Undesired behavior or behavior discriminative for punishment decreases, while desired behavior or behavior discriminative for positive reinforcement will increase. Therefore, since monitored behavior ordinarily changes in a therapeutically desired direction, self-monitoring has potential utility as a treatment technique.

Self-monitoring has been successfully employed as the sole or primary treatment modality with a wide variety of target behaviors. Monitoring has been found to reduce the rate of cigarette smoking (Lipinski et al., 1975) and alcohol consumption (Sobell & Sobell, 1973). Johnson and White (1971) demonstrated that college students who self-monitored study behavior earned significantly higher grades. In a related study, students who self-monitored their performance while studying for the Graduate Record Examination studied more and performed better than students who did not monitor (Mahoney, Moore, Wade, & Moura, 1973).

The wide range of target behaviors and patient characteristics for which self-monitoring is therapeutically effective is well represented by five single-case reports described by Maletzky (1974). Patients ranged in age from 9 to 65 years. Target behaviors included facial tics, fingernail biting, and the frantic in-class hand waving of the 9-year-old. The data for Case 1 are presented in Fig. 4.2 (this is an ABABABA design in which vertical lines have been left off the figure). The patient was a 52-year-old woman, who reported having had a 30-year history of repetitive scratching, which resulted in unsightly lesions on her arms and legs. Treatment consisted solely of recording the occurrence of scratching on a wrist counter and entering the data on a graph each evening. The effectiveness and control of this simple procedure are apparent (see Fig. 4.2). Results for the other four patients were equally positive.

The reactive effects of self-monitoring vary as a function of how monitoring is conducted and what is monitored. Anecdotal clinical data suggest that self-monitoring is most effective when the individual is required to make an overt, physical recording response such as pressing a wrist counter or making a written diary entry. Covert self-observation occurs less consistently and also is less obtrusive. The monitoring response should also be made at the time that the target response occurs, rather than cumulatively at the end of the day. Ongoing monitoring is somewhat unreliable (Lipinski & Nelson, 1974); delayed monitoring is often less reliable, as well as its having a less direct impact on behavior.

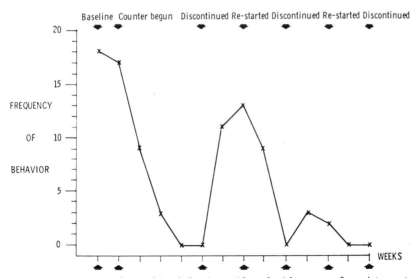

Fig. 4.2 Frequency of scratching behaviors with and without use of a wrist counter. Case 1. (Reprinted with permission from: B. M. Maletzky: *Behavior Therapy*, 5: 107, 1974.)

Finally, monitoring is often tedious and should be reinforced by the therapist in order to insure that the client complies.

When the treatment goal is reduction in rate of an undesired behavior, monitoring of intention to perform the response can be more effective than monitoring the response per se. Such pre-behavior observation interrupts the behavior flow and allows the individual to make a controlling response before the targeted response can occur. This effect was demonstrated in a weight control experiment conducted by Bellack et al. (1974). Four treatment groups were employed, and each received stimulus control instructions. In addition, one group of subjects was required to record everything they intended to eat immediately before eating; a second group of subjects recorded everything they had eaten immediately after eating. In order to insure that they actually monitored, subjects in both groups were given pocket-sized notebooks on which to monitor, along with a supply of pre-addressed envelopes; they were required to mail their monitoring records to the experimenter each day throughout the program. These subjects also attended weekly group meetings. A third group attended meetings but did not monitor, and the fourth group was a no-contact control. The intention-monitoring condition was most effective, and the post-eating monitoring condition was no more effective than the no-contact control.

As stated above, the reactive effects of self-monitoring (are presumed to) stem from the discriminative properties of the information supplied to the individual. Monitoring is most effective when the information initiates powerful controlling responses. At the beginning of any treatment program, monitoring is discriminative for self-evaluation and self-reinforcement. However, these responses are often unsystematic and are not applied contingently. In addition, people often adapt to self-produced negative feedback over time. Therefore, the reactive effects of self-monitoring are frequently short-lived. For example, Romancyzk (1974) found self-monitoring to be as effective as more elaborate treatment procedures in a 4-week weight control program, while Bellack et al. (1974) and Mahoney (1974a) found it to be no more effective than minimal treatment control conditions in longer (7–8 weeks) programs. When naturally occurring consequences quickly take over control of the behavior, or when the target response is quickly extinguished, self-monitoring may be employed as the sole treatment agent. In most situations, it is included as an adjunct to other procedures which involve more direct consequation of the target response.

Self-Reinforcement. The order in which we have presented the various self-control strategies coincidentally reflects a historical perspective of behavior therapists' emphasis on the various techniques. Initial efforts were directed toward environmental planning. As it became apparent that stimulus control instructions were often insufficient by themselves, attention shifted to the reactive effects of self-monitoring.

Systematic research and clinical reports then demonstrated that monitoring was also inadequate for modification of many dysfunctions. Consequently, in an effort to identify more powerful treatments, focus shifted to self-reinforcement. Rather than leaving consequation of behavior to chance, as with stimulus control and self-monitoring, self-reinforcement procedures establish explicit contingencies for behavior. In addition, the use of self-reinforcement often involves environmental planning (e.g., Powell & Azrin, 1968) and necessarily requires self-monitoring (behavior must be observed if it is to be consequated). Therefore, self-reinforcement procedures should be more effective than the other, less comprehensive, self-control techniques.

Clinical applications of self-imposed reinforcement procedures can be segmented into two somewhat distinct approaches. One strategy requires the individual to self-determine the criterion for reinforcement and whether or not he has met it, but the reinforcement is physically administered by an external agent. This procedure was described above in regard to the analogue studies conducted by Bandura and Perloff (1967) and Felixbrod and O'Leary (1973). The second strategy places primary emphasis on self-administration of consequences. In situations in which performance must be subjectively rated, this approach subsumes self-evaluation (as when reinforcement is contingent upon eating "appropriately" during a diet). Frequently, however, the approach involves the consequation of discrete responses on a pre-determined schedule (as when every cigarette smoked is self-punished) and no explicit self-evaluation is required.

The former procedure (self-determination of criteria) has been employed most extensively in the context of classroom token economies with children (see Chapter 6). A major difficulty with classroom token systems is that they require a substantial amount of teacher time to monitor, evaluate, and reinforce all the children. The effects of token programs also generalize poorly to non-token classrooms. It would, therefore, be desirable if children could be taught to regulate their own performance and reinforcement. Several studies have demonstrated that, with appropriate training procedures, self-regulation can occur (Bolstad & Johnson, 1972; Drabman, Spitalnik, & O'Leary, 1973; Glynn, Thomas, & Shee, 1973; Turkewitz, O'Leary, & Ironsmith, 1974). The procedure employed by Bolstad and Johnson (1972) is representative of each of the studies.

The subjects were disruptive children in the first and second grade; treatment was conducted in their regular classrooms. The children were divided into four groups: no treatment, external regulation, and two self-regulation groups. A baseline of disruptive behavior was first established for all subjects. Children in all but the no-treatment group were then placed on a therapist managed token system in which they were reinforced for decreasing their rate of disruptive behavior. In the next phase of the study the token economy was continued, and children in the two self-regulation groups were instructed to monitor their own disruptive behavior. They were, therefore, required both to determine when they were disruptive and to keep a record of each episode. If their records matched the therapist's assessment of their behavior, they were reinforced at the same level as during the previous phase of the study. However, if they were inaccurate, they were penalized by receiving fewer tokens (the penalty varied according to the degree of inaccuracy). The children in these two groups were then shifted to complete self-regulation; they were reinforced solely on the basis of their own reports. The final phase of the experiment constituted extinction for the three groups on the token system; reinforcers were no longer administered. One of the two self-regulation groups continued to self-monitor during this phase.

The results indicated that self-regulation was as effective as external regulation in maintaining lowered rates of disruption when reinforcement was provided. In addition, the children were able to observe their behavior accurately and, in general, they administered reinforcement at appropriate rates (i.e., they did not "cheat" and administer more points than they had earned). The self-regulatory effects in this study were closely tied to the use of backup reinforcers; the rate of disruptive behavior began to increase when backups were removed (even for the group that continued to monitor). However, several other studies which have used more elaborate training procedures have demonstrated that improved rates of academic and disruptive behaviors can be maintained after backups are eliminated (Drabman et al., 1973; Glynn et al., 1973; Turkewitz et al., 1974). For example, Turkewitz et al. (1974) eliminated backup reinforcers by gradually fading them out over an 18-day period rather than terminating their use all at once.

The results of this series of studies clearly demonstrates that with sufficient training, children can be taught to participate in the regulation of their own behavior. We emphasize the word "participate" rather than specifying that children can individually control their own behavior because a substantial amount of external control is provided in these applications in addition to backup reinforcers. Most children have learned, independent of the short-term classroom intervention, that they are liable to social censure or other punishment for cheating or overly generous self-reward. They also know that they can be observed without their awareness. This historical external control can supercede the experimental "freedom" from censure defined by the therapist. This effect is clearly demonstrated in the Felixbrod and O'Leary (1973) study. Children in that study gradually selected milder performance criteria over sessions as they discovered that their standards were not subject to censure. This pattern is consistent with the concept of self-reinforcement as it was described above. Self-deprivation is not expected to continue and self-reinforcement is not expected to have durable effects without periodic support by external reinforcement.

The second self-reinforcement paradigm has been employed primarily with adult outpatients. Characteristically, the patient and therapist first agree to an appropriate contingency for modifying the target behavior. The patient is then responsible for monitoring and evaluating his behavior and administering the appropriate consequence in a contingent fashion. Behavior therapy programs should always be tailored to the needs and situation of the individual client. This is especially critical with this form of self-reinforcement program, as success depends totally on the continuing cooperation of the client. The therapist can apply some control through the use of social reinforcement: praise for compliance and censure and encouragement for non-compliance. In some instances, as when money serves as the reinforcer, the therapist can retain the reinforcement in his possession (see the section below on weight control programs employing financial contingencies). However, in most instances cooperation is best assured by involving the client in treatment planning, including the identification of meaningful reinforcers and acceptable contingencies.

The self-applied consequences approach has been demonstrated in numerous uncontrolled case reports covering a wide range of target behaviors. The selection of reinforcers and mode of implementation in these programs has apparently been limited only by the imagination of the clinician and client. For example, Bucher and Fabricatore (1970) used a punishment paradigm to reduce the hallucinations experienced by a schizophrenic patient. The patient carried a portable electric shock apparatus and self-administered shocks contingent on experiencing hallucinations. Mahoney (1971) employed a similar paradigm for the treatment of an obsessional patient. However, the punishing stimulus was a heavy rubber band that the patient wore on his wrist and snapped contingently upon experiencing obsessive thoughts. Both procedures were effective.

The most frequently used form of reinforcement has involved Premack reinforcers (high probability, desired activities). Epstein and Peterson (1973) described two cases in which activity reinforcers were used in a response-cost paradigm. Case 1 was a female college student who compulsively plucked out her eyelashes under stress. She enjoyed listening to music, and a contingency was established such that she deprived herself of first 6 hours and later 12 hours of music for each eyelash plucked. Rate of eyelash plucking decreased from an average of 4 per day to 0.25 per day over 45 days of treatment. The second case (Case 3) involved a male student who shoplifted. "The reinforcement was the opportunity for the client to work at his profitable self-employed business each night. Initially, the client had to earn 2 points per day, each point being equivalent to 5 min. in a downtown store without stealing, to obtain reinforcement. The consequence of stealing was not being able to work at his business for 2 days. The amount of time was gradually increased to one-half hour per day" (Epstein & Peterson, 1973, p. 93). A similar program was employed by Watson, Tharp, and Krisberg (1972) for treatment of compulsive scratching behavior. The client earned a daily bath by engaging in behavior incompatible with scratching whenever he experienced the urge to scratch. The rate of scratching was reduced to zero after 20 days. Two recurrences over the following 18 months were quickly brought under control by reimposition of the contingency.

Most controlled investigations of the clinical effectiveness of self-consequation have focused on weight reduction. (Obesity is a convenient target as there is a substantial clinical population available, the dysfunction is appropriate for self-control interventions, and weight is an objective and easily secured dependent variable.) Several studies have examined self-imposed financial contingencies (Jeffrey, 1974; Mahoney, 1974b; Mahoney, Moura, & Wade, 1973). In the typical procedure, subjects are required to leave a financial deposit with the therapist. Portions of the deposit are made available for self-reinforcement during weekly meetings. Subjects may self-reinforce by reclaiming or forfeiting the money as a function of their evaluation of their weight loss and/or eating habits during the preceding week. Mahoney (1974b) and Mahoney, Moura, and Wade (1973) found this procedure to be highly effective. Self-reinforcement groups had significantly more weight loss than self-monitoring and no-treatment control groups. In a related study, Jeffrey (1974) compared the effectiveness of self-administered financial contingencies with parallel therapist-managed contingencies. While both procedures were equally effective during the initial treatment period, results for the self-managed procedure were more durable *after* treatment was completed. The implication of these results is that subjects administering self-reinforcement learned to manage their own behavior and, therefore, could continue to perform effectively without the therapist.

The procedure employed in these studies parallels the self-determination paradigm described above. While subjects physically administered reinforcement to themselves, therapists maintained possession of the reinforcer and limited subjects' access to it (e.g., they could only withdraw a limited amount each week). Two studies using different types of reinforcers have demonstrated that self-reinforcement can be effective with less direct external control. Bellack (1976) divided overweight subjects into four groups. All subjects received stimulus control information and were directed to keep a record of everything they ate. In addition, two groups were instructed to evaluate each meal (based on daily caloric intake goals and compliance with stimulus control guidelines) and apply self-reinforcement. Reinforcement consisted of assigning a letter grade to the meal and entering it on the monitoring record. Grades were presumed to be conditioned reinforcers for most people. Level of therapist contact was also varied; one self-reinforcement group and one non-reinforcement group mailed their monitoring records to the therapist each day and received weekly feedback (by mail). The remaining groups had no contact with the therapist after the introductory session. The results are presented in Table 4.3. Both self-reinforcement groups (SR) lost significantly more weight than their self-monitoring only (SM) counterparts, and they continued to lose weight during a follow-up period. There were no differences between therapist-contact and no-contact conditions. Thus, not only did self-reinforcement have a distinct and powerful effect on weight loss, but the level of therapist control needed to supplement that effect was negligible.

In a subsequent study, a somewhat more elaborate form of self-reinforcement was superimposed on the same basic weight control program (Bellack, Glanz, & Simon, 1976). Subjects applied either positive self-reinforcement (for appropriate eating) or self-punishment (for inappropriate eating) in successive phases of treatment. Positive reinforcement involved writing the word THIN on the monitoring record and generating a positive diet-related image for several seconds (e.g., imagining oneself wearing a smaller sized garment or being complemented by an opposite sex friend). Self-punishment consisted of writing the word FAT and generating aversive imagery (e.g., looking at one's body fat in a mirror or being unable to button a favorite garment). Both forms of reinforcement resulted in significantly greater weight loss than a non-reinforcement control condition, and the two procedures were not significantly different from one another.

The results of both analogue and applied research provide strong support for the premise that we can exert control over our own behavior. Clinical applications of self-reinforcement procedures have proven to be as effective as external control programs and more effective than similar interventions which have excluded only the self-reinforcement opera-

TABLE 4.3

Changes in Weight across Treatment[a]

Group	Change in Pounds		Percentage Change in Body Weight	
	Pre- to post-treatment	Pre-treatment to follow-up	Pre- to post-treatment	Pre-treatment to follow-up
SR-Mail	7.25	7.55	4.92	5.03
SM-Mail	4.69	3.72	2.87	2.26
SR-No contact	7.03	7.67	4.64	5.13
SM-No contact	0.39	3.60	0.04	2.63

[a] From: Bellack (1976) (Table 1).

tion. The effectiveness of self-reinforcement undoubtedly develops from and is ultimately maintained by external reinforcement. However, it has proven to be an extremely useful clinical tool that can either supplement or supplant external control in many situations. In outpatient treatment especially, the therapist has few resources available to consequate the client's behavior, and frequently the client is seen only once each week. Self-reinforcement procedures, such as described by Bellack (1976) and Bellack et al. (1976), are simple to implement and are totally portable. Thus, they can be employed to provide immediate and continual reinforcement whenever the target behavior occurs. In addition, training in self-management skills has the potential to increase the durability of therapist-produced changes and to reduce relapse rates (e.g., Jeffrey, 1974; Watson et al., 1972).

Covert Conditioning

Thoresen and Mahoney (1974) have indicated that covert (cognitive) events can serve in one of three capacities: (1) as *cues* for subsequent responses or events, as in the case of self-evaluations; (2) as *responses* which may be targets for intervention, such as obsessive thoughts; or (3) as *consequences* which have reinforcing value, such as the positive and negative images employed by Bellack et al. (1976). The role of covert events in the self-control procedures described in the preceding section can easily be categorized according to these functions. The procedures to be described in this and the subsequent section do not allow for such clear specification. Rather, they involve the compound, multiple-function use of covert activity in a manner which is often difficult to compartmentalize (this point and the organization of these sections are suggested by Mahoney [1974a]). In addition, while most self-control procedures require the manipulation of overt responses and events, the procedures to be described below place primary emphasis on covert activity for effecting change. This approach has previously been discussed in the context of fear reduction. Systematic desensitization, implosive therapy, and imaginal flooding, as well as several of the self-control approaches to fear reduction which were discussed in Chapter 3, are all based on covert conditioning procedures. Rather than being exposed to real phobic stimuli, clients undergoing each of those procedures *imagine* the stimuli. Fear is thus reduced on a cognitive basis and is expected to generalize to overt behavior. Those procedures are not characteristically classified as cognitive interventions, but with their heavy emphasis on cognitive activity they might well have been included in this chapter.

Coverant Control

The term coverant was first employed by Homme (1965) as a constraction of "covert operant" (e.g., covert response such as a self-verbalization). Homme hypothesized that the frequency of coverants could be altered by temporally pairing their occurrence with environmental reinforcers, notably Premack reinforcers (high probability behaviors; referred to as HPBs). Consider for example, a client who smokes (the HPB) and for whom it is desirable to increase the frequency of positive self-statements (coverants) such as "I am a good tennis player," or "I can play the guitar very well." (This goal is characteristic of treatment for depressed individuals and those who complain of "poor self-concepts." In both cases, such individuals typically evaluate their behavior negatively and spontaneously emit many self-critical coverants and few positive coverants.) The client would be instructed simply to emit the coverant prior to lighting a cigarette. Smoking would then reinforce the coverant. As a function of this frequent reinforcement, natural occurrence of the coverants would be expected to increase (with a resulting increase in positive mood and self-evaluation).

Several variations of this basic approach have been successfully employed with depressed and obsessively self-critical individuals (Jackson, 1972; Mahoney, 1971; Vasta, 1976). Mahoney (1971) required his client to write the coverants on small cards which were placed in a cigarette pack. The client read one of the cards each time he took out the pack. While Homme (1965) hypothesized that the HPB *reinforced* the coverant, there is some suggestion that it serves as a *cue* for emission, simply guaranteeing that it occurs at high frequency. In that regard, Vasta (1976) instructed a client to emit at least three coverants (read from index cards) per hour. This temporal cueing procedure resulted in a substantial increase in the occurrence of spontaneous coverants. This study evaluated the effects of cueing only. A critical empirical comparison of the cueing and reinforcing functions of HPBs has not yet been conducted.

In addition to altering the rate of targeted thoughts, Homme also suggested that coverant control procedures could be used to modify overt responses. He suggested that reduction of a behavior such as cigarette smoking could be accomplished by practicing a four-step response sequence. The sequence is initiated by the spontaneous emission of an undesired coverant: in this case the urge to smoke. This is followed by a negative smoking coverant such as, "Smoking will give me cancer." This response is followed by a positive non-smoking coverant such as, "I will be able to play tennis better if I stop smoking." This coverant is followed by the last response in the sequence: the HPB (e.g., drinking a cup of coffee or turning on the television). Actual rate of smoking is expected to decrease as a function of the conditioned association of non-smoking thoughts with the urge to smoke as well as the generally increased occurrence of non-smoking thoughts.

The effectiveness of this particular sequence has not received much empirical support and has also been subjected to critique on conceptual grounds. For example, Mahoney (1972) pointed out that following the urge to perform the targeted response with a reinforcer might have the paradoxical effect of increasing the frequency of such urges. However, there have been several reports of the successful use of variations of the procedure. Employing a multiple baseline analysis, Epstein and Hersen (1974) systematically reduced severe cuticle picking and lip biting in a schizophrenic patient. Cigarette smoking served as the HPB, which reinforced positive coverants (no negative coverants were employed). Cigarette smoking was subsequently reduced by following positive pipe smoking coverants (e.g., "Girls like pipe smokers.") with non-smoking HPBs. In perhaps the best controlled study to date, Horan, Baker, Hoffman, and Shute (1975) demonstrated the effectiveness of coverant control in a weight reduction program. Employing *either* positive or negative coverants, they found that the use of positive coverants was significantly more effective than the use of negative coverants. As a function of both adverse subjective reactions by subjects and the poor results, Horan et al. suggested that the use of negative coverants be excluded from future applications of coverant control techniques.

The Work of Joseph R. Cautela

Joseph R. Cautela has been one of the most vocal and influential proponents of covert behavior therapy techniques. Based more on his extensive clinical experience than on controlled research, he has argued that almost all basic conditioning paradigms can be applied effectively in clinical practice on a strictly cognitive basis. That is, rather than pairing external events (e.g., reinforcement) with overt responses (e.g., cigarette smoking), both can be presented on an imaginal basis with equal effects. Cautela has developed techniques for applying five different conditioning procedures on a covert basis.

Covert sensitization (Cautela, 1967) is an aversive conditioning procedure that is employed for reduction of undesirable target behaviors. The client first imagines himself engaging in the target response (e.g., smoking, drinking alcohol). He then superimposes the image of a highly aversive consequence or experience. For example, an alcoholic might imagine himself drinking and suddenly becoming nauseous and vomiting into his drink, over his clothes, etc. The image is then terminated and the sequence is repeated. The more vivid and aversive the image, the more effective the conditioning and the greater the conditioned aversion to the target response. Covert sensitization has been applied to a broad range of behaviors including smoking, overeating, sexual deviation, and alcoholism. The results have been variable. A more complete description of covert sensitization as well as an evaluation of empirical support for the procedure is presented in Chapter 7.

An alternative procedure for elimination of unwanted responses is *covert extinction* (Cautela, 1971a). Employed primarily for operant responses, the client repeatedly imagines himself engaging in a target response and receiving no reinforcement. In one example described by Cautela (1970a), "A teenager in a training school who expressed many psychosomatic complaints was asked to imagine he was telling the staff he had a headache or that his feet hurt, etc. but they paid no attention to him" (p. 195). Paralleling overt extinction, repeated non-reinforcement of the response, albeit in imagination, is expected to reduce the rate of occurrence of the response. Cautela suggests that this procedure is useful in situations in which it would be difficult to implement an extinction program in the natural environment. As may be apparent from the example, this approach (as well as the other covert procedures) requires a highly cooperative client.

Cautela has described two techniques for increasing the frequency of desirable responses that occur at low rates. *Covert reinforcement* entails the imagination of the low rate response followed by the imagination of a positively reinforcing event (Cautela, 1970b). As with overt reinforcement contingencies, Cautela suggests that response probability will increase following repeated conditioning trials. He has described the use of covert reinforcement for the modification of a variety of responses. One case involved a woman who compulsively folded laundered clothes over and over again before putting them away, in order to remove all possible wrinkles. She was instructed to imagine herself putting clothing away after folding only once, and then to immediately imagine a reinforcing event, for which she selected drinking tea. Subsequent scenes involved less careful folding and lack of concern about visible wrinkles.

Cautela (1970a) reported that some individuals have difficulty either identifying or clearly visualizing positive reinforcing events, but are able to visualize aversive events. He described a procedure called *covert negative reinforcement,* which is applicable for such individuals. Employing an escape conditioning paradigm (see Chapter 7), the client first imagines an aversive stimulus and then terminates that image while simultaneously initiating an image of himself performing the target response. For example, "A girl who was afraid to say anything at a party when a man walked up to her, imagined she was just about to fall off a high building (aversive stimulus) and then shifted to responding to a man's questions about her work, hobbies, etc." (Cautela, 1970a, p. 275). As with overt negative reinforcement, the target response is presumed to acquire a positive valence and occur with increased frequency due to its association with termination of an aversive state.

Covert extinction, positive reinforcement, and negative reinforcement have received scant empirical support. While each procedure has been described as effective in numerous uncontrolled case reports (e.g., Cautela, 1970a, 1970b, 1971a), their status is currently uncertain. One factor in this regard is that they are probably not effective for remediation of severe dysfunction in and of themselves. Cautela reports that he characteristically employs several of these techniques as well as other procedures (e.g., deep muscle relaxation, in vivo practice) concurrently. Therefore, critical evaluation is difficult to accomplish. The manner in which the procedures work is also uncertain. For example, covert positive reinforcement for reduction of avoidance behavior and compulsions is similar to several fear reduction techniques (recall the self-control approaches described in Chapter 3). Does the target response occur with greater frequency because it is reinforced, or is fear eliminated as a function of repeated exposure and the development of an anxiety reduction skill (the use of anxiety-inhibiting, positive imagery)? Similarly, what is the effect of unclear imagery? What is the effect of expectancy and therapist reinforcement? Further research is needed to determine the specific effects of these techniques as well as the nature of their operation.

In addition to the procedures described above, Cautela (1970b) has described a technique called *covert modeling*. Again paralleling the overt procedure from which it evolved, covert modeling entails the imagination of modeling displays rather than actual exposure to live or filmed models. For example, a snake-fearful subject might be instructed to imagine a peer approaching a box containing a snake, reaching in and picking it up, and letting it encircle his arm. In contrast to the tenuous status of the covert procedures discussed above, the operation and effectiveness of covert modeling have been well documented in a series of controlled studies conducted by Alan E. Kazdin. These studies not only demonstrate that covert modeling can be effective, but that many of the factors influencing the operation of overt modeling also influence covert modeling (see Chapter 3, for a discussion of overt modeling). Thus, Kazdin (1973, 1974a, 1974b) has shown that covert modeling can be effective for the reduction of fear and anxiety as well as for the development of new response patterns, notably assertion (Kazdin, 1974c, 1975).

Model characteristics affect the response to covert displays as they do with overt modeling. Kazdin (1973, 1974a) found greater fear reduction effects when subjects imagined coping models than when they imagined mastery models. Also, when imagined models were of similar age and sex as the subjects, there was greater fear reduction than when they were different (Kazdin, 1974a). Visualization of multiple models was found to be more effective than visualization of a single model, and the effects were greater when the models were reinforced for their behavior than when no consequences were visualized (Kazdin, 1975).

This excellent series of studies indicates that covert modeling can be an effective clinical technique. However, the relative effectiveness of covert modeling and overt treatment procedures is uncertain. Cautela, Flannery, and Hanley (1974) reported that overt and covert modeling were equally effective in the treatment of rat phobia. In contrast, Thase and Moss (1976) found that guided participant modeling (see Chapter 3) was significantly more effective than covert modeling with snake phobics. They concluded that the differential factor was in vivo exposure to snakes, rather than the nature of the modeling display per se. Consequently, they suggested that covert modeling be supplemented by in vivo exposure whenever possible. In general, this recommendation parallels our own orientation to behavior therapy, which is repeated throughout the book. Clinic-based treatment is invariably more effective when supplemented by in vivo practice.

Thought Stopping

Many people entering treatment experience recurring aversive thoughts which they are unable to control. In some instances, as with obsessions and obsessive-compulsive disturbances, ruminative thoughts are a primary manifestation. With other cases, such as phobias and depression, these thoughts (fear and self-deprecation, respectively) are often secondary aspects of the broader symptom pattern. Whether ruminations are primary or secondary, a frequently employed intervention is *thought stopping*.

Popularized by Wolpe (1958), thought stopping is a relatively simple technique in which the client is taught to make a controlling response that physically interrupts the aversive thought pattern. In its basic form, the client is instructed to initiate the target thought (often by describing it aloud). Shortly thereafter, the therapist shouts the word "Stop" out loud. The client is startled and shifts his attention to the therapist, terminating the target thought. This sequence is repeated, with the client gradually emitting the controlling response himself, first aloud and finally on a covert level. Once the controlling response is well learned, the client can, presumably, use the procedure on his own, in vivo.

The manner in which thought stopping operates is unclear. While it has been suggested that the forceful "Stop" serves as a punishing stimulus which suppresses the target thought, it seems more likely that the procedure works by distracting the client and shifting his attention. There are several possible reasons for the more lasting effects of the procedure (when they occur). Thought stopping can either reduce distress while other treatment procedures (e.g., systematic desensitization) are employed to modify the disturbance that initiates the aversive thoughts or, it may serve to extinguish a conditioned stimulus (i.e., a covert response pattern). Clients are often distressed because they cannot control such thoughts in addition to being distressed by the fact that they are aversive. By providing the client with an effective controlling response, anxiety over lack of control should be reduced. This, in turn, would make experience of the thoughts less anxiety provoking and would further increase the client's ability to exert control.

In our own experience with the simple form of thought stopping described above, we have found it to be effective in temporarily inter-rupting aversive thoughts, but not in curtailing their quick recurrence. This occurs, in part, because the individual is left in an anxious state, in which he is disorganized and the initiation of new, non-anxious thoughts is difficult. Therefore, we have employed an expanded and more systematized training program. The first step involves the identi-fication of two or three highly positive and relaxing thoughts. A fre-quent selection is: "Lying on a beach, feeling the warmth of the sun, and hearing the gentle lapping of the waves." The client is then requested to close his eyes and focus on a neutral image, such as the therapy room. Shortly after the client signals that the image is clear, the therapist shouts "Stop" and immediately presents one of the positive scenes. The therapist facilites the imagery, as in systematic desensitization. After 45–60 sec. the positive image is terminated. The sequence is repeated until the client is able to clearly visualize the positive image within 15 sec. after the stop signal is presented (usually two to three trials). Two or three trials are then conducted in which the therapist says stop with moderate voice volume, and finally in a whisper. Control is then shifted to the client. Trials are conducted until the positive image is clear within 15 sec. after the client says stop aloud. This criterion is followed by two to three trials in which the client whispers stop and, finally, says stop covertly. This series of trials is usually administered in one session. During the subsequent session, the entire procedure is repeated with the stop cue and positive imagery interfering with the anxiety-provok-ing target thoughts (e.g., the obsession).

Thus, the controlling response is first learned under non-arousing conditions, and only after it is well established is it applied to targeted thoughts. The positive imagery serves to reduce anxiety (cf. Bellack, 1973) as well as to focus attention and distract the client from the aversive image. In order to prompt the use of this controlling response in the natural environment, the client is instructed to place cue cards (bearing the word STOP) in locations having a high probability of stimulating the obsessive thought. For example, one client, who fre-quently obsessed about accidents and death while driving, was directed to tape a STOP card on the steering wheel of her car.

A parallel procedure has been described by Rimm (1973). Rather than employing positive imagery after the stop response, he has directed clients to make covert assertive responses. For example, one client was, ". . . a female suffering from insomnia, related to her fear that men, hiding in the closet, might harm her. Covert assertions included 'I *really* can take care of myself!' and 'There is nobody in that *stupid* closet!' " (Rimm, 1973, p. 466). This technique has been reported to be effective in a number of uncontrolled case reports (Hays & Waddell, 1976; Rimm, 1973). In one of the few well-controlled group studies of thought stopping, Rimm, Saunders, and Westel (1975) found thought stopping combined with covert assertion to be effective in the reduction of snake phobia.

As with most of the other covert conditioning procedures described in this section, thought stopping has not been adequately investigated with controlled research. Neither the mechanism underlying its operation nor the extent of its effectiveness are clearly understood. Nevertheless, it is a widely used technique in clinical practice. In most instances it serves as an adjunct to such techniques as flooding and negative practice with obsessive compulsive disorders, and to anxiety management training and shaping with phobias. However, in at least one study, thought stopping alone has been found to be as effective as flooding with severe obsessional disturbances (Hackman & McLean, 1975). A considerable amount of future research is needed in order to determine whether or not such widespread use is justified and how the procedure might best be applied.

Self-Verbalization Techniques

Traditional verbal psychotherapies have employed conversational techniques to modify abstract cognitive processes (e.g., feelings, attitudes) with an ultimate goal of self-understanding (often called "insight"). As behavior therapists have moved into the realm of cognition, they have objectified many of those processes and attempted to manipulate them with primarily overt, conditioning-oriented strategies (e.g., coverant control). With few exceptions, the focus has been on the manipulation of a few discrete self-verbalizations (e.g., obsessive thoughts). More recently, some behavior modifiers have expanded their focus and become interested in the manipulation of thought patterns (e.g., Goldfried, Decenteceo, & Weinberg, 1974; Meichenbaum, 1976). Rather than being trained to emit or not emit single specific self-verbalizations, clients are trained to think differently, to evaluate the environment differently, to problem solve, and to think rationally. This focus necessarily involves a greater emphasis on conversational and verbal-symbolic processes in effecting change; while a single phrase can be easily consequated, long response strings or "rational" thought sequences are much more difficult to clearly identify and manipulate externally.

At first glance, this new direction appears to swing the pendulum back to the traditional psychotherapies. However, there are several differences between what has been called Cognitive Behavior Therapy and verbal psychotherapy. *First,* there is an explicit effort to objectify and systematize the treatment process. Rather than treatment being a subjective "art," specific procedures are described (e.g., modeling, rehearsal, feedback) to be administered in a fairly specific order and form. *Second,* there is a continuing attempt to describe clients' responses objectively, rather than alluding to hypothetical processes. Thus, there is an attempt to modify internal dialogues (what the client says to himself), rather than feelings, attitudes, and the like. *Third,* cognitions are manipulated in order to reduce subjective distress *and* alter overt behavior. Treatment does not arbitrarily remain within the cognitive realm, but employs a cognitive strategy as the most effective way to modify the target response (regardless of which response modality is dysfunctional).

We have already indicated some of the many ways in which covert verbalizations can influence overt behavior (in previous chapters as well as in earlier sections of this chapter). We will now consider how this reciprocal influence process can be employed in a therapeutic manner. Kanfer and his colleagues have conducted a series of analogue studies which clearly demonstrate the controlling effects of self-verbalizations. In one of the first studies, Hartig and Kanfer (1973) brought 3- to 5-year-old children, individually, into a room containing a tableful of attractive toys. The children were then admonished to face away from the table while the experimenter temporarily left the room. In addition, some of the children were instructed to verbalize the admonition aloud while the experimenter was away; some were instructed to verbalize a nursery rhyme (as a control for verbalization, per se); and some were given no verbalization instructions. Children who verbalized the admonition were better able to resist temptation and refrain from turning around than were children in either of the other groups (which did not differ from one another).

In a subsequent study with greater clinical relevance, Kanfer, Karoly, and Newman (1975) examined the role of self-verbalization in controlling children's fear of the dark. Subjects were requested to remain in a small cubicle for as long as they were able (up to 3 min.) and with the lights dimmed to the extent they could tolerate. They were given one of three instructions for self-verbalization. "In the *competence group* the children were told to say, 'I am a brave boy (girl). I can take care of myself in the dark.' In the *stimulus group* the special words were, 'The dark is a fun place to be. There are many good things in the dark.' In the neutral group they were 'Mary had a little lamb. Its fleece was white as snow' " (Kanfer et al., 1975, p. 253). The competence group manifested greater pre- to post-training increases in ability to tolerate less illumination and to tolerate it for longer periods of time than either of the other groups. These results demonstrate not only that verbalization can control overt behavior, but that the meaning or nature of the verbalization is an important factor. This parallels previously discussed findings with modeling procedures, in which the nature of the modeled display (e.g., coping models more effective than mastery models) affects the individual's response to the model. Both sets of results underscore the importance of cognitive factors in determining the impact of operant responses.

Two of the most impressive demonstrations of the clinical possibilities of self-verbalization were described by Donald H. Meichenbaum and his associates. In the first report, Meichenbaum and Goodman (1971) trained impulsive children (7–9 years of age) to "talk to themselves" as a means of exerting control over their behavior. Training consisted of the following five-step sequence: (1) experimenter modeled performance (on one of a variety of simple tasks such as copying line patterns) including a verbal description of his behavior, (2) child performed the task while experimenter instructed him aloud; (3) child performed and instructed himself aloud, (4) child performed and whispered the instructions, and (5) child performed and repeated the instructions covertly. An example of the instructions is as follows: "Okay, what is it I have to do? You want me to copy the picture with the different lines. I have to go slow and be careful. Okay, draw the line down, down, good; then to the right, that's it; now down some more and to the left. Good, I'm doing fine so far. Remember go slow. Now back up again. No, I was supposed to go down. That's okay. Just erase the line carefully . . . Good. Even if I make an error I can go slowly and carefully. Okay, I have to go down now. Finished, I did it." (Meichenbaum & Goodman, 1971, p. 117). The major elements in this dialogue include clarification of the nature of the task, rehearsal and planning, ongoing self-guidance, and self-reinforcement. Dependent measures included pre- and post-treatment scores on a variety of standard tests in which impulsivity interferes with performance (e.g., Porteus Maze). Children undergoing this training improved significantly more than children who received practice and attention without the training and children who were simply tested twice. A subsequent study demonstrated that the self-instructional training added significantly to the effects of modeling and practice alone.

Schizophrenics exhibit many of the same performance dysfunctions as do impulsive children. For example, they are easily distracted, attend to irrelevant task dimensions, and have short attention spans. Meichenbaum and Cameron (1973) demonstrated that self-verbalization training almost identical with that employed with impulsive children could improve performance of hospitalized schizophrenic adults. In an initial study, they found that patients receiving a brief training program improved their performance on simple tasks significantly more than patients in attention-practice or no-treatment control groups. Patients in a second study received more extended training (eight 45-min. sessions). These patients were compared to a yoked practice control group. Self-instructional patients improved significantly more than the controls on such clinically meaningful measures as abstract thinking and the percentage of "sick talk" (bizarre, incoherent, or irrelevant responses) in an interview. These results were maintained at a 3-week follow-up.

The clinical populations included in both sets of studies had performance deficits based on faulty modulation of behavior. The results indicate that: (1) systematic behavioral training can be effective in developing appropriate patterns of self-verbalization in individuals who are characteristically unresponsive to verbal interventions, and (2) self-verbalization can be employed on an ongoing basis to control behavior. Despite the success of these two interventions, the difficulty of effecting durable changes in self-verbalization must be considered. Robin, Armel, and O'Leary (1975) replicated the findings of Meichenbaum and Goodman (1971). However, they reported that they were unable to get all of the children to emit the appropriate verbalizations on a consistent basis despite 20 training sessions. Children often developed idiosyncratic abbreviations which were used intermittently, and they occasionally made incorrect motoric responses while emitting the correct verbalization. As with the development of other self-regulatory behaviors (e.g., self-reinforcement procedures discussed above), extensive training, incorporating external reinforcement, is probably necessary to develop and maintain the use of systematic self-verbalization responses.

The procedures discussed thus far have focused on populations (children and schizophrenics) characterized by deficiencies in verbal self-control. Consequently, training has emphasized the development of a relatively specific series of self-verbalizations. In contrast, adults with anxiety-based disorders are presumed (by cognitive behavior therapists) to suffer from an excess of inappropriate self-verbalizations. They apply faulty labels to their behavior and experience, and have unreasonable expectations about what they and the environment should be like (Goldfried & Goldfried, 1975; Meichenbaum, 1976). For example, in evaluating male college students who were low frequency daters and reported high levels of interpersonal anxiety, Glasgow and Arkowitz (1975) concluded that the primary difficulty was the negative manner in which the students evaluated their performance, rather than a social skill deficit. Thus, no performance differences were apparent between high and low frequency daters, but the low daters consistently rated their performance as less effective.

The exact interrelationship between faulty labeling and motoric and physiologic manifestations of fear and anxiety is uncertain at this point. It seems likely that in some instances the labeling precedes and results in physiological arousal and avoidance, while in other cases the labeling is a consequence of other disturbance. In addition, once the anxiety pattern is strongly established, labeling probably does not occur in every exposure to the feared stimulus. In any case, the cognitive approach to fear reduction emphasizes manipulation of self-verbalization patterns as a vehicle for reducing dysfunction in all three response modalities.

Thus, while systematic desensitization, contact desensitization, etc. presume that cognitive change will follow motoric and physiological change, this approach presumes that the opposite sequence will occur.

Initial strategies for cognitive interventions evolved from Rational Emotive Therapy (RET), a treatment developed by Albert Ellis (1958). Ellis reasoned that the behavior of "neurotic" individuals was based on irrational thinking; they maintained myths about a perfect world and experienced distress because things were never perfect. For example, individuals with interpersonal anxiety (presumably) maintain the irrational belief that everyone must love them. When, as is invariably the case, they do not receive love (as when a prospective date turns down an invitation), they irrationally conclude they are unlovable. RET is a procedure to combat such irrational thinking and teach the client to think logically. Thus, the client is first convinced that his thinking is faulty and then taught to analyze his experience on logical grounds and substitute logical conclusions for illogical. The socially anxious individual described above would be taught to find a logical reason for the rejection (e.g., "She's a dummy for not going out with me," or "Maybe she really is busy,") and reach a more desirable conclusion (e.g., "That's her problem, I'll call someone else."). Treatment consists of a considerable amount of exhortation by the therapist, combined with modeling of appropriate analysis and self-verbalization, and practice.

While several studies have indicated that RET can be effective (e.g., Di Loreto, 1971; Trexler & Karst, 1972), both the procedures and rationale are inexplicit. There are no data to support the conjecture that individuals actually maintain such myths or that they actually *think* illogically. In fact, many individuals are quite aware that their *behavior* is illogical, but are still unable to alter it. In other instances, both the behavior and thinking are logical but are based on inaccurate perceptions, faulty data, or inappropriately high standards for self-evaluation. Thus, low frequency daters might not be aware that their performance is as good as that of high frequency daters and/or they might expect, unrealistically, to be completely calm and relaxed when meeting new people. Finally, it is also possible that the individual is unskillful, in which case his negative self-evaluation and anxiety might be justified.

Several behavioral variations of RET have been developed, in which more systematized procedures have been specified and in which the focus has been modification of labeling and self-verbalization per se rather than "rational thinking" (e.g., Goldfried et al., 1974). Meichenbaum, Gilmore, and Fedoravicius (1971) examined the effects of an "insight-oriented" treatment for modification of speech anxiety. The procedure ". . . emphasized the rationale that speech anxiety is the result of self-verbalizations and internalized sentences which are emitted while thinking about the speech situation. The Ss were informed that the goals of therapy were for each S to become aware of (gain insight into) the self-verbalizations and self-instructions which he emitted in anxiety-producing interpersonal situations and, in addition, to produce both incompatible self-instructions and incompatible behavior" (p. 413). Subjects receiving this treatment and those in a desensitization group improved significantly (and equivalently) more than subjects in several control groups on both motoric and self-report measures. In a subsequent study, Meichenbaum (1972) reported that the insight procedure supplemented by an anxiety management-type intervention was more effective than desensitization in reducing test anxiety.

In addition to evaluating results across all subjects, Meichenbaum et al. (1971) categorized subjects in terms of the breadth of their anxiety reaction: speech specific or general interpersonal anxiety. Desensitization was more effective for the former group and the insight procedure was more effective for the latter. These results once more underscore the difficulty of attempting to identify a single causal factor or treatment modality for all individuals reporting a common dysfunction.

These two studies demonstrate the overall effectiveness of self-verbalization treatments, but do not identify the specific components that were critical for change. This issue was considered in a well-designed study by Wein, Nelson, and Odom (1975). The subjects were snake-fearful college women, who were selected on the basis of poor performance on a high-demand Behavioral Avoidance Test. Five experimental conditions were employed: (1) cognitive restructuring (CR), a treatment emphasizing evaluation and re-labeling of snake-related behaviors and experiences, based on the adoption of a learning theory conception of fear and how it is developed; (2) verbal extinction (VE), a procedure emphasizing the extinction of fear through discussion and verbal recall of snake experiences, it was designed to differentiate the effects of extinction from those of cognitive restructuring in the CR group (as CR involved relabeling *and* discussion, a difference between CR and VE would suggest that relabeling was an active factor); (3) systematic desensitization (SD); (4) attention placebo control (AP); and (5) no-treatment control (NC). The first four groups received the respective treatments in six 1-hour group sessions.

The results are portrayed graphically in Fig. 4.3. The four dependent measures were the Behavioral Avoidance Test (BAT), a Fear Thermometer (FT), the S-R Inventory of Anxiousness (SRIA) which is a self-report measure of general anxiety, and heart rate (HR) during the BAT. The major results of the study are summarized as follows: "(a) CR was as effective as SD in reducing behavioral avoidance (BAT), but was superior to all other treatments in reducing self-reported fear behavior; (b) CR successfully reduced subjective anxiety in a situation involving the performance of approach behaviors (FT), as well as in a situation that did not involve the presence of a live snake (SRIA); . . . (e) there was no differential improvement among the five conditions on the measure of

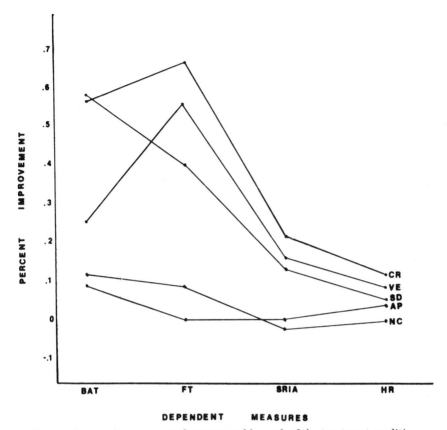

Fig. 4.3 Percent improvement demonstrated by each of the treatment conditions on the four dependent measures. (Reprinted with permission from: K. S. Wein, R. O. Nelson, and J. V. Odom: *Behavior Therapy,* 6: 459, 1975.)

heart rate; and (f) mean changes in the VE group were smaller than in the CR group on all measures that were reactive to treatments. The last finding suggests that the reattribution component of the CR technique contributes to therapeutic gains" (Wein et al., 1975, pp. 468–469). These results also suggest that CR was not effective in reducing physiological arousal. It is possible that cognitive interventions of this form are not appropriate for physiological arousal, or that such arousal might extinguish with in vivo practice (see below).

The results of this series of studies are quite promising. The development of effective behavioral interventions for cognitive dysfunctions fills one of the few remaining gaps in behavioral technology. It also demonstrates that attitudes and self-evaluations can be objectively analyzed and systematically modified. These preliminary studies must now be followed by analytical research such as occurred with systematic desensitization and social skills training (see Chapter 5). The relative contribution and most effective application of modeling, role playing, relabeling, group feedback, etc. must be determined. The range of applicability (e.g., for general versus specific anxiety, for cognitive versus motoric dysfunction) must also be determined. Finally, as with other interventions, the probable necessity of in vivo practice also needs to be considered.

Biofeedback

In previous sections we have considered applications of self-control for modification of motoric and cognitive responses. In this final section we will briefly consider self-regulatory strategies for modification of physiological responses: *biofeedback*.

The term "biofeedback" refers to a variety of procedures in which individuals are taught to become aware of (e.g., self-monitor) and control physiological responses, including heart rate, blood pressure, skin temperature, muscle tension (EMG), and the electrical activity of the brain (EEG: "alpha" training). The typical biofeedback training procedure is relatively simple. The patient is presented with either an ongoing auditory or visual stimulus reflecting the level of the targeted system. For example, heart rate might be displayed on a meter or represented by the speed of audible clicks. The patient is then instructed to attempt to change the level (e.g., heart rate) in whatever manner possible (e.g., by emitting controlling responses). Change might be accomplished by focusing on arousing or calming thoughts, concentrating on heart-produced sensations, etc. The success of any efforts is reflected by change in the feedback stimulus (e.g., meter deflection), thus providing the individual with immediate feedback with which to shape his controlling responses. In some instances, self-control is supplemented by external reinforcement for successful efforts. Clinical applications of biofeedback are based on the assumption that once the individual learns to monitor and control, he can regulate the target system in vivo.

Initial interest in this area emanated from laboratory research into the possibility and mechanisms of such control. More recently, biofeedback techniques have been applied to treatment of a host of clinical dysfunctions including: psychosomatic disorders such as tension headaches and vascular hypertension, fear reduction (by control over heart action and muscle tension), neuro-muscular disturbances (as in some cases of paralysis and Bell's palsy), epilepsy, gastrointestinal disorders (including incontinence and ulcers), and sexual disorders such as impotence (see Blanchard & Epstein, 1977, for a comprehensive review).

We will briefly consider two examples of the use of biofeedback for illustrative purposes. Blanchard and Haynes (1975) described an application of finger tip temperature feedback in a case of Raynaud's disease: " . . . a functional disorder of the cardiovascular system in which the patient experiences painful episodes of vasoconstriction in the hands and possibly the feet, which leave the extremities cold to the touch" (p. 230). The patient was a 28-year-old female. The results and sequence of treatment phases are presented in Fig. 4.4. Following baseline assessment, the patient was instructed to try (without feedback) to make her hands warmer. This was followed by feedback training. The patient observed a visual print-out of the temperature difference between her hand and forehead, and she was instructed to raise her hand temperature by attempting to move the pen. Successive phases of feedback and no feedback were then conducted followed by three follow-up phases. As shown in Fig. 4.4, feedback was effective in reducing temperature drops. Absolute level of hand temperature also increased from an average of 79° F during baseline to 88.3° F during the final follow-up. This improvement was accompanied by patient self-report of symptom reduction in the natural environment.

Reinking and Kohl (1975) examined the use of electromyograph (EMG) feedback of forehead muscle tension for inducing relaxation. College student volunteers were assigned to one of five conditions: (1) EMG feedback; (2) EMG feedback plus financial reinforcement for lowered tension; (3) deep muscle relaxation training; (4) EMG feedback plus deep muscle relaxation training; and (5) No-treatment control. Subjects in the feedback groups received live feedback (they selected either visual or auditory) and, with the exception of Group 3, were told to relax with no specific instructions other than to keep the feedback (meter or tone) within a certain range. Training continued over 12 1-hour sessions. The results on the muscle tension measure indicated that by the end of training, all four treatment groups differed significantly from the control. In addition, the three feedback conditions were significantly

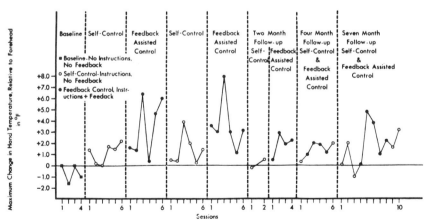

Fig. 4.4 Change in hand temperature, relative to forehead temperature, from midpoint of session-baseline to point of maximum change in experimental phase of session, on a session by session basis, for all phases of treatment. (Reprinted with permission from: E. B. Blanchard and M. R. Haynes: *Journal of Behavior Therapy and Experimental Psychiatry*, 6: 230, 1975.)

more effective that the DMR group, and were not different from one another. Thus, biofeedback was highly effective in facilitating relaxation, and the effects were not increased by the addition of reinforcement or DMR. Interestingly, all five groups reported significant and equivalent changes in self-report of relaxation

Clinical researchers are just beginning to systematically explore the operation and range of applicability of biofeedback. Success with preliminary applications holds out the promise that biofeedback training may provide a mini-revolution of new, effective interventions for both physical and "psychological" disfunctions. As might be expected with a new approach, there are many unresolved issues. Among the most prominent questions that must be empirically answered are: How can training best be conducted? What is the nature of the controlling responses (e.g., thoughts, proprioceptive feedback) that mediate change? How can the effects be generalized to the natural environment? What is the range of applicability of biofeedback techniques? Considering the excitement generated by biofeedback in both the public press and the professional literature, the answers to these questions should be forthcoming shortly.

Summary

This chapter has described the behavioral approach to self-regulation and cognition. We first discussed how behavior therapists conceptualize cognitive activity. The primary focus was on objectification and the definition of cognitive activity in terms of covert responses. These responses obey the same laws and principles as overt responses.

The model of self-regulation developed by Kanfer was then presented. The major elements are: self-monitoring, self-evaluation, and self-reinforcement. The latter is parallel to external reinforcement and depends on external reinforcement for its continued effects. Analogue literature supporting the model was presented followed by a description of clinical applications. Research indicates that self-monitoring can modify behavior on a short-term basis but that self-reinforcement interventions are more powerful and durable.

Treatments emphasizing cognitive change and cognitive approaches for altering overt responses were then considered. Procedures included were: coverant control, covert conditioning, thought stopping, and self-verbalization techniques. None of these procedures has been sufficiently researched to allow for clear conclusions about their utility. The final section briefly considered biofeedback procedures.

References

Bandura, A. Analysis of modeling processes. In A. Bandura (Ed.), *Psychological modeling: Conflicting theories*. New York: Aldine-Atherton, 1971. (a)

Bandura, A. Psychotherapy based upon modeling principles. In A. E. Bergin & S. L. Garfield (Eds.), *Handbook of psychotherapy and behavior change: An empirical analysis*. New York: John Wiley & Sons, 1971. (b)

Bandura, A. Self-reinforcement: Theoretical and methodological considerations. *Behaviorism*, 1976, in press.

Bandura, A., & Kupers, C. J. Transmission of patterns of self-reinforcement through modeling. *Journal of Abnormal and Social Psychology*, 1964, *69*, 1-9.

Bandura, A., & Perloff, B. Relative efficacy of self-monitored and externally imposed reinforcement systems. *Journal of Personality and Social Psychology*, 1967, *7*, 111-116.

Bandura, A., & Whalen, C. K. The influence of antecedent reinforcement and divergent modeling cues on patterns of self-reward. *Journal of Personality and Social Psychology*, 1966, *3*, 373-382.

Bellack, A. S. Internal versus external locus of control and the use of self-reinforcement. *Psychological Reports*, 1972, *31*, 732-733.

Bellack, A. S. Reciprocal inhibition of a laboratory conditioned fear. *Behaviour Research and Therapy*, 1973, *11*, 11-18.

Bellack, A. S. Behavior therapy for weight reduction: An evaluative review. *Addictive Behaviors*, 1975, *1*, 73-82. (a)

Bellack, A. S. Self-evaluation, self-reinforcement and locus of control. *Journal of Research in Personality*, 1975, *9*, 158-167. (b)

Bellack, A. S. A comparison of self-monitoring and self-reinforcement in weight reduction. *Behavior Therapy*, 1976, *7*, 68-75.

Bellack, A. S. Behavioral treatment for obesity: Appraisal and recommendations. In M. Hersen, R. M. Eisler, & P. M. Miller (Eds.), *Progress in behavior modification: Vol. 4*. New York: Academic Press, 1977.

Bellack, A. S., Glanz, L., & Simon, R. Covert imagery and individual differences in self-reinforcement style in the treatment of obesity. *Journal of Consulting and Clinical Psychology*, 1976, *44*, 490-491.

Bellack, A. S., Rozensky, R. H., & Schwartz, J. A comparison of two forms of self-monitoring in a behavioral weight reduction program. *Behavior Therapy*, 1974, *5*, 523-530.

Bellack, A. S., & Tillman, W. The effects of task and experimenter feedback on the self-reinforcement behavior of internals and externals. *Journal of Consulting and Clinical Psychology*, 1974, *42*, 330-336.

Blanchard, E. B., & Epstein, L. H. The clinical utility of biofeedback. In M. Hersen, R. M. Eisler, & P. M. Miller (Eds.), *Progress in behavior modification: Vol. 4*. New York: Academic Press, 1977.

Blanchard, E. B., & Haynes, M. R. Biofeedback treatment of a case of Raynaud's disease. *Journal of Behavior Therapy and Experimental Psychiatry*, 1975, *6*, 230-234.

Bolstad, O., & Johnson, S. Self-regulation in the modification of disruptive classroom behavior. *Journal of Applied Behavior Analysis*, 1972, *5*, 443-454.

Bucher, B., & Fabricatore, J. Use of patient-administered shock to suppress hallucinations. *Behavior Therapy*, 1970, *1*, 382-385.

Cautela, J. R. Covert sensitization. *Psychological Reports*, 1967, *20*, 459-468.

Cautela, J. R. Covert negative reinforcement. *Journal of Behavior Therapy and Experimental Psychiatry*, 1970, *1*, 273-278. (a)

Cautela, J. R. Covert reinforcement. *Behavior Therapy*, 1970, *1*, 33-50. (b)

Cautela, J. R. Covert conditioning. In A. Jacobs & L. Sachs (Eds.), *The psychology of private events*. New York: Academic Press, 1971. (a)

Cautela, J. R. *Covert modeling*. Paper presented at Fifth Annual Meeting of the Association for Advancement of Behavior Therapy. Washington, D. C., 1971. (b)

Cautela, J. R., Flannery, R. B., & Hanley, S. Covert modeling: An experimental test. *Behavior Therapy*, 1974, *5*, 494-502.

Davison, G. C. Counter-control in behavior modification. In L. A. Hamerlynck, L. C. Handy, & E. J. Mash (Eds.), *Behavior change: Methodology and practice*. Champaign, Ill.: Research Press, 1973.

Davison, G. C., Tsujimoto, R. N., & Glaros, A. G. Attribution and the maintenance of behavior change in falling asleep. *Journal of Abnormal Psychology*, 1973, *82*, 124-133.

Di Loreto, A. *Comparative psychotherapy*. New York: Aldine-Atherton, 1971.

Drabman, R., Spitalnik, R., & O'Leary, K. D. Teaching self-control to disruptive children. *Journal of Abnormal Psychology*, 1973, *82*, 10-16.

Ellis, A. Rational psychotherapy. *Journal of General Psychology,* 1958, *59,* 35–49.

Epstein, L. H., & Hersen, M. A multiple baseline analysis of coverant control. *Journal of Behavior Therapy and Experimental Psychiatry,* 1974, *5,* 7–12.

Epstein, L., & Peterson, G. The control of undesired behavior by self-imposed contingencies. *Behavior Therapy,* 1973, *4,* 91–95.

Felixbrod, J. J., & O'Leary, K. D. Effects of reinforcement on children's academic behavior as a function of self-determined and externally imposed contingencies. *Journal of Applied Behavior Analysis,* 1973, *6,* 241–250.

Ferster, C. B., Nurnberger, J. I., & Levitt, E. B. The control of eating. *Journal of Mathetics,* 1962, *1,* 87–109.

Fox, L. Effecting the use of efficient study habits. *Journal of Mathetics,* 1962, *1,* 76–86.

Glasgow, R. E., & Arkowitz, H. The behavioral assessment of male and female social competence in dyadic heterosexual interactions. *Behavior Therapy,* 1975, *6,* 488–498.

Glynn, E. L., Thomas, J. D., & Shee, S. M. Behavioral self-control of on-task behavior in an elementary classroom. *Journal of Applied Behavior Analysis,* 1973, *6,* 105–113.

Goldfried, M. R., Decenteceo, E., & Weinberg, L. Systematic rational restructuring as a self-control technique. *Behavior Therapy,* 1974, *5,* 247–251.

Goldfried, M. R., & Goldfried, A. P. Cognitive change methods. In F. H. Kanfer & A. P. Goldstein (Eds.), *Helping people change: A textbook of methods.* New York: Pergamon Press, 1975.

Goldiamond, I. Self-control procedures in personal behavior problems. *Psychological Reports,* 1965, *17,* 851–868.

Hackman, A., & McLean, C. A comparison of flooding and thought stopping in the treatment of obsessional neurosis. *Behaviour Research and Therapy,* 1975, *13,* 263–269.

Hartig, M., & Kanfer, F. H. The role of verbal self-instructions in children's resistance to temptation. *Journal of Personality and Social Psychology,* 1973, *25,* 259–267.

Haughton, E., & Ayllon, T. Production and elimination of symptomatic behavior. In L. P. Ullmann & L. Krasner (Eds.), *Case studies in behavior modification.* New York: Holt, Rinehart, and Winston, 1965.

Hays, V., & Waddell, K. J. A self-reinforcing procedure for thought stopping. *Behavior Therapy,* 1976, *7,* 559.

Homme, L. E. Perspectives in psychology: XXIV. Control of coverants, the operants of the mind. *Psychological Record,* 1965, *15,* 501–511.

Horan, J. J., Baker, S. B., Hoffman, A. M., & Shute, R. E. Weight loss through variations in the coverant control paradigm. *Journal of Consulting and Clinical Psychology,* 1975, *43,* 68–72.

Jackson, B. Treatment of depression by self-reinforcement. *Behavior Therapy,* 1972, *3,* 298–307.

Jeffrey, D. B. A comparison of the effects of external control and self-control on the modification and maintenance of weight. *Journal of Abnormal Psychology,* 1974, *83,* 404–410.

Johnson, S. M., & White, G. Self-observation as an agent of behavioral change. *Behavior Therapy,* 1971, *2,* 488–497.

Kanfer, F. H. Self-management methods. In F. H. Kanfer & A. P. Goldstein (Eds.), *Helping people change.* New York: Pergamon Press, 1975.

Kanfer, F. H. *The many faces of self-control, or behavior modification changes its focus.* Paper presented at Eighth International Banff Conference. Banff: Alberta, 1976.

Kanfer, F. H., & Duerfeldt, P. H. Effects of pretraining on self-evaluation and self-reinforcement. *Journal of Personality and Social Psychology,* 1967, *7,* 164–168.

Kanfer, F. H., Karoly, P., & Newman, A. Reduction of children's fear of the dark by competence-related and situational threat-related verbal cues. *Journal of Consulting and Clinical Psychology,* 1975, *43,* 251–258.

Kanfer, F. H., & Marston, A. R. Determinants of self-reinforcement in human learning. *Journal of Experimental Psychology,* 1963, *66,* 245–254.

Kazdin, A. E. Covert modeling and the reduction of avoidance behavior. *Journal of Abnormal Psychology,* 1973, *81,* 87–95.

Kazdin, A. E. Covert modeling, model similarity and reduction of avoidance behavior. *Behavior Therapy,* 1974, *5,* 325–340. (a)

Kazdin, A. E. The effect of model identity and fear-relevant similarity on covert modeling. *Behavior Therapy,* 1974, *5,* 624–635. (b)

Kazdin, A. E. Effects of covert modeling and model reinforcement on assertive behavior. *Journal of Abnormal Psychology*, 1974, *83*, 240–252. (c)

Kazdin, A. E. Reactive self-monitoring: The effects of response desirability, goal setting, and feedback. *Journal of Consulting and Clinical Psychology*, 1974, *42*, 704–716. (d)

Kazdin, A. E. Self-monitoring and behavior change. In M. J. Mahoney & C. E. Thoresen (Eds.), *Self-control: Power to the person*. Monterey, Calif.: Brooks/Cole, 1974. (e)

Kazdin, A. E. Covert modeling, imagery assessment, and assertive behavior. *Journal of Consulting and Clinical Psychology*, 1975, *43*, 716–724.

Lacey, J. I., Smith, R. L., & Green, B. A. Use of conditioned autonomic responses in the study of anxiety. *Psychosomatic Medicine*, 1955, *17*, 208–217.

Lipinski, D. P., Black, J. L., Nelson, R. O., & Ciminero, A. R. Influence of motivational variables on the reactivity and reliability of self-recording. *Journal of Consulting and Clinical Psychology*, 1975, *43*, 637–646.

Lipinski, D. P., & Nelson, R. D. The reactivity and unreliability of self-recording. *Journal of Consulting and Clinical Psychology*, 1974, *42*, 118 123.

Mahoney, M. J. The self-management of covert behavior: A case study. *Behavior Therapy*, 1971, *2*, 575–578.

Mahoney, M. J. Research issues in self-management. *Behavior Therapy*, 1972, *3*, 45–63.

Mahoney, M. J. *Cognition and behavior modification*. Cambridge, Mass.: Ballinger, 1974. (a)

Mahoney, M. J. Self-reward and self-monitoring techniques for weight control. *Behavior Therapy*, 1974, *5*, 48–57. (b)

Mahoney, M. J., Moore, B., Wade, T., & Moura, N. Effects of continuous and intermittent self-monitoring on academic behavior. *Journal of Consulting and Clinical Psychology*, 1973, *41*, 65–59.

Mahoney, M. J., Moura, N., & Wade, T. The relative efficacy of self-reward, self-punishment and self-monitoring techniques. *Journal of Consulting and Clinical Psychology*, 1973, *40*, 404–407.

Maletzky, B. M. Behavior recording as treatment: A brief note. *Behavior Therapy*, 1974, *5*, 107–111.

Mann, R. A. The behavior-therapeutic use of contingency contracting to control an adult behavior problem: Weight control *Journal of Applied Behavior Analysis*, 1972, *5*, 99–109.

Mayer, J. *Overweight: Causes, cost, and control*. Englewood Cliffs, N. J.: Prentice-Hall, 1968.

Meichenbaum, D. H. Cognitive modification of test anxious college students. *Journal of Consulting and Clinical Psychology*, 1972, *39*, 370–380.

Meichenbaum, D. H. A cognitive-behavior modification approach to assessment. In M. Hersen & A. S. Bellack (Eds.), *Behavioral assessment: A practical handbook*. New York: Pergamon Press, 1976.

Meichenbaum, D. H., & Cameron, R. Training schizophrenics to talk to themselves: A means of developing attentional controls. *Behavior Therapy*, 1973, *4*, 515–534.

Meichenbaum, D. H., Gilmore, J. B., & Fedoravicius, A. Group insight versus group desensitization in treating speech anxiety. *Journal of Consulting and Clinical Psychology*, 1971, *36*, 410–421.

Meichenbaum, D. H., & Goodman, J. Training impulsive children to talk to themselves: A means of developing self-control. *Journal of Abnormal Psychology*, 1971, *77*, 115–126.

Mischel, W., & Liebert, R. Effects of discrepancies between observed and imposed reward criteria on their acquisition and transmission. *Journal of Personality and Social Psychology*, 1966, *3*, 45–54.

Nelson, R. O., Lipinski, D. P., & Black, J. L. The effects of expectancy on the reactivity of self-recording. *Behavior Therapy*, 1975, *6*, 337–349.

Nolan, J. D. Self-control procedures in the modification of smoking behavior. *Journal of Consulting and Clinical Psychology*, 1968, *32*, 92–93.

Powell, J. R., & Azrin, N. The effects of shock as a punisher for cigarette smoking. *Journal of Applied Behavior Analysis*, 1968, *1*, 63–71.

Rachlin, H. Self-control. *Behaviorism*, 1974, *2*, 94–107.

Reinking, R. H., & Kohl, M. L. Effects of various forms of relaxation training on physiological and self-report measures of relaxation. *Journal of Consulting and Clinical Psychology*, 1975, *43*, 595–600.

Rimm, D. C. Thought stopping and covert assertion in the treatment of phobias. *Journal of Consulting and Clinical Psychology,* 1973, *41,* 466–467.

Rimm, D. C., Saunders, W. D., & Westel, W. Thought stopping and covert assertion in the treatment of snake phobics. *Journal of Consulting and Clinical Psychology,* 1975, *43,* 92–93.

Robin, A. L., Armel, S., & O'Leary, K. D. The effects of self-instruction on writing deficiencies. *Behavior Therapy,* 1975, *6,* 178–187.

Romanczyk, R. G. Self-monitoring in the treatment of obesity: Parameters of reactivity. *Behavior Therapy,* 1974, *5,* 531–540.

Schachter, S. Some extraordinary facts about obese humans and rats. *American Psychologist,* 1971, *26,* 129–144.

Sobell, L., & Sobell, M. A self-feedback technique to monitor drinking behavior in alcoholics. *Behaviour Research and Therapy,* 1973, *11,* 237–238.

Stuart, R. B., & Davis, B. *Slim chance in a fat world.* Champaign, Ill.: Research Press, 1972.

Thase, M. E., & Moss, M. K. The relative efficacy of covert modeling procedures and guided participant modeling on the reduction of avoidance behavior. *Journal of Behavior Therapy and Experimental Psychiatry,* 1976, 7, 7–12.

Thoresen, C. E., & Mahoney, M. J. *Behavioral self-control.* New York: Holt, Rinehart, & Winston, 1974.

Trexler, L. D., & Karst, T. O. Rational-emotive therapy, placebo, and no-treatment effects on public-speaking anxiety. *Journal of Abnormal Psychology,* 1972, *79,* 60–67.

Turkewitz, H., O'Leary, K. D., & Ironsmith, M. Generalization and maintenance of appropriate behavior through self-control. *Journal of Consulting and Clinical Psychology,* 1974, *43,* 577–583.

Ullmann, L. P., & Krasner, L. (Eds.), *Case studies in behavior modification.* New York: Holt, Rinehart, & Winston, 1965.

Vasta, R. Coverant control of self-evaluations through temporal cueing. *Journal of Behavior Therapy and Experimental Psychiatry,* 1976, 7, 35–37.

Watson, D. L., Tharp, R. G., & Krisber, J. Case study in self-modification: Suppression of inflammatory scratching while awake and asleep. *Journal of Behavior Therapy and Experimental Psychiatry,* 1972, *3,* 213–215

Wein, K. S., Nelson, R. O., & Odom, J. V. The relative contributions of reattribution and verbal extinction to the effectiveness of cognitive restructuring. *Behavior Therapy,* 1975, *6,* 459–474.

Wolpe, J. *Psychotherapy by reciprocal inhibition.* Stanford: Stanford University Press, 1958.

5

Social skills training

Introduction

Although the impairment of social skill seen in a variety of behavior disorders is acknowledged by most contemporary personality theorists, until very recently few attempts to directly modify social skill deficits have been reported in the psychological and psychiatric literatures. The acquisition and maintenance of requisite social skills at different developmental levels (i.e., children, adolescents, young adults, adults, etc.) play important roles in the psychological well-being of the individual. Examples at each developmental level might involve: (1) children making friends, (2) adolescents learning to interact with members of the opposite sex, (3) young adults finding suitable mates, and (4) adults interacting successfully with peers, superiors, and subordinates at work. When normal development proceeds, these skills are learned through instruction and by modeling (imitating) the behaviors of important others. However, some individuals because of their particular family and interpersonal backgrounds are less fortunate and do not learn such necessary skills. It is for these individuals that social skill treatment techniques have been designed.

Deficiencies in social skill at each of the above four developmental levels frequently result in interpersonal difficulties. Such difficulties may be observed at home, at school, at work, or during the course of recreational activities. Depending on the degree of skill deficit, interpersonal rebuff may be minor or may result in social isolation, as in the case of the withdrawn chronic schizophrenic patient or the withdrawn depressive patient.

The developmental consequences of skill deficits have been known now for many years. That is, skill deficits first seen in the formative years still display their negative effects in adulthood. Kagan and Moss (1962), in a longitudinal study, examined the relationship of stable childhood characteristics to adult behavior. They reported that, "Passive withdrawal from stressful situations, dependency on the family, ease of anger arousal, involvement in intellectual mastery, social interaction anxiety, sex-role identification, and pattern of sexual behavior in adulthood were each related to reasonably analogous dispositions during the early childhood years" (p. 266).

Developmental difficulties in heterosocial skill, for example, often make their first appearance when the adolescent reaches the dating stage in high school and early in college. Some males do not know how to ask a girl for a date. Others do not know how to talk to the girl when on the date. Still others do not know how to pursue the relationship after the first date. Similarly, some girls do not know how to respond to the male's positive advances at varying stages in the dating relationship. Also, in accordance with trends toward the "liberated woman," there are some women who do not know how to properly approach suitable males. The contribution of skill deficits to heterosexual relations in the dating situation (i.e., minimal dating) in college populations has recently attracted considerable research attention (e.g., Twentyman & McFall, 1975). In the Twentyman and McFall study it was demonstrated that confident as opposed to shy college males (based on self-reports of confidence in heterosexual interactions) evidenced considerably more skill in simulated (i.e., role-played) dating interactions.

Absence of skill in social situations has also been related to a variety of clinical syndromes such as depression and schizophrenia. When comparing depressed versus non-depressed individuals in small group settings, it was found that depressed individuals were significantly less skillful socially (Libet & Lewinsohn, 1973). That is, those who were depressed took longer to respond, initiated fewer conversations, tended to focus primarily on one person in the group, and proportionately fewer of their statements toward others were positive than was typical of their non-depressed counterparts. Similarly, Eisler, Miller, and Hersen (1973, 1973b), working with psychiatric inpatients, found that highly skilled (i.e., assertive) versus poorly skilled (i.e., unassertive) individuals within this population could be reliably differentiated on a number of verbal and nonverbal behaviors. Still more recently, Hersen and Bellack (1976c) have reviewed and documented the important relationship of social skill deficit and chronicity of psychiatric disorder.

Historical Basis

Social skill training techniques (frequently referred to as assertive training) are now commonplace in the practice of behavior modification. But what are the origins of these techniques? When reviewing the historical basis the impetus seems to have come from two directions. The *first* stems from the clinical work of pioneers in behavior modification such as Andrew Salter (1949), Joseph Wolpe (1958), and Arnold Lazarus (1971). These three clinicians were involved in developing assertive training techniques to help individuals overcome inhibitions in interpersonal relations. Specifically, Wolpe (1969) has stated that such treatment ". . . is required for patients who in interpersonal contexts have unadaptive anxiety responses that prevent them from saying or doing what is reasonable and right" (p. 61). According to Wolpe, then, the individual knows what to do in a given situation but the high level of anxiety interferes with his saying or doing the right things. Broadly speaking, treatment is directed toward teaching these individuals how to deal better in a large variety of interpersonal situations. Situations may range from learning how to ask a girl out for a date, to saying "No" to a persistent salesman, to expressing appreciation to a friend for a favor done. More will be said about the specifics of assertive training in subsequent sections.

The *second* historical impetus derives from the work of Edward Zigler and his colleagues (e.g., Phillips & Zigler, 1961; Zigler & Levine, 1973; Zigler & Phillips, 1960) relating psychiatric disorder to social competence. Other workers in the field have also commented on the relationship of psychiatric disorder and social skill. For example, Gladwin (1967) states: ". . . that in order to become effective the psychologically inadequate person not only needs to relieve his anxieties and correct his maladaptive behavior but also to learn alternative success-oriented ways of behaving in society" (p. 87). Also from the treatment standpoint, in a recently completed 25-year project at The Johns Hopkins University, improvement in social skills of patients was one of two positive effects of brief psychotherapy (Frank, 1974).

But despite occasional acknowledgements of the important relationship of psychiatric disorder and social competence, it is Zigler and his colleagues who have done the painstaking research needed in the area. In an extended series of studies spanning the last 20 years, Zigler and his colleagues have documented a number of interesting relationships. However, the most basic finding may be summarized as follows: "The higher the patient's level of social competence before being hospitalized, the better his/her chance of succeeding in the community after being discharged from the hospital." Thus, patients who had finished high school, worked, married, and showed a rapid onset of symptoms before hospitalization did better following discharge than those who had not finished high school, worked, or married, and who had developed their symptoms slowly over time. It quickly became apparent that level of social competence before being hospitalized was the critical factor. That is, prehospitalization level of social competence turned out to be a better predictor of post-hospital adjustment than the psychiatric diagnosis given or the particular type of treatment received.

Unfortunately, until recently the findings reported by Zigler and colleagues have had little impact on approaches used in treatment. Indeed, only recently have the clinical implications of these findings been recognized (Hersen & Bellack, 1976b, 1977) and put into practice (Hersen & Bellack, 1976a; Hersen, Eisler, & Miller, 1973a).

Definitions of Social Skill

When an individual is perceived by his acquaintances as being effective in his social interactions, they label him as "socially skilled." On the other hand, the individual who is perceived as being ineffective in his social interactions is frequently labeled as "socially unskilled." However, in making such judgments we all have our unique biases, and from the psychological point of view some more unified definitions are needed. As will be seen later in our discussion on measurement of social skill, even more precise definitions are needed. But for the time being, let us examine some more global definitions that have appeared in the literature.

Wolpe (1969) and many others (e.g., Hersen & Bellack, 1977) have used the words assertive and social skill interchangeably. For example, Wolpe (1969) points out that, "The word *assertive* is applied to the outward expression of practically all feelings other than anxiety. Experience has shown that such expression tends to inhibit anxiety. Assertiveness usually involves more or less aggressive behavior, but it may express friendly, affectionate, and other non-anxious feelings" (p. 61). Wolpe distinguishes between "hostile" negative assertiveness and "commendatory" (positive) assertiveness. The following represents an example of "hostile" assertiveness: "I've been waiting at this counter for 10 minutes now; please wait on me." Conversely, an example of "commendatory" assertiveness might be: "Thank you for going out of your way to help me; it's much appreciated."

Lazarus (1971), in his definition, is more intent on differentiating assertiveness from aggression, particularly as aggression has negative connotations such as *outbursts of hostility*. "The difference between assertion and aggression should . . . be noted, since outbursts of hostility, rage, or resentment usually denote pent-up or accumulated anger rather than the spontaneous expression of healthy emotion. Habits of emotional freedom imply the ability to give honest feedback (i.e., to show one's true feelings, and to do so in a frank and open manner). Emotional freedom opposes hypocrisy, phoniness, and deception. Contrary to the popular belief, the result of emotional freedom is not alienation or increased vulnerability, but decreased anxiety, close and meaningful relationships, self-respect, and social adaptivity" (pp. 115–116). In short, Lazarus is saying that honest communication will not lead to punishment but, to the contrary, should result in better interpersonal relations.

Argyris (1965, 1968) speaks of social skill when referring to an individual's effectiveness within the context of a larger group of individuals. Libet and Lewinsohn (1973) also defined social skill, but their definition is based on work with depressed subjects. They consider social skill ". . . as the complex set of behaviors making up the ability both to emit behaviors which are positively or negatively reinforced and not to emit behaviors which are punished or extinguished by others" (p. 304). That is, the socially skilled individual is highly rewarded for his social initiatives as he receives repeated approval from his peers.

As might be expected, we too have our own definition of social skill, which reflects our interest in treating unassertive psychiatric patients. "We therefore emphasize an individual's ability to express both positive and negative feelings in the interpersonal context without suffering consequent loss of social reinforcement. Such skill is demonstrated in a large variety of interpersonal contexts (that range from family to employer-employee relationships), and involves the coordinated delivery of appropriate verbal and nonverbal responses. In addition, the socially skilled individual is attuned to the realities of the situation and is aware when he/she is likely to be reinforced for his/her efforts. Thus, at times the socially skilled individual may have to forego the expression of 'hostile' assertiveness if such expression is likely to result in punishment or social censure" (Hersen & Bellack, 1977). Given this definition, we recognize that the context of a given situation will determine effectiveness of the individual's response. Context might vary such as introducing oneself to an attractive member of the opposite sex at a party, thanking a friend, or asking a waiter to return an uncooked steak. In addition, as previously noted, the politics or realities of the situation will also determine the style and quality of the response. We certainly think twice about telling our boss to "go to hell" when slighted or wronged, especially if we value our jobs. To the contrary, the truly socially skilled individual will be able to effectively communicate his upset to his boss without inappropriately offending him or risking the possibility of being fired. The socially skilled individual is interested in communicating feelings, at times requests changes in the interpersonal partner's behavior, but tends to elicit a minimum of hostility and retaliation in return.

Measurement of Social Skill

As was noted in Chapter 1, an important feature that distinguishes behavior modification from other treatment approaches is the emphasis on empiricism. By empiricism, we mean that the therapist or clinical researcher *is* concerned whether or not his treatment techniques have brought about positive changes in his patient that can be measured and documented. Taking this one step further, by documentation we refer to the difference between a post-treatment and pretreatment measurement of some aspect of a patient's behavior. Here we are talking about improvement in a given social skill deficit. Measurement or assessment is, therefore, central to both clinical and research activities. A number of different strategies or techniques have been applied to social skills. We will discuss major approaches and issues in this section.

Self-Report

As with other behavioral problems, there are three basic ways of measuring social skill deficits. The *first* follows a time-honored tradition and simply involves the individual's self-report of his behavior (i.e., what he does and how he feels about it). This could involve a structured interview or the individual's written responses to a standardized questionnaire (e.g., responses to yes-no items or ratings of items, say on a 1–5-point scale). The Wolpe-Lazarus (1966) Assertiveness Scale is representative of the self-report method of assessing social skill. This scale consists of 30 items that are answered in yes-no fashion. Sample items are as follows: "Are you inclined to be overapologetic?" "Do you usually try to avoid 'bossy' people?" "Do you generally express what you feel?" "Are you able openly to express love and affection?" (p. 41). Such questions can be used individually to assess problem areas and the effects of treatment or the questions can be compiled into a total scale score (0–30).

Motoric

The second strategy to assess an individual's social skill deficit is to actually observe him in an interpersonal situation in his specific environment (i.e., at home, work, or school). This is labeled as a naturalistic observation. However, frequently, either for practical or because of ethical limitations (i.e., the invasion of privacy), this will not be possible. An alternative, then, is to have the individual simulate (play act) the interaction under laboratory conditions, usually through *role playing*. This is referred to as an analogue measurement technique. Examples of both naturalistic and analogue measures are provided below. Both, however, involve the assessment of motoric behavior.

Naturalistic Observation. As an example of a semi-naturalistic measure of social skill, Hersen, Turner, Edelstein, and Pinkston (1975) observed a patient who was in group psychotherapy, through a one-way mirror. This patient was a chronic schizophrenic showing extremely withdrawn behavior. That is, when spoken to he answered in monosyllables and he rarely began a conversation on his own. Individual social skills training was, therefore, directed toward improving his conversational skills. Observations of this patient in group psychotherapy, then, simply consisted of counting the number of times (per group session) that he initiated conversation with another member of the group.

A more naturalistic measure of social skill has been used by McFall and Marston (1970) during the course of evaluating the effects of assertive training with college students. Following a brief period of assertive training, each of the students received a telephone call from a "high pressure" salesman who was trying his best to convince the student to purchase some magazines. What each student did not know was that this "salesman" was, in reality, a confederate (i.e., a stooge) trained by the experimenter. The students' responses to this "salesman" were tape recorded and later rated on a number of dimensions: overall social skill or poise in dealing with this call, length of time before the student began to resist the salesman and assert himself/herself, and total time that the telephone call lasted (i.e., before the student terminated the call). This type of measure would appear to be the most useful, especially since the student is unaware that his/her social skills (i.e., the ability to resist sales pressure) are under evaluation. However, the very fact that he/she is unaware presents an ethical-methodologic problem in that "deception" has been used. Of course, after the completion of the study all students who participated were specifically informed of the "true" nature of the telephone call. Interestingly, *none* of the students refused post hoc to give the experimenter permission to use tapes of the telephone conversation for research purposes.

Analogue Role Playing. A series of 14 interpersonal situations was developed by Eisler, Miller, and Hersen (1973b) to measure assertiveness. This measure is known as the Behavioral Assertiveness Test (BAT). Each of the 14 situations in the BAT requires that the subject being tested respond in an assertive manner while role playing. The 14 situations vary, but in each case the subject is hypothetically being thwarted. To give a semblance of realism to the test, the subject is seated next to a role model who delivers a pre-determined prompt (see below). The subject is then expected to respond (role play) to that prompt while being videotaped. Prior to the prompt the entire situation is narrated by the therapist or experimenter.

An example follows:

"*Narrator:* 'You're in a restaurant with some friends. You order a very rare steak. The waitress brings a steak to the table which is so well-done it looks burned.' *Role Model Waitress:* 'I hope you enjoy your dinner sir.'" (p. 296).

In response to the prompt given by the waitress, an unassertive individual might simply say: "Thank you, it looks fine." On the other hand, the more assertive individual might say: "I ordered the steak rare. This one is well-done. I enjoy my steak rare. Please get me another one that is cooked rare." In so responding, not only is the assertive individual expressing dissatisfaction with the way the steak was prepared, but he is making a specific request that the order be repaired. In addition to the content of the verbal message delivered to the waitress, the truly assertive individual will usually speak in an appropriately loud voice, with sufficient affect (modulation and intonation), and with proper gestures and facial expression. Also, he does not hesitate or stammer and responds to the prompt with some rapidity (i.e., short latency of response). Some of the specific components of the overall response just mentioned can be codified and specific target measures can be identified and rated retrospectively from the taped responses of subjects.

In the Eisler et al. (1973b) study, several verbal and nonverbal behaviors were rated: duration of looking (eye contact), smiles, duration of reply, latency of response, loudness of speech, fluency of speech, compliance content (i.e., if the subject does not resist the role model's position), requests for new behavior (e.g., "get me a new steak cooked rare"), affect, and overall assertiveness (a more global judgment of the efficacy of the subject's response). In this study, differences between high and low overall assertiveness subjects were examined. "Those who are perceived as being assertive tend to respond to interpersonal problems quickly and in a strongly audible voice with marked intonation. The results also demonstrated that highly assertive individuals do not automatically accede to the demands of others and are more likely to request that the interpersonal partner change his behavior. There was a tendency for high assertive Ss to respond verbally at greater length than low assertive Ss. . ." (p. 199). In addition, this study showed that ratings of subjects' overall assertiveness was moderately correlated with their responses to the Wolpe-Lazarus Assertiveness Scale (previously described). That is, what a subject said he did was related to how he appeared to others.

The 14 situations that make up the BAT require the expression of hostile or negative assertion. In a subsequent study, Eisler, Hersen, Miller, and Blanchard (1975) added scenes requiring the expression of "commendatory" (positive) assertion as well. This test is known as the Behavioral Assertiveness Test-Revised (BAT-R). An example is provided below:

"Narrator: 'You are the leader of the company bowling team. Your team is slightly behind when one of the men on your team makes three strikes in a row to even up the score. You are really proud of him.' *He says:* 'How did you like that one?'" (p. 332)

In response to the question, an example of "commendatory" assertion might be: "That's terrific; you're really great in the clutch." This kind of response would certainly be rated higher on overall assertiveness than, for instance, one including a mere: "That's fine."

Physiological

There is no direct physiological measure of social skill. Rather, the physiological measures that have been used (e.g., heart rate and pulse rate) reflect a subject's anxiety or arousal in a potentially threatening situation. A typical clinical example might involve the following. Let us consider the case of a shy and socially anxious male college student. This student has met an attractive girl in one of his classes and, despite his usual shyness, he is sufficiently attracted so that he plans to telephone her for a date. As he is about to telephone his throat feels dry, his palms are sweaty, and his heart is pounding. In a recent study, Borkovec, Stone, O'Brien, and Kaloupek (1974) experimentally confirmed this clinical description. Thus, when high and low anxious (with respect to being with a member of the opposite sex) college men were evaluated in a laboratory situation where they were instructed to interact with a female confederate (a research assistant), high anxious males evidenced significantly greater physiological arousal; that is, their heart rate showed greater increases than low anxious subjects. Similar findings were reported by Twentyman and McFall (1975), using pulse rate as the measure, when comparing heterosexually confident and heterosexually shy college males.

Measurement of Specific Problem Areas

In the preceding sections we have examined the three response systems in which social skill deficits may be measured (i.e., the self-report, the motoric, and the physiological). In the following sections we will examine how social skill deficits have been measured behaviorally for three specific problem areas: unassertive but otherwise normal children, heterosexually shy college students, and depressed clients. In each of the three categories we will focus our attention on how the individuals respond in analogue or real situations requiring socially skilled behavior.

Unassertiveness in Children

In a recent study, Bornstein, Bellack, and Hersen (in press) evaluated and modified social skill deficits in four unassertive children, ranging from 8 to 11 years of age. Of 12 such children originally described by their teachers as: "Excessively cooperative, passive, shy, unassertive, and conforming," four were found to be deficient in targeted behaviors. These targets, identified during role playing, were poor eye contact when interacting with the role model, short speech duration in response to prompts, inaudible responses, and an inability to ask the role model to alter his/her behavior. To give the reader a flavor for how these children appeared, the following represents a description of our first subject:

"Subject 1 was an 8-year-old female third grader referred because of her difficulty relating to peers. She was described as passive, experienced difficulty expressing anger when appropriate, and was unable to refuse unreasonable requests. In addition, she was oversensitive to criticism and rarely volunteered in class" (Bornstein, Bellack, & Hersen, in press).

To evaluate these children, a modification of the BAT (Eisler et al., 1973b) and BAT-R (Eisler et al., 1975) was devised so as to be suitable to their age levels. Nine scenes were developed, five involving role playing with a same sex model and four with a cross-sex model. These nine scenes constitute the Behavioral Assertiveness Test for Children (BAT-C). All of the scenes involve the expression of "hostile" (negative) assertion. Again, as in the case of the BAT and BAT-R, the responses to these scenes are videotaped and later rated by judges for targeted behaviors. Presented below are two scenes, the first involving a response to a female model and the second to a male role model:

"*Narrator:* 'Imagine you need to use a pair of scissors for a science project. Betty is using them, but promises to let you have them next. But when Betty is done she gives them to Ellen.' *Prompt:* 'Here's the scissors, Ellen.'"

"*Narrator:* 'Imagine you're playing a game of four squares in gym. You make a good serve into Barry's square. But he says that it was out and keeps the ball to serve.' *Prompt:* 'It's my turn to serve!'" (Bornstein et al., in press).

When the BAT-C is used to evaluate "hostile" assertiveness in children, the therapist reads the scene (i.e., he functions as the *Narrator*), the role model delivers the prompt, and then the child gives his/her response. The nine scenes are usually presented to the child as a game-like procedure in which he/she will be asked to imagine situations that will require his/her responding to various slights and frustrations. To date, most children readily accept this rationale and are quite cooperative.

Although the BAT-C appears to have some "face" validity (i.e., the scenes appear to represent possible examples of negative interactions that school children might be exposed to), the test has not yet received formal validation. However, a study is currently under way by the present authors to obtain empirical confirmation of this test's validity. In this study "commendatory" (positive) assertion is also being evaluated.

Heterosexual Skills in College Males

Arkowitz, Lichtenstein, McGovern, and Hines (1975) describe a three-part behavioral interaction sequence for evaluating heterosexual skills in college males. The *first* part of the evaluation consists of the subject's role playing in 10 social situations (adapted from the work of Rehm & Marston, 1968) that are tape recorded. These situations are known as the Taped Situation Test (TST). Each of the audiotaped situations is narrated by a male. A female then reads the dialogue, and after a pre-recorded signal the subject being assessed is asked to respond. His responses are recorded with a second tape recorder. These 10 situations are quite similar in format to the BAT scenes, previously described.

An example of one of the scenes from the TST appears below:

"*Male Narrator:* 'At a party, you go over to a girl and ask her to dance'."

"*Female Voice:* 'I'm not really much of a dancer'."

"*Subject:* (He is expected to respond at this point)."

In the Arkowitz et al. (1975) study, responses to the 10 scenes were rated on two measures: (1) latency of response, and (2) mean number of words per scene for TST responding.

The *second* part of the evaluation involves the subject's interacting with a female confederate (an attractive and socially skilled female undergraduate who serves as a research assistant to the experimenter) for a 10-min. time period. The subject's task consists of talking to the female in order to get "to know her further," as if it were an actual social situation. The female confederates participating in this evaluation had previously been given instructions on how to respond in order to stand-ardize the situation for all of the males being assessed. "They were instructed to be moderately positive with all subjects, but to let the burden of the conversation fall on the subject. For this purpose, the confederates were trained to limit their utterances to 5 sec. or less and to avoid initiating any topics of conversation unless there was a silence in the conversation of 10 sec. or more" (Arkowitz et al., 1975, p. 5). These interactions are then observed from behind a one-way mirror by trained judges who code the behaviors as follows: male talk time, number of verbal reinforcements, male head nods, number of male smiles, male gazing (i.e., length of eye contact per interaction), and verbal content. Verbal content consists of statements, questions, or responses. Re-sponses are coded with respect to restatement, acknowledgement, agreement, or disagreement.

The *third* part of the evaluation involves the subject's now telephon-ing this same female confederate (from the laboratory room to the female confederate's room). His stated objective is to ask her out for a date following a hypothetical (imagined) meeting with her earlier dur-ing the day. This conversation is limited to 5 min. and also is recorded. The female confederate follows the same tactics she used in the preced-ing 10 min. in vivo conversation. In addition, she is instructed to role play accepting the date. Audiotapes of the telephone conversation are rated for: (1) male talk time, and (2) total length of the conversation if less than the allotted 5 min.

Depression

Although the relationship between social skill and depression had been acknowledged by other clinical researchers (e.g., Weissman, Paykel, & Klerman, 1972; Weissman, Paykel, Siegel, & Klerman, 1971), it is Lewinsohn and his colleagues (Lewinsohn, 1975; Libet & Lewinsohn, 1973) who have focused attention on this particular area. The Lewinsohn group is especially concerned with social skill as they hypothesize that the depressed person, because of such skill deficits, is unable to obtain the positive reactions (i.e., positive reinforcement) needed from the environment. It is further hypothesized, then, that the absence of positive reactions from significant others *may* lead to depression. As pointed out in the introductory section, Libet and Lewinsohn (1973) present evidence that depressed subjects are ". . . lower than controls on a number of operational measures of social skill (i.e., activity level, interpersonal range, rate of positive reactions emitted, and action latency)" (p. 304).

It will be recalled that Lewinsohn (1975) has defined social skill primarily "as the ability to emit behaviors that are positively reinforced by others" (p. 41). Therefore, it is not surprising that observations of depressed individuals' behaviors have taken place within small group settings (e.g., self-study groups) and at home within the family setting (e.g., Lewinsohn & Shaffer, 1971). Although in the Lewinsohn coding system many behaviors related to social skill have been studied, there are five primary targets for investigation. The *first* involves the total *rate of behavior* emitted by the individual. That is, how many verbal interactions within a group in a 1-hour period will the depressed individual initiate (these data are presented as rate per hour)? The *second* is labeled *interpersonal efficiency*. This definition refers to the number of behaviors an individual elicits from others in relation to how many behaviors he/she emits. Let us illustrate what is specifically meant here. If in a group a given individual emits four statements to individual A and four statements to individual B, and receives four comments in reply from individual A but only one comment from individual B, his/her interpersonal efficiency is less with individual B. Lewinsohn (1975) points out that depressives are not as interpersonally efficient as are normal controls. The *third* target concerns *interpersonal range*. The socially skilled individual is able to interact with a large number of individuals while eliciting an equally large number of responses from most of these individuals. This does not hold in the depressed client, whose interpersonal range is restricted. A *fourth* target involves measurement as to whether an individual's behavior is positive toward those with whom he/she interacts. This is specifically measured as the *rate of positive reactions* directed toward others per session (group or at home). In this realm, depressed clients tend to be less positive than their nondepressed counterparts. Finally, the *fifth* measure is termed *action latency*. Libet and Lewinsohn (1973) define this ". . . as the amount of elapsed time between a reaction by another person to an individual's verbal behavior and a subsequent action by that individual" (p. 306).

It should be noted that all of the above categories of response related to social skill (and many others) can be rated reliably by trained observers (Lewinsohn, 1975). Moreover, the particular setting used is easy to arrange (any group or family situation held constant over observation periods). In addition, trained judges can make their ratings relatively unobtrusively. Thus, a useful coding system has been devised for studying social skill deficits in depressed individuals.

Clinical Issues

Now that we have examined the origins of social skills training, listed some of the definitions of social skill currently being used, and presented some examples of how social skill deficits are measured for different populations, it should be useful to consider what actually takes place during social skills treatment. However, it is probably obvious that the particular treatment that is used will be adapted to the particular disorder under consideration. Certainly, the treatment approach will vary considerably for the chronic schizophrenic (who has experienced many and repeated long-term hospitalizations) manifesting a series of skill deficits and the mildly neurotic middle-class housewife who experiences anxiety in interpersonal relations.

In the case of our chronic schizophrenic, his skill deficits may be due to either: (1) a faulty learning history wherein needed skills for social survival were never learned, or (2) a function of his disorder and the negative impact of institutionalization over many years. In either case, a re-educative approach in which the therapist is cast in the role of the teacher and the patient as student would seem appropriate. Thus, the therapist would actually show the patient (model for him), give verbal instruction, provide corrective feedback (positive and negative), administer praise contingent on an approximation of a current response, and have the patient practice his developing repertoire. This is a slow and arduous process that requires much practice on the part of the patient and considerable patience on the part of the therapist, particularly as literally thousands of trials may be needed (see Hersen & Bellack, 1976b, 1977; Hersen et al., 1975). With the chronic patient who shows poor social skill the therapist cannot assume that the patient knows *"what to do, how to do it, and when to do it."* To the contrary, experience shows that the conservative approach is to be preferred and that the patient must be taught an entirely new behavioral repertoire.

On the other hand, with our middle-class housewife who experiences inhibition of expression in her interpersonal dealings, it is generally safe to assume that she knows *"what to do, how to do it, and when to do it,"* but it is anxiety that interferes with her responding appropriately. It follows, then, from a careful behavioral analysis, that this patient will require treatment directed toward reducing the anxiety component of her disorder (e.g., relaxation training and/or assertive training done gradually in hierarchical fashion in order to minimize any discomfort or interference due to anxiety). We will discuss this at greater length in subsequent sections.

Definition of Clinical Strategies

During the clinical course of assertive training the therapist will employ a number of strategies, at times in sequence and at other times concurrently. These strategies are: instruction, feedback, modeling, behavior rehearsal (i.e., role playing), social reinforcement, and graduated "homework" assignments. Let us now define each of the specific strategies that comprise assertive training.

Instruction

Instruction simply involves telling the client or patient that he is expected to engage in a specific behavior at a given time. For example, the therapist might say to his patient: "When role playing with me the scene with your father, look at me when you are talking and speak up so that I can hear you clearly." As noted experimentally (Hersen, Eisler, Miller, Johnson, & Pinkston, 1973b), clear instructions can lead to rapid acquisition of such discrete behaviors as eye contact and loudness of speech.

Feedback

Feedback refers to the therapist's comments on the patient's behavior following an instructional set to change and an attempt to implement the instructional set. An example might be: "This time when we role played the scene with your father you looked at me 90% of the time, but you still did not speak loudly enough." In this therapist's comment both positive ("you looked at me 90% of the time") and negative ("but you still did not speak loudly enough") feedback are incorporated. Simple positive and negative feedback has been demonstrated to lead to marked behavioral change in behavioral studies (e.g., Bernhardt, Hersen, & Barlow, 1972; Eisler, Hersen, & Miller, 1974).

Modeling

There are instances when instructions and feedback (even when applied systematically and repeatedly) do not lead to behavioral change.

This frequently occurs when the patient has never performed the behavior or has had very few opportunities to perform it. In some cases the patient may have never learned the behavior in the first place. In any event, here the therapist must actually display (i.e., model) the behavior for the patient and then ask him to imitate. The use of modeling has proven effective for patients who have limited repertoires (e.g., Hersen & Bellack, 1976a; Hersen et al., 1975), particularly for the more complex aspects of assertiveness such as asking the interpersonal partner to change his behavior (see Hersen et al., 1973b). Both live (Hersen & Bellack, 1976a) and videotaped models (e.g., Hersen, Eisler, & Miller, 1974) have been used.

Behavior Rehearsal

"Behavior rehearsal is a procedure whereby more desirable responses to interpersonal conflict situations are practiced under the supervision of the therapist" (Eisler & Hersen, 1973, p. 112). In addition to conflict situations, practice in expressing positive feelings ("commendatory" assertion) takes place during behavior rehearsal. Such practice sessions occur in the clinic or in the consulting room, with the therapist and patient role playing a variety of social situations (e.g., BAT scenes).

Social Reinforcement

Social reinforcement simply involves praising the patient, contingent on an approximation of a desired target response. Social reinforcement is usually intertwined with feedback. For example, when the therapist says: "You looked at me 90% of the time when talking; that's very good," both feedback ("you looked at me 90% of the time") and social reinforcement ("that's very good") are communicated to the patient at the same time. During the clinical application of assertive training much social reinforcement is used as the patient's responses begin to approximate the therapist's criterion for change. Thus, a given targeted response is gradually *shaped* by the use of social reinforcement. There is no doubt that social reinforcement is a very powerful behavioral change strategy (e.g., Hersen, Gullick, Matherne, & Harbert, 1972; Kallman, Hersen, & O'Toole, 1975).

Homework Assignments

It should now be obvious that behavior modification in general and assertive training in particular are task-oriented approaches to treatment. Thus, during assertive training an important part of the procedure is to have the patient practice his newly developing repertoire of responses in his natural environment (at home, at work, or at school).

The heterosexually anxious college male might be instructed simply to telephone two different girls during the 1-week interim between treatment sessions. The socially anxious housewife might be instructed to telephone a neighbor and invite her over for coffee. Of course, this would follow appropriate role playing in the therapist's office. The withdrawn schizophrenic on the psychiatric ward might be asked to initiate three comments in the next group psychotherapy session. When "homework" assignments are given to patients they should be geared in such a way that when these patients practice their newly developed responses in their natural environments they will be positively reinforced for their efforts. This is quite important inasmuch as rebuff from the environment when the patient initially tries out new responses may lead to a setback in treatment. Usually the skilled and practiced clinician is able to gauge (on the basis of carefully evaluating the patient during role playing sessions in the office situation) how effective the patient will be in a particular situation in the environment. As the patient gains confidence in his new abilities and is successful in implementing homework assignments, more difficult types of assignments are then given to him to perform.

Assertive Training When Anxiety Inhibits Performance

The present writers have developed a treatment protocol for the patient whose anxiety interferes with the expression of skilled responses (both positive and negative). For most of these patients, they currently have, or at one time did possess, the requisite responses in their repertoires. However, their present level of anxiety is sufficiently intense so as to prevent the full expression of their feelings in a variety of interpersonal situations. The protocol to be outlined below is akin to a strategy known as *rehearsal-desensitization,* first introduced by Piaget and Lazarus (1969). However, our protocol involves a time-limited approach that usually consists of 12–15 sessions conducted over a 12–15-week period.

Material for training sessions is derived from interview data in addition to being based on an analysis of relevant self-report scales and performance on the BAT-R (Eisler et al., 1975). In the initial two sessions, BAT-R-like scenes specifically tailored to the patient's particular interpersonal deficiencies (e.g., interactions with spouse, children, parents, friends, employees, strangers, casual acquaintances, etc.) are constructed. Material in these scenes focuses on the patient's transactions in his environment with significant others, who provide social reinforcement or who have the potential for providing social reinforcement. The scenes are selected so that they present the opportunity for training in the expression of positive and negative feelings. Expression of such feelings in these contexts may then lead to reciprocal reinforcement by others in the environment. For example, the patient who has a high rate of complaining to a spouse about his behavior but who rarely provides the spouse with any positive feedback (even though deserved) is taught a new mode of interaction (in which the patient responds more positively to the spouse's positive initiatives). Conversely, the patient who is unable to stand up for his rights in marital situations or is unable to set limits with his children is taught how to express himself effectively in order to bring about the necessary changes in others in the environment. Thus, he is taught how to achieve greater mastery over his environment through the coordinated delivery of the verbal and nonverbal components of his communications.

The scenes are typed on 5″ x 8″ cards and are ranked in order of difficulty: i.e, how much difficulty or anxiety the patient might experience carrying out such behavior in vivo. Separate hierarchies for positive and negative scenes are established. (See Table 2.1 in Chapter 2, for examples of such hierarchies in treating anxiety conditions.) Number of scenes in a hierarchy for a particular patient will obviously vary, but should range from 10–20 scenes for each patient for each of the positive and negative categories.

Assertive training is first directed toward those scenes (interpersonal situations) that are least threatening to the patient. Following initial observation of role played scenes, alternative methods of responding to the same situation may be modeled by the therapist. Instructions, feedback, and social reinforcement are administered by the therapist to improve performance of targeted behaviors during behavior rehearsal sessions. Attention is directed to the specific components comprising social skill (e.g., duration of eye contact, smiles, duration of reply, latency of response, loudness of speech, appropriate affect, ratio of speech disturbances to duration of speech, compliance content, requests for new behaviors, praise, appreciation, spontaneous positive behavior). As the patient begins to master the scenes on the low end of the hierarchy, more difficult aspects of the patient's interactions are tackled, thus progressing up the hierarchy of scenes. Although this is done in a graduated progression, there are some patients whose anxiety is so great that even the scenes on the lower end of the hierarchy will lead to performance inhibition. For those patients a course of systematic desensitization prior to assertive training is recommended (Wolpe, 1973).

Homework assignments (e.g., standing up to one's spouse, praising one's child) are determined through therapist-patient discussion. These homework assignments are given weekly and are designed so that the environment reinforces the patient's initial attempts at expressing positive and negative feelings (see Hersen et al., 1973a; Wolpe, 1969). That is, at first, homework assignments consist of actually carrying out behaviors depicted in the scenes on the lower end of the hierarchy. This procedure should insure maximal generalization of effects into the environment. As the patient improves and obtains environmental support, homework assignments are gradually increased in difficulty.

The typical training session consists of the following sequence: (1) the patient reports on the ability to carry out homework assignments and environmental reactions to new behaviors, (2) the patient reports any new difficulties that may have arisen since the last session, (3) more effective behaviors for dealing with such new difficulties are identified and the new difficulties are included in a revised hierarchy of scenes, (4) the patient practices scenes higher up on the hierarchy, the therapist instructs, provides feedback, models, administers social reinforcement, and the patient practices again, etc., and (5) the therapist and patient discuss new homework assignments. All of the above are conducted in a "positive" atmosphere in which the therapist provides systematic social reinforcement for the step-wise progress seen during the course of a session and from one session to the next.

Case Description

A clinical case description of rehearsal-desensitization is presented below:

> "Mrs. T. was a plump, soft-spoken housewife of 37 years who, during her initial interview, never once established eye contact with the therapist. Her presenting complaint involved a fear of crowds, particularly in situations where attention might be focused on her. It soon became apparent however, that Mrs. T.'s functioning was severely impaired in nearly all interpersonal situations. She complained of chronic depression and severe anxiety which three years of 'existential therapy' had been unable to overcome. When the therapist suggested assertive training as a possible starting point, Mrs. T. smiled sadly and said that such a method had been attempted by a previous 'behavior therapist.' She explained that she was simply unable to carry out her previous therapist's instructions.
>
> The therapist then described rehearsal-desensitization to Mrs. T. He suggested that in this way she might acquire assertive skills, at her own pace, within the safety of the consulting room. Mrs. T. expressed initial doubt as to the outcome of the procedure, but finally agreed to give it a try.
>
> The next four sessions were used to complete the behavior analysis and to build an appropriate hierarchy. During this time the therapist was extremely supportive and gentle with Mrs. T., in order to gain her trust and confidence, and to establish a relationship between them conducive to optimal rehearsal-desensitization. A 24-item hierarchy was constructed along a continuum of progressively more assertive behavior in the presence of one other person. The lower end of the hierarchy consisted of such items as: maintaining eye contact with herself in a mirror while speaking; maintaining eye contact with the therapist while silent. Middle-hierarchy

items were: complaining to a waiter about food and asking a stranger on the street for directions. High-anxiety items involved expressing and defending an opinion, discussing a controversial topic, and expressing a novel idea regarding teaching methodology to a supervisor, in a loud, clear voice.

Mrs. T. had considerable difficulty with several of the items, but the hierarchy was completed to the mutual satisfaction of patient and therapist after 14 sessions. Concurrently she reported substantial improvements in her reactions to similar real-life situations.

Phase 2 of therapy involved the completion of a similar hierarchy consisting of graded behavioral interactions with two or more persons. Secretaries, research assistants, and other departmental personnel were employed in the behavioral rehearsal. Mrs. T. needed only seven sessions to complete a 15-item hierarchy, and subsequently reported marked improvements outside the consulting room. Her depression vanished and she referred to herself as a 'new woman with a renewed interest in living.'

To check the validity of this report, the therapist accompanied Mrs. T. on a shopping trip one afternoon. During this time he encouraged such *in vivo* behaviors as initiating a conversation with a stranger, criticizing the manners of a salesgirl, and returning an item she had just bought. Mrs. T. needed little encouragement. Although reporting a certain amount of anticipatory anxiety, she was more than willing to test her new skills. In addition, she initiated several 'assertive performances' on her own.

Mrs. T. was accompanied by her husband to the final consultation. He stated that the change in Mrs. T. was 'amazing,' that she seemed happier than he had ever known her to be, and that she was now a 'much more interesting person to live with.' . . .

Mrs. T. terminated therapy after a total of 28 sessions. A six-month follow-up indicated that her assertive behavior had become even more pronounced (Piaget & Lazarus, 1969, pp. 265–266).

Skills Training for the Chronic Patient

The present writers have also developed a protocol for the treatment of the chronic patient who exhibits marked deficits in social skill. However, at this time the approach is in its experimental stages (e.g., Hersen & Bellack, 1976a, 1976b), and its overall efficacy has not yet been established. It might be noted that when treating the chronic patient the major focus is on the deficit aspect of the disorder rather than on indications of anxiety. This is largely because the deficits seen are so enormous and so basic.

Although there are some major differences in using the social skills approach with the anxiety-bound patient and the chronic patient (usually a schizophrenic), aspects of the protocol described in the previous sections are applicable with the chronic patient. However, the pace of treatment is slower and the goals of treatment are much more limited in scope. Many more trials are needed to achieve even minimal improvement in single target behaviors. Indeed, for the chronic patient, treatment is directed toward one behavior at a time (e.g., increased eye contact when talking) until sufficient mastery has been achieved. Then, the treatment proceeds to a second target (e.g., duration of speech) until a given criterion has been attained, but booster treatment is maintained for the first target (e.g., eye contact). This strategy is pursued until all the targets have reached criterion.

The primary reason for focusing on one behavior is that generally the chronic psychiatric patient will find it difficult to process successfully more than one stimulus at a time. Moreover, to achieve success (even dealing with one behavior at a time) each of the new behaviors must be *overlearned* in order to insure some permanence of the effect. By contrast, with the less chronically impaired patient several target behaviors can be brought under control concurrently.

A further description of our experimental approach with chronic patients will appear in the next section.

Experimental Support for the Skills Approach

The empirical verification of the social skills approach has been accomplished with three types of research strategies. In the *first,* usually short-term treatment analogues, the various component techniques (e.g., instructions, modeling, practice) that comprise assertive training have been compared. These studies indicate which of the component techniques is most effective, alone and in combination with others. The *second* research strategy involves the evaluation of social skill techniques in single case experimental designs (see Chapter 1 for a description of this approach). Here the patient or client serves as his own control. The *third* research strategy consists of a comparison of social skills training with other treatment approaches. We will examine the research findings for these three strategies in the succeeding sections.

Analogue Designs

In the short-term treatment studies (usually consisting of two to four 1-hour treatment sessions) the individual and combined effects of the component techniques of assertive training have been assessed. These evaluations are based on pre-post differences on self-report, motoric, and physiological indices. The value of these studies does not lie on the clinical changes brought about, but rather in an identification of the active ingredients in assertive training. Analogue designs have used college students as subjects (e.g., Kazdin, 1974; McFall & Marston, 1970) as well as psychiatric patients (Eisler, et al., 1973a; Goldstein, Martens,

Hubben, van Belle, Shaaf, Wiersma, & Goedhart, 1973; Hersen, Eisler, & Miller, 1974).

Let us first examine the studies conducted by McFall and his colleagues (McFall & Lillesand, 1971; McFall & Marston, 1970; McFall & Twentyman, 1973), using college students as subjects. In the first study, McFall and Marston (1970) compared four groups of subjects: (1) *Behavior Rehearsal with Performance Feedback*, (2) *Behavior Rehearsal without Performance Feedback*, (3) *Placebo-Therapy*, and (4) *No-Treatment*. Behavior rehearsal simply involved practicing negative assertion. The *Behavior Rehearsal* group *with Performance Feedback* listened to audiotapes of their responses. The *Behavior Rehearsal* group *without Performance Feedback* spent an equal amount of time "reflecting" on their responses. The *No-Treatment* group was put on a "waiting list."

Forty-two unassertive subjects participated in this experiment. The first three groups received four 1-hour sessions held over a 2–3-week period. The *No-Treatment* group received pre- and post-testing at the same time intervals as the other three groups. Pre-post testing involved a behavioral test, filling out self-report questionnaires, and pulse rate measures taken before and after the behavioral test, both pre and post. The results of this study indicated that both of the behavior rehearsal groups had improved performance on the behavioral, self-report, and pulse rate measures. The *Behavior Rehearsal* group *with Performance Feedback* did somewhat better than the group *without Performance Feedback*. In addition, 2 weeks after the completion of the experiment all subjects were contacted by an experimenter posing as a telephone salesman who was attempting to sell magazines. (This procedure has been described at some length in a previous section). The ability to resist the salesman was greater for the two experimental groups combined (*Behavior Rehearsal with* and *without Performance Feedback*) than the two control groups combined (*Placebo-Therapy* and *No-Treatment*).

In a subsequent study, McFall and Lillesand (1971) compared three treatment conditions: (1) *Overt Rehearsal with Modeling and Coaching*, (2) *Covert Rehearsal with Modeling and Coaching*, and (3) *Assessment-Placebo Control*. Overt rehearsal involved "rehearsing aloud" whereas covert rehearsal involved "imagining" the responses to BAT-like situations. Coaching here was analogous to a combination of instructions and feedback. Training consisted of only two sessions, with emphasis toward teaching the unassertive subjects to refuse unreasonable requests. The results of this study showed that contrasted to the *Assessment-Placebo* group, both of the *Behavior Rehearsal* groups (*Overt* and *Covert*) evidenced significant improvements in negative assertive responding on self-report and behavioral measures. The *Covert Rehearsal with Modeling and Coaching* group showed the greatest improvement. However, in this study the results did not appear to generalize beyond the laboratory situation when evaluated with the telephone follow-up test (i.e., the persistent magazine salesman).

McFall and Twentyman (1973) conducted the third of this series of short-term (two sessions) treatment studies with unassertive college students. Four specific experiments were run and yielded the following results: (1) behavior rehearsal and coaching accounted for most of the treatment effects found, (2) the addition of modeling to behavior rehearsal (with or without coaching) did not lead to further improvements, and (3) no differences among overt, covert, or covert plus overt rehearsal were found.

Many other short-term treatment studies with unassertive college students have been conducted (e.g., Friedman, 1971; Rathus, 1973). Although length and type of treatment have varied in these studies, a number of conclusions can be reached when these studies are considered together with those conducted by McFall and his colleagues. (1) Assertive training when contrasted to placebo treatment and no treatment produces rapid change in targeted behavioral measures. (2) Changes in self-report measures of assertiveness, anxiety, and physiological indices are less dramatic than overt behavioral changes. This is primarily a function of the length of the treatment (e.g., the longer the treatment the greater the likelihood that pre-post differences in self-reports will approach those seen in the motoric area). (3) In spite of the brevity of analogue treatment, there is evidence that some of the behavioral changes are maintained at follow-up assessments. (4) Although conclusions derived from such short-term studies in which college students are used as subjects have somewhat limited generalizability to actual clinical populations, it is possible to assess the relative efficacy of specific techniques within the limitations of the framework. The most active ingredients in assertive training appear to be behavior rehearsal, coaching, modeling (overt and covert), and performance feedback. With respect to modeling, the McFall and Twentyman (1973) investigation clearly showed that modeling when added to an already potent combination (behavioral rehearsal and coaching) did not result in further improvements. It would seem that with undergraduate populations, instructional control coupled with guided practice (i.e., coaching and behavior rehearsal) may be sufficient to facilitate appropriate assertive responding" (Hersen & Bellack, 1976b).

A similar set of analogue treatment studies, with psychiatric patients as subjects has been conducted by Hersen and his colleagues (Eisler et al., 1973a; Hersen, Eisler, & Miller, 1974; Hersen, Eisler, Miller, Johnson, & Pinkston, 1973). In their first study, Eisler et al. (1973a) compared three groups: (1) *Modeling,* (2) *Practice-Control,* and (3) *Test-Retest.* Subjects in the *Modeling* condition practiced negative assertive responses (on five BAT scenes) and observed an assertive videotaped model during four treatment sessions. Subjects in the *Practice-Control* condition simply practiced negative assertion during four treatment sessions but were not exposed to the videotaped model. *Test-Retest* subjects did not practice their responses nor did they observe the model.

The results of this study indicated that the *Modeling* group showed significant improvement on five of eight components of assertion (as evaluated with five BAT scenes on a pre-post basis). There were no differences found between the *Practice-Control* and *Test-Retest* groups, suggesting "that in cases where response deficits exist (lack of assertiveness), repeated exposure to the difficult situation alone does not change behavior" (Eisler et al., 1973, p. 5).

In a subsequent study, Hersen et al. (1973b), following the same experimental format, added two groups (*Instructions, Modeling plus Instructions*). *Instructions* consisted of telling the subject how to improve his performance (e.g., "Make sure you talk long enough. . . . Look at her when you talk. Tell her how you want things changed to make the situation better. Tell her what you expect her to do" [Hersen et al., 1973b, p. 447]). Thus, the study compared the following five groups: (1) *Test-Retest,* (2) *Practice-Control,* (3) *Instructions,* (4) *Modeling,* and (5) *Modeling plus Instructions.* In addition to evaluating responses to five BAT scenes, pre-post differences on the Wolpe-Lazarus Assertiveness Scale were examined. The results of this study indicated that the *Modeling plus Instructions* condition was equal or superior to the *Instructions* or *Modeling* conditions on five of the seven components of assertion. *Instructions* and *Modeling* alone resulted in greatest improvement in two of the components. As in the previous study, no differences were found between the *Practice-Control* and *Test-Retest* conditions. This again confirms the notion that with behavioral deficits the patient *must be taught a new response.* Also, there were *no* pre-post differences on the Wolpe-Lazarus Assertiveness Scale.

In the final study in this series, Hersen, Eisler, and Miller (1974) evaluated generalization effects. It was found that there was generalization from trained items (BAT scenes on which subjects received treatment) to untrained items (BAT scenes on which subjects did not receive treatment). However, the effects of treatment did not generalize to a totally new situation independent of the training. Again, the results of this study showed that there were no differences between *Practice-Control* and *Test-Retest* conditions, lending still further support to the contention that patients with behavioral deficits require re-education and practice in order to show improvement.

Other investigators have also conducted short-term treatment analogues with psychiatric patients (e.g., Goldsmith & McFall, 1975; Gutride, Goldstein, & Hunter, 1973). The results of these studies when taken together with those conducted by Hersen and colleagues lead to the following conclusions: (1) The skills approach when compared to placebo treatment or no treatment results in significant pre-post differences in targeted measures. (2) Instructions combined with modeling seem to be a potent treatment combination. (3) Practice in the absence of instructions or modeling *will not* lead to behavioral change in psychiatric subjects who evidence gross behavioral deficits. (4) The evidence with respect to changes in self-reports of assertiveness is unclear. However, again, the short-term nature of these studies does not allow for definitive conclusions. (5) There seems to be some evidence for unprogrammed generalization from trained to untrained items, but the evidence is somewhat contradictory from one type of situation requiring social skill to a totally different one requiring skilled responses. It is clear that if generalization is to be pronounced, clinicians will have to program its occurrence. That is, the patient will have to be taught how to respond successfully in a wide variety of situations. Also, the social environment will have to be *primed* to reinforce such social initiatives by the patient.

Single-Case Experiments

Recently the social skills approach has been evaluated in single case experimental designs. A large variety of disorders have been treated with assertive training and assessed using single case methodology. Included are: (1) shy and withdrawn children (Bornstein et al., in press), (2) marital discord (Eisler, Miller, Hersen, & Alford, 1974), (3) passive-aggressive disorders (Eisler, Hersen, & Miller, 1974), (4) unassertiveness in the work situation (Eisler, in press), (5) explosive behavior (Foy, Eisler, & Pinkston, 1975; Frederiksen, Jenkins, Foy, & Eisler, 1976), (6) skill deficits associated with schizophrenia (Edelstein & Eisler, 1976; Hersen & Bellack, 1976a; Hersen et al., 1975) and (7) depression (Lewinsohn & Atwood, 1969). Let us examine two examples of this experimental approach.

Bornstein et al. (in press) evaluated the effects of social skills training in four unassertive children ranging in age from 8 to 11. Treatment success was evaluated in each case with a multiple baseline strategy. During baseline assessments (three times in the 1st week) subjects were administered the Behavioral Assertiveness Test for Children (BAT-C). (This measure was previously described in an earlier section). On the basis of their responses to the nine scenes in the BAT-C, specific targets for each subject were selected* (see Fig. 5.1). Targets for Subject 1 were: eye contact, loudness of speech, and requests for new behavior. Following baseline assessment, social skills treatment was administered three times weekly for 15–30-min. sessions. During the 1st week, training was directed toward increasing eye contact, in the 2nd week toward increasing loudness of speech, and in the 4th week toward increasing number of requests.

Training was applied to six of the nine BAT-C scenes. Three remained untreated and served as the generalization scenes. Training in a typical session was as follows: "(1) The therapist presented one of the scenes

---

* During probe sessions the therapist presented a scene, the role model delivered a prompt, and then the subject responded to the role model. Responses were videotaped and rated retrospectively for target behaviors and overall assertiveness.

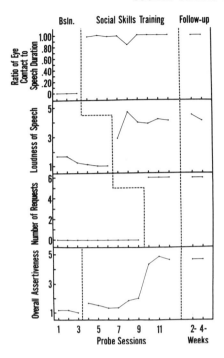

Fig. 5.1 Probe sessions during baseline, social skills treatment, and follow-up *training* scenes for Jane. A multiple baseline analysis of: ratio of eye contact to speech duration, loudness of speech, number of requests, and overall assertiveness. (Reprinted with permission from: M. R. Bornstein, A. S. Bellack, and M. Hersen: *Journal of Applied Behavior Analysis,* in press.)

from the BAT-C, the model delivered a prompt, and the subject responded. (2) The therapist provided the subject with feedback. . . . (3) The therapist then discussed feedback with the subject. . . . (4) The role models then modeled responses, with specific attention to the target behavior. (5) Specific instructions were then given by the therapist concerning the target behavior, followed by the subject responding a second time. (6) Rehearsal continued for a scene until the therapist felt that the criterion for that target behavior had been reached. (7) Training then advanced to a new interpersonal situation, proceeding in a similar fashion through all training scenes" (Bornstein et al., in press). Following completion of training, follow-up probes were conducted 2 and 4 weeks post-treatment.

Probe session data for the six training scenes are presented in Fig. 5.1. An examination of this figure indicates that there were marked increases for each targeted behavior following application of social skills training. In addition, overall assertiveness increased gradually over the 3 weeks of training. Moreover, 2- and 4-week follow-up probes suggest that the effects were durable.

Data for the three generalization scenes are presented in Fig. 5.2.

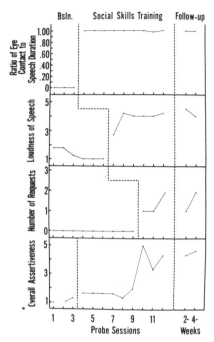

Fig. 5.2 Probe sessions during baseline, social skills treatment, and follow-up *generalization* scenes for Jane. A multiple baseline analysis of: ratio of eye contact to speech duration, loudness of speech, number of requests, and overall assertiveness. (Reprinted with permission from: M. R. Bornstein, A. S. Bellack, and M. Hersen: *Journal of Applied Behavior Analysis,* in press.)

This figure shows that data followed a similar pattern to those seen in Fig. 5.1, thus indicating that the results generalized from *trained* to *untrained* items.

The above-mentioned results were repeated in three other subjects. Although this study represents the first study demonstrating efficacy of the social skill approach with children, considerably more research is needed. One area of study involves the extent of generalization. That is, do the effects of skill training in unassertive children generalize beyond the analogue task and into their natural environments? The second question is: Can these results be repeated with a more disturbed patient population of children? Both questions await empirical study and confirmation of these initial findings.

Our second example of the single case experimental approach involves a multiple baseline analysis of social skills training in two chronic schizophrenics (Hersen & Bellack, 1976a). One of the patients was a 27-year-old, single, white male who was rather withdrawn, extremely anxious, avoided eye contact, and stuttered. A baseline analysis of this patient's responses to eight of the BAT scenes confirmed our initial evaluation and yielded the following targets for modification: eye contact, speech disruptions, appropriate smiles, compliance, and appropriate affect.

The procedures described in our first case example were generally followed here. However, skills training (instructions, feedback, and modeling) was applied to both positive and negative behaviors and was administered about five times weekly (30–90-min. sessions) over a 4-week period. Follow-up probes were obtained at 2-, 4-, 6-, and 8-week intervals. The results of this multiple baseline are presented in Fig. 5.3. Data indicate effectiveness of the social skill approach for all of the targeted behaviors. Overall assertiveness gradually increased over treatment. In addition, follow-ups show the durability of the treatment. Similar results were noted for the second schizophrenic patient so treated. However, these results lead to a number of questions: (1) Does training generalize from one set of items to another? (2) Does training generalize from one type of situation (i.e., the laboratory) to another? (3) How long do the effects of treatment persist? The present authors are

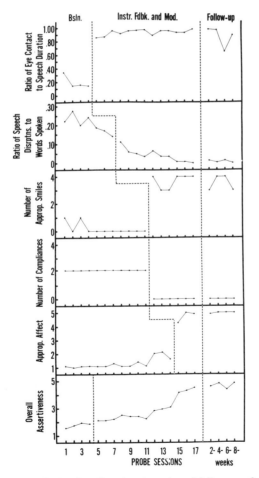

Fig. 5.3 Probe sessions during baseline, treatment, and follow-ups for Subject 2. Data are presented in blocks of eight scenes. (Reprinted with permission from: M. Hersen and A. S. Bellack: *Journal of Applied Behavior Analysis,* 9: 239, 1976.)

currently investigating these issues and, to date, have evidence confirming the first question.

Controlled Group Outcome Studies

The studies to be described in this section point toward the utility of the skills training approach. Indeed, in most of the studies the skills approach appears to be superior to both control conditions and to other treatments. However, the conclusions must be tempered inasmuch as treatments tend to be brief and follow-ups are generally not extensive. Let us now briefly review the evidence.

In an early study, Lazarus (1966) compared three different approaches for improving social and interpersonal problems in psychiatric outpatients. Patients in each of the following groups received a maximum of four 2-hour sessions: behavior rehearsal, non-directive psychotherapy, and direct advice. Lazarus was the therapist for each of the approaches and also rated improvement (behavior rehearsal-92%, direct advice-44%, non-directive psychotherapy-32%). However, considering the fact that Lazarus served both as therapist and rater, the possibility for bias cannot be discounted.

In a more recent and more elegantly controlled study, Goldsmith and McFall (1975) compared interpersonal skill training, a pseudotherapy control condition, and an assessment-only control using psychiatric inpatients as subjects. The skills group and pseudotherapy group each received three sessions of treatment. The skills approach was found to lead to significantly greater pre-post differences than the two control conditions on behavioral and self-report measures. Moreover, skills training resulted in generalization to a "real-life context."

In another study, Percell, Berwick, and Beigel (1974) compared group assertive training (using behavior rehearsal) and a "relationship-control" condition, with 24 psychiatric outpatients as the subjects. Each of the groups received eight sessions of treatment. The superiority of the assertive training group was evidenced by increased ratings of overall assertiveness, decreased anxiety scores, and increased self-acceptance scores. Based on these data, the experimenters concluded, " . . . that a behavior therapy, assertive training, is able to improve a client's self-concept and reduce his general level of distress as well as modify his social and interpersonal behavior" (Percell, Berwick, and Beigel, 1974, p. 504).

In an interesting study, using a complicated experimental design, Argyle, Bryant, and Trower (1974) also compared the social skills approach with more traditional psychotherapy. Pre-post evaluations indicate that both treatments led to improved social skill behavior. However, the psychotherapy patients had received twice as much treatment. More important was the fact that at the 1-year follow-up, therapeutic effects were better maintained by the group that had received social skills training.

Curran and Gilbert (1975) evaluated the relative efficacy of systematic desensitization and interpersonal skills training with "date anxious" college students. Both behavioral treatments were contrasted to a "minimal contact" control condition. Subjects in each of the two behavioral groups received eight 90-min. treatment sessions over a 9-week period. Self-report and behavioral measures of anxiety and social skill were obtained at the end of treatment and at the 6-month follow-up. The results showed that both of the behavioral groups evidenced significant improvement in anxiety over the control condition. However, only the interpersonal skills training group evidenced improvements in dating skill performance in the behavioral tests.

In summary, these and other studies indicate the promise of the social skill approach to treatment of interpersonal difficulties. However, as noted in the beginning of this section, further research in this area will be needed before conclusive statements can be made safely.

Summary

In this chapter we have traced the historical roots of the current impetus for social skills training. This impetus appears to stem from two directions: (1) the clinical work of Arnold Lazarus, Andrew Salter, and Joseph Wolpe, and (2) the studies by Edward Zigler relating psychiatric disorder to social competence. The various definitions of social skill have been presented and the methods for assessing social skill were outlined. Examples of self-report, motoric, and physiological measures were given.

We have also detailed the clinical applications of social skill treatment for anxiety-based disorders and skill deficit-based disorders. Experimental support for the skills approach was documented. Experimental studies representing analogue designs, single case designs, and group controlled comparisons were reviewed.

References

Argyle, M., Bryant, B., & Trower, P. Social skills training and psychotherapy. *Psychological Medicine*, 1974, *4*, 435–443.

Argyris, C. Explorations in interpersonal competence-I. *Journal of Applied Behavioral Science*, 1965, *1*, 58–83.

Argyris, C. Conditions for competence acquisition and therapy. *Journal of Applied Behavioral Science*, 1968, *4*, 147–177.

Arkowitz, H., Lichtenstein, E., McGovern, K., & Hines, P. The behavioral assessment of social competence in males. *Behavior Therapy*, 1975, *6*, 3–13.

Bernhardt, A. J., Hersen, M., & Barlow, D. H. Measurement and modification of spasmodic torticollis: An experimental analysis. *Behavior Therapy*, 1972, *3*, 294–297.

Borkovec, T. D., Stone, N. M., O'Brien, G. T., & Kaloupek, D. G. Evaluation of a clinically relevant target behavior for analog outcome research. *Behavior Therapy*, 1974, *5*, 503–513.

Bornstein, M. R., Bellack, A. S., & Hersen, M. Social skills training for unassertive children. *Journal of Applied Behavior Analysis,* in press.

Curran, J. P., & Gilbert, F. S. A test of the relative effectiveness of a systematic desensitization program and an interpersonal skills training program with date anxious subjects. *Behavior Therapy,* 1975, *6,* 510–521.

Edelstein, B., & Eisler, R. M. Effects of modeling and modeling with instructions and feedback on the behavioral components of social skills of a schizophrenic. *Behavior Therapy,* 1976, *7,* 382–389.

Eisler, R. M. Assertive training in the work situation. In J. D. Krumboltz & C. E. Thoresen (Eds.), *Counseling methods.* New York: Holt, Rinehart, & Winston, in press.

Eisler, R. M., & Hersen, M. Behavioral techniques in family-oriented crisis intervention. *Archives of General Psychiatry,* 1973, *28,* 111–116.

Eisler, R. M., Hersen, M., & Miller, P. M. Effects of modeling on components of assertive behavior. *Journal of Behavior Therapy and Experimental Psychiatry,* 1973, *4,* 1–6. (a)

Eisler, R. M., Hersen, M., & Miller, P. M. Shaping components of assertiveness with instructions and feedback. *American Journal of Psychiatry,* 1974, *131,* 1344–1347.

Eisler, R. M., Hersen, M., Miller, P. M., & Blanchard, E. B. Situational determinants of assertive behaviors. *Journal of Consulting and Clinical Psychology,* 1975, *43,* 330–340.

Eisler, R. M., Miller, P. M., & Hersen, M. Components of assertive behavior. *Journal of Clinical Psychology,* 1973, *29,* 295–299. (b)

Eisler, R. M., Miller, P. M., Hersen, M., & Alford, H. Effects of assertive training on marital interaction. *Archives of General Psychiatry,* 1974, *30,* 643–649.

Foy, D. W., Eisler, R. M., & Pinkston, S. G. Modeled assertion in a case of explosive rage. *Journal of Behavior Therapy and Experimental Psychiatry,* 1975, *6,* 135–137.

Frank, J. D. Therapeutic components of psychotherapy: A 25-year progress report of research. *Journal of Nervous and Mental Disease,* 1974, *159,* 325–342.

Frederiksen, L. W., Jenkins, J. O., Foy, D. W., & Eisler, R. M. Social skills training in the modification of abusive verbal outbursts in adults. *Journal of Applied Behavior Analysis,* 1976, *9,* 117–125.

Friedman, P. H. The effects of modeling and role-playing on assertive behavior. In R. D. Rubin, H. Fensterheim, A. A. Lazarus, & C. M. Franks (Eds.), *Advances in behavior therapy.* New York: Academic Press, 1971.

Gladwin, T. Social competence and clinical practice. *Psychiatry,* 1967, *30,* 30–43.

Goldsmith, J. B., & McFall, R. M. Development and evaluation of an interpersonal skill-training program for psychiatric inpatients. *Journal of Abnormal Psychology,* 1975, *84,* 51–58.

Goldstein, A. P., Martens, J., Hubben, J., van Belle, H. A., Shaaf, W., Wiersma, H., & Goedhart, A. The use of modeling to increase independent behaviour. *Behaviour Research and Therapy,* 1973, *11,* 31–42.

Gutride, M. E., Goldstein, A. P., & Hunter, G. F. The use of modeling and role playing to increase social interaction among asocial psychiatric patients. *Journal of Consulting and Clinical Psychology,* 1973, *40,* 408–415.

Hersen, M., & Bellack, A. S. A multiple baseline analysis of social skills training in chronic schizophrenics. *Journal of Applied Behavior Analysis,* 1976, *9,* 239–245. (a)

Hersen, M., & Bellack, A. S. Social skills training for chronic psychiatric patients: Rationale, research findings, and future directions. *Comprehensive Psychiatry,* 1976, *17,* 559–580. (b)

Hersen, M., & Bellack, A. S. Assessment of social skills. In A. R. Ciminero, K. S. Calhoun, & H. E. Adams (Eds.), *Handbook for behavioral assessment.* New York: John Wiley & Sons, 1977.

Hersen, M., Eisler, R. M., & Miller, P. M. Development of assertive responses: Clinical, measurement, and research considerations. *Behaviour Research and Therapy,* 1973, *11,* 505–521. (a)

Hersen, M., Eisler, R. M., & Miller, P. M. An experimental analysis of generalization in assertive training. *Behaviour Research and Therapy,* 1974, *12,* 295–310.

Hersen, M., Eisler, R. M., Miller, P. M., Johnson, M. B., & Pinkston, S. G. Effects of practice, instructions, and modeling on components of assertive behavior. *Behaviour Research and Therapy,* 1973, *11,* 443–451. (b)

Hersen, M., Gullick, E. J., Matherne, P. M., & Harbert, T. L. Instructions and reinforcement in the modification of a conversion reaction. *Psychological Reports,* 1972, *31,* 719–722.

Hersen, M., Turner, S. M., Edelstein, B. A., & Pinkston, S. G. Effects of phenothiazines and social skills training in a withdrawn schizophrenic. *Journal of Clinical Psychology*, 1975, *31*, 588-594.

Kagan, J., & Moss, H. A. *Birth to maturity; A study in psychological development*. New York: John Wiley and Sons, 1962.

Kallman, W. M., Hersen, M., & O'Toole, D. H. The use of social reinforcement in a case of conversion reaction. *Behavior Therapy*, 1975, *6*, 411-413.

Kazdin, A. E. Effects of covert modeling and model reinforcement on assertive behavior. *Journal of Abnormal Psychology*, 1974, *83*, 240-252.

Lazarus, A. A. Behaviour rehearsal vs. non-directive therapy vs. advice in effecting behaviour change. *Behaviour Research and Therapy*, 1966, *4*, 209-212.

Lazarus, A. A. *Behavior therapy and beyond*. New York: McGraw-Hill, 1971.

Lewinsohn, P. M. The behavioral study and treatment of depression. In M. Hersen, R. M. Eisler, & P. M. Miller (Eds.), *Progress in behavior modification: Volume 1*. New York: Academic Press, 1975.

Lewinsohn, P. M., & Atwood, G. E. Depression: A clinical-research approach. *Psychotherapy: Theory, Research and Practice*, 1969, *6*, 166-171.

Lewinsohn, P. M., & Shaffer, M. The use of home observations as an integral part of the treatment of depression: Preliminary report and case studies. *Journal of Consulting and Clinical Psychology*, 1971, *37*, 87-94.

Libet, J. M., & Lewinsohn, P. M. Concept of social skill with special reference to the behavior of depressed persons. *Journal of Consulting and Clinical Psychology*, 1973, *40*, 304-312.

McFall, R. M., & Lillesand, D. B. Behavior rehearsal with modeling and coaching in assertion training. *Journal of Abnormal Psychology*, 1971, *77*, 313-323.

McFall, R. M., & Marston, A. R. An experimental investigation of behavior rehearsal in assertive training. *Journal of Abnormal Psychology*, 1970, *76*, 295-303.

McFall, R. M., & Twentyman, C. T. Four experiments on the relative contributions of rehearsal, modeling, and coaching to assertion training. *Journal of Abnormal Psychology*, 1973, *81*, 199-218.

Percell, L. P., Berwick, P. T., & Beigel, A. The effects of assertive training on self-concept and anxiety. *Archives of General Psychiatry*, 1974, *31*, 502-504.

Phillips, L., & Zigler, E. Social competence: The action-thought parameter and vicariousness in normal and pathological behaviors. *Journal of Abnormal and Social Psychology*, 1961, *63*, 137-146.

Piaget, G. W., & Lazarus, A. A. The use of rehearsal desensitization. *Psychotherapy: Theory, Research and Practice*, 1969, *6*, 264-266.

Rathus, S. A. Instigation of assertive behavior through videotape-mediated assertive models and directed practice. *Behaviour Research and Therapy*, 1973, *11*, 57-65.

Rehm, L. P., & Marston, A. R. Reduction of social anxiety through modification of self-reinforcement: An instigation therapy technique. *Journal of Consulting and Clinical Psychology*, 1968, *32*, 565-574.

Salter, A. *Conditioned reflex therapy*. New York: Capricorn, 1949.

Twentyman, C. T., & McFall, R. M. Behavioral training of social skills in shy males. *Journal of Consulting and Clinical Psychology*, 1975, *43*, 384-395.

Weissman, M. M., Paykel, E. S., & Klerman, G. L. The depressed woman as mother. *Social Psychiatry*, 1972, *7*, 98-108.

Weissman, M. M., Paykel, E. S., Siegel, R., & Klerman, G. L. The social role performance of depressed women: Comparisons with a normal group. *American Journal of Orthopsychiatry*. 1971, *41*, 390-405.

Wolpe, J. *Psychotherapy by reciprocal inhibition*. Stanford, Calif.: Stanford University Press, 1958.

Wolpe, J. *The practice of behavior therapy*. New York: Pergamon Press, 1969.

Wolpe, J. Supervision transcript: V — Mainly about assertive training. *Journal of Behavior Therapy and Experimental Psychiatry*, 1973, *4*, 141-148.

Wolpe, J., & Lazarus, A. A. *Behavior therapy techniques*. New York: Pergamon Press, 1966.

Zigler, E., & Levine, J. Premorbid adjustment and paranoid-nonparanoid status in schizophrenics. *Journal of Abnormal Psychology*, 1973, *82*, 189-199.

Zigler, E., & Phillips, L. Social effectiveness and symptomatic behaviors. *Journal of Abnormal and Social Psychology*, 1960, *61*, 231-238.

6

Operant approaches with children

Introduction

The behavioral revolution has come closest to fruition in the application of operant conditioning techniques with children. The use of operant techniques is now relatively commonplace in institutions for the mentally retarded, in psychiatric hospitals, in classrooms, and in mental health clinics. The behavior disorders of children clearly have been more responsive to behavioral interventions than to any other form of treatment (Levitt, 1963; O'Leary, Turkewitz, & Taffel, 1973; Patterson, 1974).

The range of success has been as extensive as the magnitude of the changes obtained. At one extreme, children previously considered unreachable (e.g., those with childhood schizophrenia) have been socialized with intensive conditioning programs. At the other end of the spectrum, infants have been quickly taught to stop making discrete responses (e.g., chronic vomiting that is life threatening) and have been toilet trained in periods as brief as 1 day. Considerable success has also been achieved in teaching parents and teachers to employ operant procedures. This training has been designed not only to modify current dysfunctions in the home and classroom, but to prevent future disturbance by creating effective living and learning environments.

Aside from the power of operant conditioning procedures per se, there are two factors that have led to their great success in work with children. *First,* with the exception of childhood schizophrenia, the behavioral dysfunctions of children are fairly resilient. Children have simply not lived long enough to have developed highly overlearned responses with a broad network of compensating and maintaining factors. *Second,* adults (e.g., teachers and parents) control many of the most potent reinforcers for children: attention and approval, food, money, and access to activities such as television. Thus, in contrast to many potential but in practice unworkable interventions with adults, operant procedures can be readily applied with children.

The literature on operant interventions with children is more extensive than for any other topic covered in this book. One of us counted 14 professional-level books and as many non-professional how-to-do-it books on his bookshelf. Therefore, our approach to this chapter will differ somewhat from that of the other chapters. Rather than presenting what by necessity would have to be a scant review of all areas of application, we will describe major techniques in a general way and provide a few representative examples.

The first section will describe procedures for removing behavioral deficits: primarily positive reinforcement. The second section, on behavioral excesses, will consider extinction procedures and punishment. We will then consider a broad-band approach encompassing a variety of operant procedures: the token economy. The fourth section will focus on the role of parents in behavioral interventions. The final section pertains to one of the most critical issues facing behavior modifiers: the ethical and legal considerations attendant upon "control" of children.

Behavioral Deficits

Behavioral deficits comprise any response that occurs at insufficient rate or strength, that has less than adequate form, or that fails to occur at appropriate times (see Chapter 1). Many dysfunctions can be clearly conceptualized as deficits. Asocialized child schizophrenics are deficient in speech (they often do not speak coherently at all) and they often fail to imitate (model) adults as much as "normal" children. Academic failures of children can often be caused by skill deficiencies such as reading problems. In other cases, deficits can be masked by more obvious and aversive behavioral excesses. Thus, truancy can be viewed as a low rate of school attendance rather than a high rate of absence. Children who are disruptive and often out of their seats in the classroom can be defined as deficient in time spent on task (i.e., paying attention) and in time spent in seat. This differentiation is more than terminological. As will be seen in this and the subsequent section, the intervention of choice will vary considerably as a function of how the target behavior is defined.

There are innumerable potential reasons for behavioral deficits. However, most deficits can be categorized according to three major classes or factors. *First,* the environment might not provide adequate prompts (S^Ds) for the child to emit a response already in his repertoire. *Second,* a response in the repertoire might be prompted, but fails to appear because its occurrence is not maintained by reinforcement. *Third,* the response simply might not be in the child's repertoire (i.e., a skill deficit). Frequently, two or all three of these factors appear in combination.

Prompting

Problems that can be ascribed solely to insufficient prompts are the simplest to modify. The basic remediation strategy involves supplying the child with a cue for appropriate behavior. Krumboltz and Krumboltz (1972) provide several clear examples of simple, direct prompting. In one case, a 15-year-old boy ignored his parents' guests at a party. When questioned about his apparent rudeness, he stated that he thought no conversation was appropriate as he was not attending the party. The parents then explained that a polite "Hello" was appropriate, and he easily complied at their next party. The effectiveness of this verbal cue reflects a common source of parent-child conflict. Adults often presume that children know quite a bit more about their environment and the way in which they are expected to behave than they actually do know. In many instances adults function as if children were able to read their minds (e.g., "He should know I'm busy and can't be interrupted," or "She should have known I wanted her to come straight home from school"). However, childhood is a period of socialization in which children must learn where and when different behaviors are appropriate. Provision of informative prompts serves a necessary educative function as well as structuring the environment so that the child knows the response that is required.

Children do not anticipate future events and contingencies as well as adults. Time sense, ability to delay gratification, etc. develop slowly throughout childhood. Time cues are often helpful in preparing the child for a particular event or forewarning him of an impending response requirement. "Dinner will be ready in 5 minutes," or "You may watch television for 15 more minutes and then it will be time for bed," are much more apt to result in appropriate cooperative responses than will requests for immediate interruption of ongoing activities or retrospective punishment for failure to judge time accurately. Similarly, cooperation can often be secured by structuring the child's activities around time constraints. Bedtime can be set on the hour or half hour rather than in the middle of a television program. The child can be asked to help set the table or simply to stay at home rather than going out to play 15 minutes before dinner.

Physical prompts are sometimes helpful in addition to or in lieu of verbal prompts. Consider the frequent scene of a child running up and down the aisles of a toy store, touching and requesting every toy in sight. By specifying limits (e.g., "We are looking for a water pistol.") and holding the child's hand or walking with a hand on his shoulder, considerable control can be maintained. Both cues structure the situation; the physical contact is a prompt for walking slowly and staying near the parent.

One of the most effective forms of prompting is the use of consistent rules (Smith & Smith, 1964). The term rule is a colloquial expression for contingency. By making the child aware of what is expected of him, developing a consistent pattern of responses to his behavior as well as consistent limits, he is much more likely to make appropriate responses. (We will consider the component of rules involving consequences below.) One of us recently worked with the parents of Bobby, a 4-year-old boy who was described as "impossible to manage and a consistent discipline problem." The parents also reported that he was unresponsive to punishment and would never cooperate. After careful interviewing and review of a 2-week monitoring diary kept by the parents, the primary areas of conflict were identified as dinner time and bedtime. These two periods overlapped and usually dragged on from 6:30–10:00 P.M. each evening. The family began dinner at 6:30 and Bobby was taken up for a bath and bed as soon as he finished eating. During dinner he was constantly in and out of his chair, under the table, etc., and he rarely finished in less than $1\frac{1}{2}$ hours. This behavior naturally generated considerable conflict, including threats and pleading by the parents. The conflict then carried over to bath and bedtime, with the parents often spanking him and screaming at him until he finally fell asleep (probably from exhaustion). Our analysis suggested that the dinner behavior was maintained as it delayed bedtime. The intervention was quite simple and involved establishment of an appropriate set of rules. Bobby was told that dinner would begin at 5:30 and that he would have up to 30 min. to eat. At that time (or when he finished) his plate would be removed and he would be allowed to play or watch television until 7:00. He would then be bathed and put to bed, and one of the parents would read him a story. The intervention was totally effective within 3 days. By structuring the environment in a manner appropriate for both Bobby *and* his parents, cooperative behavior was easily established and maintained. (This procedure employed playtime and reading as sources of positive reinforcement for Bobby. However, the reinforcement was not contingent upon any response, and was, therefore, secondary to the rule and time change.)

When prompts are first established they should be used frequently and as closely as possible to the time when the behavior is desired. Thus, in the case of Bobby, the parents announced the rule each evening just before dinner. Once the new response is established, the prompt can be *faded* out (Gelfand & Hartmann, 1975). That is, it is gradually presented with decreased frequency such as every third night for 1 week, then once per week for 1 month, and then eliminated entirely as long as the response is maintained at an appropriate rate or form. In addition, as the prompt is designed to be of help to the child, it should be presented with a positive voice tone rather than as a threat. In many instances it is appropriate (and helpful) to work out a rule or structure jointly with the child. For example, Bobby might have preferred to watch television from 5:30–6:00 and have 1/2 hour less of playtime after dinner.

Positive Reinforcement

Prompting is rarely effective by itself when appropriate responses do not lead to some reinforcement or when the child lacks the skill to make the desired response (O'Leary & O'Leary, 1976). In either of those instances, prompting is used in conjunction with positive reinforcement. Positive reinforcement is the intervention of choice wherever it promises to be effective. In addition to being what is probably the most powerful behavior change technique available, it also lacks many of the aversive ramifications and ethical constraints associated with extinction and punishment procedures. It is generally recommended that positive reinforcement be included either as primary intervention or as a supplemental procedure in all operant programs.

In its basic form, positive reinforcement procedures follow what has frequently been referred to as "Grandma's Rule" to reflect the common sense simplicity of the approach (Becker, 1971). The child is first given a prompt specifying the contingency and is reinforced immediately (or as soon as possible) after performing the response. For example, "You may watch television after you finish your homework," or "You will receive your allowance if you walk the dog every day this week." Most clinical and classroom applications involve elaborations of this "if-then" contingent relationship.

One of the most critical factors is the selection of an appropriate reinforcer. There are four basic classes of reinforcement: primary reinforcers (food, drink), social reinforcers (e.g., attention and approval), desired activities, and valued concrete materials (e.g., money, toys). In addition, as will be discussed in the section on token economies, any stimulus (e.g., token, star, point) that represents one of the above reinforcers can also be positively reinforcing. In order to be effective, a "reinforcer" must, in fact, be reinforcing to the individual child. This was made clear to one of our graduate students who attempted to use M&M's to reinforce a child who was allergic to chocolate. The reinforcing value of any stimulus can rarely (if ever) be determined on an ipso facto basis. The child should be carefully observed and significant adults should be interviewed to determine appropriate reinforcers.

There are a number of other guidelines which we will describe briefly at this point. (1) The reinforcer should not be available to the child noncontingently either from the therapist or from other sources. Consider offering a small allowance to an adolescent who has a well-paying part-time job! (2) When the reinforcer must be administered at a high rate, as when reinforcing language development, it should be available in small quantities to avoid satiation. Hence the popularity of M&M's and corn flakes rather than candy bars. (3) At the beginning of any program, reinforcement should be administered immediately after an acceptable response. The schedule of reinforcement can then be thinned over time such that increasing levels or rates of performance are required and the delay between the response and reinforcement is increased. (4) If the child is not capable of making a completely adequate response at first, the response should be shaped by reinforcing successive approximations to the criterion level. (5) When reinforcement is to be administered over extended periods of time, several different reinforcers should be offered so as to insure that the child will always find at least one item sufficiently motivating. This procedure has been referred to as a "Reinforcement Menu" (Homme, Csanyi, Gonzales, & Rechs, 1970) and is typified by most token economies.

Social reinforcers are among the most broadly applicable and desirable forms of reinforcement. Social stimuli such as attention, affection, and approval develop powerful reinforcing value for most children because of the close association of positive social interaction with nourishment, safety, and physical comfort during infancy and early childhood (Lovaas & Newsom, 1976). While the strength of social reinforcement from adults decreases in adolescence, it is extremely powerful for most younger children. It also has the advantage of being a "natural" source of reinforcement (Baer & Wolf, 1970; O'Leary, Poulos, & Devine, 1972). In contrast to such "extrinsic" reinforcers as money and toys, approval and attention are administered regularly (albeit not always contingently) in the natural environment. Thus, it is easier to maintain their use for extended periods of time and they avoid many of the negative social value implications of extrinsic reinforcement (see section on ethical issues below).

An interesting example of the use of social reinforcement was reported by Buell, Stoddard, Harris, and Baer (1968). The subject was Polly, a 3-year-old girl attending a nursery school. Polly was brought to the attention of Buell et al. because she failed to interact appropriately with peers and she engaged in a variety of immature behaviors. She rarely played with other children in school, preferring instead to "hang on teacher's coattails" and she often used baby talk rather than age-appropriate speech. The behavior selected as a target was utilization of outdoor play equipment. At the time of referral, Polly used the equipment very infrequently. Buell et al. hypothesized that increased play with the equipment would result in greater contact with other children, and thus increase social interaction.

The experimental design and results are portrayed graphically in Fig. 6.1. The baseline period lasted 5 days, during which time teachers interacted with Polly in their characteristic manner. Despite periodic requests for Polly to use the play equipment, her rate of use was almost zero. The next phase involved reinforcement and priming for play on the equipment. *Priming* is a form of prompting in which the individual is induced to engage in the initial steps of a response sequence. It is employed in situations (as with Polly) in which the initial rate of a target response is zero or very low (as little or no reinforcement would otherwise be received). In the case of Polly, teachers physically placed her on a piece of equipment and held her there for 30 sec. Reinforcement consisted of staying nearby, touching her, giving verbal approval, and talking about the play for as long as she remained on the equipment. This phase lasted for 9 days and resulted in a substantial increase in time spent on equipment.

Reinforcement was then continued while priming was terminated. After an initial decrease, rate of play again rose to a high level. The controlling effect of social reinforcement was demonstrated by subse-

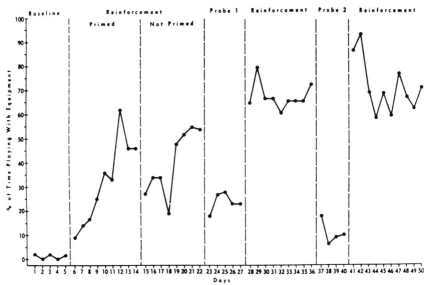

Fig. 6.1 The development of outdoor equipment use by priming and reinforcement procedures, probed by noncontingent reinforcement. (Reprinted with permission from: J. Buell, P. Stoddard, F. R. Harris, and D. M. Baer: *Journal of Applied Behavior Analysis*, 1: 167, 1968.)

quent phases in which reinforcement was withdrawn (Probe 1 and Probe 2) and reinstated. Overall, rate of play increased from 2% during baseline to 70% during the final reinforcement phase.

As hypothesized, appropriate interactions with other children increased during the course of treatment. Polly engaged in age-appropriate levels of physical contact, conversation, and cooperative play with other children by the end of the intervention. In addition, the use of baby talk and other immature behaviors disappeared. This pattern of changes represents what Baer and Wolf (1970) have referred to as "trapping." The child is first engaged in a situation through an artificial contingency. Natural reinforcers (e.g., peer contact) then take over and maintain the new behavior. The artificial reinforcement can then be removed or maintained on a very thin schedule. The trapping strategy, obviously fosters maintenance and generalization and should be considered whenever possible.

Social reinforcement has also been used effectively with children suffering from severe dysfunctions. Hall and Broden (1967) described the successful treatment of three children with organic brain injuries. The third child was a 9-year-old boy with perceptual and motor problems and speech difficulties. He was also impulsive and had frequent temper tantrums. The target behavior (selected by teacher request) was social activity with other children; he generally remained isolated or demanded teacher attention. Treatment involved teacher approval, conversation, and physical proximity contingent upon social play with peers. Treatment was conducted in an ABAB format. Social play increased from an average rate of 16.8% in baseline to 51.2% during the first treatment phase. The rate fell to 11.9% during the withdrawal phase and quickly returned to 57.4% when reinforcement was reinstated. A 3-month follow-up was conducted, by which time the child had been transferred to a different school. Nevertheless, he was observed to engage in social play at a rate of 65.7% during recess period. Not only was treatment effective but the changes maintained and generalized to a new environment. It seems likely that the trapping phenomenon occurred with this child as it did with the case of Polly.

As stated above, most children learn to value social attention (and consequently to model adult behavior) naturally during early childhood. This frequently does not take place for psychotic and severely mentally retarded children. Intense conditioning procedures must be employed to establish social control over their behavior. Primary reinforcers, often facilitated by mild deprivation before training sessions, are typically the only source of positive control which is effective with these children (Risley & Wolf, 1967). Training programs based on the application of contingent food reinforcement have been developed to teach fundamental self-help skills such as toilet training (Hundziak, Maurer, & Watson, 1965), and social imitation (Lovaas, Freitas, Nelson, & Whalen, 1967).

The work conducted by O. I. Lovaas and his colleagues at U.C.L.A. provides a classic model of the intensive shaping and prompting required in work with psychotic children. Lovaas et al. (1967) described a procedure for developing imitative behavior (i.e., teaching children to imitate adults). Children were reinforced with small bits of food (Sugar Flakes) for imitating (or approximating) therapist performance on a series of tasks ranging from playing with toys to more complex responses. "The training procedure relied very heavily on initial prompting and continuous food reinforcement for correct behavior, and subsequent fading of prompts and shifts to partial reinforcement. . . . *E* (the attending adult) would engage in a particular behavior (the training or discriminative stimulus). If the child did not exhibit (match) this behavior within 5 sec. *E* would prompt the response. In other words, *E* would do whatever was necessary and convenient for the child to complete the response. Most often, prompts consisted of physically moving the child through the desired behavior. For example, if the adult demonstrated the placement of a ball in a cup and the child failed to imitate this behavior upon its first presentation, *E* would take the child's hand with the ball and move it toward the cup, and by releasing his grip on the child's hand, cause the ball to fall within the cup. On subsequent trials, *E* would gradually fade the prompt. . . . For example, *E* might gradually lessen his hold on the child's hand, and then merely touch the child's hand, then his elbow, then his shoulder, and finally only emit the behavior to be imitated" (Lovaas et al., 1967, pp. 173–174). Once the response was established, reinforcement was also faded for responses on which the child required prompting. After simple imitation was established, training was shifted to imitation of more complex responses including self-help skills, game playing, appropriate sex-role behavior, drawing and printing, and non-verbal components of communication.

It should be pointed out that such training required thousands of trials and the children never reached totally "normal" levels of functioning. However, this pioneering work underscores two critical issues. *First,* no child (or adult) should be considered untreatable. Given adequate resources and appropriate interventions, even grossly disturbed individuals can be given a better, if not normal, life. *Second,* operant techniques (in this case positive reinforcement and shaping) have sufficient power to modify even the most dysfunctional behavior if they are used in a systematic, contingent manner.

Material and activity reinforcers have been used most frequently in the context of token reinforcement systems. Administering a material reinforcer contingent on each and every performance of a target response would be both expensive and inconvenient. For example, even if a classroom teacher could give a child a toy whenever he attended to his work, receipt of the toy would undoubtedly distract him from on-task behavior. Similarly, many activities used as reinforcers (e.g., going on trips, watching favored television shows) are not available at the times when target responses are performed. In the typical token system, the child receives a token, point, star, etc. contingent upon some response and "buys" the material reinforcer or activity after he has sufficient earnings. Comprehensive token systems will be discussed in a subsequent section. We will, however, describe two examples of circumscribed procedures here.

Walker and Buckley (1968) employed material reinforcers with Phillip, a 9-year-old boy who exhibited low rates of attending behavior in the classroom. Attempts to alter the behavior in the classroom were unsuccessful due to the large number of distracting stimuli in the complex classroom environment. Therefore, treatment was conducted in a small room for 40 min. a day. Phillip was presented with programmed learning material on arithmetic. After a stable baseline of on-task behavior was established, Phillip was told that he would hear a click, representing a point, after a brief period during which he remained on task. If he earned 160 points during the session, he would receive a model. Duration of attending behavior necessary to earn points was increased gradually over sessions from 30 sec. to 60, 120, 240, 480, and finally 600 sec. Points were administered at the rate of 1 per 30 sec.; thus, he eventually received 20 points for meeting the 600-sec. criterion. Percentage of attending behavior rose from 33% during baseline to 93% during reinforcement and fell to 44% during a subsequent extinction phase. Phillip was then returned to his classroom and a generalization program was initiated. A recording form was placed on his desk each day, and his teacher reinforced him by administering points contingent on his attending for variable periods averaging 30 min. (a variable-interval schedule). Attending behavior rapidly returned to levels of 90%.

Barrish, Saunders, and Wolf (1969) employed a variety of reinforcers in a system labeled the "Good Behavior Game." The subjects were 24 children in a fourth grade classroom. Rather than applying individual contingencies to each child, Barrish et al. employed group contingencies. That is, rules were established for the entire class and the behavior of individual children resulted in group-wide consequences. The class was first divided into two teams and the system was explained as a game in which the teams would compete each day. The rules, which were designed to reduce out-of-seat and talking-out behavior, were as follows.:

"(1) No one was to be out of his seat without permission. . . . Permission could be obtained only by raising the hand and being called on by the teacher.
(2) No one was to sit on his desk or on any of his neighbors's desks.
(3) No one was to get out of his seat to move his desk or scoot (sic) his desk.
(4) No one was to get out of his seat to talk to a neighbor. This also

meant there was to be no leaning forward out of a seat to whisper.

(5) No one was to get out of his seat to go to the chalkboard (except to sign out for the restroom), pencil sharpener, waste basket, drinking fountain, sink, or to the teacher without permission.

(6) When the teacher was seated at her desk during study time, students could come to her desk one at a time if they had a question.

(7) No one was to talk without permission. Permission could be obtained again only by raising the hand and being called on by the teacher.

(8) No one was to talk while raising his hand.

(9) No one was to talk or whisper to his neighbors.

(10) No one was to call out the teacher's name unless he had permission to answer.

(11) No one was to make vocal noises" (pp. 120–121).

A scorecard was maintained on the chalkboard. Whenever a child was observed violating the rules, his team received a point. The team with the fewest points each day won a variety of reinforcers including: privilege to wear a victory tag, stars next to each child's name on a chart, lining up first for lunch, and a 30-min. free time period during which special projects were completed. If both teams received fewer than five points, all children shared in the reinforcement. The effectiveness of the game in controlling disruptive behavior was assessed by implementing it in a multiple baseline fashion across mathematics and reading periods as well as by a withdrawal during mathematics. The design and results are presented in Fig. 6.2.

Baselines were first established in both periods for the two target behaviors: talking-out and out-of-seat. The game was then administered during mathematics only, and the two behaviors declined from averages of 96% and 82% to 19% and 9%, respectively. No change occurred during reading. In the next phase, the game was discontinued during mathematics and was applied during reading. As expected, disruption dropped sharply in reading and returned to baseline during mathematics. In the fourth phase, the game was reinstituted, with dramatic effects, during the mathematics period. Throughout the study both teams "won" 82% of the time when the game was in effect.

This study has several important and practical implications for behavior control in the classroom. The procedure was highly effective and demonstrates that class-wide management can be achieved with positive consequences. The game employed reinforcers that were natural to the classroom and provides an example of a system that is both inexpensive and designed to facilitate maintenance. Finally, by applying group-wide contingencies, it was relatively easy for the teacher to implement the procedure without disturbing her teaching activities. On the other hand, some caution is advised in the use of group contingencies. Two children in the class were not responsive to the program. They had to be removed from the system so that their teams were not continually

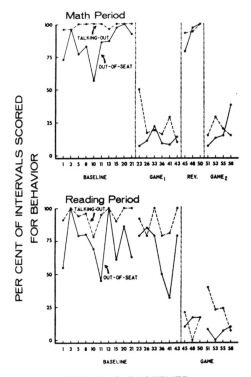

Fig. 6.2 Percent of 1-min. intervals scored by an observer as containing talking-out and out-of-seat behaviors occurring in a classroom of 24 fourth-grade school children during math and reading periods. In the baseline conditions the teacher attempted to manage the disruptive classroom behavior in her usual manner. During the game conditions out-of seat and talking-out responses by a student resulted in a possible loss of privileges for the student and his team. (Reprinted with permission from: H. H. Barrish, M. Saunders, and M. M. Wolf: *Journal of Applied Behavior Analysis*, 2: 119, 1969.)

punished for their disruption. While it was not reported by Barrish et al., children in other group programs have been observed to chastise and threaten one another for rule violations (see Axelrod, 1973). Any such side effects would have serious negative implications for continued use of the program. Either termination or major revision would be necessary.

This section has described interventions in which positive reinforcement has been the sole form of treatment. Subsequent sections will consider the use of positive reinforcement in token economies, in parent-managed programs, and in conjunction with other techniques.

Behavioral Excesses

Behavioral excesses are responses that occur at inappropriately high rates, with too great intensity, or that occur at inappropriate times (including responses which should not occur at all). Examples include the self-abusive responses of psychotic children, physical aggression, stealing, and disruptive behavior in the classroom such as distracting peers and hyperactivity. As with behavioral deficits, there are numerous possible reasons for excesses. One major category consists of highly overlearned classically conditioned responses such as tics, fear, or anxiety. The most frequently employed interventions for reducing children's anxiety are systematic desensitization and modeling procedures. The reader is referred back to Chapters 2 and 3, respectively, for a discussion of these procedures.

The second major category entails operant responses that are maintained by reinforcement. In some cases, children have appropriate responses in their repertoire, but inappropriate responses require less effort or result in greater reinforcement. For example, it has frequently been shown that negative forms of attention such as shouting and threats can maintain disruptive behavior when cooperative behavior is not reinforced with positive attention (O'Leary, Kaufman, Kass, & Drabman, 1970; Thomas, Becker, & Armstrong, 1968). In other cases, the child does not have a particular appropriate response in his repertoire and has simply learned to perform an inappropriate response. A third subcategory involves situations in which the child has not learned to modulate what is otherwise an appropriate response. Thus, a response might be performed at the wrong time, in the wrong place, or too powerfully. Running, shouting, and playful wrestling are often appropriate in the schoolyard, but are considered excesses when performed by a hyperactive child in the classroom, or when the wrestling causes physical injury.

The two primary strategies for reducing behavioral excesses are extinction (which is often paired with positive reinforcement for appropriate responses) and punishment. We will describe the two approaches in sequence.

Extinction

Extinction is a straightforward procedure in which the reinforcement maintaining the inappropriate response is withheld. As the child continues to perform the response without receiving reinforcement, the response strength gradually weakens until the response ceases to occur at all. Extinction is most effective with relatively new responses and with those maintained on a very rich reinforcement schedule. Responses maintained on thin or very intermittent schedules are highly resistant to extinction. A functional analysis of the behavior is absolutely critical when using extinction. If the actual maintaining factor is not identified, the response will continue to be reinforced and extinction will not occur. In addition, the reinforcement must be totally eliminated. If the response is reinforced even intermittently, there is a possibility that it will be established more strongly.

There are also a number of limitations and undesirable concomitants of extinction procedures which must be considered before beginning an extinction program. *First,* extinction works gradually. It is often not the treatment of choice when the target response is harmful to the child or others (e.g., self-injurious behavior) or when it cannot be tolerated by the environment (e.g., as with stealing or operant vomiting). In that regard, the early stages of extinction procedures often result in a burst of higher frequency responding and the latter stages are accompanied by a temporary recovery of the response (spontaneous recovery). *Second,* adults responsible for administering extinction procedures (parents, teachers, nurses) often find it exceedingly difficult to ignore aversive behavior. Imagine enduring the seemingly endless tantrums of a 5-year-old child. *Third,* while extinction is not usually considered to be an aversive procedure, many children do experience it as aversive and respond with negativism and hostility. Our own clinical experience suggests that this reaction is more frequent when the target response has a long history and when the child does not have an alternative response with which to secure positive reinforcement. Therefore, it is desirable to provide positive reinforcement for alternative appropriate responses whenever possible (see below).

The effects of extinction can be clearly seen in the withdrawal phase (second A phase) of most studies on positive reinforcement employing ABAB designs (e.g., Barrish et al., 1969; Walker & Buckley, 1968). Two illustrative examples of the use of extinction alone were reported by Hart, Allen, Buell, Harris, and Wolf (1964). The subjects were two male nursery school children who exhibited inappropriately high rates of operant crying. Hart et al. distinguished between two forms of crying: respondent and operant. The former is an appropriate classically conditioned response to pain or stress. Operant crying, on the other hand, is not a response to an aversive experience but is maintained by environmental consequences: primarily adult attention. The two children in this study exhibited operant crying episodes at rates between 5 and 10 times per morning. Treatment for both children was conducted in ABAB fashion. B phases consisted of teachers' ignoring all instances of operant crying, including walking away if approached by the child. In both cases crying dropped to less than two episodes per day within 5 days, returned to baseline levels during the withdrawal phase, and dropped to almost zero after extinction was reinstituted.

Some of the difficulties associated with extinction procedures are demonstrated in a study by Madsen, Becker, and Thomas (1968). We will consider two of their subjects, Cliff and Frank, who were in the same second grade class. Both boys had a record of disruptive behaviors in school including lack of response to teachers, out-of-seat behavior, and annoying other children. Cliff and Frank were observed for 20 min. per day, 3 days each week during the study. Target behaviors consisted of a variety of inappropriate responses including: making noises, motor responses (such as getting out of seat, running in the room), disturbance of other children or their property, and disobeying teachers or being off task. The experimental phases and results are presented in Fig. 6.3. During the baseline assessment the teacher attempted to control the children in her usual manner, which emphasized disapproval and criticism for inappropriate behavior. During the first intervention phase, she established a series of rules governing behavior. No consequences were provided during this phase. In the next phase, rules were repeated and the teacher attempted to ignore all disruptive behavior (extinction). In the fourth phase, social reinforcement (praise) was added to rules and ignoring. The fifth phase involved a return to baseline and was followed by reinstatement of rules, praise, and ignoring.

The introduction of rules had a minimal effect on the children's behavior. The addition of ignoring had the paradoxical effect of increasing the rate of inappropriate behavior. The teacher reported this phase of the procedure to be very unpleasant, and despite receiving training by Madsen et al. she was unable to totally ignore the boys' disruptions. Her rate of disapproval responses decreased from one per minute in previous phases to an average of three in 4 min. While this difficulty limits the conclusions that may be reached about extinction effects, it does reflect some of the limitations associated with extinction programs.

The rate of inappropriate behavior dropped sharply when praise was added to rules and ignoring. The controlling effect of this combined program is shown by the increase of disruption during the return to

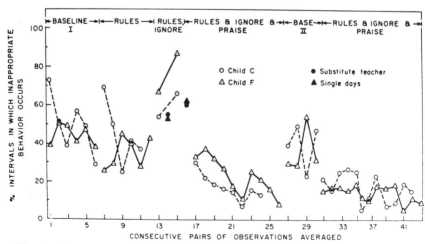

Fig. 6.3 Inappropriate behavior of two problem children in Classroom A as a function of experimental conditions. (Reprinted with permission from: C. H. Madsen, Jr., W. C. Becker, and D. R. Thomas: *Journal of Applied Behavior Analysis*, 1: 139, 1968.)

baseline and subsequent decrease when the program was reinstituted. The combination of extinction of a target behavior while simultaneously providing positive reinforcement of an alternative (usually incompatible) desired response is a form of Differential Reinforcement of Other schedule (DRO). In laboratory work, DRO implies reinforcement of *any* response other than the target. However, the customary clinical-educational applications focus on increasing particular appropriate responses. As stated above, extinction is characteristically combined with DRO.

Of all the behaviors which behavior therapists have been called upon to modify, self-injurious responses are among the most dangerous and most distressing to the environment. This response pattern includes severe face slapping, head banging, eye gouging, self-biting and scratching, etc. It is frequently seen in psychotic and severely retarded children. These children cause so much damage to themselves that they often must be placed in restraints such as football helmets, padded arm splints, etc. Two learning hypotheses have been offered to account for this behavior (Bachman, 1972; Lovaas & Newsom, 1976). Both hypotheses are based on the assumption that these children are unable to find appropriate responses to secure adequate stimulation and reinforcement in the environment. In one case, the self-injurious behavior is thought to be maintained by social reinforcement attendant upon the behavior. The second possibility is that the behavior is self-stimulatory and functions to avoid aversive stimulation from the environment or compensates for an insufficiency of environmental stimuli. It is possible that the two sources of response maintenance accurately explain the behavior of different children or that one (or both) are invalid.

The social reinforcement hypothesis has received indirect support from studies in which extinction and DRO have been effective in reducing the rate of self-injurious behavior. An example of this approach with a severely retarded child was described by Peterson and Peterson (1968). The subject was an institutionalized 8-year-old boy who engaged in severe self-destructive behavior. His face, arms, and legs were covered with scabs and bruises resulting from hitting himself on the face and head and banging on chairs, walls, etc. Self-injurious behavior ranged from 21.6 to 32.8 responses per minute during baseline. Treatment was conducted in a small room at mealtime. The child was reinforced verbally and with small bits of food contingent on 3–5-sec. periods of no self-hitting. When self-hitting did occur, the experimenter turned his back for 10 sec. This procedure was continued for 10 sessions, during which time self-destruction decreased to an average of 14.2 responses per minute. Treatment was then altered. Rather than the experimenter turning away from the child contingent upon self-destructive behavior, the child was directed to walk away from the experimenter. Food and social reinforcement were again provided for behaviors other than self-hitting. Response rate first dropped during this intervention, then briefly rose to baseline levels, and declined gradually over the next 20 sessions until it finally dropped out entirely. The response rate increased dramatically during a brief withdrawal period, and quickly returned to zero when treatment was reinstated. Thus, DRO and extinction were effective in controlling the response. However, the child performed a high number of self-destructive responses during the course of extinction. As will be discussed in the next session, there is some evidence that self-abusive behavior can be eliminated more rapidly with the use of punishment procedures (Bachman, 1972; Corte, Wolf, & Locke, 1971).

Punishment

Punishment is probably the most controversial of all behavioral techniques. It has been associated with conceptual critiques suggesting that it has highly specific effects lacking in durability and that it teaches the individual what *not* to do, but does not teach him what *to* do. It has also been criticized on the more value-oriented grounds that it is dehumanizing and unacceptably aversive given the power of positive reinforcement techniques. While these admonitions are not entirely unfounded, the use of punishment techniques has had a resurgence since the mid-1960s. Applied research has demonstrated that punishment can be highly effective and durable, and that when used judiciously it can reduce human suffering and dysfunction efficiently and with considerably less pain than would be otherwise experienced (Azrin & Holz, 1966; Gardner, 1969; Johnston, 1972).

Punishment is operationally defined as a procedure which results in a decreased rate of a target response contingent on the presentation or removal of a stimulus (the punisher) (Johnston, 1972). Punishment is characterized by its effect (reducing response rate), rather than by the nature of the stimulus producing the effect. Punishment should be distinguished from extinction and negative reinforcement. In contrast to the *active* nature of punishment procedures, extinction reduces response rate by the *passive* omission of positive reinforcement. Negative reinforcement has the effect of *increasing* response rate by *removing* an aversive stimulus.

The use of punishment by behavior therapists in clinical and educational programs should also be differentiated from its use by parents, teachers, and courts in society at large. When used by such "nonprofessionals," punishment often serves less to alter the child's behavior than to gain retribution and express anger. In that context, the aversive aspects of punishment are the most meaningful attributes. Thus, it is not surprising that children frequently learn to circumvent or reduce punishment by stating that a spanking did not hurt or that they did not want a withheld reinforcer anyway. Punishment does not have to be physically painful or extremely aversive in order to be effective. Furthermore, it is typically more effective when administered dispassionately and with the benefit of the child in mind rather than the person administering the punishment.

Punishment techniques can be divided into two general categories: (1) procedures that involve the presentation of some (aversive) stimulus, and (2) procedures that involve the removal of some (positive) stimulus (Gardner, 1969). The first category includes verbal admonitions, scowls, slaps, electric shock, and overcorrection (see below and Chapter 7). Removal procedures are exemplified by response cost and time-out from positive reinforcement (both procedures will be described below). We will consider the use of punishment in the classroom first, followed by examples of punishment for the suppression of self-stimulatory behavior. A more systematic analysis of punishment and other aversive procedures will be presented in Chapter 7.

Verbal punishment, such as disapproval and reprimands, probably constitutes the most widely used form of behavior control in the classroom. Despite the demonstrated effectiveness of positive social reinforcement, rates of disapproving reponses by teachers are consistently greater than rates of approving responses (O'Leary & O'Leary, 1976; White, 1976). While teachers must be receiving some reinforcement for this behavior, it is not at all certain that they are actually controlling students with their approach. When used inappropriately, "punishing" stimuli can have the paradoxical effect of increasing the occurrence of the target response. Thomas, Becker, and Armstrong (1968) showed that disapproval responses increased disruptive behavior while approval responses for appropriate behavior led to a decrease in disruption. In a related study, Madsen, Becker, Thomas, Koser, and Plager (1968) found that contingent "Sit down" commands increased standing responses while praise for sitting lowered the rate of standing. (Some of the possible reasons for this phenomenon will be discussed at the conclusion of this section in the context of guidelines for effective use of punishment.)

Some forms of verbal punishment can be effective when used appropriately. O'Leary, Kaufman, Kass, and Drabman (1970) compared the effects of loud and soft reprimands for the control of a variety of behaviors including noises, aggression, and time off task and out-of-seat responses. Loud reprimands were the usual control responses of teachers in the study and consisted of critical responses audible to the entire class. Soft reprimands were similar in content, but were verbalized such that they were audible only to the disruptive child. Employing a series of ABAB replications, O'Leary et al. found that soft reprimands decreased disruptions and loud reprimands increased the rate of disruptive behavior.

Many teachers report that they can control behavior effectively simply by pointing or staring at an offending child with hands on hips. A variant of this approach was examined experimentally by Hall, Axelrod, Foundopoulos, Shellman, Campbell, and Cranston (1971). The subject was Andrea, a 7-year-old resident at an institute for the mentally retarded. She repeatedly pinched and bit herself, classmates, and teachers. The intervention consisted of teachers pointing at her and shouting , "No!" whenever she exhibited the aversive response. Rate of biting and pinching decreased from an average of 71.8 per day during baseline to 5.44 per day during treatment. Subsequent return to baseline and reapplication of treatment demonstrated control over the response, which stabilized at less than three episodes per day. In addition, anecdotal teacher reports indicated that as the response rate decreased, positive social interactions increased and Andrea was no longer avoided by her classmates.

In another example of traditional classroom disciplinary techniques, Hall et al. (1971) employed staying after school as a punishment for out-of-seat behavior. The subjects were 10 boys in a class for emotionally disturbed children. Out-of-seat behavior for the group aveaged 23 instances per reading and mathematics session during baseline. Being out-of-seat without permission was then consequated by requiring the child to stay after school for 5 min. The response was reduced to an average of 2.2 occurrences during 10 treatment sessions. Subsequent withdrawal and treatment phases demonstrated the controlling effects of the contingency. This procedure is a form of punishment referred to as *response cost* (Kazdin, 1972).

As the name implies, response cost is a procedure in which the child pays a penalty by losing some positive reinforcer contingent on inappropriate behavior. The most common example of response cost is the use of fines for parking and traffic violations. By having to remain after school, children in the Hall et al. study lost playtime or free time that they would otherwise have enjoyed. Response cost contingencies are ordinarily combined with DRO procedures. For example, Repp and Dietz (1974) reinforced the appropriate classroom behavior of a 13-year-old retarded boy with stars and removed all stars earned during each session contingent on inappropriate responses. Similarly, Schmidt and Ulrich (1969) reinforced second grade children for being quiet with extra gym time. Simultaneously, out-of-seat behavior was punished by loss of gym time.

Response cost has been used most frequently in token reinforcement systems. Without discussing the details of the token procedures, we will consider one illustrative example of token response cost at this point: a study by Axelrod (1973). The subjects were 31 mentally retarded students in two special-education classes. Target behaviors included out-of-seat responses and a number of child-specific disruptive acts. Response cost was administered as both a group and individual contingency at different points during the study. When the group contingency (GC) was in effect the teacher wrote the numbers 0–25 on the chalkboard. Whenever a child was observed making an inappropriate response, the highest number was erased and the child's name was written on the blackboard. At the end of the 1-hour contingency period, each child in the class received a number of tokens corresponding to the highest number remaining on the board. The tokens were exchangeable for candy and toys. Thus, the children began each session with 25 tokens and lost them for disruption. The individual contingency (IC) paralleled GC except that each child's name was written on the board at the beginning of the period; only the child making the disruptive response lost points.

The experimental design and results are presented in Fig. 6.4. One class received treatment conditions in the following order: baseline, IC, baseline, GC, baseline. The second class received baseline, GC, baseline, IC, baseline. Both contingencies were highly effective in the two classes. The individual and group contingencies were equally effective. Disruption in the two classes dropped from 173.6 and 141.6 disruptions per session to 19.8 and 8.2 disruptions during IC and 20.4 and 8.6 disruptions during GC. The dramatic recovery during the second and third baselines demonstrates the controlling effects of the two contingencies.

The group contingency was easier to administer than the individual contingency as the teacher did not have to keep 31 separate tallies. While it was not employed here, group contingencies also provide the

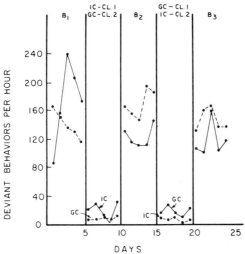

Fig. 6.4 The number of undesirable behaviors performed by each class during the 25 experimental sessions. Measurements were conducted for a 1-hour period. The *unbroken line* represents Class I (*Cl. 1*), and the *dashed line* Class II (*Cl. 2*). B_1, B_2, and B_3 are the three baseline phases, with *IC* and *GC* denoting individual and group contingencies, respectively. (Reprinted with permission from: S. Axelrod: *Behavior Therapy*, 4: 83, 1973.)

possibility of using a single, group-wide reinforcer such as a class trip or free time. However, GC was associated with an undesired side effect. Children in the second class were observed to make 14 verbal threats to one another during the 5 days in which the GC was in effect (the first class was not observed for this response). No threats were made during IC. Such social pressure might be a central factor in the operation of group contingencies. Whether central or secondary, their occurrence indicates that caution is necessary when group contingencies are applied.

Response cost involves the permanent withdrawal of some amount of positive reinforcement. *Time-out* (from positive reinforcement) is a related procedure in which the individual is temporarily removed from a current source of reinforcement. A prototypic example is requiring a child to stand in a corner for several minutes. In educational and institutional settings, a small, empty time-out room is often employed so that the child is physically removed from the class, dining hall, etc. For example, Drabman and Spitalnik (1973) employed a 10-min. time-out period in a small, dimly lit, soundproof music practice room. The aversive punishing aspect of time-out is presumed to be the removal from positive reinforcement, rather than the noxious aspects of isolation and the setting in which the child is placed. Thus, it is critical that the child be removed from reinforcement if time-out is to be effective. A child who experiences a classroom as aversive will not decrease disruptive behavior as a consequence of time-out from the classroom. Similarly, sending a child to his room at home will not be effective if the room contains a television, toys, etc. On the other hand, the child need not (and should not!) be placed in a physically noxious setting such as a cage or pen.

A wide variety of forms and durations of time-out have been used successfully. Barton, Guess, Garcia, and Baer (1970) employed time-out from food to modify the inappropriate table manners and eating behavior of institutionalized retarded children. Stealing food was consequated by removal from the dining hall for the remainder of the meal. Other behaviors were successfully modified by removal of food trays for periods of only 15-sec. It is of interest that despite the concerns of the nursing staff, this procedure did not result in the children losing weight because of excessive food deprivation.

Another interesting example of brief time-out was described by Sachs (1973). Ricky, a 13-year-old hyperactive child, exhibited a variety of self-stimulatory responses including repetitive guttural sounds and hand gestures. Treatment was administered in the context of individual tutoring sessions conducted by undergraduate students. The behavior was not affected by two initial contingencies: verbal punishment ("No") and time-out consisting of placing Ricky behind a piano. Control was established by having the tutor turn away from him for 30-sec., contingent on self-stimulatory behavior (i.e., time-out from social contact). In addition, the tutor did not turn back until Ricky had been quiet for 30-sec. This latter contingency is frequently employed when children are disruptive or have tantrums when placed in time-out.

Time-out has been employed to suppress harmful and self-injurious behaviors with mixed results. Risley (1968) reported that social isolation from parents was not effective for reducing the climbing behavior of an autistic child despite the strong suggestion that parental attention was maintaining this dangerous activity. On the other hand, Tate and Baroff (1966) reported the successful use of time-out for the self-injurious behavior of Sam, a 9-year-old autistic boy. Sam had been engaging in increasingly severe self-abuse since the age of four. At the time of treatment he had detached retinas in both eyes and a hematoma (blood clot) on his forehead as a result of head banging. Treatment was conducted within an ABAB design in daily 20-min. sessions. During all sessions, Sam was taken on a walk by two experimenters who each held one of his hands. Self-injurious behaviors (SIBs) were ignored during the two A phases and consequated by time-out during B phases. Time-out consisted of both experimenters releasing Sam's hands until no SIBs occurred for 3 sec. Rate of SIBs decreased from 6.6 per min. during the first baseline to 1.0 per min. during the second time-out phase.

Despite this marked reduction, the danger to Sam's eyes of any further SIBs made continuation of this procedure untenable. Therefore, treatment was shifted to the use of contingent electric shocks. The shocks were painful but not harmful. The rate of SIBs was reduced to 0.04 per min. on the 1st day of shock, 0.06 on the 2nd day, and 0.03 on the 3rd day. At the time that Tate and Baroff wrote their article, the contingency had been effective for 6 months and there had been no SIBs for the last 20 days of that period. At this point in time, electric shock appears to be the treatment of choice for SIB (Birnbrauer, 1976; Lovaas & Newsom, 1976). We will further consider some of the positive and negative attributes of shock in Chapter 7.

The final punishment procedure to be considered is *overcorrection* (Foxx & Azrin 1972, 1973). "The general rationale of the Overcorrection procedure is (1) to overcorrect the environmental effects of an inappropriate act, and (2) to require the disruptor intensively to practice overly correct forms of relevant behavior. The method of achieving the first objective of correcting the effects of the disruption is designated as Restitutional Overcorrection, and consists of requiring the disruptor to correct the consequences of his misbehavior by having him restore the situation to a state vastly improved from that which existed before the disruption. For example, an individual who overturned a table would be required both to restore the table to its correct position and to dust and wax the table. The method of achieving the second objective of practicing correct behaviors is designated as Positive Practice Overcorrection.

For example, the disruptor who overturned the table would also be required to straighten and dust all other tables and furniture in the room. This latter requirement teaches the disruptor the correct manner in which furniture should be treated" (Foxx & Azrin,1973, p. 2).

This procedure, which has only recently been developed, is a promising approach because it teaches appropriate behavior, is not overly noxious, and is comparatively easy to administer in a variety of situations. Foxx and Azrin (1973) have demonstrated the effectiveness of overcorrection in reducing a variety of self-stimulatory behaviors of mentally retarded children including mouthing of objects, head weaving, and hand clapping (these responses are presumed to be functionally similar to SIBs). One of the children was Barbara, an 8-year-old girl who was enrolled as an outpatient in a day-care program. "She continuously mouthed objects by picking them up and touching them to her mouth or placing them inside her mouth. If the object was too heavy to lift she would sit or stand beside it and mouth it with her lips, mouth, and tongue" (p. 3).

After first demonstrating that overcorrection could reduce this behavior in a circumscribed setting, Foxx and Azrin attempted to eliminate it entirely throughout the school day. Overcorrection consisted of a 2-min. period during which Barbara was told "No," her teeth and gums were brushed with a toothbrush that had been immersed in mouthwash, and her outer lips were cleaned with a washcloth. The results are presented in Fig. 6.5. Mouthing behavior occurred more than 80% of the time during baseline sessions despite the fact that teachers employed a DRO procedure for non-self-stimulatory behaviors. Overcorrection had an almost immediate effect, reducing mouthing to almost zero within 10 days. The behavior stabilized at a zero rate and overcorrection was discontinued. During the succeeding 3 months, the behavior increased substantially and quickly dropped out again when overcorrection was reinstated. Shortly thereafter, a verbal warning was added and overcorrection was applied only if the behavior continued or if it recurred during the same half-day session. As can be seen, this natural contingency was highly effective in maintaining the response over the next 3 months. Barbara's mother reported that during treatment, frequency of mouthing at home increased. The mother was then taught to use overcorrection and she subsequently reported that instances of mouthing had become very rare.

We have discussed a variety of different punishment techniques in this section, all of which have been shown to be effective for suppressing at least some behaviors with some children. None of the procedures (no procedure of any form) is universally effective even when applied appropriately. However, even the circumscribed effectiveness of punishment techniques can be attained only with judicious selection of cases and careful application of the techniques. Johnston (1972) has suggested a set of guidelines for employing punishment:

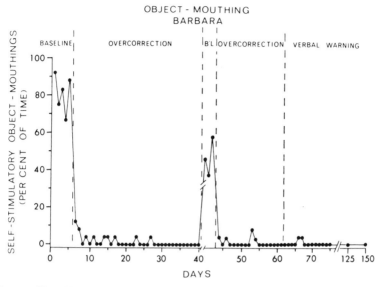

Fig. 6.5 The effect of the Overcorrective Oral Hygiene and Verbal Warning procedures on the self-stimulatory object-mouthing of a severely retarded child. The ordinate
is labelled in terms of the percent of time samples in which mouthings were observed.
The first *slash marks* on the abscissa indicate a 3-month period. During the baseline
periods, no contingencies were in effect for mouthing. (Reprinted with permission from:
R. M. Foxx and N. H. Azrin: *Journal of Applied Behavior Analysis*, 6: 1, 1973.)

"(a) The initial intensity of the punishing stimulus should be as
great as possible and continued intensities should also be at the
highest reasonable levels.

(b) The punishing stimulus should be delivered for each occurrence
of the response to be punished or as frequently as possible.

(c) The impact of the punishing stimulus on the subject should allow
no unauthorized means of escape from contact with the stimulus.

(d) However, an alternative response should be available which will
result in the same reinforcement as the punished response but
which will not receive the punishing stimulus.

(e) Similarly, where there is no alternative response available, the
subject should have the opportunity to respond in a different situation in which the same reinforcement is earned but in which that
response is not punished.

(f) If mild intensities of punishment are used, long periods of
punishment should be avoided.

(g) The delivery of the punishing stimulus should not be associated
differentially with the presentation of reinforcement; rather it
should be a signal that a period of extinction is in progress for the
punished response.

(h) The level of motivation to make the punished response should be
decreased.

(i) A conditioned punishing stimulus may be used to decrease the
frequency of a response by pairing a neutral stimulus with the

noxious punishing stimulus and by then presenting the conditioned punishing stimulus immediately following the response" (p. 1034).

These guidelines are designed not simply to aid the therapist, but to maintain the dignity of the child in two ways. *First,* they guarantee that punishment is as effective as possible in as short a time as possible. *Second,* they insure that the child is not simply punished, but that he is also provided with positive reinforcement (guidelines d and e). *When positive reinforcement procedures cannot be used in lieu of punishment, they should always be used in conjunction with punishment.* Guidelines g and i deserve special mention. Punishment can result in an increase in the target response if it is discriminative for subsequent positive reinforcement (guideline g). This phenomenon often occurs when parents, feeling guilty about overly severe or impulsive punishment, attempt to make amends by being overly solicitous or offering special treatment after punishment. Guideline i suggests that a discriminative stimulus for punishment be established by pairing a warning word or gesture with the punishing stimulus. Once such a cue is established, the actual punishing stimulus can be used with much less frequency.

Token Economies

A token economy (TE) is a miniature socioeconomic system in which an attempt is made to reproduce in a special setting (such as a classroom) the contingent response-reinforcement relationships found in the real world. Thus, members of a TE must earn reinforcers by making appropriate responses, rather than receiving them noncontingently. Conversely, their efforts do not go unrewarded as they often do in a noncontingent system. Similarly, rule violations in the TE result in penalties (such as response cost).

As with any operant program, the first step in developing a TE is to define target behaviors. Contingencies are then established in which tokens serve as the basic form of reinforcement. Tokens might be stars, points, check marks, poker chips, or any other convenient indicator of earnings. Tokens serve as a medium of exchange for back-up reinforcers: activities and materials having strong reinforcing value.

The economy includes varying levels of payment (and fines) for different responses and varying costs of back-up reinforcers. As in the real world, the TE participant earns tokens throughout the day (week, etc.) and can either save them or use them to purchase desired reinforcers. By using tokens as an intermediary in the response-reinforcement chain, a number of behaviors for a number individuals can be more easily consequated than if back-up reinforcers were administered directly and immediately for every targeted response.

Token economies run the gamut from miniature systems in which only one behavior is consequated and one back-up reinforcer (such as a trip) is available, to large scale residential token environments in which everything from combed hair to work productivity is maintained on a contingent basis (e.g., basic reinforcers such as food and a bed are purchased). There is a great deal of similarity between token programs in different settings and across populations. The reader is referred to Chapter 8 for a more extensive discussion of TE procedures. We will confine our discussion here to a few examples of token systems which are unique to work with children (i.e., classroom token economies).

K. Daniel O'Leary and Wesley C. Becker are noted for their research efforts concerning classroom token economies. They have conducted a series of studies demonstrating the effectiveness of this approach as well as elucidating some of the major parameters of their operation (Kuypers, Becker, & O'Leary, 1968; O'Leary & Becker, 1967; O'Leary, Becker, Evans, & Saudargas, 1969). The third study in the series (O'Leary et al., 1969) is quite representative of their approach. Data were collected for seven children in a class of 21 second graders in a public school. Target behaviors consisted of seven categories of disruptive behavior including motor behaviors (out-of-seat), aggressive behaviors, disturbing another's property, disruptive noise, turning around, verbalization (when not permitted), and inappropriate tasks.

The implementation of token economies typically involves a number of nontoken procedures such as stating rules, structuring the educational process, and social reinforcement. This study included several control phases designed to examine the contribution of tokens above and beyond these other factors. The study was conducted in eight phases (see Fig. 6.6). Experimental procedures were implemented daily in the afternoon and generalization effects were assessed in the morning.

During the 6-week Base Period, the classroom teacher was instructed to manage the children in her usual manner. The second phase, Classroom Rules, lasted 3 weeks during which time the teacher regularly announced non-consequated rules such as: "We sit in our seats," and "We raise our hands to talk." During the third phase, Educational Structure, the teacher reorganized the class program into four 30-min. topic sessions. In the fifth stage, social reinforcement (Praise) for appropriate behavior and extinction (Ignore) for inappropriate behavior were added to rules and structure.

The token economic system was added to previous manipulations in the sixth phase. Tokens consisted of points entered in a small book on each child's desk. The children could earn between 1 and 10 points at each of four times during the afternoon. Points were administered on a somewhat subjective basis, according to occurrence of disruptive behavior and improvement over behavior on previous days. (While it is usually desirable to maintain an objective criterion, this procedure was adopted to make it simple for one teacher to administer the system for

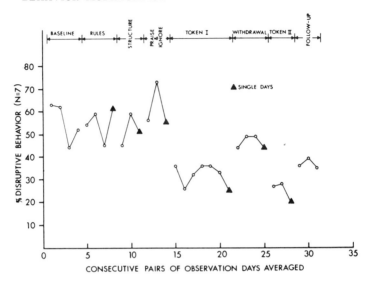

Fig. 6.6 Average percentage of combined disruptive behavior of seven children during the afternoon over the eight conditions: Base, Rules, Educational Structure, Praise and Ignore, Token I, Withdrawal, Token II, Follow-up. (Reprinted with permission from: K. D. O'Leary, W. C. Becker, M. B. Evans, and R. A. Saudargas: *Journal of Applied Behavior Analysis*, 2: 3, 1969.)

an entire class.) Back-up reinforcers consisted of a variety of material reinforcers (candy, pennants, dolls, toy trucks, etc.) ranging in value from two to thirty cents. The economic system was designed to gradually increase the delay between receiving and spending tokens.

> "During the initial four days, the children were eligible for prizes just after their fourth rating at approximately 2:30. Thereafter, all prizes were distributed at the end of the day. For the first ten school days the children could receive prizes each day. There were always two levels of prizes. During the first ten days, a child had to receive at least twenty-five points to receive a two to five cent prize (level two prizes). For the next six days, points were accumulated for two days and exchanged at the end of the second day. When children saved their points for two days, a child had to receive fifty-five points to receive a ten cent prize or seventy points to receive a twenty cent prize. Then, a six-day period occurred in which points were accumulated for three days and exchanged at the end of the third day. During this period, a child had to receive eighty-five points to receive a twenty cent prize or one hundred and five points to receive a thirty cent prize. Whenever the prizes were distributed, the children relinquished all their points" (O'Leary et al., 1969, p. 6).

The token system remained in effect for 5 weeks and was followed by a 5-week withdrawal period during which time the other procedures remained in effect. The token system was then reinstated for 2 weeks and the token back-up delay was again faded in. The final month of the study involved a follow-up period. Rules, praise, and educational structure remained in effect, but the token economy was severely restricted. Stars and occasional pieces of candy were administered for appropriate behavior, but no other back-up reinforcers were available.

The results are portrayed graphically in Fig. 6.6. As can be seen, disruptive behavior was reduced only during token phases. In addition, statistical analyses indicated that disruptive behavior was significantly lower during both token phases than during each of the other phases with the exception of follow-up. Thus, while disruptive behavior did increase when back-up reinforcers were removed, the increase was not statistically significant. Disruptive behavior during the follow-up was significantly lower than during any of the non-token phases. The shift from extrinsic back-up reinforcers to more natural reinforcers appears to have been an effective procedure for maintaining the effects of the program. On the other hand, there was little generalization of either the teacher's behavior or the children's behavior from afternoon to morning sessions. The teacher was not consistent in her use of praise and ignoring, and the rate of disruptive behavior did not decrease during the morning.

As previously discussed, generalization must be programmed, not expected to occur automatically. If behavior is a function of its consequences, it is not logical to presume that behavior will change when no consequences are applied. Fading out of back-up reinforcers (while adding natural reinforcers) is one of the most frequently employed strategies for attaining generalization (i.e., maintenance over time) within the same setting. The application of social reinforcers is not only socially desirable, but appears to be a necessary (if not sufficient) condition for maintaining changes when back-ups are withdrawn (Kuypers et al., 1968; O'Leary, Poulos, & Devine, 1972; Walker, Hops, & Fiegenbaum, 1976).

An alternative strategy for producing behavioral maintenance involves training children to use self-control techniques. As discussed in Chapter 4, there have been several demonstrations of the ability of children to take over control of token systems with little loss of treatment gains (e.g., Drabman, Spitalnik, & O'Leary, 1973; Glynn, Thomas, & Shee, 1973). While positive effects have generally been limited to periods in which back-up reinforcers were available, Drabman et al. (1973) found changes in periods without back-ups as well. The development of improved techniques for building self-control skills promises to facilitate increased generalization across time and settings.

Our discussion of generalization thus far has emphasized stimulus generalization: the transposition of a response from one setting to another or across time. Another form of generalization is response generalization: the transposition of effects within one setting to other response forms. This is primarily of issue in regard to the effects on academic performance of reducing disruptive behavior. The ultimate goal of schooling is education. It is generally presumed that disruptive behavior decreases learning by distracting the offending student, his peers, and the teacher from academic activity. Therefore, decreased disruption is expected to result in increased academic performance (i.e., response generalization). Unfortunately, this has not generally been found to occur; academic performance has not consistently improved as disruption has decreased (O'Leary & O'Leary, 1976).

An alternative treatment strategy is to focus the token economy on academic performance instead of, or in addition to, disruptive behavior. This approach is illustrated in a study by Ayllon and Roberts (1974). The study was conducted in a fifth grade classroom of an urban public school. Ayllon and Roberts were consulted by the school principal as the class was so disruptive that two teachers together were unable to control the 38 children. The five most disruptive children in the class were selected as subjects for observation and modification. Two classes of behaviors were selected as targets. Disruptive behavior consisted of being out-of-seat, talking out, and motor activity which interfered with other student's studying. Academic behavior consisted of performance on daily reading tests (the children were all deficient in reading skills). Both classes of behavior were assessed during daily (15 min.) testing sessions. The token economy is described in Table 6.1.

Points could be earned for accurate performance on the reading tests and expended for back-up reinforcers on a daily or weekly basis. Reinforcers were identified by observing the children and identifying their most preferred activities. Those reinforcers which were available to only one child at a time were sold at auction. In contrast to the extrinsic reinforcers employed by O'Leary et al. (1969), all reinforcers were natural to the classroom environment.

The effectiveness of the token economy was assessed with an ABAB design. The results are presented in Fig. 6.7. Both target categories averaged between 40% and 50% during baseline. Reading accuracy increased to 70% during the first token phase, dropped sharply during the withdrawal phase, and rose to 85% when the token system was reinstated. As expected, the results for disruptive behavior were exactly the opposite. Disruption dropped to 15% during the first token phase, increased to 40% during the withdrawal phase, and dropped back to 5% when the token system was reinstituted. These results provide a clear indication that response generalization can be accomplished and suggest that greater attention be paid to remediation of academic difficulties in disruptive classes (cf. Winett & Winkler, 1972).

However, Ayllon and Roberts caution that this sequence will not always follow. In some situations, disruptive behavior might have to be decreased prior to (or in conjucnction with) academic training in order to get children to attend to the academic program. This might be especially

TABLE 6.1

Information Sheet for Academic Performance Criteria and Back-up Reinforcers Cost[a]

Points Earning Criteria for Fifth-Grade Reading Class
1. 80% correct on workbook assignments = 2 points
2. 100% correct on workbook assignments = 5 points

Back-up Reinforcers	
Daily	
1. Access to game room (per 15 minutes)	2 points
2. Extra recess time (10 minutes)	2 points
3. Buy a ditto master	2 points
4. Have ditto copies run off (per copy)	1 point
5. Review grades in teacher's book	5 points
6. Reduce detention (per 10 minutes)	10 points
7. Change cafeteria table	15 points
8. Have the lowest test grade removed	20 points
9. Become an assistant teacher	Auction
Weekly	
1. See a movie	6 points
2. Have a good work letter sent to parents	15 points
3. Become the classroom helper for one week	Auction
4. Become the ball captain for one week	Auction
5. Do bulletin board (will remain up for three weeks)	Auction

[a] From: Ayllon and Roberts (1974) (Table 1).

true in situations in which academic deficits are severe and extensive remediation (as well as incentives) is required. It is also of interest that while the procedure resulted in response generalization, it did not result in stimulus generalization. There was no change in disruptive behavior except during the 15-min. reading test. A program for overall classroom change would have to be more extensive.

In concluding this section, we would like to emphasize some of the critical factors about token programs. There is little, if any, doubt that token systems are highly effective in easily and inexpensively modifying a broad range of behaviors of both individual children and entire classrooms. Nevertheless, they are not effective with all children, and to this point, achieving generalization across time and settings has been exceedingly difficult. In addition, token systems based on extrinsic reinforcers should be considered a temporary intervention, to be substituted by natural reinforcers (social and activity) as soon as possible (O'Leary et al., 1972). Finally, "A token program is not a magical procedure to be applied in a mechanical way. It is simply the tool within a larger set of tools available to the teacher concerned with improving the behavior of children" (Kuypers et al., 1968, p. 108).

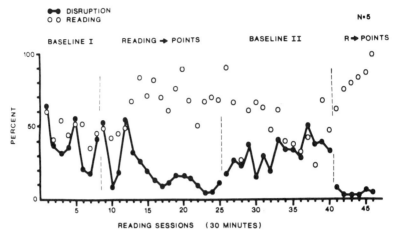

Fig. 6.7 Mean percent disruption and mean percent correct on reading assignments for the five target students. Each point represents 30 min. of assignment time. (Reprinted with permission from: T. Allyon and M. D. Roberts: *Journal of Applied Behavior Analysis*, 7: 71, 1974.)

Parents as Change Agents

Parenting is one of the most difficult functions for anyone to fulfill, and yet few people in our society receive any training or direction as to how to be an effective parent. It is not surprising, therefore, that a significant (probably overwhelming) proportion of the behavior problems of children are manifested in the home. Traditionally, the responsibility for parent-child conflict and the "misbehavior" of problem children has been placed on the child (family therapy models are an obvious exception). The typical pattern has been for the parents to bring the child to a mental health worker who proceeds to treat the child (e.g., play therapy). Any collateral parental involvement has usually involved intermittent meetings to inform them of progress and to help reduce their distress. The behavioral approach to home problems has generally shifted the focus to the parents. Since the child's behavior is viewed as being a function of his environment, undesirable behavior (as well as desirable behavior) is ascribed to the behavior of the parents, who are the primary sources of control and reinforcement. Thus, changing the child's behavior requires that the parents' responses to the child be altered first.

The primary form of intervention for problems in the home has been to train the parents to behave more effectively in relation to the child. Many of the same techniques used to modify behavior in other contexts have been employed to modify parent behavior, including instruction and feedback, modeling, shaping, and positive reinforcement. In this section we will consider examples of two general training strategies: (1) training parents to implement somewhat specific techniques with the goal of modifying specific child behaviors, and (2) training in the broader technique of contingency contracting, with the goal of more extensive modification of parent-child interaction.

Problem-Specific Interventions

Parents have been successfully trained to employ almost every form of intervention described above in the context of classroom and institutional programs. We have already discussed several examples. Recall the cases of Bobby, whose parents were taught to apply rules about dinner and bathtime, and of Barbara (Foxx & Azrin, 1973), whose mother was taught to apply overcorrection. Strober and Bellack (1975) worked with the mother of an impulsive, overaggressive child. In addition to training the mother to employ social reinforcement and response cost (for television viewing time), they successfully taught her to use a cognitive intervention strategy. Whenever her son showed signs of losing control, she physically held him and instructed him to make verbal self-controlling statements until he was calmed, analogous to the procedure employed by Meichenbaum and Goodman (1971) (see Chapter 4).

McKenzie, Clark, Wolf, Kothera, and Benson (1968) involved parents in a program to improve the academic skills of children with learning disabilities. They first attempted to apply a totally in-school token system, which was not effective. In an effort to incorporate more powerful reinforcers, they had the children's parents provide allowances (at home) contingent on weekly grade reports. This approach was most effective.

In general, there is little difference either in procedure or in the effectiveness of intervention techniques irrespective of the individual who carries them out (e.g., parents, teachers, Ph.D. psychologists). The most critical factors are with respect to who controls the relevant reinforcers and how appropriately and contingently they are applied. We will describe one further example of parent-implemented programs in greater detail, as it demonstrates some of the major postive consequences of parent-oriented interventions.

A frequent source of parental complaint is that their children are oppositional: that they refuse to obey commands, do household chores, cooperate at bedtime, etc. From a behavioral perspective, the parents of such children have not learned appropriate techniques for securing cooperation and/or they are inadvertently reinforcing non-compliance. Wahler (1969) described a parent-oriented intervention for two oppositional children which employed time-out and DRO. One of the children, Billy, was a 6-year-old boy. He rarely interacted with his parents.

Indeed, most interchanges involved parents' attempts (generally futile) to curtail his inappropriate behavior or get him to comply with some directive.

Home observation sessions were conducted once per week in the evening. Sessions lasted 40 min., during which time the parents were instructed to give Billy directions to perform simple household chores. Training was initiated following a baseline period in which the parents exerted control in their customary manner. Four training sessions ranging from 30–65 min. were conducted immediately before the weekly observation sessions (the parents of the second child required seven sessions, 30–105 min. in length). Parents were first instructed in the principles of reinforcement theory and then taught to use social reinforcement for cooperation and time-out for opposition. Time-out consisted of 5 min. in Billy's bedroom. The trainer provided additional instructions and feedback during actual periods of parent-child interaction.

Treatment was conducted in ABAB fashion; the results are presented in Fig. 6.8. The measure of oppositional behavior consisted of any indication of non-compliance during the 10 sec. following any parental command or request. As shown in the upper portion of the figure, the

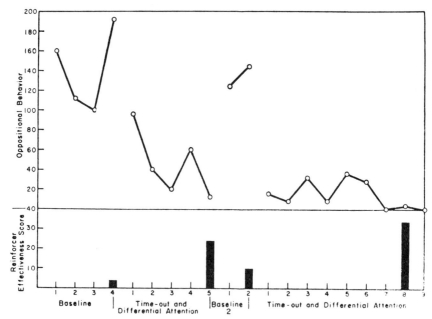

Fig. 6.8 Number of Billy's 10-sec. oppositional units and parental reinforcer effectiveness scores over baseline and treatment periods. All observations were made during 40-min. sessions held once a week in Billy's home. Reinforcer effectiveness scores were obtained through a choice task (see text) conducted at the end of certain observation sessions. (Reprinted with permission from: R. G. Wahler: *Journal of Applied Behavior Analysis*, 2: 159, 1969.)

intervention was quite effective in a brief period of time. The parents were requested to employ and monitor these procedures throughout the week as well as during observation sessions. They reported that Billy's cooperative behavior had increased throughout the day. During the first 2 weeks of the intervention they reported using time-out 63 times, while only 2 time-outs were needed during the final 4 weeks of the study.

When contingency procedures are first described to them, parents frequently react negatively, anticipating that the rigidity of the approach will alienate their children. In fact, children's response to their parents' new consistency and firmness is often quite the opposite. This is evidenced in the reinforcer effectiveness scores presented in the lower portion of Fig. 6.8. These scores reflect a measure of the reinforcing value of the parents for Billy. The scores were derived from a simple task in which the parents first observed Billy dropping marbles into one of two holes in a box. After determining which hole he preferred, they began to apply social reinforcement whenever he dropped a marble into the non-preferred hole. Thus, the more reinforcing he found the parents, the more marbles he would place in the non-preferred hole. As can be seen, effectiveness scores *increased* during the contingency phases and *decreased* when the contingency was removed.

In addition, Billy also spent considerably more time interacting with his parents during the week. There are two factors that (probably) account for this phenomenon with other children as well as with *Billy*. *First,* by reducing the child's inappropriate behaviors, negative parent-child interactions occur less frequently and animosity is decreased. *Second*, by teaching parents to apply positive social reinforcement, the quality of interactions is improved, and affection and reinforcement value is increased. Both factors contribute to parents' and child's liking each other more.

Contingency Contracting

Training parents to employ specific techniques to modify specific behaviors has been quite effective. However, there is little reason to presume that parents so trained are more effective at preventing or curtailing different forms of conflict than are untrained parents. If the source of distress is highly specific and the parent is otherwise effective in controlling his/her child, a specific intervention might be sufficient. On the other hand, many parents are deficient in behavior control skills and require more broad-based training if new problems are to be avoided. The treatment of choice for such parents is referred to as training in contingency management or contingency contracting.

This approach is well represented by the work of Gerald R. Patterson and his colleagues at the Oregon Research Institute (Patterson, 1974; Patterson, Reid, Jones, & Conger, 1975; Wiltz & Patterson, 1974). These investigators have developed and evaluated a systematic training program which can be administered to parents individually or in groups. The core of the program is presented to parents in one of two programmed-learning texts developed by Patterson (Patterson, 1971; Patterson & Gullion, 1968). The material is then elaborated during training sessions by modeling and role playing as well as didactic instruction. Parents are taught simple assessment techniques including how to define and pinpoint sources of disruption. They are presented with a behavioral conception of human behavior and taught techniques for employing positive reinforcement and some simple punishment procedures. Once they have mastered these preliminaries (as determined by tests, homework assignments, role playing, and self-report), training shifts to the development and implementation of contingency contracts.

Contingency contracts are the basic vehicle employed for behavior change. They are (generally) written agreements between parent and child that specify: (1) a requisite behavior that the child is expected to perform, and (2) a positive consequence which is to be received upon compliance, and (often) a negative consequence for non-compliance. A simple contract might specify that the child is to walk the dog for 10 min. when he returns home from school, to be reinforced by a weekly allowance. A more elaborate contract could involve a home-based token economy in which points are earned for a variety of behaviors, and a reinforcement menu is provided for back-up reinforcers.

Instructing parents in contracting procedures has several advantages over the simple presentation of an array of consequation procedures. *First,* by requiring specific planning, it encourages the parents to critically examine their own needs and preferences in relation to the child and his behavior, rather than impulsively imposing rules and consequences. *Second,* contracting entails negotiation with the child, which allows him to express his own feelings and facilitates a more positive interaction than arbitrarily imposed rules. *Third,* by maintaining a written record, both parents and child can remain clear as to exactly what the behavioral criteria and consequences are, rather than allowing either component to be gradually and covertly modified.

As might be apparent, development of effective contracting skills is far from easy. In addition to weekly meetings in the clinic, telephone calls and home visits are frequently employed to determine sources of difficulty, demonstrate appropriate techniques, and provide reinforcement to the parents for their efforts. Initial efforts are restricted to a few, easily modified behaviors articulated in simple contracts. Many parents are resistant to this form of intervention, preferring instead that the mental health worker treat their child directly. Patterson et al. (1975) suggest that contingencies be applied to parents in order to secure cooperation. For example, the therapists may retain financial deposits, which are returned contingent upon attendance, and the parents must present completed homework assignments (such as assessment data) or sessions are cancelled.

This fundamental approach has been demonstrated to be most effective in numerous studies by the Patterson group as well as by other research groups in different parts of the country (Alexander & Parsons, 1973; O'Leary, Turkewitz, & Taffel, 1973; Tharp &Wetzel, 1969). Unlike some behavioral interventions, which have been evaluated primarily in specialized research settings, parent training has proven to be effective with nonrecruited clinic referrals in community clinic settings (O'Leary et al., 1973; Kent & O'Leary, 1976). There are several indications that the effects of parent training generalize. Extended follow-ups have demonstrated that behavior changes maintain well (e.g., Alexander & Parsons, 1973; Patterson, 1974). In addition, the behavior of siblings of referred children (who have been the focus of treatment) has been shown to change in positive directions after parent training (Arnold, Levine, & Patterson, 1975). This finding suggests that parents have been able to apply creatively what they have learned without the direct guidance of the therapist. Finally, parent training programs are efficient and economical, typically requiring only 10–30 hours of professional contact per family or group of families. Patterson et al. (1975) suggest that paraprofessionals can be trained to conduct parent training programs and that two out of three families can be helped significantly.

These positive conclusions do not indicate that all questions about parent training have been answered. There have been several reports in which seemingly well-conducted programs have led to disappointing results (Ferber, Keeley, & Shemberg, 1974; Weathers & Liberman, 1975). Future research efforts are needed to determine the types of parents for whom the approach is applicable (currently, lower socioeconomic status parents appear to be less responsive than middle- and upper-class parents). The range of behavior problems that are responsive to this intervention is also uncertain (e.g., boys who steal have been less effectively treated than boys who are aggressive and noncompliant). Despite these questions, the development of behavioral parent training programs has provided a dramatic advance in the alleviation of parent-child conflict and distress.

Ethical Issues

The general discussion of ethical issues in Chapter 1 provides a background for considering ethics in work with children. However, there are several issues that are either unique to the treatment of children or are especially relevant in that context. Perhaps the most critical factor pertains to the determination of target behaviors and a treatment plan. With the occasional exception of severely disturbed or retarded inpatients, it is encumbent upon the therapist working with adult clients to secure their informed consent for his program. The client helps to determine and agrees with the plan and goals of treatment, and he is free to terminate at any point. This is not the case with children. They are not voluntary referrals to treatment, and are not free to determine what, if anything, they want from treatment or when it should end. The therapist is engaged by parents, schools, or institutions, and he is ordinarily expected to secure *their* informed consent and work toward *their* goals for the child. Such parental and school control is sanctioned by society, which expects and permits parents and schools to socialize and control children.

In most instances, this form of control works to the benefit of the child and the therapist is not in conflict. For example, there is little question that self-injurious behavior should be controlled, that a child should not steal or set fires, and that learning academic material is beneficial. However, this is not always the case. While there are not many parents who wish their children to be taught to steal (cf. *Oliver Twist*), it is not unusual for parents to expect excessive levels of obedience and an absence of "normal" childhood spontaneity and exuberance. Similarly, schools generally have the best interests of children in mind, but often demand undue conformity and establish rules (such as no talking in hallways) more for their own convenience than for the good of the child (McIntire, 1974). While adherence to the value system of society at large will sometimes aid in determining what is appropriate (e.g., with stealing), the behavior therapist must frequently rely on his own personal and professional value system in determining which behaviors he is willing to establish or curtail (Tharp & Wetzel, 1969).

Inappropriate requests can sometimes be modified by providing parents with normative information about child development and suggesting alternative goals. Many parents do not know what to expect and accept from their children and can profit from education as well as contingency techniques. School personnel can be taught to restructure the learning environment to promote cooperation through increased student enjoyment and success, rather than through repressive discipline and outmoded teaching practices. When the parents or school persist in making unreasonable demands, the therapist must decide if the child would benefit even from a less than perfect intervention (e.g., quiet and conformity might be better than expulsion). However, the behavior therapist should be prepared to refuse to intervene in some situations.

The age of the child must also be considered in this context. Parents and schools justifiably have more control over young children than over adolescents. Teenagers should generally be regarded more like adults, capable of providing their own informed consent, than like children. Even with younger children, it is generally advisable to discuss goals and treatment plans rather than impose the intervention. Children can often be helpful in selecting appropriate reinforcers and punishing consequences as well as in suggesting how the home or school environment can be altered to facilitate appropriate behavior (e.g., what time they would like to eat dinner, or how they would like to study arithmetic).

Another aspect of interventions with children that has been the subject of substantial controversy is the use of extrinsic reinforcers. Some of the major objections that have been raised against the use of extrinsic reinforcers include: it is bribery; it teaches greed; it reduces the effectiveness of alternative (natural) means of control; it teaches the child to be bad; and good behavior should be intrinsically rewarding (see, O'Leary et al., 1972). In addition, it has been suggested that token reinforcement systems reduce intrinsic interest in tasks so reinforced (Levine & Fasnacht, 1974). Many of these criticisms may be justified when extrinsic reinforcement programs are used inappropriately, excessively, or in isolation. However, adherence to the guidelines of appropriate usage makes these critiques invalid.

Administering rewards *before* a target response or to induce an inappropriate response is bribery. Token rewards administered *after* socially desirable behavior is no more bribery than receiving a salary for a week's work. Many critics of token programs believe that children should be "good" and should achieve in school simply because those behaviors are moral and appropriate. While intrinsic reinforcement and moral self-guidance are desirable ideals, there is no indication that they are sufficient to motivate the behavior of all (or any) children. In any case, it is illogical to arbitrarily preclude the use of extrinsic reinforcement to shape appropriate behavior when intrinsic reinforcement has not been sufficient (as is the case with children referred for treatment). We have previously indicated that token procedures should be supplemented by natural reinforcers and be faded out as quickly as possible. Intrinsic interest in tasks and the effectiveness of natural forms of control are not reduced when these guidelines are followed (e.g., Feingold & Mahoney, 1975).

The final issue to be considered is the use of punishment. There is little doubt that punishment procedures can be effective. However, effectiveness alone is not a sufficient reason for their widespread use. Of all behavioral techniques, punishment has the greatest likelihood of misuse. Many people find it easier to apply punishment than to expend the effort to identify and apply positive reinforcement procedures for behavior incompatible with the undesired response. Punishment is also attractive because its impact is often more quickly visible than the effects of positive reinforcement. Finally, punishment can be a form of aggression and retribution, which are frequently the natural responses to the anger engendered by undesirable child behavior.

We have already considered some of the mechanical guidelines for effective use of punishment. There are several other guidelines which need to be adhered to when punishment is being considered: (1) Punishment should not be used when positive procedures can be as effective. If there is any doubt, positive procedures should be employed first and punishment applied only if positive procedures have been unsatisfactory. This is especially true when highly aversive procedures are at issue (e.g., electric shock). (2) Consultation with colleagues and relevant others (e.g., parents, institutional staff, and ethics review committees) is advised before and during punishment programs to aid in determining when the use of punishment is justified. (3) When a decision is made to use punishment the mildest form of punishment that might be effective should be selected, and punishment should be terminated as soon as possible.* (4) Punishment should only be used when it is clearly for the benefit of the child (e.g., to suppress self-injurious behavior). Punishment should not be used to enforce compliance with institutional rules (Brown, Wienckowski, & Stolz, 1975). (5) Caution is urged when parents, school personnel, etc. are taught to use punishment procedures. Providing admonitions about limited reliance on punishment techniques is not sufficient. The behavior therapist must make a subjective judgment about the possibility of misuse of the procedures after training is completed. If there is a reasonable probability of misuse, the individuals should not be instructed in the use of punishment. (6) The use of corporeal punishment (e.g., spanking, paddling) should be avoided. This is perhaps the most subjective guideline. Spanking is widely used in the home, and paddling is not uncommon in the schools. Nevertheless, its effectiveness is unknown. There are several factors that are generally suggested for avoiding its use. Corporeal punishment is dehumanizing to the child (imagine your feelings at being placed over a teacher's knee!) and teaches him to use physical aggression to control the behavior of others. It can rarely be used dispassionately and, therefore, it is difficult to apply it contingently and avoid extreme administration. Finally, other forms of punishment, which have proven to be effective, do not have these negative side effects.

---

* This recommendation might appear to be in conflict with Johnston's (1972) guideline (a) that initial intensities of punishing stimuli should be as great as possible. However, they are complementary. The *form* of punishment selected should be the mildest that can be effective (e.g., time-out is less aversive than electric shock, individual response-cost contingencies are less aversive than group contingencies). However, once a form is selected it should be applied with sufficient intensity to insure its effectiveness. Individuals can adapt to intensely punishing stimuli if they are first presented with an ineffective level which is gradually increased in an effort to secure response suppression (Church, 1963). This is not to suggest that an extreme level should be presented. Rather, the behavior therapist should begin the program with a level that research data and his own experience suggest has a high likelihood of being effective without being excessive.

Summary

The focus of this chapter has been on operant techniques for modifying the behavior of children. We first considered alleviation of behavioral deficits. The primary approaches discussed in that section were prompting and positive reinforcement. Guidelines for using positive reinforcement were provided along with examples of a variety of reinforcement techniques.

The next section considered reduction of behavioral excesses and described the use of extinction procedures, DRO, and punishment. A variety of punishment procedures were discussed, including verbal reprimands, time-out, response cost, electric shock, and overcorrection. The use of positive reinforcement in conjunction with extinction and punishment was emphasized. The use of all three procedures was further elaborated in the section on token economies. Two different strategies for conducting token programs were described, and major issues associated with the use of token programs were discussed.

The application of operant techniques in the home was then described. Two strategies for home intervention were discussed: training parents to apply specific techniques for modifying specific behaviors and training in contingency contracting as a general parental skill. The work of G. R. Patterson was emphasized.

The final section focused on ethical considerations when applying operant techniques. Three major issues were considered: (1) problems in securing informed consent for programs and in determining appropriate treatment goals, (2) controversy over the use of extrinsic reinforcement, and (3) ethical constraints for the use of punishment. Guidelines for dealing with all three issues were presented.

References

Alexander, J. F., & Parsons, B. V. Short-term behavioral intervention with delinquent families: Impact on family process and recidivism. *Journal of Abnormal Psychology,* 1973, *81,* 219–225.

Arnold, J. E., Levine, A. G., & Patterson, G. R. Changes in sibling behavior following family intervention. *Journal of Consulting and Clinical Psychology,* 1975, *43,* 683–688.

Axelrod, S. Comparison of individual and group contingencies in two special classes. *Behavior Therapy,* 1973, *4,* 83–90.

Ayllon, T., & Roberts, M. D. Eliminating discipline problems by strengthening academic performance. *Journal of Applied Behavior Analysis,* 1974, *7,* 71–76.

Azrin, N. H., & Holz, W. Punishment. In W. K. Honig (Ed.), *Operant behavior: Areas of research and application.* New York: Appleton-Century-Crofts, 1966.

Bachman, J. A. Self-injurious behavior: A behavioral analysis. *Journal of Abnormal Psychology,* 1972, *80,* 211–224.

Baer, D. M., & Wolf, M. M. The entry into natural communities of reinforcement. In R. Ulrich, T. Stachnik, & J. Mabry (Eds.), *Control of human behavior. Vol. 2: From cure to prevention.* Glenview, Ill.: Scott, Foresman and Co., 1970.

Baer, D. M., & Wolf, M. M. The entry into natural communities of reinforcement. In R. Ulrich, T. Stachnik, & J. Mabry (Eds.), *Control of human behavior. Vol. 2: From cure to prevention.* Glenview, Ill.: Scott, Foresman and Co., 1970.

Barrish, H. H., Saunders, M., & Wolf, M. M. Good behavior game: Effects of individual contingencies for group consequences on disruptive behavior in a classroom. *Journal of Applied Behavior Analysis*, 1969, *2*, 119-124.

Barton, E. S., Guess, D., Garcia, E., & Baer, D. M. Improvement of retardates' mealtime behaviors by timeout procedures using multiple base-line techniques. *Journal of Applied Behavior Analysis*, 1970, *3*, 77-84.

Becker, W. C. *Parents are teachers: A child management program*. Champaign, Ill.: Research Press, 1971.

Birnbrauer, J. S. Mental retardation. In H. Leitenberg (Ed.), *Handbook of behavior modification and behavior therapy*. Englewood Cliffs, N. J.: Prentice-Hall, 1976.

Brown, B. S., Wienckowski, L. A., & Stolz, S. B. *Behavior modification: Perspective on a current issue*. U. S. Department of Health, Education, and Welfare Publication No. (ADM) 75-202, Washington, D. C.: U. S. Government Printing Office, 1975.

Buell, J., Stoddard, P., Harris, F. R., & Baer, D. M. Collateral social development accompanying reinforcement of outdoor play in a preschool child. *Journal of Applied Behavior Analysis*, 1968, *1*, 167-173.

Church, R. M. The varied effects of punishment on behavior. *Psychological Review*, 1963, *70*, 369-402.

Corte, H. E., Wolf, M. M., & Locke, B. J. A comparison of procedures for eliminating self-injurious behavior of retarded adolescents. *Journal of Applied Behavior Analysis*, 1971, *4*, 201-213.

Drabman, R., & Spitalnik, R. Social isolation as a punishment procedure: A controlled study. *Journal of Experimental Child Psychology*, 1973, *16*, 236-249.

Drabman, R., Spitalnik, R., & O'Leary, K. D. Teaching self-control to disruptive children. *Journal of Abnormal Psychology*, 1973, *82*, 10-16.

Feingold, B. D., & Mahoney, M. J. Reinforcement effects on intrinsic interest: Undermining the overjustification hypothesis. *Behavior Therapy*, 1975, *6*, 367-377.

Ferber, H., Keeley, S., & Shemberg, K. Training parents in behavior modification: Outcome of and problems encountered in a program after Patterson's work. *Behavior Therapy*, 1974, *5*, 415-419.

Foxx, R. M., & Azrin, N. H. Restitution: A method of eliminating aggressive-disruptive behavior of retarded and brain-damaged patients. *Behaviour Research and Therapy*, 1972, *10*, 15-28.

Foxx, R. M., & Azrin, N. H. The elimination of autistic self-stimulatory behavior by overcorrection. *Journal of Applied Behavior Analysis*, 1973, *6*, 1-14.

Gardner, W. I. Use of punishment procedures with the severely retarded: A review. *American Journal of Mental Deficiency*, 1969, *74*, 86-103.

Gelfand, D. M., & Hartmann, D. P. *Child behavior analysis and therapy*. New York: Pergamon Press, 1975.

Glynn, E. L., Thomas, J. D., & Shee, S. M. Behavioral self-control of on-task behavior in an elementary classroom. *Journal of Applied Behavior Analysis*, 1973, *6*, 105-113.

Hall, R. V., Axelrod, S., Foundopoulos, M., Shellman, J., Campbell, R. A., & Cranston, S. S. The effective use of punishment to modify behavior in the classroom. *Educational Technology*, 1971, *11*, 24-26.

Hall, R. V., & Broden, M. Behavior changes in brain-injured children through social reinforcement. *Journal of Experimental Child Psychology*, 1967, *5*, 463-479.

Hart, B. M., Allen, K. E., Buell, J. S., Harris, F. R., & Wolf, M. M. Effects of social reinforcement on operant crying. *Experimental Child Psychology*, 1964, *1*, 145-153.

Homme, L., Csanyi, A. P., Gonzales, M. A., & Rechs, J. R. *How to use contingency contracting in the classroom*. Champaign, Ill.: Research Press, 1970.

Hundziak, M., Maurer, R. A., & Watson, L. S. Jr. Operant conditioning in toilet training of severely retarded boys. *American Journal of Mental Deficiency*, 1965, *70*, 120-124.

Johnston, J. Punishment of human behavior. *American Psychologist*, 1972, *27*, 1033-1054.

Kazdin, A. E. Response cost: The removal of conditioned reinforcers for therapeutic change. *Behavior Therapy*, 1972, *3*, 533-546.

Kent, R. N., & O'Leary, K. D. A controlled evaluation of behavior modification with conduct problem children. *Journal of Consulting and Clinical Psychology*, 1976, *44*, 586-596.

Krumboltz, J. D., & Krumboltz, H. B. *Changing children's behavior*. Englewood Cliffs, N. J.: Prentice-Hall, 1972.

Kuypers, D. S., Becker, W. C., & O'Leary, K. D. How to make a token system fail. *Exceptional Children*, 1968, *35*, 101–109.

Levine, F. M., & Fasnacht, G. Token rewards may lead to token learning. *American Psychologist*, 1974, *29*, 816–820.

Levitt, E. E. Psychotherapy with children: A further evaluation. *Behaviour Research and Therapy*, 1963, *1*, 45–51.

Lovaas, O. I., Freitas, L., Nelson, K., & Whalen, C. The establishment of imitation and its use for the development of complex behavior in schizophrenic children. *Behaviour Research and Therapy*, 1967, *5*, 171–181.

Lovaas, O. I., & Newsom, C. D. Behavior modification with psychotic children. In H. Leitenberg (Ed.), *Handbook of behavior modification and behavior therapy*. Englewood Cliffs, N. J.: Prentice-Hall, 1976.

Madsen, C. H., Jr., Becker, W. C., & Thomas, D. R. Rules, praise and ignoring: Elements of classroom control. *Journal of Applied Behavior Analysis*, 1968, *1*, 139–150.

Madsen, C. H., Becker, W. C., Thomas, D. R., Koser, L., & Plager, E. An analysis of the reinforcing function of "sit down" commands. In R. K. Parker (Ed.), *Readings in educational psychology*. Boston: Allyn & Bacon, 1968.

McIntire, R. W. Guidelines for using behavior modification in education. In R. Ulrich, T. Stachnik, & J. Mabry (Eds.), *Control of human behavior. Vol. 3: Behavior modification in education*. Glenview, Ill.: Scott, Foresman and Co., 1974.

McKenzie, H. S., Clark, M., Wolf, M. M., Kothera, R., & Benson C. Behavior modification of children with learning disabilities using grades as tokens and allowances as back-up reinforcers. *Exceptional Children*, 1968, *34*, 745–752.

Meichenbaum, D. H., & Goodman, J. Training impulsive children to talk to themselves: A means of developing self-control. *Journal of Abnormal Psychology*, 1971, *77*, 115–126.

O'Leary, K. D., & Becker, W. C. Behavior modification of an adjustment class: A token reinforcement program. *Exceptional Children*, 1967, *33*, 637–642.

O'Leary, K. D., Becker, W. C., Evans, M. B., & Saudargas, R. A. A token reinforcement program in a public school: A replication and systematic analysis. *Journal of Applied Behavior Analysis*, 1969, *2*, 3–13.

O'Leary, K. D., Kaufman, K. F., Kass, R. E., & Drabman, R. The effects of loud and soft reprimands on the behavior of disruptive students.

O'Leary, K. D., Poulos, R. W., & Devine, V. T. Tangible reinforcers: Bonuses or bribes. *Journal of Consulting and Clinical Psychology*, 1972, *38*, 1–8.

O'Leary, K. D., Turkewitz, H., & Taffel, S. Parent and therapist evaluation of behavior therapy in a child psychological clinic. *Journal of Consulting and Clinical Psychology*, 1973, *41*, 279–283.

O'Leary, S. G., & O'Leary, K. D. Behavior modification in the school. In H. Leitenberg (Ed.), *Handbook of behavior modification and behavior therapy*. Englewood Cliffs, N. J.: Prentice-Hall, 1976.

Patterson, G. R. *Families: Applications of social learning to family life*. Champaign, Ill.: Research Press, 1971.

Patterson, G. R. Interventions for boys with conduct problems: Multiple settings, treatments, and criteria. *Journal of Consulting and Clinical Psychology*, 1974, *42*, 471–481.

Patterson, G. R., & Gullion, M. E. *Living with children: New methods for parents and teachers*. Champaign, Ill.: Research Press, 1968.

Patterson, G. R., Reid, J. B., Jones, R. R., & Conger, R. E. *A social learning approach to family intervention (Vol. 1)*. Eugene, Oreg.: Castalia, 1975.

Peterson, R. F., & Peterson, L. R. The use of positive reinforcement in the control of self-destructive behavior in a retarded boy. *Journal of Experimental Child Psychology*, 1968, *6*, 351–360.

Repp, A. C., & Deitz, S. M. Reducing aggressive and self-injurious behavior of institutionalized retarded children through reinforcement of other behaviors. *Journal of Applied Behavior Analysis*, 1974, *7*, 313–325.

Risley, T. R. The effects and side effects of punishing the autistic behaviors of a deviant child. *Journal of Applied Behavior Analysis*, 1968, *1*, 21–34.

Risley, T. R., & Wolf, M. Establishing functional speech in echolalic children. *Behaviour Research and Therapy*, 1967, *5*, 73–88.

Sachs, D. A. The efficacy of time-out procedures in a variety of behavior problems. *Journal of Behavior Therapy and Experimental Psychiatry*, 1973, *4*, 237–242.

Schmidt, G. W., & Ulrich, R. E. Effects of group contingent events upon classroom noise. *Journal of Applied Behavior Analysis*, 1969, *2*, 171–179.

Smith, J. M., & Smith, D. E. P. *Child management: A program for parents and teachers*. Ann Arbor, Mich.: Ann Arbor Publishers, 1964.

Strober, M., & Bellack, A. S. Multiple component behavioral treatment for a child with behavior problems. *Journal of Behavior Therapy and Experimental Psychiatry*, 1975, *6*, 250–252.

Tate, B. G., & Baroff, G. S. Aversive control of self-injurious behavior in a psychotic boy. *Behaviour Research and Therapy*, 1966, *4*, 281–287.

Tharp, R. G., & Wetzel, R. J. *Behavior modification in the natural environment*. New York: Academic Press, 1969.

Thomas, D. R., Becker, W. C., & Armstrong, M. Production and elimination of disruptive classroom behavior by systematically varying teacher's behavior. *Journal of Applied Behavior Analysis*, 1968, *1*, 35–45.

Wahler, R. G. Oppositional children: A quest for parental reinforcement control. *Journal of Applied Behavior Analysis*, 1969, *2*, 159–170.

Walker, H. M., & Buckley, N. K. The use of positive reinforcement in conditioning attending behavior. *Journal of Applied Behavior Analysis*, 1968, *1*, 245–250.

Walker, H. M., Hops, H., & Fiegenbaum, E. Deviant classroom behavior as a function of combinations of social and token reinforcement and cost contingency. *Behavior Therapy*, 1976, *7*, 76–88.

Weathers, L., & Liberman, R. P. Contingency contracting with families of delinquent adolescents. *Behavior Therapy*, 1975, *6*, 356–366.

White, M. A. Natural rates of teacher approval and disapproval in the classroom. *Journal of Applied Behavior Analysis*, 1976, *4*, 367–372.

Wiltz, N. A., & Patterson, G. R. An evaluation of parent training procedures designed to alter inappropriate aggressive behavior of boys. *Behavior Therapy*, 1974, *5*, 215–221.

Winett, R. A., & Winkler, R. C. Current behavior modification in the classroom: Be still, be quiet, be docile. *Journal of Applied Behavior Analysis*, 1972, *5*, 499–504.

7

Aversive techniques

Introduction

There is a vast literature on the use of aversive techniques for a variety of clinical problems in different kinds of applied settings. Indeed, many chapters (e.g., Barlow, 1972; Hallam & Rachman, 1976; Sandler, 1975) and entire books (e.g., Rachman & Teasdale, 1969) have been written on this topic. Therefore, in this chapter we will focus on a presentation of the major aversive techniques currently used in day-to-day practice. These techniques have been used primarily to modify behavioral excesses that may involve self-injury, harm, or substance abuse (e.g., head banging in retardates, chronic vomiting and sneezing, alcoholism and other addictions), and for those disorders that are considered to be socially reprehensible (e.g., sexual deviations such as pedophilia, exhibitionism, cross-dressing, incest, etc.).*

We will first present a very brief historical introduction of the early use of aversion therapy both in the United States and Russia. Then, we will examine the specific techniques in light of the operant conditioning (punishment), classical conditioning, avoidance training, and escape training models. We will focus on the use of electric shock, covert sensitization, time-out, overcorrection, and response cost. For each of

---

* Recent theoretical expositions (e.g., Begelman, 1975; Davison, 1976) do not subsume homosexuality under this category (i.e., being socially reprehensible). Nonetheless, "treatment" of homosexuality with aversion therapy has been and still is commonplace.

the techniques, we will present the rationale and a clinical description of its application and discuss the range of applicability with respect to types of disorders. Recent empirical support for each of the techniques will also be presented, with illustrations taken from the clinical research literature. In addition, some of the inherent limitations and possible side effects (positive and negative) of the various treatment strategies will be examined.

A brief section of this chapter will be devoted to a comparative evaluation of some of the aversive techniques presented and assessed in preceding sections. Finally, but hardly least of all, we will consider the critical ethical implications and limitations of the use of aversion therapy. Given the general public's highly emotional reaction to the application of aversive techniques (reinforced by fictionalized accounts such as *A Clockwork Orange* by Anthony Burgess), it certainly behooves the conscientious behavior therapist to evaluate the therapeutic, legal, ethical, and moral issues surrounding the use of any given aversive technique. Thus, in this final section we will outline the various ethical and moral dilemmas concerning the utilization of aversion therapy both with adults and children.

Historical Antecedents

The oft quoted saying: "There is nothing new under the sun" is in many ways most applicable to the field of aversion therapy. A simple examination of an individual's interactions with his environment indicates that a multitude of aversive events can potentially take place on a daily basis. This point has been aptly underscored by Kazdin (1975). "Indeed, aversive techniques are deeply enmeshed in many social institutions including government and law (e.g., fines and imprisonment), education (e.g., failing grades on exams, expulsion, and probation), religion (e.g., damnation), international relations (e.g., military coercion), and normal social intercourse (e.g., discrimination, disapproval, humiliation, and social stigma). Routine interactions of most individuals with both physical and social environments result in aversive events ranging from a burn on a hot stove to verbal abuse from an acquaintance" (p. 146).

What, then, is the major difference between these kinds of aversive events and the application of aversion therapy? Quite simply, in the case of aversion therapy, the aversive stimuli are presented in a planned and systematic fashion in order to decelerate certain types of behavior (i.e., surplus behavior). Although punishment techniques are employed, the obvious goal *is not* punishment per se. Quite to the contrary, the terminal goal is rehabilitation or improvement in the patient's psychological condition. Despite the fact that the distinction between fortuitous and planned environmental aversion and aversion therapy is quite clear to all behavioral practitioners, behavior therapists have not been fully successful in conveying this distinction to others (e.g., colleagues holding non-behavioral theoretical persuasions, the general public).

Although the greatest surge of interest in aversion therapy has taken place in the last two decades (see Barlow, 1972; Hallam & Rachman, 1976; Rachman & Teasdale, 1969), there were several earlier attempts at applying aversive strategies with both alcholics and homosexuals. Let us examine some of these applications. For example, in the early part of this century, Kantorovich (1929) reported a study conducted at the Leningrad Psychiatric Hospital in which he described the use of electrical aversion with a group of 20 alcoholics. Treatment consisted of pairing alcohol with a strong electrodermal stimulus (a punishment paradigm), using 5–20 sessions per patient. Of the 20 patients so-treated, 14 had remained abstinent at the follow-up assessments conducted 3 weeks to 20 months after conclusion of aversion therapy. By contrast, 7 of 10 patients in a control condition receiving hypnosis and medication rapidly returned to their former drinking habits post-treatment.

Also using electrical stimulation, Max (1935) shocked his homosexual patient contingent on his imagining homosexual activities. During the course of this treatment, Max found that high intensity shocks were much more effective in decreasing the "emotional value" of the homosexual stimuli than corresponding low intensity shocks. In describing the results of this case, Max referred to improvements seen over a 3-month period as "cumulative."

Apparently, Max's brief note on the clinical use of electrical stimulation did not attract much attention in the therapeutic world, as attested by reports featuring the use of chemical aversion in the 1930s, 1940s, and early 1950s. The most ambitious clinical trial of chemical aversion has been conducted by Voegtlin and his colleagues (Lemere & Voegtlin, 1950; Voegtlin, Lemere, Broz, & O'Halleren, 1941) at the Shadel Sanitorium in Seattle, Washington. Close to 5,000 alcoholics have been treated with chemical aversion by this clinical research group, first using apomorphine and then with emetine (both drugs are emetics and induce nausea and vomiting).

As our succeeding account will undoubtedly indicate, the use of emetics in chemical conditioning treatments is aesthetically unpleasing, and probably accounts for the loss of popularity of this treatment strategy in recent years. In any event, the objective of the treatment procedure was to pair the taste, smell, and sight of alcohol with nausea and vomiting. Treatment was conducted in a soundproof room and first involved an injection of emetine in a dose *insufficient* to elicit vomiting. However, after the injection the alcoholic would be asked to taste, smell, and swallow about 4 oz. of whiskey. This, then would lead to nausea and vomiting. In some instances (after vomiting) the patient was also requested to drink a small quantity of beer, which contained an additional emetic to prolong the period of nausea. Treatment sessions would typically last about 45 min., with four to six sessions conducted over a 2-week interval. To insure maximal "conditioning," other alcoholic beverages would also be paired in such fashion with the emetic.

Following the 2-week treatment period, booster sessions were administered at 6- and 12-month intervals or when a given patient once again might experience an urge to drink. Despite the unpleasantness of the procedure, the results appeared to be remarkably good given our current standards of success.* Lemere and Voegtlin (1950) reported that 44% of their patients (over 4,000) remained abstinent; in some cases follow-ups extended for 10 years. Of the relapses, 878 patients received further treatment, with a 39% success rate being achieved. When the original treatment successes and the successful re-treatment of initial relapses are combined, a total abstinence rate of 51% emerges. Not only is this an excellent rate of success for this most resistive treatment problem, but the extensive and long-term follow-ups are unparalleled in the field. The earlier results were recently cross-validated by Wiens, Montague, Manaugh, and English (1976, in press).

Basic Treatment Paradigms

There are four basic treatment paradigms that have been used during the course of aversion therapy. As noted in our Introduction, they are: (1) operant conditioning (punishment), (2) classical conditioning, (3) avoidance training, and (4) escape training. Although, theoretically, there are some unique features in each of the paradigms, in practice specific aspects of each may be found in a given technique. This point will be further elaborated as we describe each of the paradigms.

Punishment

In the punishment paradigm, the aversive stimulus (be it electrical or verbal) immediately follows the occurrence of the undesirable behavior. Specifically, in the case of alcoholism, the patient may be given a painful electric shock contingent on his actually drinking the alcohol. In contrast to the classical conditioning paradigm, here (in the punishment paradigm) the patient *actually engages* or imagines engaging in the undesirable behavior. Therefore, in the case of the alcoholic, the patient

---

* It should be noted that this sample of alcoholics is somewhat atypical with respect to social class (higher than the average alcoholic) and with regard to the generally good motivation for treatment (greater than the average alcoholic). However, these two variables notwithstanding, the results obtained are still most exceptional.

will actually pour a drink, pick up the glass, and begin to drink the alcohol prior to receiving the electric shock. The objective, of course, is to decrease the rate of drinking behavior to zero when abstinence is the stated treatment goal. As noted by Azrin and Holz (1966), punishment is "a process similar to positive reinforcement in terms of its determinants, but opposite in terms of the direction of behavioral change" (p. 339).

It is clear, however, that some elements of classical conditioning are operating in the punishment model. Barlow (1972) points out that, "These two procedures are often confused and are in fact difficult to separate since during punishment classical conditioning is also taking place. Each time a response is punished, the sensory cues associated with the behavior are being paired with the aversive stimuli in a classical conditioning paradigm. If drinking a glass of whiskey is punished by shock, then seeing and smelling whiskey are also being paired with the aversive stimuli" (p. 92).

Perhaps a clearer or "purer" example of the punishment paradigm can be illustrated by the use of electric shock contingent on self-abusive behavior evidenced in retarded children (Lovaas & Simmons, 1969). In this study, the elements found in the classical conditioning model were apparently minimized, and response-contingent shock served to suppress self-destructive behavior. However, here too it is conceivable that cues associated with punishment were classically conditioned as well.

Classical Conditioning

As was noted in Chapter 2, classical fear conditioning follows procedures developed by Pavlov. Thus, in actual practice, the stimulus that elicits the maladaptive behavior will be repeatedly paired with an aversive stimulus. In the case of alcoholism, the stimulus may be a glass of whiskey (or a picture of one), the maladaptive behavior is abusive drinking, and the aversive stimulus may be electrical, chemical, or verbal. More specifically, the sight or smell of alcohol might be repeatedly paired with a painful electrical shock. Theoretically, as a function of "conditioning," anxiety or fear now become associated with the sight, smell, or taste of the once pleasurable stimulus (i.e., the whiskey), thus leading to diminution or complete cessation of drinking. Also, at the physiological level, an actual conditioned autonomic nervous system response (e.g., increased heart rate) may develop and should appear upon presentation of the whiskey.

Avoidance Training

In this paradigm the patient learns to avoid the aversive stimulus (programmed at a standard time interval following presentation of the maladaptive stimulus) by actually removing (i.e., avoiding) the pleasurable albeit maladaptive response. For example, in the case of a homosexual being shown slides of "attractive" male nudes, he may *avoid* receiving a painful electric shock by pressing a switch that turns off the slide (e.g., Feldman & MacCulloch, 1965). Or, for our alcoholic, he may similarly avoid such electric shock by refusing a drink or pushing it away. In either case, it is assumed that the refusal or avoidance response is reinforced as it reduces anxiety (related to fear of shock) and avoids pain. In consequence, by repeating such trials many times the individual will begin to avoid the formerly pleasurable stimulus (e.g., alcohol, sexual contact with males) in his natural environment.

Escape Training

Escape training is a variant of the avoidance procedure which, in addition, contains elements of the punishment paradigm. More specifically, in the escape training situation the patient is able to *terminate* the aversive stimulus by engaging in a behavior that is more adaptive than the maladaptive response. This paradigm has been used with occasional success in treating alcoholics (e.g., Blake, 1965; Miller & Hersen, 1972). For example, in the case of our alcoholic, he may be asked to sip but avoid swallowing his favorite drink. Electric shock is then administered contingently upon this sip (this is the punishment aspect). However, shock is terminated *only* when he spits out the alcohol (this is the *escape* training aspect). Analogously, in the case of the homosexual, shock would be applied contingently upon his viewing the slide of a nude male and is terminated when the slide is turned off by the patient. A common variant of escape training employed with homosexuals is aversion relief. In this procedure termination of the aversive stimulus is paired with presentation of slides of nude women; the female slides become positive because of their pairing with "aversion relief."

Electric Shock

In discussing the use of electric shock in behavior therapy, we first must underscore the fact that it is of the nonconvulsive variety. This is in contrast to the application of electroconvulsive therapy (ECT), which is a psychiatric treatment used for severe depression (when antidepressant drugs appear ineffective) and less frequently used with some of the schizophrenic reactions (particularly catatonic excitement). Presently, nonconvulsive electric shock is one of the most commonly employed of the aversive stimuli. One of the reasons for its frequent usage is that it is a more precise aversive stimulus than the chemical agents (apomorphine or emetine). That is, the intensity of the stimulus and the length of its application are directly under the therapist's control. Similarly, the interval between the patient's deviant approach behavior (e.g., drinking alcohol, imaginally engaging in a homosexual act) and the actual onset of the shock is also within the therapist's control. By contrast, such controls are lacking when chemical aversion is used (e.g., the therapist *does not* have precise control over the time interval between an injection of apomorphine and its nausea-producing effect). Moreover, the use of electrical stimulation is aesthetically less displeasing than chemical aversion (see Rachman & Teasdale, 1969).

In practice, electric shock (nonconvulsive) is administered through two electrodes placed either on the forearm, fingertips, or calf, fastened with elastic or cloth strips. Electrode paste is often used to increase conductance and to prevent occurrence of possible burns. As individual patients have unique thresholds for shock level, the intensity of the shock is adjusted in each case. Also, because individuals do adapt to shock intensity, levels may have to be increased from one treatment session to the next. This can be determined by observing the magnitude of the patient's reflexive response to shock. Finally, it should be recognized that since the electric shock is painful (albeit safe), patients frequently do not comply with the treatment or may prematurely terminate treatment.

We might also note that in this section we will refer to the use of nonconvulsive electrical stimulation as electric shock. However, elsewhere the terms electrical stimulation and electrical aversion have been used interchangeably with electric shock of nonconvulsive intensities. To be absolutely correct, the term electrical aversion should be used only with respect to the case of electrical shock in the classical conditioning paradigm.

In the succeeding sub-sections we will examine the use of electric shock while illustrating its application for a variety of disorders. For purposes of clarity, the illustrations will be categorized under the four primary aversive paradigms (punishment, classical conditioning, avoidance training, escape training). Following these case illustrations, we will present a more general discussion of the issues involved in using electric shock as a behavior-therapeutic technique.

Punishment Training

In recent years behavior therapists have occasionally turned their attention to the treatment of medical disorders (e.g., persistent vomiting in infants and adults of a non-medical etiology) that were considered to be of life-threatening proportions (see Cunningham & Linscheid, 1976; Kohlenberg, 1970; Lang & Melamed, 1969; Sajwaj, Libet, & Agras, 1974). With the exception of the Sajwaj, Libet, and Agras (1974) study, response-contingent shock was used as the aversive stimulus. Let us examine the most recently published case involving the elimination of chronic vomiting in an infant by using contingent electric shock in a punishment paradigm.

Cunningham and Linschied (1976) report the case of a 9¹/₂-month-old male infant who was hospitalized for malnutrition and weight loss due to ruminative vomiting (a life-threatening disorder in which the infant vomits, chews, and reswallows his food). The patient's symptomatology was first noted at the age of 6 months, and within 2 weeks it worsened to the point where hospitalization was required. As no physical etiology was determined, the patient was given a diagnosis of "psychogenic rumination." Over the next 3¹/₂ months a variety of medical and psychological approaches failed to control the rumination. Therefore, in light of the patient's deteriorating condition, it was decided to try an aversive procedure.

The punishment procedure simply consisted of shocking the patient (electrodes attached loosely to his calf), contingent on observations of rumination. These shocks were of a 0.5 sec. duration given at 1-sec. intervals. Shocks were terminated whenever rumination ceased. Shock level was initially set at 0.5 milliamperes and increased in steps of 0.5 milliamperes until a 4.5-milliampere level was reached. At this intensity the child whimpered when shocked, but rumination stopped altogether. To insure generalization of treatment effects, shocks were administered to the child in several settings (e.g., in bed, in his walker, in a simulated home environment) and with a variety of observers present.

Introduction of contingent electric shock on the 1st day resulted in a decrease of rumination episodes from a baseline level of 36 to 4. Over the 14 days of treatment, number of rumination episodes per day was somewhat variable but in the low range. Not only had ruminating decreased substantially but amount regurgitated was also greatly decreased. In addition, a marked improvement in the child's social behavior was observed (cried less, babbled again, showed increased motor activity).

The results of treatment presented with respect to daily weight appear in Fig. 7.1. A sharp linear increase in weight to 19 lbs. was noted during treatment. At the 6-month follow-up the child weighed 30 lbs., with no further evidence of rumination. At an earlier (3-month) follow-up evaluation the patient had evidenced normal social and motor development. It should be pointed out that similar successes using contingent electric shock had been reported by Lang and Melamed (1969) and Kohlenberg (1970) for such persistent vomiting in an infant and a 21-year-old retardate, respectively.

In the next study to be presented, some of the problems inherent in the use of electric shock will be documented. These include the small proportion of adult subjects willing to participate in this kind of treatment in addition to the active avoidance and/or escape of the procedure for those who *are* willing to volunteer. Powell and Azrin (1968) were interested in reducing cigarette smoking in three subjects (two graduate students and one professor), using a specially designed cigarette case

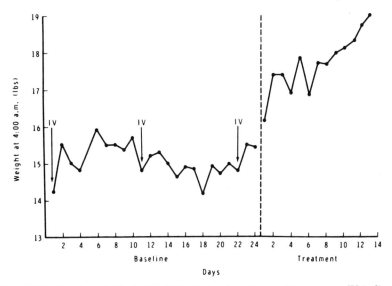

Fig. 7.1 Patient's weight at 4:00 A.M. during baseline and treatment. *IV* indicates days on which intravenous feedings were required. (Reprinted with permission from: C. E. Cunningham and T. R. Linscheid: *Behavior Therapy*, 7: 231, 1976.)

that delivered a shock when opened; it also activated a counter for purposes of data collection. Of 20 subjects initially contacted only three finally completed the experiment.

There were five distinct experimental phases in this study. The first consisted of the subjects' self-recording number of cigarettes smoked. In the second phase, subjects read literature concerning the hazards of smoking. In phase three, the cigarette case (containing shock aparatus) was worn but shock was not activated when the case was opened for purposes of taking out a cigarette. In the fourth phase, subjects did receive shock contingent on opening the case. Finally, in the fifth phase, the apparatus was worn but shock was again deactivated.

The results of this study indicated that during the first three phases rate of cigarette smoking was essentially unchanged. The specific results for phase four appear in Figs. 7.2 and 7.3. Examination of Fig. 7.2 shows that smoking rate decreased as a function of increasing shock intensity. However, a concurrent measure of duration of time the apparatus was worn (Fig. 7.3) indicates a decrease for subjects one and two as a function of the intensity of the shock stimulus. A slight increase was observed for subject three. In the final phase of experimentation, when shock was discontinued, rate of smoking returned to the pre-punishment level.

Based on these rather disappointing results, Powell and Azrin (1968) question the practical utility of using electric shock for the problem of cigarette smoking. They contend that, "For the subjects who did com-

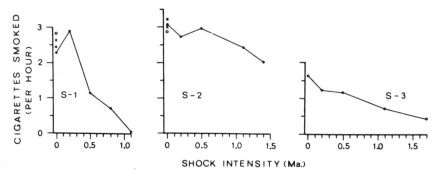

Fig. 7.2 Rate of smoking as a function of punishment intensity. *Open circles* represent written self-reports. Points designated *X* represent written self-reports after review of health hazard literature. The *closed circles* not connected by the line represent redeterminations. (Reprinted with permission from: J. Powell and N. Azrin: *Journal of Applied Behavior Analysis*, 1: 63, 1968.)

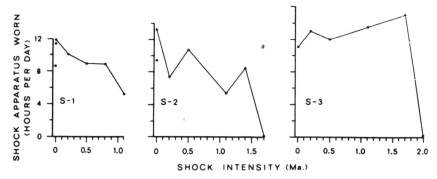

Fig. 7.3 Duration that shock apparatus was worn as a function of punishment intensity. *Points not connected* by the line represent redetermined points. Lower point for S-1 represents the first redetermination; upper point the second redetermination. (Reprinted with permission from: J. Powell and N. Azrin: *Journal of Applied Behavior Analysis*, 1: 63, 1968.)

plete the experiment, the shock punisher produced escape or avoidance reactions: as the punishment intensity increased, the duration decreased for which the subjects would remain in contact with the punishment contingency decreased (sic); ultimately, an intensity was reached at which they refused to experience it altogether. Thus, it seems that the use of aversive stimulation can result in the unwanted by-product of decreased participation on the part of subjects, or in the most extreme instance, in their terminating all such participation" (p. 69).

Next we will examine the use of electric shock in suppressing the self- and other-destructive behaviors of autistic and retarded childen (cf. Birnbrauer, 1968; Lovaas & Simmons, 1969; Risley, 1968). Rather than focusing on one study, we will abstract the general findings obtained in the three aforementioned papers, citing the immediate beneficial effects of shock, the concurrent improvements in pro-social behaviors exhibited by these children, and the limitations concerning generalization of effects. Research in this area is of paramount importance considering the magnitude of self-inflicted injury (e.g., head banging, arm banging, face beating, biting of arms, wrists, shoulders, etc.) and destructive behaviors (biting and breaking furniture, biting and hitting others). Due to such behaviors these children are frequently institutionalized, thus depriving them of parental attention and love. Moreover, as destructive behavior persists in the institutional setting, these children tend to be physically restrained and/or placed in seclusion, thereby further inhibiting their motoric and psychological development. Although pharmacological treatments are applied, success of medication in reducing destructive behavior is not great.

In the typical punishment paradigm used to decrease destructive behavior, a painful electric shock is administered contingent upon evidence of such behavior. An attempt is made to minimize the interval between the behavior and the shock to about 1 sec. Because of the rapid motility of these children, a portable shock apparatus has been used. Lovaas and Simmons (1969) describe it as follows: "The inductorium was a 1-ft. long rod with two electrodes, 0.75 in. apart, protruding from its end. The shock, delivered from five 1.5-v flashlight batteries, had spikes as high as 1400 v at 50,000 ohms resistance. It was definitely painful to the experimenter, like a dentist drilling on an unanaesthetized tooth, but the pain terminated when shock ended" (p. 149). (Much to the dismay of critics of this behavioral approach, the inductorium has been used primarily in the past as a "cattleprod.")

The results of the studies indicate that destructive behavior (self and other) can be rapidly suppressed, particularly when the level of shock is at a high intensity. However, treatment effects tend to be stimulus bound. That is, destructive behavior will remain suppressed in the presence of the therapist that applied shock but not in the presence of a second therapist who has not applied shock. Also, treatment effects in one environment do not automatically generalize to a new environment. (The procedure must be repeated in the second environment as well.) Similarly, generalization from one form of destructive behavior to a second type of destructive behavior tends to be weak. Here too, the procedure has to be repeated for each of the behaviors. Pairing a loud "No" or "Don't" before onset of shock and then using it by itself in the absence of shock to control the behavior is effective only at times. On the more positive side (and contrary to theoretical expectation), there appear to be some beneficial side effects of punishment, including improved eye and body contact with the therapist as well as decreases in inappropriate behaviors such as crying, whining, and facial grimacing. Reasons for and mechanisms underlying such improvements in concurrent behaviors are not known. Finally, although the short-term effects of treatment appear promising, less is known about the durability of response-contingent shock in the absence of teaching these children more adaptive behaviors. Despite these limitations, as stated in Chapter 6, this approach has had the most rapid and extensive effects on self-abusive behavior.

The punishment paradigm has also been employed in the treatment of sexual deviation (e.g., Marks & Gelder, 1967). Sexual deviations so treated include: fetishism, transvestism, pedophilia, homosexuality, voyeurism, etc. The course of treatment is well illustrated by a representative case from the series of five patients treated by Marks and Gelder (1967). The patient was a 21-year-old, unmarried male university student who had been cross-dressing (accompanied by masturbation) in women's clothing since the age of 13. He had never experienced intercourse and did not have any girlfriends. As the patient was particularly fond of cross-dressing using panties, pyjamas, a skirt and blouse, and a slip, these stimuli were used during the course of assessment and treatment. The patient's erectile response to these stimuli was measured with a penile transducer (see Chapter 9), while attitudes toward these same sexually arousing stimuli were measured with a self-report inventory (the Semantic Differential).

During baseline assessment erectile strength to women's clothing and to a photograph of a nude woman were obtained. These data appear in the first bar graph on the bottom part (Patient B) of Fig. 7.4. Treatment consisted of shocking the patient (arm or leg) while he looked at or touched one of the garments. There were 20 trials for each piece of clothing, with shock administered on 75% of the trials. After six sessions of treatment (shock for panties) no erection to panties occurred, even after 3 min. of exposure (see Patient A, Fig. 7.4). Then, pyjamas (three sessions), skirt and blouse (six sessions), and slip (three sessions) were treated in succession in a multiple baseline format. Interestingly, erectile response to the nude female was still very much present, even after erections to women's clothing has been eliminated. This, then, shows the *extreme specificity* of the treatment with respect to the particular stimulus under consideration.

Although the other patients treated by Marks and Gelder (1967) also showed specificity of treatment effects, they were not as pronounced as in this illustrative case. Concurrent with changes in erectile strength were changes in attitude (deviant sexuality now devalued) as well as improvements in the patients' general lives including heterosexual adjustment. However, extensive and detailed follow-up data are not provided.

An interesting application of the use of electric shock for alcoholics (in a punishment paradigm) was presented by Wilson, Leaf, and Nathan (1975). Using an experimental analysis research design (subjects serving as their own controls in a variety of conditions), the effects of

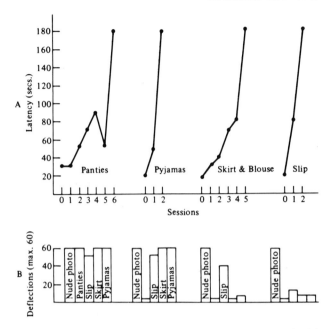

Fig. 7.4 Specificity of autonomic changes (Patient B). (Reprinted with permission from: I. M. Marks and M. G. Gelder: *British Journal of Psychiatry*, 113: 711, 1967.)

experimenter-administered shock and self-administered shock were evaluated in four chronic alcoholics. Throughout all phases of treatment, subjects were given free access to alcohol but with a maximal consumption of 30 oz. a day and a 10-min. interval between each 1-oz. drink. The first phase consisted of 2 days of baseline observation and a "recovery day." In the next phase (experimenter-administered shock) a 2-sec. shock (3–10 milliamperes) was administered following each 1-oz. drink that was consumed. The third phase involved a return to baseline. During the fourth phase subjects were requested to self-administer shock, also following each 1 oz. of alcohol consumed. However, shock here was administered on a variable ratio schedule (VR 2, VR 4, VR 20) to determine whether it could be faded out while alcohol consumption remained low. (VR 2 means that on the average the subject was able to drink 2 oz. before being shocked; VR 4 means that on the average the subject was able to drink 4 oz. before being shocked, etc.) In the fifth phase baseline conditions were reinstated. In the sixth and final phase self-administered shock was reinstituted on a 100% schedule.

The results of this experimental analysis are presented in Fig. 7. 5. Examination of these data indicate relatively high levels of consumption for all subjects during baseline. As expected, experimenter-administered punishment markedly reduced consumption, which returned to baseline levels when it was discontinued in the next phase. Self-administered shock seemed to be effective in the fourth phase, but alcohol

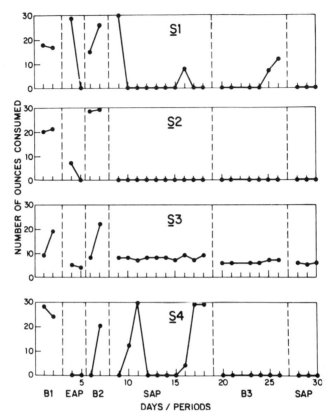

Fig. 7.5 Total number of ounces of alcohol consumed by each subject across baseline (*B*) drinking, experimenter-administered (*EAP*), and self-administered punishment (*SAP*) conditions. (Reprinted with permission from: G. T. Wilson, R. C. Leaf, and P. E. Nathan: *Journal of Applied Behavior Analysis*, 8: 13, 1975.)

consumption was variable for *S*1 and *S*2. A return to baseline in phase five indicates zero levels of consumption for *S*2 and *S*4, a low level of consumption for *S*3, and an initially low but then increasing level of consumption for *S*1. In the final phase, self-administered shock once again seemed to be effective in reducing consumption.

In summary, this experimental analysis clearly documents the suppressing effects of both experimenter- and self-administered shock. In a separate experimental analysis, also presented in this report, Wilson, Leaf, and Nathan (1975) demonstrated that the suppressing effects of shock *were not* due to placebo effects or those of experimental demand. In this latter analysis, self-administered shock was somewhat superior to experimenter-administered shock. Although these analyses suggest the promise of the punishment paradigm in decreasing alcohol consumption on a short-term basis, studies evaluating the long-term effects of such treatment have yet to be done.

Classical Conditioning

In reviewing the literature on the use of electric shock, it becomes clear that there are relatively few studies that totally fit the "classical" conditioning paradigm.* To the contrary, most involve at least some elements of the punishment model in that electric shock follows a semi-active response (e.g., conjuring up a deviant sexual fantasy, tasting alcohol) on the part of the sexual deviate or alcoholic. However, there are two important studies that do approximate our definition of the classical conditioning paradigm. Moreover, these two studies are of particular interest as the investigators in each case ascertained whether a conditioned physiological response (heart rate, skin resistance) to deviant sexual and alcoholic stimuli was observed following treatment.

Hallam and Rachman (1972) applied electrical aversion therapy to seven sexual deviates. Therapy sessions lasted 30–60 min., and ranged from 12–25 sessions for the seven patients. Treatment consisted of having the patient imagine fantasies of the deviant sexual stimulus or act. Shock was presented to the patient's leg following his signal that the deviant image was clear. In some cases, slides were used to stimulate fantasy. Deviant scenes were presented in hierarchical fashion (least to most arousing), with a trial for a given scene terminated when it failed to arouse the patient sexually or when latency to fantasy was greater than a few minutes. Shock was administered during 80% of the trials.

The patients' autonomic responses (i.e., heart rate) to deviant fantasies were evaluated before and after aversion treatment. Follow-ups for the seven patients ranged from 3 to 11 months. Four of the seven patients so treated were successes. It appeared that successfully versus unsuccessfully treated patients were differentiated on the basis of "time required to imagine deviant sexual material." After treatment, all seven patients showed accelerated cardiac response (increased heart rate) to deviant sexual fantasy material. This suggests the possibility of a classically conditioned response. Indeed, Hallam and Rachman (1972) argue that, "The lengthening of latencies to deviant fantasy production after aversion for sexual deviation suggests a specific learning mechanism" (p. 180).

In contrast to the above, Hallam, Rachman, and Falkowski (1972) were unable to find a conditioned cardiac or skin resistance response for a group of alcoholics who received electric shock contingent on viewing slides of alcoholic stimuli and such shock contingent on tasting, smelling, and seeing their preferred drink. Consistent with classical condi-

---

* An exception, of course, is the very brief clinical report presented by McGuire and Vallance (1964). Classical conditioning techniques have also been used as part of more comprehensive behavioral programs (e.g., Marshall, 1973) or in comparative analyses (e.g., Feldman & MacCulloch, 1971; McConaghy, 1975).

tioning theory, it had been expected that following electrical aversion: (1) alcoholics would evidence conditioned heart rate responses to alcoholic stimuli, (2) similarly, they would evidence conditioned galvanic skin resistance responses to alcoholic stimuli, and (3) they would report *anxiety* in response to such stimuli. However, none of these hypotheses was substantially borne out. Evidence post-treatment for cardiac or skin resistance conditioning was absent. Successes (whether from the aversion therapy group or the control group) "showed a significant heart rate sensitivity to alcoholic stimuli." Also, contrary to expectation, alcoholic stimuli post-treatment did not elicit "anxiety." At best, these stimuli were viewed as "distasteful," but this change in attitude was unrelated to successful outcome.

Thus, the reasons for the success or lack thereof of electrical aversion with alcoholics remains unclear. Hallam, Rachman, and Falkowski (1972) conclude by saying that, "we would like to suggest that cognitive theorists are likely to find early joy if they concentrate on the treatment of alcoholism whereas conditioning theorists may do better with therapy for sexual disorders" (p. 13). In addition, a more recent study (Russell, Armstrong, & Patel, 1976) evaluating the effects of electrical aversion therapy for cigarette smoking also failed to provide evidence for the clinical conditioning model.

Avoidance Training

Avoidance training procedures have been used by Feldman and his colleagues (Feldman & MacCulloch, 1964, 1965; Feldman, MacCulloch, Mellor, & Pinschof, 1966; MacCulloch, Feldman, & Pinschof, 1965) in the treatment of homosexual patients. The specific treatment used by this team of researchers is known as "Anticipatory Avoidance Training" and involves a series of distinct procedures. First, the homosexual patient is asked to rate a series of slides of men (clothed and unclothed) from least to most attractive. Then, a series of slides of women is similarly rated. Treatment proper consists of having the patient initially view the "least" attractive male slide while attached to electrodes leading to an electric stimulator. (The patient is asked to view each slide as long as he finds it attractive.) If the patient views the slide for more than 8 sec. and does not press a switch that turns off the slide, he receives a painful electric shock. When he finally does depress the switch the shock is terminated (this is an *escape* trial). Soon the patient learns to *avoid* the shock by depressing the switch before the 8 sec. have elapsed. On some trials when he successfully *avoids* shock, termination of the male slide is associated with a female slide (most attractive) being projected.

After three successful avoidance responses have been carried out by the patient, a pre-determined schedule of reinforcement is followed.

One-third of all avoidance responses result in no shock. One-third of avoidance responses are ineffective. That is, the male slide remains on for 8 sec. and the patient receives a brief shock. Finally, one-third of the avoidance trials involve a delay of the slide being switched off, but within the 8-sec. time limit. The three types of trials are randomized within sessions as are the inter-trial intervals. In all, 30 trials are given per session, each session lasting about 20 min. Over the sessions, the hierarchy of male slides (least to most attractive) and female slides (most to least attractive) is presented.

In one of the first reports stemming from this clinical trial (Feldman & MacCulloch, 1965), efficacy of the treatment strategy appeared to be much better with patients between the ages of 30–40 as opposed to those over 40. In the next report (MacCulloch, Feldman, & Pinschof, 1965), response latencies for avoidance in successfully treated patients were longer and displayed a more regular learning curve pattern than those of the unsuccessfully treated patients. Of two successes reported, one of the patients showed definite evidence of a conditioned pulse rate response to presentation of the male slides. In a third report (Feldman et al., 1966), evidence is presented indicating that 23 patients showed improvement on the Sexual Orientation Method (a well-designed self-report measure) while nine patients did not show improvement.

Applying anticipatory avoidance training techniques to four alcoholics, MacCulloch, Feldman, Orford, and MacCulloch (1966) were unable to replicate their initial successes with this diagnostic category. (In fact, the sub-title of their article is: "A record of therapeutic failure.") Essentially, the same procedures were applied here as in the treatment of the homosexuals. Instead of slides of males, those of alcoholic stimuli (e.g., photographs of beer and liquor), in addition to viewing actual liquor and listening to a tape recording inviting the patient to drink, were substituted. Similarly, instead of using slides of females as the "relief" (from shock) stimuli, slides of "orange squash" were so substituted. The four alcoholics were given 10–46 sessions of treatment, treatment ending when the hierarchy of alcoholic stimuli had been completed.

All four patients were therapeutic failures and resumed drinking. Evaluation of response latencies showed considerable fluctuation over trials; pulse rate data did not reveal a tendency toward a conditioned response. In attempting to account for this failure, the investigators consider the possibility that alcoholics display a "pathological biochemical necessity" for alcohol and that treatment should involve more than just the visual and auditory sensory modalities for the alcoholic.

Although anticipatory avoidance training procedures do not seem to be effective in the treatment of chronic alcoholism, other applications of avoidance training have resulted in the development of "social drinking" in some alcoholics (Lovibond & Caddy, 1970; Mills, Sobell, & Schaefer, 1971). For example, Lovibond and Caddy (1970) describe a technique whereby alcoholics are taught to discriminate blood alcohol concentration (BAC) levels. (Blood alcohol level is the criterion used by police to determine "drunkenness" in the context of traffic violations. Presumably, BAC is one of the cues non-alcoholics use to determine when to stop drinking.) Treatment involves the patient's drinking at a steady rate until a BAC level of 0.065 is reached (usually over a 1½-hour period). Throughout training the patient is asked to estimate his BAC level and is given periodic feedback based on a breathalyzer reading. The patient is instructed that he may drink but that he will receive painful shocks (5–7 milliamperes of 1–6-sec. duration) if he exceeds the criterion BAC level (0.065%). Thus, the therapeutic task is to *avoid* being shocked (administered on 80% of the trials in which the stated level is exceeded). After 6–12 sessions (30–70 shocks having been administered) treatment is discontinued. During the course of treatment the patient learns those cues (e.g., skin on cheeks tightening, or ears pop at a given BAC level) that discriminate his social drinking from abusive drinking.

Of 31 patients (experimental group) receiving this treatment, 21 were considered to have reached their goal of social drinking (16–60-week follow-ups). A comparison with a control condition (patients receiving contingent shock prior to reaching a 0.065% BAC level and sporadically after exceeding this criterion) revealed a smaller drop-out rate for the experimental subjects. In addition, experimentals versus controls evidenced a significantly smaller post-hospital consumption rate of alcohol. Lovibond and Caddy (1970) note that, "rather than developing a marked aversive reaction to alcohol, many successfully treated subjects appear to lose the desire to drink after the first few glasses" (p. 437).

Mills, Sobell, and Schaefer (1971) taught their experimental subjects (13 hospitalized male alcoholics) to drink like social drinkers (i.e., small sips, small amounts, mixed drinks). Their patients had free access to alcohol during experimental drinking sessions and could *avoid* painful electric shocks (30% above or at individual pain thresholds) by behaving like social drinkers. This within hospital analysis indicated that four patients were able to learn during the first treatment session; the other nine patients required 12–14 sessions before they approximated the drinking habits of social drinkers.

In summary, avoidance training procedures seem to offer promise in shaping social drinking habits in some alcoholics. However, anticipatory avoidance training procedures as described by MacCulloch et al. (1966) do not seem to be effective either with respect to clinical follow-up or in terms of establishing conditioned responses at the physiological level.

Escape Training

Blake (1965, 1967) has used an escape paradigm in the treatment of alcoholics. In this treatment the patient is instructed to sip but not to swallow his favorite drink. Concurrent with his taking a sip the patient receives a painful electric shock. When the patient spits out the alcohol into a bowl the shock is terminated. This, then, constitutes the escape trial. In Blake's (1965) first study shock was administered on 50% of the trials, with full treatment averaging 4.93 hours per patient.

Of 37 patients receiving escape training in combination with relaxation training, 54% were considered to be sober at the 6-month follow-up, while 52% of 25 patients were described as sober at the 12-month follow-up. In a separate report (Blake, 1967), an escape training plus relaxation group was considered to have done somewhat better (but not statistically so) than an escape training only group.

In a more recent evaluation, Miller and Hersen (1972) describe the results of a single-case analysis in which the escape paradigm was used. Two alternating baseline and treatment phases and a 6-month follow-up showed the positive effects of electric shock in suppressing drinking as measured in a laboratory drinking task. However, in a still more recent series of single-case analyses, Wilson, Leaf, and Nathan (1975) were unable to show the positive effects of electric shock, using a free operant drinking measure. Similar difficulties in confirming their earlier successes during the escape training paradigm were also encountered by Miller, Hersen, Eisler, and Hemphill (1973). In this study three treatment groups comprised of 10 alcoholics each were compared: (1) high shock paired with alcohol sips, (2) low shock paired with alcohol sips, and (3) group therapy in which "confrontation" was the major therapeutic ingredient. Pre-post analyses failed to reveal significant differences among the groups in terms of either decreased consumption on a laboratory drinking task or with regard to changes in attitude toward the alcohol. However, trends (albeit non-significant) were found in favor of the high shock group.

In two other controlled group studies (Vogler, Ferstl, Kraemer, & Brengelman, 1975; Vogler, Lunde, Johnson, & Martin, 1970) conducted in the United States and Germany, evidence for the usefulness of the escape training paradigm with alcoholics is presented. However, methodological difficulties in both studies do not permit clear cut conclusions. Indeed, Vogler et al. (1975) conclude that aversion therapy in itself will not suffice to produce lasting sobriety in alcoholics. To the contrary, aversive techniques will have to be combined and supplemented with treatment strategies that enable the alcoholic to reduce stress and deal more effectively with his interpersonal environment.

Summary and Conclusions

The foregoing reviews clearly indicate that electric shock can be used effectively to decelerate a variety of deviant approach behaviors. In general, it would seem that application of electric shock as the aversive stimulus has resulted in greater success with sexual deviates than with alcoholics. As pointed out by Wilson and Davison (1969), psychophysiological studies suggest that some cues may be more appropriately applied with particular response systems; namely, the use of chemical aversion with alcoholics. Thus, with clinical problems involving consumption (e.g., alcoholism, obesity), at least at the theoretical level, use of nausea-producing agents such as emetine and apomorphine would be expected to produce superior results. Consider, for example, the comparatively excellent results obtained by Lemere and Voegtlin (1950) in their extensive clinical trial with alcoholics. To date, such high rates of success have not been achieved with electric shock (with or without the added benefit of booster treatment).

Perhaps one of the most critical questions regarding the use of electric shock (irrespective of the paradigm followed) is: why does it work when it does? In a recent review, Hallam and Rachman (1976) concluded: "The widely accepted notion that conditioning, and especially classical conditioning plays a significant role in the effectiveness of aversion therapy was critically examined, and the lack of empirical evidence was noted. Patients who develop conditioned fear or anxiety after electrical aversion therapy are rare exceptions. Indifference to, or an alteration in the perceptual quality of the stimulus paired with shock is the more common outcome" (p. 218). Indeed, it is obvious that the patient (i.e., adults and most children) *is* able to discriminate the situation in which the deviant response will result in shock and that situation (extra-therapeutic) where it will not. The specific effects of electric shock were most clearly documented in the studies (previously described) by Risley (1968) and Birnbrauer (1968). In attempting to determine the reasons why these deviant responses will remain suppressed, some writers (e.g., Miller et al., 1973) postulate the patient's use of cognitive-mediational processes. However, although such theoretical speculation would seem to have high face validity, such explanation remains strictly at the theoretical level in the absence of empirical support.

The long-term effects of electric shock have not been carefully studied at this point. Although on a priori grounds it would seem that booster treatments would enhance such long-term successes, the needed controlled group studies are still forthcoming. Also, the importance of teaching such patients alternative and positive responses, although clearly articulated (e.g., Barlow, 1973), have rarely been carried out. (This point applies equally well to the other aversive methods used and is not at all peculiar to electric shock alone).

Finally, it should be noted that many of the variables that contribute to the maximal efficacy of the punishment stimulus (cf. Azrin & Holz, 1966; Kazdin, 1975) have been ignored by clinical researchers when carrying out their treatments. These include the following: (1) the punishing stimulus should be intense, (2) the punishing stimulus should be introduced at full strength, not gradually, (3) delay of punishment should be minimized, (4) continuous punishment (100% schedule) is more effective than a partial schedule (e.g., 80%), (5) the punished response should not be reinforced concurrently, (6) the entire sequence of events leading to a deviant response should be punished, particularly the earlier parts of the response chain, and (7) as already mentioned, the punishing stimulus will be more effective if alternative positive responses are systematically reinforced. It is quite possible that if the above strictures were religiously and systematically attended to in treatment paradigms, then greater suppression of deviant behavior and permanence of results might ensue.

Covert Sensitization

Covert sensitization is a verbal aversion technique in which unpleasant scenes (usually nausea and vomiting) are paired imaginally with scenes of deviant approach behavior (Cautela, 1966, 1967). This technique has been used in the treatment of a variety of sexual deviations (Barlow, Leitenberg, & Agras, 1969; Harbert, Barlow, Hersen, & Austin, 1974; Maletzky, 1974), alcoholism (Ashem & Donner, 1968; Hedberg & Campbell, 1974), and obesity (Janda & Rimm, 1972). In recent years this technique has received wide application, not only because of some of its documented successes, but because: (1) it does not require any equipment (as in the case of electric shock), (2) it can be safely administered in the consulting room, and (3) it can be self-administered by the patient or client when booster treatment is needed.

A careful evaluation of covert sensitization indicates that aspects of the punishment, classical conditioning, and escape paradigms are operating throughout its administration. We will first describe the clinical application of covert sensitization and then point out in which way the aforementioned paradigms may be contributing to the efficacy of the technique.

In typical clinical practice the patient is first taught relaxation after the behavioral assessment has been completed (see Cautela, 1967). This usually requires three to four sessions. Then the patient is given the rationale for the technique and is instructed in visualization (imagery). The state of relaxation often permits the patient to visualize more clearly. Next the therapist will begin to describe scenes involving the deviant approach behavior (e.g., abusive drinking), and completion or near completion of the act (i.e., imaginally) will lead to nausea and vomiting (as vividly described by the therapist). Cautela recommends that the aversive stimuli (nausea and vomiting) should be presented on a continuous basis (100% schedule) contingent on the deviant act and thoughts of engaging in the act. (This is the punishment aspect of covert sensitization.)

An example of a typical narrative for an alcoholic is presented below:

"You are walking into a bar. You decide to have a glass of beer. You are now walking toward the bar. As you are approaching the bar you have a funny feeling in the pit of your stomach. Your stomach feels all queasy and nauseous. Some liquid comes up your throat and it is very sour. You try to swallow it back down, but as you do this, food particles start coming up your throat to your mouth. You are now reaching the bar and you order a beer. As the bartender is pouring the beer, puke comes up into your mouth. You try to keep your mouth closed and swallow it down. You reach for the glass of beer to wash it down. As soon as your hand touches the glass, you can't hold it down any longer. You have to open your mouth and you puke. It goes all over your hand, all over the glass and the beer. You can see it floating around in the beer. Snots and mucous come out of your nose. Your shirt and pants are full of vomit. The bartender has some on his shirt. You notice people looking at you. You get sick again and vomit some more and more. You turn away from the beer and immediately start to feel better and better. When you get out into clean fresh air you feel wonderful. You go home and clean yourself up" (Cautela, 1967, pp. 461–462).

The latter part of the presentation, when the alcoholic leaves the barroom and begins to feel better, represents the escape aspect of the technique. Here the patient engages in an incompatible but more desirable alternative behavior. In some cases, hierarchies of scenes involving the deviant behavior are developed. With alcoholics, covert sensitization may have to be repeated for each type of beverage that is typically consumed. Similarly, for the obese, separate application of covert sensitization for each fattening food may be required.

In addition to pairing the nauseous scene with deviant approach behavior in the therapist's office, the patient is asked to practice this association twice a day at home (10–20 trials each time). Many patients report that soon the sight or thought of alcohol (or other deviant stimuli and acts) results in their feeling nauseous (Ashem & Donner, 1968). This, then, is the classical conditioning component of the procedure. That is, alcohol now has become the CS for the CR of nausea. This association is presumed to enable the patient to *avoid* engaging in the undesirable action. The range of treatment sessions is from about 10–20, and in some cases booster sessions are also needed to ensure greater permanence of results (e.g., Harbert et al., 1974).

Clinical Research

Let us now examine some of the single-case and group comparison studies that have evaluated the use of covert sensitization as a treatment strategy. Barlow, Leitenberg, and Agras (1969) applied covert sensitization to a pedophile and a homosexual, using a single-case experimental design to evaluate the results. Two self-report measures served as the dependent variables. The first simply involved the patient reporting his number of deviant urges per day. The second was a daily card sort measure in which the patient rated the desirability of deviant approach behavior (i.e., pedophilia or homosexuality). Using an A-BC-B-BC design, four experimental phases were followed: Baseline, Acquisition, Extinction, Reacquisition. Following Baseline assessment (A) the two patients were administered standard covert sensitization treatment in Acquisition (BC). The Extinction phase (B) simply consisted of continuation of covert sensitization procedures but with the "nauseous" scene removed. Reacquisition (BC) involved the reinstatement of the nauseous scene. As data for both patients were similar, we will present the figure for the first patient only (Fig. 7.6). Examination of covert sensitization in Acquisition reveals a marked decrease in pedophilic urges and a devaluation of pedophilic acts (Card Sort Score). In Extinction the trends were reversed when the nauseous scene was omitted. Finally, in Reacquisition, the reinstatement of the nauseous scene effected a renewed improvement. Barlow et al. (1969) conclude that, "The results indicated that verbal description of a nauseous scene was an effective stimulus, and that pairing the scene with scenes of the undesired behavior was responsible for declines in deviant sexual behavior" (p. 597).

Harbert et al. (1974) describe the case of a 52-year-old man who had

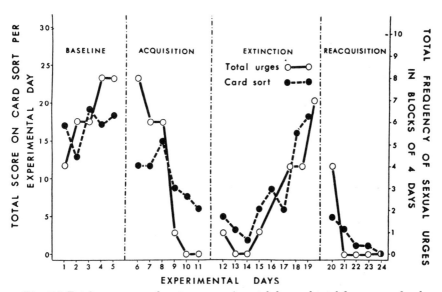

Fig. 7.6 Total score on card sort per experimental day and total frequency of pedophilic sexual urges in blocks of 4 days surrounding each experimental day. (Lower scores indicate less sexual arousal.) (Reprinted with permission from: D. H. Barlow, H. Leitenberg, and W. S. Agras: *Journal of Abnormal Psychology*, 74: 597, 1969.)

continued an incestuous relationship with his 17-year-old daughter for about 5 years. Dependent measures in this study also involved card sort ratings (both the deviant and non-deviant aspects of the patient's relationship with the daughter were rated). In addition, penile circumference change scores in response to slides of the daughter and audiotaped descriptions of sexual activity with the daughter were obtained in the laboratory.

Following baseline assessment standard covert sensitization treatment (consisting of scenes of incest paired with nausea and vomiting) was administered. However, nausea and vomiting proved to be ineffective aversive stimuli for this patient. Therefore, the aversive scene was changed to one in which the patient was discovered engaging in incestuous activity by his current wife, father-in-law, or beloved family priest. An example of this approach is presented for illustration below:

"You are alone with your daughter in your trailer. You get the feeling that you want to caress your daughter's breasts. So you put your arm around her, insert your hand in her blouse and begin to caress her breasts. Unexpectedly the door to the trailer opens and in walks your wife with Father X (the family priest). Your daughter immediately jumps up and runs out the door. Your wife follows her. You are left alone with Father X. He is looking at you as if to ask for some explanation of what he has just seen. Seconds pass, but it seems like hours. You think of what Father X must be thinking as he stands there staring at you. You are very embarrassed and want to say something, but you can't seem to find the right words. You realize that Father X can no longer respect you as he once did. Father X finally says, 'I don't understand this; this is not like you.' You begin to cry. You realize that you may have lost the love and respect of both Father X and your wife, which are very important to you. Father X asks, 'Do you realize what this has done to your daughter?' You think about this and you hear your daughter crying; she is hysterical. You feel like you want to run, but you can't. You are miserable and disgusted with yourself. You don't know if you will ever regain the love and respect of your wife and Father X" (Harbert et al., 1974, p. 82).

Results of this treatment are presented in Figs. 7.7 and 7.8. Examination of these data shows the positive effects of covert sensitization treatment including follow-up assessments. However, as some recidivism was noted at the 3-month follow-up, covert sensitization treatment was readministered for a 3-week period (booster treatment). At the 6-month follow-up the patient was doing well. Fig. 7.8 shows the discriminating effects of covert sensitization treatment. That is, the patient learned to de-value the deviant part of his relationship with his daughter while being able to retain positive feelings about the non-deviant aspects of the relationship with her.

A variation of the covert sensitization procedure, labeled "assisted"

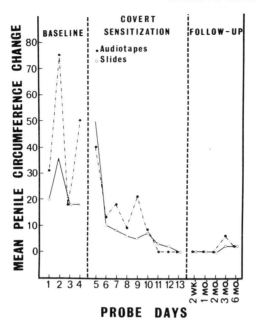

Fig. 7.7 Mean penile circumference change to audiotapes and slides during baseline covert sensitization, and follow-up. (Reprinted with permission from: T. L. Harbert, D. H. Barlow, M. Hersen, and J. B. Austin: *Psychological Reports*, 34: 79, 1974.)

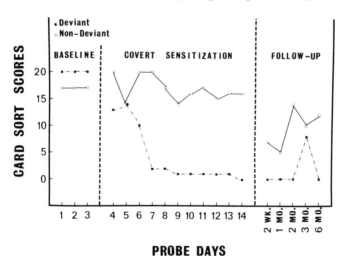

Fig. 7.8 Card sort scores on probe days during baseline covert sensitization, and follow-up. (Reprinted with permission from: T. L. Harbert, D. H. Barlow, M. Hersen, and J. B. Austin: *Psychological Reports*, 34: 79, 1974.)

covert sensitization, has been used by Maletzky (1974) in the treatment of exhibitionism. "Assistance" is provided by presenting a malodorous but harmless substance, valeric acid, at "critical points" during verbal descriptions of the aversive stimulus. This clinical trial involved 10 exhibitionists who received 11–19 treatment sessions each as well as booster treatment at 3-, 6-, and 12-month follow-up intervals. Outcome data were based on self- and observer-reports in addition to a "temptation test" in which an attractive female assistant presented herself in situations where the patients might expose themselves. All but one patient passed the "temptation" test; this patient, then, received an additional 10 treatment sessions and subsequently was able to pass a second "temptation" test. Despite the uncontrolled nature of this study, the results do appear to be promising, particularly in light of independently obtained confirmation of the patients' self-reported improvements. Moreover, none of the 10 patients treated had been apprehended by the authorities at the 1-year follow-up.

Bellack (1974) described a procedure referred to as covert aversion relief; as the title implies, the technique entails both covert sensitization and an aversion relief component. Bellack reported successful application of the procedure with a 22-year-old male homosexual who had no history of satisfactory heterosexual experience. "The patient was first put into deep relaxation. The therapist then described a nightclub and directed the patient to form an image of an attractive male, imagine himself slowly approaching the figure, become increasingly dizzy and nauseous and finally vomiting on him. . . . The relief image was an attractive woman with whom the patient interacted. Over repetitions, the interaction involved increasingly intense sexual activity, culminating in intercourse" (Bellack, 1974, p. 436). Results (based on self-report data) were quite positive. The ABAB sequence indicated that behavior change was under control of the treatment. Follow-up over 2 years indicated that the patient had since married and maintained an exclusively heterosexual pattern.

Janda and Rimm (1972) report using covert sensitization in the treatment of obesity with some success. A group of overweight subjects receiving six sessions of covert sensitization was compared with a group receiving six sessions of "realistic attention-control" treatment and a no-treatment control condition. Following treatment, three covert sensitization subjects verbalizing "intense" reaction to the procedure evidenced a mean weight loss of 21 lbs. in contrast to the three subjects who did not appear to be so affected by the treatment (mean weight loss of 2.3 lbs.). However, overall differences among groups immediately post-treatment were not significant. On the other hand, at the 6-week follow-up the covert sensitization group had lost a mean of 11.7 lbs., the "realistic attention-control group" had gained a mean of 2.3 lbs., and the untreated controls evidenced a mean weight loss of 0.9 lbs. These differences *were* statistically significant.

Although these results are encouraging, the small number of subjects participating in this experiment and relatively brief follow-up period do not permit firm conclusions about the full efficacy of covert sensitization with this clinical population. To the contrary, a most recent review of the behavioral approach to obesity does not indicate considerable empirical support for covert sensitization (see Bellack, 1977, in press).

As noted previously (Cautela, 1967), there are clinical indications that covert sensitization may be useful in the treatment of alcoholics. Such initial success was presented by Anant (1967) in his description of a series of cases so treated. Subsequently, Ashem and Donner (1968) compared a group of alcoholics who received standard covert sensitization (forward classical conditioning), a pseudo-conditioning group (backward classical conditioning), and a no-contact control. Despite the investigators' intent to conduct backward classical conditioning (UCS-nausea before the CS-alcohol), patients in this group made the CS-UCS connection during training. Therefore, the forward and "backward" conditioning subjects were combined and contrasted to the no-treatment controls. This comparison yielded significant differences between experimental subjects and control subjects at the 6-month follow-up. That is, none of the eight control group alcoholics was abstinent; by contrast, 6 of 15 experimental group alcoholics were abstinent.

More recent investigations (e.g., Wilson & Tracey, 1976), however, do not support the earlier clinical and experimental findings. On the contrary, Wilson and Tracey (1976) found both covert sensitization and escape training (using electric shock) relatively ineffective in suppressing drinking when contrasted to a punishment technique (also involving electric shock). This study is representative of the more carefully run experiments (currently being conducted) in which actual drinking measures are obtained "in a semi-naturalistic laboratory setting." Thus, as in the case of obesity, the present evidence for covert sensitization as a viable treatment strategy for alcoholism is not compelling.

Covert sensitization has also been applied as one of many behavioral treatment techniques to reduce smoking behavior (e.g., Lawson & May, 1970; Sipich, Russell, & Tobias, 1974). Although covert sensitization is not less effective than other procedures in effecting reductions in smoking behavior, the absolute smoking decrement achieved with this technique is small (see Lichtenstein & Danaher, 1976, for a comprehensive review). Thus, as was previously articulated (Hunt & Matarazzo, 1973), the primary problem confronting researchers in this area is not response suppression, but response maintenance (i.e., the prevention of relapse). Unfortunately, to date, covert sensitization therapy has not played a very successful role in this respect.

To summarize, then, as in the case of most of the newer treatment applications, the earlier reports on covert sensitization yielded better results than the more recent ones. Either this is a function of initial enthusiasm or better research currently being done. Our survey would indicate that the latter is probably the case. Overall, covert sensitization seems to be effective in the treatment of sexual deviation (e.g.,

Callahan & Leitenberg, 1972; Harbert et al., 1974; Maletzky, 1974). Of course, as aptly underscored by Barlow (1973), aversion techniques, in and of themselves, will not result in permanent changes in the absence of teaching the patient alternative behaviors.

With respect to obesity, alcoholism, and smoking, the results are much less encouraging. It still behooves proponents of covert sensitization therapy to demonstrate its viability as a useful treatment strategy for these clinical problems. Finally, with respect to sexual deviation, obesity, alcoholism, and smoking, the long-term effects of covert sensitization (with and without booster treatments) still warrant considerably greater documentation.

Overcorrection

Overcorrection can best be classified as a punishment procedure that involves two steps. Implementation of the first step consists of having the individual correct the environmental consequences of his behavior. That is, the environment is to be restored to its former level. For example, in the case of a child who exhibits a tantrum and throws food on the floor, he would be required to "clean up the mess." The second step in the procedure consists of having the individual restore the environment to a "better-than-normal" state (Foxx & Azrin, 1973). For example, our child who tantrums, throws food on the floor, and then "cleans up the mess," might also be required to polish the same floor or clean up the floor of a second room.

Overcorrection procedures, originally developed by Azrin and Foxx, have been successfully applied in the treatment of autistic behavior (e.g., Azrin, Kaplan, & Foxx, 1973), enuresis (Azrin, Sneed, & Foxx, 1973), agitative-disruptive conduct (Webster & Azrin, 1972), self-injurious behavior (Harris & Romanczyk, 1976), scavenging behavior in retardates (Foxx & Martin, 1975), as well as in the case of toilet training (e.g., Foxx & Azrin, 1973). In this section we will illustrate the use of overcorrection for a number of behavioral problems and will point out both the positive (e.g., Foxx & Martin, 1975) and negative (e.g., Epstein, Doke, Sajwaj, Sorrell, & Rimmer, 1974; Rollings, Baumesiter, & Baumeister, 1977, in press) side effects of the procedure.

Illustrations

Azrin and Wesolowski (1974) describe the use of an overcorrection procedure, labeled theft reversal, for 34 severely and profoundly retarded adult residents of a state facility. The particular problem at hand was the residents' stealing behavior, which most notably involved taking food from one another and stealing from each other's personal dresser. Episodes of such stealing were reliably recorded, and during the first 5 days of the study, whenever a theft was observed, the resident was simply required to return the item (i.e., simply correction). During the next 20 days of the study, not only was the resident required to return the item stolen, but he was also required to give the "victim" an "additional item identical to the one stolen" (i.e., theft reversal).

As can be seen in Fig. 7.9, during simple correction a high rate of theft was still noted. Institution of theft reversal in the second phase resulted in dramatic decreases, which remained at zero levels after theft reversal was in force for only 4 days. In evaluating the results, Azrin and Wesolowski (1974) suggest four reasons for the success of the procedure. *First,* reinforcement for theft is ended by taking any stolen item from the thief. *Second,* theft reversal is punishing in that the resident is required to exert effort to obtain an additional item for his victim. *Third,* the theft reversal procedure involves time-out from reinforcement as the thief is interrupted from his activities for a given period of

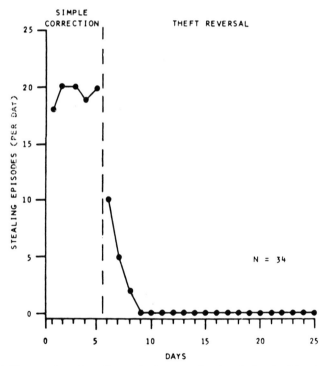

Fig. 7.9 The number of stealing episodes committed each day by 34 retarded adult residents in an institution. During the 5 days of simple *correction,* the thief was required to return the stolen item. During the theft-reversal (overcorrection) procedure (subsequent to the *vertical dashed line*), the thief was required to give the victim an additional item identical with the one stolen, also returning the stolen item. The stealing episodes consisted of stealing food items from the other retarded residents during commissary periods. (Reprinted with permission from: N. H. Azrin and M. D. Wesolowski: *Journal of Applied Behavior Analysis,* 7: 577, 1974.)

time. *Fourth,* a re-educative aspect involves practice of a positive action (i.e., returning items and giving new items to the victim).

Azrin and Wesolowski (1974) also point out that, "On a theoretical basis, the theft-reversal procedure can be expected to be effective with nonretarded persons since the same reasons noted above for the effectiveness of the procedure apply to the normal person" (p. 580). However, this contention has not been empirically evaluated to date.

Foxx and Martin (1975) used overcorrection strategies in the treatment of four profoundly retarded adults who evidenced pica behavior (ingesting non-nutritive substances such as cigarette butts) and coprophagy behavior (ingesting feces). Obviously, both of these behaviors have serious medical repercussions and represent a health hazard for the individual so involved. In one study (a multiple baseline analysis), baseline, physical restraint, and overcorrection phases were compared. Baseline simply involved assessment of the rate of scavenging episodes per day. Physical restraint consisted of placing the resident in a mesh bag for 30 min. following each scavenging episode. In the case of coprophagy, overcorrection involved the following: The resident was first guided to a toilet bowl and encouraged to spit out the feces into the bowl. She was then required to spend 10 min. brushing her mouth, teeth, and gums with a soft toothbrush soaked in an oral antiseptic. Next, she spent 10 min. washing her hands and fingernails in warm soapy water. Finally, she was returned to the area where she was found ingesting feces and required to mop that area with a disinfectant. Very similar procedures were instituted for pica behavior.

The results of this procedure for two female residents appear in Fig. 7.10. Examination of the figure indicates that mere physical restraint did not result in elimination of scavenging behavior. However, institution of overcorrection led to almost total elimination of coprophagy and pica behavior for both residents.

Side Effects

Despite the impressive results obtained in our two illustrations, previous investigations, and in two more recent reports (Foxx, 1976; Harris & Romanczyk, 1976), there are a number of studies emerging in which negative side effects of the overcorrection procedure have been documented. These reports underscore the importance of monitoring concurrent behaviors (i.e., nontarget behaviors) in addition to those targeted for modification. For example, Epstein et al. (1974) developed "hand" overcorrection procedures in order to decrease self-stimulatory behaviors in two children diagnosed as schizophrenic. In both children, the "hand" overcorrection procedure resulted in suppression of the inappropriate hand movements and also in some behaviors that were topographically dissimilar (inappropriate verbalizations). In one child, as

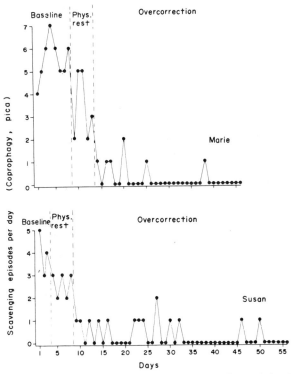

Fig. 7.10 The effect of physical restraint and overcorrection training in the scavenging for feces and trash of two profoundly retarded females. During the baseline conditions no contingencies were in effect for scavenging. During the physical restraint conditions, the women were placed in a mesh restraining bag for 30 min. whenever they scavenged. The overcorrection training was 30 min. in duration. The upper portion of the figure shows the treatment course for Marie; the lower portion shows the treatment course for Susan. (Reprinted with permission from: R. M. Foxx and E. D. Martin: *Behavior Research and Therapy*, 13: 153, 1975.)

inappropriate self-stimulation decreased, appropriate play increased. However, in the second child, inappropriate foot movements increased concurrently with suppression of inappropriate hand movements.

Similarly, Rollings et al. (1977, in press) found that application of overcorrection procedures to suppress stereotyped body rocking in one severely retarded individual led to increased responding in a different collateral behavior (head-nodding). In the second retardate, suppression of head-weaving behavior appeared to be related to an increase in the subject's "emotional" behaviors. Also, the results are mixed with respect to durability of the effects of treatment. For example, although rocking behavior was lower at the 6-month follow-up than in baseline, the rate of the behavior was higher at that point than at the completion of treatment. In addition, little evidence for generalization was found from the training to the ward setting. Finally, degree of response suppression was related to trainer-subject proximity. Close trainer-subject proximity was related to greater degree of response suppression, suggesting that the trainer became a conditioned aversive stimulus and/or a discriminative cue for punishment.

On the other hand, Foxx and Martin (1975) documented positive benefits of the overcorrection procedures used with their subjects who engaged in pica and coprophagy. Not only was response suppression noted, but these four retarded residents showed improved health (intestinal parasites were controlled, improved appetite, gained weight, etc.) and evidenced improved interactions with both staff and other residents. "This integration provided the scavengers with an increased number of positive social interactions with other residents and staff and a greater exposure to potentially reinforcing appropriate activities" (p. 162).

In summary, overcorrection seems to be a powerful behavior change procedure that can result in both positive and negative side effects. The particular circumstances under which desirable and undesirable side effects occur have not been clearly defined at this time. However, as the procedure is relatively new, these issues and those of durability would not be expected to have been resolved. Once again, then, further research should lead to needed clarification with regard to time, setting, and subject characteristics that result in the optimal application of this treatment strategy.

Time-Out

Time-out or time-out from positive reinforcement (Kazdin, 1975) is also a punishment procedure. When applied contingently upon undesirable behavior, access to positive reinforcement is withdrawn for a given amount of time. For example, a psychiatric patient who resides on a token economy ward and engages in temper outbursts might be removed to a room devoid of stimulation for a 15-min. period contingent on each episode. During these 15 min., not only will he be in a non-stimulating environment, but access to privileges (e.g., watching television) as well as the opportunity to earn points in the economy will be withheld.

There is an extensive literature on time-out procedures (see Kazdin, 1975; Leitenberg, 1965) used in the treatment of both adults and children. As some of the time-out procedures with children have already been described in Chapter 6, we will focus here on their application to adult disorders.

Illustrations

Cayner and Kiland (1974) report the successful use of time-out with three schizophrenic patients. In each case a brief 5-min. time-out period (applied contingently) led to elimination of the patient's inappropriate behavior (disruptive social behaviors, "tirade-tantrum" behavior, self-mutilating behavior). The time-out area was a 7 ft. by 11 ft. room that was empty with the exception of a bed and mattress. Staff members applying the procedure wore small buzz timers, signaling them when the time-out period was completed. In each of the three cases described, contingent use of time-out led to a near zero level of the deviant behavior targeted for change. For two of the three patients, such decreases in aberrant behavior resulted in their being discharged from the hospital. The third patient was transferred to another unit in the same hospital. Cayner and Kiland (1974) note the various benefits of using brief time-out in the psychiatric hospital:*

> "Various intrinsic characteristics of brief time out facilitate its use. First, the procedure has clear cut rules which can be easily followed and understood by patients and ward personnel. Second, there is avoidance of long and punitive isolation. The fact that the approach is only mildly aversive makes it acceptable to patients and staff. The temporary inconvenience of a time out does not elicit the angry and resentful responses that other methods of behavioral control sometimes engender. Third, brief 5-min. time out provides up to 12 learning trials per hour. This permits repeated opportunities to test environmental contingencies in a relatively brief period of time and facilitates learning. Finally, the method requires little staff time and automatically provides objective data regarding the effectiveness of the therapeutic intervention" (p. 145).

In an interesting set of studies (Bigelow, Liebson, & Griffiths, 1974; Griffiths, Bigelow, & Liebson, 1974), contingent time-out procedures were effective in reducing alcohol consumption in alcoholics given free access to 95-proof ethanol (1 oz.) mixed with 2oz. of orange juice. In one study, the subjects (chronic alcoholics being treated in an experimental unit at the Baltimore City Hospitals) were given access to 17 drinks (as described above) between 12:00 noon and 11:00 P.M. daily (baseline phase). In the next phase, contingent social time-out, each drink resulted in a 40-min. time-out period from social interactions (e.g., no talking, playing cards or pool with other patients; only minimal contact allowed with the staff). However, watching television was allowed during time-out. This experimental phase was then followed by a return to baseline conditions. The same A-B-A experiment was subsequently repeated, except that access to television was withdrawn in both base-

---

* In this connection, brief-time out needs to be distinguished from the more extended social isolation procedures used for disruptive patients (known as seclusion). Seclusion, *does* involve many of the same characteristics as time-out in that access to positive reinforcement is withdrawn. However, seclusion practices in psychiatric settings frequently require forceful removal of the patient and are maintained for extended periods of time (at times, hours). Also, the clear cut contingent aspects in time-out are not always as apparent when seclusion is implemented.

line and contingent social time-out phases. Thus, in the no television condition the importance of social interaction as a positive reinforcer was heightened.

The results of this experimental analysis appear in Fig. 7.11. Under the full privileges condition, time-out resulted in some suppression of drinking. However, under the no television condition, suppression of drinking was reduced to zero during contingent social time-out. The results obtained here indicate that, "Although social interactions are apparently not solely responsible for maintaining alcoholics' drinking, the current study has demonstrated that social contingencies can effectively suppress drinking under certain conditions . . . . The demonstrated control by social contingencies in the current study suggest that manipulation of social factors may provide one important component of control for the development of alcoholism treatment programs" (Griffiths et al., 1974, p. 333).

Some of the specific parameters of time-out were recently examined by Kendall, Nay, and Jeffers (1975) in a study with acting-out male adolescent delinquents. Acting out involved verbal aggression, physical aggression, noncompliance, and out-of-area behavior. Using a successive treatments design, 5- and 30-min. time-out periods were compared. When presented before the 30-min. time-out, 5-min. contingent time-out periods were successful in suppressing verbal aggression and out-of-area behavior, and to some extent physical aggression. On the other hand, when 5-min. time-outs followed 30-min. time-outs, the aforementioned

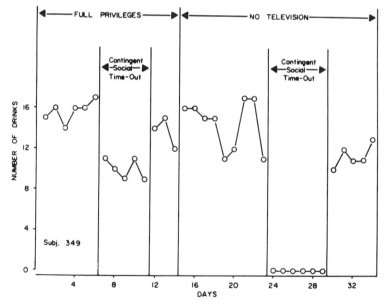

Fig. 7.11 Daily data for subject 349. (Reprinted with permission from: R. Griffiths, G. Bigelow, and I. Liebson: *Behavior Research and Therapy*, 12: 327, 1974.)

behaviors were not suppressed. To the contrary, rates of verbal and physical aggression exceeded baseline levels.

Comment

Time-out is probably an effective punishment strategy for a number of reasons. *First,* it removes the individual from the very situation that may be reinforcing the undesirable behavior in the first place. *Second,* the individual is placed in a situation (i.e., time-out room) whereby access to positive reinforcement (e.g., the ability to earn points on a token economy ward) is withdrawn. *Finally,* in the case of the assaultive individual (who is unable to control his behavior once the aggressive sequence has begun), time-out prevents possible physical harm to the individual in question, others in the environment, and the physical environment itself.

Despite the advantages of using time-out for disruptive behavior, there are some distinct disadvantages for certain classes of individuals. For example, Kazdin (1975) has argued that time-out, when used in the case of the withdrawn patient, may be unwarranted, particularly as the opportunities for social interaction are obviously withheld. Thus, for the withdrawn patient, whose behavior may require a punishment procedure, a response cost strategy (see the next section) may represent a better choice.

It should also be noted that short periods of time-out tend to be effective. Indeed, there is some evidence that lengthening the time interval of time-out will not necessarily increase its efficacy (see White, Nielson, & Johnson, 1972).

Response Cost

Response cost represents yet another type of punishment procedure. Its application involves the imposition of a stated penalty (e.g., fines) or loss (e.g., tokens, points, privileges, material goods) contingent on inappropriate or undesirable behavior. As noted by Kazdin (1975), fines (e.g., as a parking or speeding ticket) represent a type of response cost of which we are all familiar. In contrast to time-out, response cost *does not* involve a particular time limit as to withdrawal of reinforcement. But, on the other hand, for the individual who resides in a token economy and who is repeatedly fined (response costed) for some rule violation, these fines (cumulatively) may lead to decreased motivation to a point where he no longer attempts to earn tokens by exhibiting positive behavior. (Financially, he is bankrupt.) In these instances, application of time-out may be the treatment of choice.

Response-cost procedures have been used to decrease emission of undesirable behaviors in a wide variety of laboratory, educational, and

clinical settings with an equally wide variety of child and adult populations (see Kazdin, 1972). (The use of response cost procedures will be
discussed in Chapter 8 in relation to the token economy).

Illustrations

Let us very briefly review a few applications of response-cost procedures to several problem behaviors and then present some general
conclusions as to the "status of the art" with respect to this procedure.
Kazdin (1971) used a token reinforcement strategy to increase the
productivity of an adult retardate employed in a sheltered workshop.
However, in spite of increased productivity her rate of bizarre ("psy-
chotic-like") verbalizations remained at a high level. Only when tokens
earned for work were then lost contingently upon emitting such verbalizations was a decreased rate observed. Siegel, Lenske, and Broen (1969)
evaluated the effects of response-cost procedures in decreasing speech
disfluencies in five "normal-speaking college students." Each of these
students had been promised $2.00 per experimental session to partake in
the study. Response cost, then, consisted of a one penny loss per dis-
fluency (as indicated on a screen in front of the subject) noted during a
15-min. period in which the subject was expected to speak ad libitum
(i.e., spontaneously). Not only were disfluencies reduced to minimal
levels during this task, but such decreases were also observed during
the course of a second task (reading for about 15 min.) wherein the
punishment contingency was not imposed.

In an interesting variation of the aforementioned study, Lanyon and
Barocas (1975) compared the effects of contingent monetary loss (response cost) and contingent monetary gain (positive reinforcement) on
stuttering in four adult male stutterers. As *both* contingencies resulted
in decreased speech disfluencies, it was concluded that, "the effect of
observing and recording instances of stuttering was more powerful than
the money" (p. 786) (i.e., the feedback aspects of each contingency). In
the second part of this study, however, only monetary gain (not monetary loss) proved to be effective in increasing fluency. Thus, the response-cost contingency in these instances was not the effective ingredient leading to behavioral change.

In recent work, Mann (1972, 1976) has shown how the threat of
response-cost implementation led to substantial weight losses in overweight adult subjects. Mann's procedure consists of establishing a contract with the overweight subject stipulating that he is to surrender a
"series of valuables" to the therapist. These "valuables" are returned
one at a time contingent on reaching weight level goals agreed upon by
both the therapist and client. Response cost here would involve forfei-
ture of "valuables" if the criterion were not successfully met. Despite the
apparent short-term success of this procedure, the long-term effects as to

stability and change in eating habits are unclear (e.g., some subjects took diuretics the day before each weigh-in so as to ensure their meeting the criterion).

Current Status

As with many of the punishment procedures currently employed by behavior modifiers, the long-term effects of response cost have not been fully evaluated (see Kazdin, 1972, 1975). In general, behaviors suppressed with response cost tend to stay suppressed after the response cost contingency has been lifted. Moreover, some of the undesirable side effects, at times observed when other punishment procedures are implemented, have not appeared when response cost has been applied. However, insufficient data are currently available to warrant complete support of the above conclusions (Kazdin, 1972, 1975).

Other Aversive Techniques

In this section we will briefly list and describe a number of other aversive techniques that have been applied by behavior modifiers with some success. However, with the exception of Antabuse (disulfiram), used with alcoholics, the majority of these techniques are relatively new and still require considerably greater empirical support than currently available.

For example, a technique known as shame aversion therapy (Serber, 1970) or assertive behavior rehearsal (e.g., Wickramasekera, 1976) has been applied to sexual exhibitionists. During the treatment, the patient (as previously agreed upon) is asked to *expose* himself in the clinic under controlled conditions. According to Wickramasekera (1976), "The goal is to elicit and 'demythologize' any autistic fantasies that may cognitively mediate the exhibitionism in the natural habitat. Conditions are arranged to increase the probability that the patient will take a pedestrian, critical, and analytic view of what he is doing during the act of 'exposure' " (p. 167). Wickramasekera states that of 20 patients so treated none has relapsed, with follow-up extending to 7 years in some cases.

Foreyt and Kennedy (1971) describe an aversive procedure in which overweight subjects' favorite foods were paired repeatedly with a variety of noxious odors. Although differences in weight loss between experimental and control subjects were significant at the conclusion of treatment, after 48 weeks such differences no longer reached statistical significance. Moreover, the total number of subjects used in this experiment ($N = 12$) does not allow for much generality of the results.

Lando (1975) recently compared two aversive methods for the modification of smoking behavior: (1) *excessive smoking* (at least twice the usual rate consumed), and (2) *rapid smoking* (one puff per 6 sec.). Although both experimental groups evidenced a statistically significant treatment effect after six sessions when compared with control procedures, these effects had disappeared at the 12-month follow-up assessment. Indeed, as in most attempts to modify smoking, relapse appeared across both experimental and control conditions. Only 20% of the subjects were abstinent after 12 months.

A number of studies (Alford & Turner, 1976; Bucher & Fabricatore, 1970; Turner, Hersen, & Bellack, 1977, in press) have shown that electric shock, applied contingently, can lead to response suppression of hallucinations in schizophrenics whose symptomatology remains uncontrolled in spite of phenothiazine medication. However, a sufficient number of such patients have not yet been treated in this fashion to warrant firm conclusions about the long-term effects of the procedure.

Sajwaj, Libet, and Agras (1974) described a single-case analysis of an aversive strategy to control life-threatening rumination in a 6-month-old infant. The technique simply involved squirting a small amount of lemon juice in the infant's mouth contingent on ruminations or evidence of its precursors. The strategy was effective and resulted in suppression of rumination, an increase in weight, and discharge from the hospital. However, as only one case was presented here, further work and comparative analyses with contingent electric shock are obviously warranted.

Although the administration of Antabuse (disulfiram) for alcoholism is considered to be primarily a medical approach to the problem, the approach includes several aspects of aversion therapy. As noted by Barlow (1972), "Theoretically, Antabuse is an aversive treatment since drinking is suppressed by the threat of the Antabuse reaction" (p. 104). This Antabuse reaction consists of nausea and vomiting when the alcoholic drinks concurrently with taking Antabuse pills. Thus, a major problem with Antabuse is the question of the patient's motivation for treatment (i.e., will he/she take the pills as prescribed?). That is, unless the patient is intent on being abstinent, he obviously will cease taking the Antabuse and then resume his drinking. Despite the aforementioned limitations, success rates with Anatabuse have generally been quite good for patients with the following characteristics: " . . . age more than 40, high motivation, high social stability, compulsive personality traits, and an ability to form dependent relations" (Lundwall & Baekeland, 1971, p. 392).

A rather unusual application of aversion therapy in the treatment of hydrocarbon inhalation addiction (i.e., a paint-sniffer) was reported by Blanchard, Libet, and Young (1973). The patient, a 19-year-old male, had been so addicted for about 7 years and had proved refractory to most psychologic and psychiatric interventions. In this single-case analysis, standard covert sensitization and apneic aversion were evaluated. The apneic aversion procedure is described as follows:

"This treatment was conducted by an anesthesiologist . . . . The patient was told that he was to receive an injection which might affect his breathing and which might cause him to begin to dislike paint sniffing. Then he was seated on a table, and an intravenous saline drip was started. He then proceed to spray paint into a bag and bring to his face to inhale. At this point, the anesthetist, from behind a screen, added 20 mg of succinylcholine chloride (Anectine) to the injection, which caused paralysis and apnea within approximately 20 sec. Apnea was allowed to continue for approximately 30 sec before he was artificially respirated" (Blanchard et al., 1973, p. 385).

Objective (i.e., a "smell preference test") and self-report measures were taken repeatedly during baseline and experimental phases. Although initial application of covert sensitization led to some improvement, more rapid and dramatic changes were observed after apneic aversion (four apneic aversion sessions). However, the experimental design does not permit a clear evaluation as to whether apneic aversion was the agent responsible for behavioral change (i.e., decrease in the patient's paint-sniffing behavior). Nonetheless, the 1-year follow-up indicated maintenance of improvement following the patient's discharge from the hospital.

This study obviously raises some interesting ethical considerations that will be discussed in the final section of this chapter.

Comparative Analyses

A review of the aversion therapy literature shows that there are several well controlled studies in which the relative effectiveness of specific techniques has been evaluated for given disorders. Among the disorders considered are sexual deviation (Callahan & Leitenberg, 1972; Feldman & MacCulloch, 1971), alcoholism (Wilson & Tracey, 1976), and antisocial behavior (Burchard & Barrera, 1972). A detailed evaluation of additional studies is well beyond the scope of the present chapter. However, we will examine the four aforementioned investigations that are representative of both group comparison and single-case designs.

Callahan and Leitenberg (1972) compared the effects of contingent electric shock (punishment paradigm) and covert sensitization for two exhibitionists, one transvestite-transsexual, two homosexuals, and one pedophilic homosexual. Treatments were evaluated using penile plethysmograph readings and subjective reports of deviant sexual urges. Single-case experimental designs were used, with each of the two aversive techniques applied to each of the patients but in counter-balanced order. That is, for three of the patients contingent shock was applied first; for the other three patients covert sensitization was applied first. When possible, each technique was introduced twice during the course of treatment.

Although the results seemed to favor covert sensitization treatment over contingent shock with respect to penile circumference change measures, these differences were not substantial. On the other hand, covert sensitization appeared to be more effective in suppressing sexual urges than contingent electric shock. Follow-ups ranging from 4–18 months for given patients were reported. In general, the effects of treatment were highly positive for five of the six patients so treated.

Feldman and MacCulloch (1971) describe an extensive group comparison outcome study in which two types of electrical aversion therapy (classical conditioning and avoidance conditioning) were contrasted to a psychotherapy control condition for homosexual subjects. The results of this study indicate that both the avoidance paradigm and the classical conditioning paradigm resulted in approximately 60% success (i.e., change in sexual preference). By contrast, the psychotherapy control led to only a 20% change in sexual preference.

A comparative evaluation of aversive imagery (covert sensitization), electrical escape conditioning, and contingent electric shock (punishment) for chronic alcoholics has recently been reported by Wilson and Tracey (1976). In this study, 11 subjects were evaluated in single-case experiments in which treatments were presented in counter-balanced orders. The effects of treatment were monitored repeatedly in a "semi-naturalistic laboratory setting" in which alcoholic subjects had access to alcohol. Covert sensitization and electric escape conditioning proved to be relatively ineffective in suppressing drinking and did not appear to differ from one another. On the other hand, the punishment paradigm resulted in substantial suppression of drinking behavior, even when a self-shock phase was introduced. However, subjects "preferred" the covert sensitization procedure as indicated by the lower dropout rate when this strategy was being applied.

Burchard and Barrera (1972) compared the effects of time-out and response cost in suppressing antisocial behavior in six mildly retarded adolescents in a token economy program. Not only were the two punishment procedures contrasted, but different levels of each were evaluated (e.g., 30 tokens response cost versus 30 min. time-out versus 5 tokens response cost versus 5 min. time-out). Using a within subject analysis design, it was found that the higher levels of response cost and time-out were significantly more effective in suppressing antisocial behavior than the lower levels of the punishment for five of six subjects. Moreover, the higher levels of punishment proved to increase in their suppressive value over time. By contrast, the suppressive value of the lower levels of punishment diminished over time. No substantial differences between response cost and time-out were noted.

In discussing these results, Burchard and Barrera comment on the advantages and disadvantages of each of the procedures. Although these issues have been discussed in the sections on Time-Out and Response

Cost, we will recapitulate here. For example, time-out does not permit the subject to continue earning tokens or to evidence improved behavior in the "difficult" stimulus situation. However, when response cost is applied, the subject is still in position to continue earning tokens by emitting desired behaviors, thus providing him with a new learning experience (i.e., he is able to rectify his behavior in a given situation). Of course, if numerous response costs are administered, the subject may be in such debt that his motivation to further earn tokens by exhibiting positive behavior is decreased. We previously have likened this condition to financial "bankruptcy."

Ethical Issues

It should be apparent to the reader, at this point, that the degree of control exerted by aversive techniques over a given individual's inappropriate behavior is not quite as great as professionals of other theoretical persuasions and the general public might currently presume. That is, the almost instantaneous changes (i.e., presumably conditioned) described in fictionalized accounts such as in *A Clockwork Orange* are simply not seen in our respective clinical, rehabilitation, and educational settings in *real life*. Not only are these remarkably rapid changes infrequently seen at the applied clinical level, but unfortunately there are few empirical data supporting the extreme clinical powers of these treatment strategies. However, there certainly *are* data suggesting the potential utility of these techniques for some behavioral problems. Irrespective of the particular efficacy of a given aversive technique, the mere fact that *it is aversive* raises the question of ethical and moral values. That is, under what circumstances is a specific aversive technique to be administered? Related questions are: who administers the technique and to whom is the procedure applied?

Although it would be nice to present definitive answers to the above questions, our present state of scientific-ethical-moral-legal development does not allow for such specificity. However, we will look at some of the relevant issues in relation to specific techniques and given circumstances under which their use might benefit clients and patients. (See also Chapters 1 and 6.)

One objection raised against the use of aversive procedures is that for some applications, the recipient of the technique will suffer pain (e.g., electric shock in a punishment paradigm; possibly nausea in a verbal aversion paradigm). Begelman (1975) presents cogent arguments against labeling an aversive procedure as unethical simply because pain in and of itself is involved. He contends that,

> "The argument that aversive procedures per se are unethical because they involve pain or discomfort to clients or patients is totally

without validity. Indeed, if the absence of pain were a necessary condition of any treatment procedure, we all would have succumbed to one or another variety of infections, conditions we have been immunized from by *painful* inoculations. . . Obviously, the conscientious administration of an aversive procedure is hardly undertaken with the sole aim of inflicting pain on clients. It is undertaken with the ultimate goal of ameliorating a behavioral problem, and in this sense, the pain involved is incidental. The relevant point is that no treatment procedure involving pain as a direct or indirect consequence of the methods employed can be declared unethical on the abstract base alone" (pp. 184–185).

Let us illustrate the above argument with a concrete example. If it can be documented that contingent electric shock applied to a retarded and institutionalized head-banger will lead not only to suppression of the head banging (which obviously can result in irreparable tissue damage), but that a positive side effect is increased socialization, is the institution of the aversive procedure warranted? In this instance, we think that it is! The use of electric shock here would also be warranted with regard to yet another ethical concern that is frequently raised (i.e., "the human dignity of the individual involved"). Again, using our illustration, the typical institutionalized "head-banger" who exhibits a high rate of the behavior is often placed in physical restraints, thus resulting in further social isolation. Not only does this represent an insult to human dignity (when more effective procedures, albeit aversive, are available and documented empirically), but the individual's possibility of learning new behaviors is impeded. (We already have noted how restraints result in prolonged social isolation.)

A much more persuasive argument against the use of aversive strategies is the *possibility* of their being *misapplied* and *abused*. (However, this concern can be raised in regard to any therapeutic endeavor or modality. Note, for instance, the Liberman and Davis (1975) argument that drugs *can* and *have* been used in some psychiatric settings as punishing agents.) With respect to abuse, some important elements need to be examined. *First*, before an aversive procedure is implemented, have alternative positive behavioral and pharmacological procedures been considered and attempted? *Second*, if the answer to the first question is yes, has the patient been informed of the nature of the aversive procedure that is about to be carried out? (In this connection, it is not clear whether the paint-sniffer, to whom apneic aversion had been administered in the Blanchard et al. [1973] report, received the full benefits of informed consent. That is, were all the details and effects of the procedure clearly articulated to the patient?) Has the patient willingly agreed to comply, with the stipulation that treatment be stopped without negative repercussions of any kind to him if and when he so desires? In the case of the child, has parental consent been obtained? In the case of the institutionalized individual who, because of his disorder, is unable to make an *informed decision*, have the ethical-legal guidelines of the institution been followed? If no such guidelines exist, has the prevailing clinical-ethical-moral-legal practice in the community of professionals been observed?

Third, is the practitioner who is applying the aversive procedure competent (by training and experience) to administer it in a safe and judicious manner? At present, there is no formal certification of behavior therapists, although the issue has often been raised (cf. Agras, 1973). Indeed, this is a subject that has aroused much controversy within the respective behavior therapy organizations. As the matter now stands, unfortunately there is no professional or legal challenge to any individual who so labels himself a *behavior therapist* without proper credentials. Although licensing and certification laws do exist for psychologists, psychiatrists, social workers, and psychiatric nurses, the specificity of the technical approach used in the psychotherapies is not covered by these respective laws. Thus, the potential for abuse and misuse, of behavioral techniques in general and aversive procedures in particular, remain high.

Fourth, but related to the third point raised above, is the question of whether the correct technique is being administered to the appropriate type of problem. Again, the issues of training and competence are paramount here. It is clear that the potential for abuse (occasionally documented in the public media with bold headlines) is very much present. Being a relatively new approach, the guidelines indicating what constitutes adequate behavioral training and practice have not been delineated to any great degree. On the other hand, good clinical practice and some common sense should prevail in any therapeutic endeavor. Perhaps, these need to be spelled out more concretely.

Fifth, a hallmark of the behavioral tradition has been measurement and a general concern for documentation. This is probably even more important when an aversive procedure is applied for at least two reasons: (1) Especially when pain is involved, it behooves the therapist to demonstrate with data the efficacy of the procedure. (2) As there is some evidence that negative side effects may occur (see Kazdin, 1975) when aversive procedures are used, the measurement and documentation of concurrent behaviors in addition to the behavior(s) targeted for modification seem warranted. If the treated behavior improves when the aversive procedure is applied and a concurrent behavior deteriorates, it would seem that either the aversive technique should be discontinued or an additional technique should be applied to prevent such deterioration in the concurrent behavior. In either case, repeated evaluation of progress is critical.

Before concluding this section, there are three additional points that bear some discussion. *First*, although some of the short-term effects of aversion therapy are known, the long-term suppressive effects (if any) of the aversive techniques *are not known*. Strictly from an ethical perspective, these long-term effects must be documented if the respective aversive techniques are to be fully legitimized in the future. Thus, longitudinal research studies will have to be undertaken to answer these questions.

Second, it should be noted that in their zeal to document the initial successes of their technical applications, the earlier behavior therapists tended to employ aversive techniques with a primary goal being suppression of the undersirable behavior. However, in consideration of our increased concerns about patients' social skills (see Hersen & Bellack, 1976, 1977, in press), it is clear that mere suppression of deviant behavior may not be enough. The complete behavioral treatment requires teaching the patient new ways of adapting to the environment once deviant behaviors have been extinguished. Consider, for example, the pedophile whose deviant sexuality may have been suppressed with some aversive procedure. Despite such suppression, he obviously still experiences sexual urges. Should not the therapist also begin teaching our pedophilic patient what an appropriate sexual object is and how to make the approach? We think yes!

Third, and finally, is a more subtle ethical issue recently raised by Davison (1976) in a thoughtfully presented paper entitled: "Homosexuality: The ethical challenge." In this paper, Davison suggests the interesting thesis that many homosexuals (frequently the recipients of aversive techniques) seek to change their sexual orientation not because of a "real wish to change," but because of prevailing societal pressures to conform to the basic standard. Although this raises a complicated issue as to whether homosexuality may yet represent another expression of sexuality (cf. Davison, 1976) or a pathological condition (cf. Bieber, 1976), it behooves the "thinking" behavior therapist to evaluate the motivation of such patients or clients who seek out behavioral treatment where an aversive procedure may be implemented.

Summary

The purpose of this chapter has been to familiarize the reader with some of the major aversive techniques that are currently being used by behavior therapists in a variety of applied settings. In so doing, some of the historical antecedents to contemporary behavioral practice were first identified. Then, a description of the four primary paradigms (operant conditioning, classical conditioning, avoidance training, escape training) used was provided.

Specific technical applications were considered including: electric shock, covert sensitization, overcorrection, time-out, and response cost. In each case the technique was described in some detail, with illustrations taken from the clinical research literature. Additional aversive procedures (not listed above) were also described. Some examples of positive and negative side effects of specific techniques were documented. Also, four examples of comparative analyses of aversive techniques were provided in which group comparison and single-case research designs were used. Finally, the intricate ethical issues inherent in the use of aversion therapy were presented and discussed.

References

Agras, W. S. Toward the certification of behavior therapists. *Journal of Applied Behavior Analysis*, 1973, *6*, 167–173.

Alford, G. S., & Turner, S. M. Stimulus interference and conditioned suppression of auditory hallucinations. *Journal of Behavior Therapy and Experimental Psychiatry*, 1976, *7*, 155–160.

Anant, S. A note on the treatment of alcoholics by a verbal aversion technique. *Canadian Psychologist*, 1967, *80*, 19–22.

Ashem, B., & Donner, L. Covert sensitization with alcoholics: A controlled replication. *Behaviour Research and Therapy*, 1968, *6*, 7–12.

Azrin, N. H., & Holz, W. C. Punishment. In W. K. Honig (Ed.), *Operant Behavior*. New York: Appleton-Century-Crofts, 1966.

Azrin, N. H., Kaplan, S. J., & Foxx, R. M. Autism reversal: Eliminating stereotyped self-stimulation of retarded individuals. *American Journal of Mental Deficiency*, 1973, *78*, 241–248.

Azrin, N. H., Sneed, T. J., & Foxx, R. M. Dry bed: A rapid method of eliminating bedwetting (enuresis) of the retarded. *Behaviour Research and Therapy*, 1973, *11*, 427–434.

Azrin, N. H., & Wesolowski, M. D. Theft reversal: An overcorrection procedure for eliminating stealing by retarded persons. *Journal of Applied Behavior Analysis*, 1974, *7*, 577–581.

Barlow, D. H. Aversive procedures. In W. S. Agras (Ed.), *Behavior modification: Principles and clinical applications*. Boston: Little, Brown and Co., 1972.

Barlow, D. H. Increasing heterosexual responsiveness in the treatment of sexual deviation: A review of the clinical and experimental evidence. *Behavior Therapy*, 1973, *4*, 655–671.

Barlow, D. H., Leitenberg, H., & Agras, W. S. Experimental control of sexual deviation through manipulation of the noxious scene in covert sensitization. *Journal of Abnormal Psychology*, 1969, *74*, 597–601.

Begelman, D. A. Ethical and legal issues of behavior modification. In M. Hersen, R. M. Eisler, & P. M. Miller (Eds.), *Progress in behavior modification: Vol. 1*. New York: Academic Press, 1975.

Bellack, A. S. Covert aversion relief and the treatment of homosexuality. *Behavior Therapy*, 1974, *5*, 435–437.

Bellack, A. S. Behavioral treatment for obesity: Appraisal and recommendations. In M. Hersen, R. M. Eisler, & P. M. Miller (Eds.), *Progress in behavior modification: Volume 4*. New York: Academic Press, 1977, in press.

Bieber, I. A discussion of "Homosexuality: The ethical challenge." *Journal of Consulting and Clinical Psychology*, 1976, *44*, 163–166.

Bigelow, G., Liebson, I., & Griffiths, R. Alcoholic drinking: Suppression by a brief time-out procedure. *Behaviour Research and Therapy*, 1974, *12*, 107–115.

Birnbrauer, J. S. Generalization of punishment effects: A case study. *Journal of Applied Behavior Analysis*, 1968, *1*, 201–211.

Blake, B. G. The application of behaviour therapy to the treatment of alcoholism. *Behaviour Research and Therapy*, 1965, *3*, 75–85.

Blake, B. G. A follow-up of alcoholics treated by behaviour therapy. *Behaviour Research and Therapy*, 1967, *5*, 89–94.

Blanchard, E. B., Libet, J. M., & Young, L. D. Apneic aversion and covert sensitization in the treatment of a hydrocarbon inhalation addiction: A case study. *Behavior Therapy and Experimental Psychiatry*, 1973, *4*, 383–387.

Bucher, B., & Fabricatore, J. Use of patient-administered shock to suppress hallucinations. *Behavior Therapy*, 1970, *1*, 382–385.

Burchard, J. D., & Barrera, F. An analysis of timeout and response cost in a programmed environment. *Journal of Applied Behavior Analysis*, 1972, *5*, 271–282.

Callahan, E. J., & Leitenberg, H. Aversion therapy for sexual deviation: Contingent shock and covert sensitization. *Journal of Abnormal Psychology*, 1972, *81*, 60–73.

Cautela, J. R. Treatment of compulsive behavior by covert sensitization. *Psychological Record*, 1966, *16*, 33–41.

Cautela, J. R. Covert sensitization. *Psychological Reports*, 1967, *20*, 459–468.

Cayner, J. J., & Kiland, J. R. Use of brief time out with three schizophrenic patients. *Journal of Behavior Therapy and Experimental Psychiatry*, 1974, *5*, 141–145.

Cunningham, C. E., & Linscheid, T. R. Elimination of chronic infant ruminating by electric shock. *Behavior Therapy*, 1976, *7*, 231–234.

Davison, G. C. Homosexuality: The ethical challenge. *Journal of Consulting and Clinical Psychology*, 1976, *44*, 157–162.

Epstein, L. H., Doke, L. A., Sajwaj, T. E., Sorrell, S., & Rimmer, B. Generality and side effects of overcorrection. *Journal of Applied Behavior Analysis*, 1974, *7*, 385–390.

Feldman, M. P., & MacCulloch, M. J. A systematic approach to the treatment of homosexuality by conditioned aversion: Preliminary report. *American Journal of Psychiatry*, 1964, *121*, 167–171.

Feldman, M. P., & MacCulloch, M. J. The application of anticipatory avoidance learning to the treatment of homosexuality. *Behaviour Research and Therapy*, 1965, *2*, 165–183.

Feldman, M. P., & MacCulloch, M. J. *Homosexual behavior: Therapy and assessment.* Oxford: Pergamon Press, 1971.

Feldman, M. P., MacCulloch, M. J., Mellor, V., & Pinschof, J. M. The application of anticipatory avoidance learning to the treatment of homosexuality – III: The sexual orientation method. *Behaviour Research and Therapy*, 1966, *4*, 289–299.

Foreyt, J. P., & Kennedy, W. A. Treatment of overweight by aversion therapy. *Behaviour Research and Therapy*, 1971, *9*, 29–34.

Foxx, R. M. Increasing a mildly retarded woman's attendance at self-help classes by overcorrection and instruction. *Behavior Therapy*, 1976, *7*, 390–396.

Foxx, R. M., & Azrin, N. H. The elimination of autistic self-stimulatory behavior by overcorrection. *Journal of Applied Behavior Analysis*, 1973, *6*, 1–14.

Foxx, R. M., & Martin, E. D. Treatment of scavenging behavior (coprophagy and pica) by overcorrection. *Behaviour Research and Therapy*, 1975, *13*, 153–162.

Griffiths, R., Bigelow, G., & Liebson, I. Suppression of ethanol self-administration in alcoholics by contingent time-out from social interactions. *Behaviour Research and Therapy*, 1974, *12*, 327–334.

Hallam, R. S., & Rachman, S. Theoretical problems of aversion therapy. *Behaviour Research and Therapy*, 1972, *10*, 341–353.

Hallam, R. S., & Rachman, S. Current status of aversion therapy. In M. Hersen, R. M. Eisler, & P. M. Miller (Eds.), *Progress in behavior modification: Volume 2.* New York: Academic Press, 1976.

Hallam, R. S., Rachman, S., & Falkowski, W. Subjective, attitudinal, and physiological effects of electrical aversion therapy. *Behaviour Research and Therapy*, 1972, *10*, 1–13.

Harbert, T. L., Barlow, D. H., Hersen, M., & Austin, J. B. Measurement and modification of incestuous behavior: A case study. *Psychological Reports*, 1974, *34*, 79–86.

Harris, S. L., & Romanczyk, R. G. Treating self-injurious behavior of a retarded child by overcorrection. *Behavior Therapy*, 1976, *7*, 235–239.

Hedberg, A. G., & Campbell, L. A comparison of four behavioral treatments of alcoholism. *Journal of Behavior Therapy and Experimental Psychiatry*, 1974, *5*, 251–256.

Hersen, M., & Bellack, A. S. Social skills training for chronic psychiatric patients: Rationale, research findings, and future directions. *Comprehensive Psychiatry*, 1976, *17*, 559–580.

Hersen, M., & Bellack, A. S. Assessment of social skills. In A. R. Ciminero, K. S. Calhoun, & H. E. Adams (Eds.), *Handbook for behavioral assessment.* New York: John Wiley & Sons, 1977, in press.

Hunt, W. A., & Matarazzo, J. D. Three years later: Recent developments in the experimental modification of smoking behavior. *Journal of Abnormal Psychology*, 1973, *81*, 107–114.

Janda, L. H., & Rimm, D. C. Covert sensitization in the treatment of obesity. *Journal of*

Abnormal Psychology, 1972, *80*, 37–42.

Kantorovich, N. V. An attempt of curing alcoholism by associated reflexes. *Novoye v Refleksologii i Fiziologi Nervnoy Sistemy*, 1929, *3*, 436.

Kazdin, A. E. The effects of response cost in suppressing behaviour in a pre-psychotic retardate. *Journal of Behavior Therapy and Experimental Psychiatry*, 1971, *2*, 137–140.

Kazdin, A. E. Response cost: The removal of conditioned reinforcers for therapeutic change. *Behavior Therapy*, 1972, *3*, 533–546.

Kazdin, A. E. *Behavior modification in applied settings*. Homewood, Ill.: Dorsey Press, 1975.

Kendall, P. C., Nay, W. R., & Jeffers, J. Timeout duration and contrast effects: A systematic evaluation of a successive treatments design. *Behavior Therapy*, 1975, *7*, 609–615.

Kohlenberg, R. J. The punishment of persistent vomiting: A case study. *Journal of Applied Behavior Analysis*, 1970, *3*, 241–245.

Lando, H. A. A comparison of excessive and rapid smoking in the modification of chronic smoking behavior. *Journal of Consulting and Clinical Psychology*, 1975, *43*, 350–355.

Lang, P. J., & Melamed, B. G. Case report: Avoidance conditioning therapy of an infant with chronic ruminative vomiting. *Journal of Abnormal Psychology*, 1969, *74*, 1–8.

Lanyon, R. I., & Barocas, V. S. Effects of contingent events on stuttering and fluency. *Journal of Consulting and Clinical Psychology*, 1975, *43*, 786–793.

Lawson, D. M., & May, R. B. Three procedures for the extinction of smoking behavior. *Psychological Record*, 1970, *20*, 151–157.

Leitenberg, H. Is time-out from positive reinforcement an aversive event? A review of the experimental evidence. *Psychological Bulletin*, 1965, *64*, 428–441.

Lemere, F., & Voegtlin, W. An evaluation of the aversion treatment of alcoholism. *Quarterly Journal of Studies on Alcohol*, 1950, *11*, 199–204.

Liberman, R. P., & Davis, J. Drugs and behavior analysis. In M. Hersen, R. M. Eisler, & P. M. Miller (Eds.), *Progress in behavior modification: Volume 1*. New York: Academic Press, 1975.

Lichtenstein, E., & Danaher, B. G. Modification of smoking behavior: A critical analysis of theory, research, and practice. In M. Hersen, R. M. Eisler, & P. M. Miller (Eds.), *Progress in behavior modification: Volume 3*. New York: Academic Press, 1976.

Lovaas, O. I., & Simmons, J. Q. Manipulation of self-destruction in three retarded children. *Journal of Applied Behavior Analysis*, 1969, *2*, 143–157.

Lovibond, S. H., & Caddy, G. Discriminated aversive control in the moderation of alcoholics' drinking behavior. *Behavior Therapy*, 1970, *1*, 437–444.

Lundwall, L., & Baekeland, F. Disulfiram treatment of alcoholism. *Journal of Nervous and Mental Disease*, 1971, *153*, 381–394.

MacCulloch, M. J., Feldman, M. P., Orford, J. F., & MacCulloch, M. L. Anticipatory avoidance learning in the treatment of alcoholism: A record of therapeutic failure. *Behaviour Research and Therapy*, 1966, *4*, 187–196.

MacCulloch, M. J., Feldman, M. P., & Pinschof, J. M. The application of anticipatory avoidance learning to the treatment of homosexuality – II: Avoidance response latencies and pulse rate changes. *Behaviour Research and Therapy*, 1965, *3*, 21–44.

Maletzky, B. M. "Assisted" covert sensitization in the treatment of exhibitionism. *Journal of Consulting and Clinical Psychology*, 1974, *42*, 34–40.

Mann, R. A. The behavior-therapeutic use of contingency contracting to control an adult behavior problem: Weight control. *Journal of Applied Behavior Analysis*, 1972, *5*, 99–109.

Mann, R. A. The use of contingency contracting to facilitate durability of behavior change: Weight loss maintenance. *Addictive Behaviors*, 1976, *1*, 245–249.

Marks, I. M., & Gelder, M. G. Transvestism and fetishism: Clinical and psychological changes during faradic aversion. *British Journal of Psychiatry*, 1967, *113*, 711–729.

Marshall, W. L. The modification of sexual fantasies: A combined treatment approach to the reduction of deviant sexual behavior. *Behaviour Research and Therapy*, 1973, *11*, 557–564.

Max, L. Breaking up a homosexual fixation by the conditioned reaction technique. *Psychological Bulletin*, 1935, *32*, 734.

McConaghy, N. Aversive and positive conditioning treatments of homosexuality. *Behaviour Research and Therapy*, 1975, *13*, 309–319.

McGuire, R. J., & Vallance, M. Aversion therapy by electric shock: A simple technique.

British Medical Journal, 1964, *1*, 151–153.

Miller, P. M., & Hersen, M. Quantitative changes in alcohol consumption as a function of electrical aversive conditioning. *Journal of Clinical Psychology*, 1972, *28*, 590–593.

Miller, P. M., Hersen, M., Eisler, R. M., & Hemphill, D. P. Electrical aversion therapy with alcoholics: An analogue study. *Behaviour Research and Therapy*, 1973, *11*, 491–497.

Mills, K. C., Sobell, M. B., & Schaefer, H. H. Training social drinking as an alternative to abstinence for alcoholics. *Behavior Therapy*, 1971, *2*, 18–27.

Powell, J., & Azrin, N. The effects of shock as a punisher for cigarette smoking. *Journal of Applied Behavior Analysis*, 1968, *1*, 63–71.

Rachman, S., & Teasdale, J. *Aversion therapy and behaviour disorders: An analysis.* Miami: University of Miami Press, 1969.

Risley, T. R. The effects and side effects of punishing the autistic behaviors of a deviant child. *Journal of Applied Behavior Analysis*, 1968, *1*, 21–34.

Rollings, J. P., Baumeister, A. A., & Baumeister, A. A. The use of overcorrection procedures to eliminate the stereotyped behaviors of retarded individuals: An analysis of collateral behaviors and generalization of suppressive effects. *Behavior Modification*, 1977, in press.

Russell, M. A. H., Armstrong, E., & Patel, U. A. Temporal contiguity in electric aversion therapy for cigarette smoking. *Behaviour Research and Therapy*, 1976, *14*, 103–124.

Sajwaj, T., Libet, J., & Agras, S. Lemon-juice therapy: The control of life-threatening rumination in a six-month-old infant. *Journal of Applied Behavior Analysis*, 1974, *7*, 557–563.

Sandler, J. Aversion methods. In F. II. Kanfer & A. P. Goldstein (Eds.), *Helping people change.* New York: Pergamon Press, 1975.

Serber, M. Shame aversion therapy. *Journal of Behavior Therapy and Experimental Psychiatry*, 1970, *1*, 213–215.

Siegel, G. M., Lenske, J., & Broen, P. Suppression of normal speech disfluencies through response cost. *Journal of Applied Behavior Analysis*, 1969, *2*, 265–276.

Sipich, J. F., Russell, R. K., & Tobias, L. L. A comparison of covert sensitization and "nonspecific" treatment in the modification of smoking behavior. *Journal of Behavior Therapy and Experimental Psychiatry*, 1974, *5*, 201–203.

Turner, S. M., Hersen, M., & Bellack, A. S. Effects of social disruption, stimulus interference, and aversive conditioning on auditory hallucinations. *Behavior Modification*, 1977, in press.

Voegtlin, W. L., Lemere, F., Broz, W. R., & O'Halleren, P. Conditioned reflex therapy of chronic alcoholism. *Quarterly Journal of Studies on Alcohol*, 1941, *2*, 505–511.

Vogler, R. E., Ferstl, R., Kraemer, S., & Brengelmann, J. C. Electrical aversion conditioning of alcoholics: One year follow-up. *Journal of Behavior Therapy and Experimental Psychiatry*, 1975, *6*, 171–173.

Vogler, R. E., Lunde, S. E., Johnson, G. R., & Martin, P. L. Electrical aversion conditioning with chronic alcoholics. *Journal of Consulting and Clinical Psychology*, 1970, *34*, 302–307.

Webster, D. R., & Azrin, N. H. Required relaxation: A method of inhibiting agitative-disruptive behavior of retardates. *Behaviour Research and Therapy*, 1972, *11*, 67–78.

White, G. D., Nielson, G., & Johnson, S. M. Timeout duration and the suppression of deviant behavior in children. *Journal of Applied Behavior Analysis*, 1972, *8*, 111–120.

Wickramasekera, I. Aversive behavior rehearsal for sexual exhibitionism. *Behavior Therapy*, 1976, *7*, 167–176.

Wiens, A. N., Montague, J. R., Manaugh, T. S., & English, C. J. Pharmacologic aversive counterconditioning to alcohol in a private hospital: One year follow up. *Journal of Studies on Alcohol*, 1976, in press.

Wilson, G. T., & Davison, G. C. Aversion techniques in behavior therapy: Some theoretical and metatheoretical considerations. *Journal of Consulting and Clinical Psychology*, 1969, *33*, 327–329.

Wilson, G. T., Leaf, R. C., & Nathan, P. E. The aversive control of excessive alcohol consumption by chronic alcoholics in the laboratory setting. *Journal of Applied Behavior Analysis*, 1975, *8*, 13–26.

Wilson, G. T., & Tracey, D. A. An experimental analysis of aversive imagery versus electrical aversive conditioning in the treatment of chronic alcoholics. *Behaviour Research and Therapy*, 1976, *14*, 41–51.

8

Token economic techniques for psychiatric patients

Introduction

As noted in Chapter 2, the token economy is one of two behavioral approaches that has received widespread attention among both the behaviorists and non-behaviorists. Its popularity as a rehabilitative procedure is indicated by its extensive application in a large variety of treatment and educational settings (the interested reader should see Kazdin, 1975, for an extensive recent review of the research literature). Specifically, token economic techniques have been used in such diverse settings as psychiatric hospitals (Carlson, Hersen, & Eisler, 1972), prisons (Bassett, Blanchard, & Koshland, 1975), the military (Colman & Baker, 1969), institutions for the delinquent (Cohen & Filipczak, 1971), institutions for the retarded (Girardeau & Spradlin, 1964), class-rooms (Walker & Buckley, 1974), and half-way houses (Henderson & Scoles, 1970).

Although there definitely are distinctive differences among the target institutions listed above, there are some unique principles underlying the development and implementation of token economies in each of these settings. The specific features that characterize token economic management will be identified and defined in subsequent sections. In so doing, we will focus on the application of token economies in psychiatric hospitals. Applications of token economies in the home and classroom situations have already been outlined in Chapter 6. Also, special applications of token reinforcement strategies for families of delinquent children and in the case of marital discord will be presented in Chapters 9 and 10.

Despite the frequent direct and indirect attacks on total institutions such as the large state psychiatric facilities (e.g., Goffman, 1961; Hersen, 1976; Szasz, 1963), such settings have proved to be fertile "testing grounds" for operantly oriented psychologists interested in tackling difficult applied problems.* Thus, we will trace the development of the token economy vis-à-vis the typical day-to-day operation of the large and poorly staffed state hospital. We will first trace the genesis of the token economy from the early basic research of Lindsley and Skinner (1954) on the effects of reinforcement in adult psychotics, to the initial application of operant principles to individual patients (e.g., Ayllon & Michael, 1959), to the ward-wide applications that later followed (e.g., Ayllon & Azrin, 1965).

Subsequent sections in this chapter will then deal with the more contemporary issues facing the field today. Included are questions of evaluation, comparative efficacy of the token economy with respect to other treatment approaches, issues of generalization to extra-treatment settings (i.e., the natural environment), and the ethical limitations inherent in the token economy system of ward management.

The Institutional Setting

In the typical state psychiatric hospital facility there are patients displaying a wide variety of disorders and an equally wide array of symptomatic manifestations. Most of the disorders are severe. Included are highly disturbed neurotics, the retarded, severe character disorders, organics, alcoholics, drug addicts, schizophrenics, manics, depressives, etc. Some of the patients may be assaultive or overactive; others may at times be homicidal; and still others may be suicidal. A large proportion of all of these patients can be described as chronic. That is, most of them have had numerous prior psychiatric hospitalizations. In many cases the patients are so well known to the hospital authorities that immediately upon admission they are returned to their previous units or wards. Frequently, after many admissions and re-admissions, these patients show less initiative about being discharged into the community and gradually become "permanent" residents of the institution. (Staff, too,

---

* Of course, it can be argued (see Hersen, 1976) that establishment of the token economy may never have occurred in the first place if conditions in large psychiatric institutions were not so woefully inadequate. If active treatment were given instead of custodial care, the work of operant psychologists in these settings might have taken a different direction.

become discouraged and "give up.") As the years go by, this type of patient begins to lose contact with the community, family, and friends. After a period of prolonged isolation from the community the patient begins to deteriorate with respect to the usual social amenities (e.g., bathing, grooming, appearance, table manners, salutations, etc.). This phenomenon has been labeled institutionalization (see Goffman, 1961; Ullmann, 1967). Many of the so-called "back wards" of the state hospital house such patients. Indeed, in most state hospitals chronic patients constitute the majority.

In addition to the above, a major problem in state hospitals is the low staff to patient ratio.* The problem is more acute at the professional levels. For example, physician (often not even a psychiatrist) to patient ratios of 1 to 500 are more frequently the rule rather than the exception. Equally poor staff to patient ratios are found with respect to nurses, psychologists, social workers, etc. (Exceptions to these low staff to patient ratios are often found only in the admission units, where increased numbers of staff function in diagnostic and brief treatment capacities.)

Given this state of affairs, it should be apparent that the chronic psychiatric patient receives little clinical attention and/or active psychotherapeutic treatment. In this system, nursing assistants tend to have the greatest number of interactions with the chronic patient during the course of the typical hospital day. Ironically, the nursing assistant is, for the most part, the least well schooled, trained, or motivated to function in a "therapeutic" manner with the patient. It is little wonder, then, that nursing assistants tend to ignore positive behavior emitted by patients while systematically attending to their negative behaviors. Let us consider the following. The passive or "well-behaved" chronic psychiatric patient who "goes about his business" without causing any disturbance on the unit is generally ignored, particularly for any *positive* initiatives that he may exhibit. By contrast, the "difficult" patient who causes disturbances on the ward frequently elicits an enormous amount of attention from doctors (when in evidence), nurses, nursing assistants, and other patients. The aforementioned, although prototypic, represents behavior modification in reverse. "Deviant" behavior receives attention, hence increasing the likelihood of its recurrence. "Positive" behavior is ignored, thus leading to its extinction.

Unprogrammed and Programmed Reinforcement

Evaluation of naturally occurring reinforcement contingencies on the

---

* Problems of housing large numbers of chronic psychiatric patients and low staff to patient ratios are also seen in federal institutions. However, the extent of the problem is somewhat less severe.

psychiatric ward were examined in the now classic Gelfand, Gelfand, and Dobson (1967) study. Specifically, these investigators studied the reactions of nurses, nursing assistants, and non-study patients to the behaviors emitted by six chronic and severely disturbed psychotic patients (the study patients). These observations were made on a psychiatric ward in a relatively well-staffed Veterans Administration Hospital.*
Behavior of the six study patients was rated on a 5-point scale, ranging from highly inappropriate (e.g., incoherent speech) to highly appropriate (e.g., joking appropriately with a staff member). Responses to the study patients were identified as: (1) *positive attention* (e.g., social approval, praise, etc.), (2) *negative attention* (e.g., negative reaction, refuses to comply), or (3) *ignore* (looks or walks away). Ratings of responses to these six study patients by staff and other patients on the ward were made by independent judges (several psychology graduate students) who observed interactions very closely. Thirty-three behavior reinforcement sequences between study patients and staff and study patients and other patients were observed.

The results of this investigation are summarized in Table 8.1. An examination of the top part of the table shows that other patients ignored inappropriate behavior 79% of the time while rewarding it only 12% of the time. Comparable data for nursing assistants were 64% and 30%. Nurses rewarded inappropriate behavior 39% of the time. When good behavior modification is conceptualized as ignoring inappropriate behavior while rewarding it at a minimum, it is clear that the other patients were the *better* "behavioral engineers" and that staff members (nursing assistants and nurses) were a poor second and third.

Examination of the middle portion of the table indicates that nurses rewarded appropriate behavior 68% of the time, followed by other patients (56%), and then nursing assistants (44%). Considering nurses' positive reactions to both inappropriate and appropriate behavior, it appears that they are indiscriminate in their applications of reinforcement. That is, they do not practice differential reinforcement. Similarly, nursing assistants indiscriminantly seem to *ignore* both inappropriate and appropriate behavior.

Examination of the bottom portion of the table indicates that appropriate behavior was reinforced with positive attention 61% of the time. Inappropriate behavior was reinforced with positive attention 26% of the time. An even more detailed examination of the data showed that the greater the severity of disturbance evidenced by a given study patient, the more inappropriate the response to his behavior.

The implications of these data are very clear. Staff in the psychiatric hospital are not providing the optimal reinforcement contingencies for

---

* The results of this study bear directly on the larger institutions where, because of increased patient to staff ratios, even less attention is given to patients' positive initiatives.

TABLE 8.1

Summary of Results from Gelfand, Gelfand, and Dobson (1967)

	Inappropriate Behavior	
	Ignore	Reward
Other patients	79%	12%
Nursing assistants	64%	30%
Nurses	Data not presented	39%
	Appropriate Behavior	
		Reward
Nurses		68%
Other patients		56%
Nursing assistants		44%
	All Other Instances	
		Positive attention
Appropriate behavior		61%
Inappropriate behavior		26%

their patients. "Patients' desirable responses were, on the whole, inadequately rewarded while their psychotic behavior was intermittently reinforced" (Gelfand et al., 1967, p. 205). This latter point is especially important inasmuch as there are countless numbers of studies showing that intermittent reinforcement (in this case sporadic attention to patients' "deviant" responses) results in strengthened resistance to extinction. Thus, *deviant response patterns are unwittingly being maintained by the staff.*

What, then, are the conclusions and recommendations based on this study? Gelfand et al. (1967) present arguments for instituting changes in the psychiatric hospital, with specific recommendations concerned with the training of nurses and nursing assistants in operant techniques:

"First, the nursing assistants, who have more contact with patients than do other staff members, are using behavior control techniques which are not maximally effective in producing desirable behavior changes. It would be most beneficial for the patients if hospital staff-members, and particularly the nursing assistants, could receive intensive training in reinforcement techniques.

Since the nurses are the group most influential in the training and supervision of the nursing assistants, it is undoubtedly the nurses' attitudes and practices which are the most important to change. In an attempt to increase their therapeutic effectiveness, psychiatric nurses have adopted a psychodynamic treatment approach which has led them to respond warmly to their patients regardless of the patients' behavior. However, their well-intended treatment interventions most probably serve to reinforce the very problem behavior they are attempting to alleviate. Because the nurses are not acquainted with reinforcement principles and therefore cannot visualize the role they might play in a behavioristic treatment program, many nurses view such procedures with considerable suspicion and unjustified alarm. Psychologists working in hospitals and graduate schools of nursing can play a major role in instructing nurses in reinforcement principles and, more important, in training them in the actual use of behavior modification techniques. Once a nurse has had the highly gratifying experience of having produced dramatic improvements in her patients' behavior, it is likely that she will adopt with enthusiasm a treatment approach which allows her to play such a pivotal role in the lives of people she is charged to help" (Gelfand et al., 1967, pp. 206–207).

Directly following some of the suggestions made by Gelfand et al. (1967), Trudel, Boisvert, Maruca, and Leroux (1974) recently compared unprogrammed reinforcement of patients' behaviors in two wards (one with and one without token economy). In the ward administering standard hospital treatment there were nine nursing assistants (mean years of experience = 9.66) for 48 patients. Other than training initially provided by the hospital, nurses and nursing assistants were not exposed to further instruction for the purposes of this study. Ward treatment here was described as "active." There were 11 nursing assistants (mean years of experience = 8.27) for 49 patients in the token economy unit. Staff in this unit had been exposed to a 6-month training period in operant technology and had worked on the ward 2 years before initiation of the study. The investigation, itself, consisted of a partial replication of the Gelfand et al. (1967) work in which staff (nursing assistants) responses to appropriate and inappropriate patient behaviors were carefully observed and recorded. These observations were carried out on the control ward (standard psychiatric treatment) and the token economy ward.

The results of this study are presented in Table 8.2. Examination of

TABLE 8.2

Unprogrammed Reactions of Staff to Behaviors of Patients in Wards with and without Token Economy[a]

	Appropriate Behaviors		Inappropriate Behaviors	
	Ward with token economy	Ward without token economy	Ward with token economy	Ward without token economy
Positive attention	54.41%	8.33%	19.23%	15.09%
Negative attention	0.0%	0.0%	0.0%	1.88%
Behaviors ignored	45.58%	91.66%	80.76%	83.01%

[a] From: Trudel et al., 1974 (Table 1).

the table indicates that nursing assistants reinforced (i.e., positive attention) appropriate behavior more frequently (ratio of 6.5 to 1) in the token ward than in the control ward. Nursing assistants in the control ward ignored appropriate behaviors 91.66% of the time while nursing assistants trained in behavioral principles ignored appropriate behaviors only 45.58% of the time. Positive attention to inappropriate behaviors was not substantially different for the two wards (token ward = 19.23%; control = 15.09%). Similarly, negative attention (i.e., punishment) across wards and appropriate and inappropriate behavior was similar. Finally, there were similar data with regard to inappropriate behavior ignored for the two units (token ward = 80.76%; control ward = 83.01%).

This study clearly demonstrates the advantages of training staff in operant technology with respect to the differential reinforcement of appropriate behavior. However, nursing assistants trained in operant principles still *evidenced* a substantial percentage (19.23%) of reinforcing inappropriate behavior displayed by patients. It would appear that contingency management of staff (e.g., reinforcing staff for applying correct reinforcement strategies) may very well provide a solution for this residual problem (see Ayllon & Azrin, 1968; Katz, Johnson, & Gelfand, 1972; Panyan, Boozer, & Morris, 1970).

Historical Impetus

Now that we have described the ward atmosphere (which still persists in many small and large psychiatric institutions) that provided the basis for the current interest in token economic management and treatment (e.g., Stenger & Peck, 1970), we will examine some of the historical developments leading to the establishment of the initial token economy for psychiatric patients (Ayllon & Azrin, 1965). It is of some interest that the token economy is one of the few currently applied behavioral approaches that can be traced directly to operant work conducted not only in the human laboratory (e.g., Lindsley & Skinner, 1954) but in the animal laboratory as well (Cowles, 1937; Wolfe, 1936). For example, Wolfe (1936) demonstrated that tokens could function as generalized secondary reinforcers in chimpanzees when such tokens were first paired with primary reinforcement. Specifically, chimpanzees were taught to insert poker chips (i.e., the tokens) into a slot using food reinforcers (delivery of a grape contingent on the appropriate motor response). Later, Wolfe showed that delivery of the token was able to control a lever-pulling response. Similarly, Cowles (1937) used poker chips (initially paired with edibles) to effect pattern, size, and color discriminations in his chimpanzee subject. Chips earned were subsequently "traded in" by the animal for edibles dispensed from a vending machine. Thus, the analogue to the token economy, in which patients earn tokens that can later be exchanged for a variety of commodities including edibles, is very clear in both studies.

Laboratory Applications

Another historical antecedent for the token economy is found in Lindsley's early operant studies with adult psychotics (see Lindsley, 1956, 1960; Lindsley & Skinner, 1954). Paralleling some of the operant work done with animals (e.g., Skinner, 1938), Lindsley showed that a variety of simple motor responses (e.g., lever-pulling) of adult psychotics could be controlled using differing schedules of reinforcement. Such motor responses were reinforced with a number of stimuli: candy, cigarettes, pictures, etc. In somewhat later work, Lindsley (1960), still using rate of performance on simple motor tasks, differentiated response characteristics of psychotics and normal adults. Psychotic adults were more likely to evidence the following: (1) low and erratic response rates, (2) pauses in responding, and (3) temporary periods of lowered responding.

Single-Case Applications

Concomitant and subsequent to Lindsley's early efforts, Ayllon and his colleagues (e.g., Ayllon, 1963; Ayllon & Haughton, 1962, 1964; Ayllon & Michael, 1959) began to apply principles of operant psychology with demonstrated success for chronic psychiatric patients who were residents in large state institutions. Almost all of the problems tackled by Ayllon and his associates had proved refractory (i.e., resistive) to most traditional psychotherapeutic and medical (i.e., pharmacological) interventions. In each of the studies to be described below, a single behavioral principle was followed to modify targeted behaviors in individual patients.

Ayllon and Michael (1959) taught nursing staff to function as "behavioral engineers" in dealing with problematic behaviors exhibited by their patients. Nurses were first taught how to pinpoint, identify, measure, and record "undesirable" behaviors. Then they were taught a variety of simple behavioral procedures such as extinction, differential attention (concurrent reinforcement of positive and ignoring of negative patient behaviors), stimulus satiation, and contingent punishment. Let us illustrate more specifically with one of the cases from this series. One of the chronic patients, Lucille, had the annoying habit of entering the nurses' office on an average of 16 times a day, primarily for trivial reasons. Such intrusion interfered with ongoing work and had persisted for a 2-year period of time. "Frequently, she was taken by the hand or pushed back bodily into the ward. Because the patient was classified as mentally defective, the nurses had resigned themselves to tolerating her behavior" (Ayllon & Michael, 1959, p. 326). A straightforward behavioral analysis of the situation simply suggested that the nurses' contingent attention to this patient probably maintained and intensified the behavior. Therefore, an approach consisting of ignoring her when she entered the nurses' station (i.e., extinction) was recommended. Within the 7th week of the extinction program such uninitiated visits had diminished to about two per day.

Ayllon and Haughton (1964) demonstrated the effects of contingent social reinforcement and cigarettes given contingently on two classes of verbal behavior — "psychotic" or "neutral" responses. The subject of this experimental analysis was a 47-year-old female who was diagnosed as chronic schizophrenic and who had been hospitalized for 16 years. Her verbal behavior involved numerous references to "the Royal Family," "King George," and "Queen Elizabeth." These "delusional" statements had persisted for 14 years in spite of a bilateral prefrontal lobotomy and pharmacological treatment. The experiment proper followed a period of baseline observation during which time ward staff maintained records of interactions with the patient and content of planned 3-min. conversations. For 75 days after baseline, "psychotic" responses were reinforced with social attention and cigarettes; "neutral" responses (e.g., "it's nice today") were systematically ignored. Then, for 90 days the contingencies were reversed. "Neutral" responses were reinforced and "psychotic" verbalizations were ignored. The resulting data clearly indicated that reinforcement not only maintained a given response class ("psychotic" or "neutral") but actually increased its rate of occurrence. Similarly, extinction procedures applied systematically worked equally well in reducing "psychotic" or "neutral" verbal behavior when applied contingently to each.

Ayllon and Haughton (1964) also showed how social reinforcement contingencies were able to control the rate of somatic complaints in two additional patients. On the basis of this study and others conducted by Ayllon, it was concluded that, "Just as it is possible to eliminate the patient's maladaptive behaviors, it is also possible to bring them back and maintain them. The powerful effectiveness of the environment in molding behaviors must not be underestimated. Hence, the hospital environment in which the patient lives must become a therapeutic environment no longer in abstract and empty words, but in deed. The future of such an attempt lies, therefore, in a concerted effort toward 'programmed therapy' " (Ayllon & Haughton, 1964, pp. 96–97).

Initial Ward-Wide Applications

The studies cited above involved applications of operant psychology to individual psychiatric cases. In the studies to be presented in this section, a unified set of contingencies was developed to deal with problematic behaviors evidenced by an entire ward of patients. This kind of program was described by Ayllon and Haughton (1962) to improve promptness and attendance at meals. Prior to instigation of the program, chronic psychiatric patients hospitalized on the experimental ward missed meals and required considerable nursing assistant attention (usually in the form of reminding, "nagging," and physical direction) in order for them to appear on time. In the first part of the study, serving of meals was made contingent upon entering the dining area within stated time limits. Allotted time was gradually reduced from 30 to 5 min. Application of this contingency resulted in a high level of (prompt) meal attendance in contrast to baseline levels. The second part of the study consisted of pairing food (as the reinforcer) with social behavior. Patients were first expected to deposit one penny in a slot before entering the dining area. (Pennies had been distributed to all patients by the staff prior to meal time.) Next, patients were expected to display a cooperative social response before receiving the penny needed for admission. This simply involved two patients pressing two buttons simultaneously (activating a light-buzzer arrangement) before receiving the needed admission charge (i.e., the penny). Not only did all patients except one evidence the required social response, but staff noted a concurrent increase in the patients' social interchanges. Many of the patients had previously been described as withdrawn and "out of contact."

In a separate study also involving ward-wide application of contingencies, Ayllon and Azrin (1964) evaluated the individual and combined effects of instructions and reinforcement (consisting of extra milk and other extra foods viewed as desirable). The target behavior here involved correct utensil selection while patients were waiting in line for their meals. Although both instructions and reinforcement resulted in improved performance over baseline levels, the combination of instructions and reinforcement led to the best results.

To summarize, these two studies showed that a number of contingencies applied uniformly to chronic psychiatric patients on a ward-wide basis yielded marked improvements in targeted behaviors. Thus, the stage was set for institution of a still more formal and complicated application of uniform contingencies to an entire ward of such chronic patients (i.e., the token economy).

The Token Economy (Ayllon & Azrin, 1965)

Ayllon and Azrin (1965) described the development and application of the first formal token economy. This program was conducted at Anna State Hospital in Illinois on a ward housing female, chronic psychiatric patients ranging in age from 24 to 74. The primary target response in this demonstrational study (consisting of six specific experiments or analyses of behavior) was work performance in the hospital both on and off the ward. Prior to the beginning of the study, baseline assessment revealed that work performance was generally at a low level. When the program was instituted, patients were given the opportunity to earn metal tokens contingent on engaging in work behavior on and off the ward (e.g., *grooming assistant*-patient helps wash and groom less able patients; *assistant janitor*-patient helps maintain cleanliness of ward using ordinary housekeeping skills; *waitress*-patient washes dishes and helps clean up dining room after meals and commissary). Tokens earned could then be exchanged for privileges and luxuries three times a day at the commissary (e.g., trip to town with an escort-100 tokens; private audience with social worker-100 tokens; personal cabinet-2 tokens; choice of television program-3 tokens).

The six experimental analyses clearly showed that when privileges were given on a contingent basis (if sufficient numbers of tokens were earned) high levels of work performance were maintained. By contrast, when tokens were given non-contingently (i.e., free tokens at the beginning of the day) work performance quickly decreased to very low levels for most patients. Let us illustrate this point by presenting one of the graphs taken from Experiment III (Ayllon & Azrin, 1965, p. 373). Examination of Fig. 8.1 indicates that on days 1–20, when token reinforcement was contingent upon performance, the 44 patients worked a total of about 45 hours per day. When token reinforcement was *not* contingent upon performance, by day 35 these same 44 patients were working a total of only 1 hour per day. Finally, on days 41–60, when the token reinforcement contingency was reintroduced, work performance again returned to a total of about 45 hours per day for the 44 patients.

Thus, the controlling effects of token reinforcement with respect to work performance were dramatically established during contingent versus non-contingent experimental phases. Other experimental demonstrations presented in this report indicated that job preference (i.e., which of the several jobs available on or off the ward the patient would select) could be modified. This was accomplished by: (1) presenting tokens for a non-preferred job while giving *no* tokens for the preferred job, and (2) presenting larger reinforcement (more tokens) for the non-preferred job.

In examining the efficacy of their program, Ayllon and Azrin (1965) note how success cut across a variety of patient characteristics. "The effectiveness of the reinforcement program was not restricted by any identifiable trait or characteristic of the patients. The primary limitation was the patient who had lost almost all behavior. Age had no discernible limit on effectiveness. Subjects' ages ranged from 24–74 years. Nor was IQ a limitation. Three mental defectives were treated (including one Mongoloid) as well as many high school graduates and one college graduate. No particular type of diagnosis proved to be

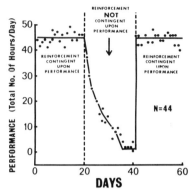

Fig. 8.1 The total number of hours of the on-ward performance by a group of 44 patients, Experiment III. (Reprinted with permission from: T. Ayllon and N. H. Azrin: *Journal of the Experimental Analysis of Behavior*, 8: 357, 1965.)

especially restrictive; the diagnoses included manic-depression, paranoid schizophrenia, and one diagnosis attributable to syphilitic encephalitis. Length of hospitalization of the patients was as little as 1 year and as long as 37 years" (p. 381).

Characteristics of All Token Economies

Before continuing with our survey of the token economy, it will be useful to examine more specifically the principles underlying its clinical application. We will identify the basic characteristics of all token economies (i.e., adult or child; classroom or psychiatric ward, etc.) and will also provide definitions of frequently used terms and concepts connected with its functioning.

Premack Principle

All token economies involve the direct application of the Premack Principle. Very succinctly, the Premack Principle states that a high frequency behavior can be used to reinforce the occurrence of a low frequency behavior. By linking a high frequency behavior in such a way that its occurrence immediately follows the occurrence of a low frequency behavior, the rate of our low frequency behavior can actually be increased. Let us present an example of this principle looking at high and low frequency behaviors exhibited by the chronic psychiatric patients described by Ayllon and Azrin (1965). *First,* it was obvious that *work* was a *low frequency* behavior. *Second,* it was equally obvious that *drinking coffee* or *watching television* were two *high frequency* behaviors engaged in by these patients. Thus, to apply the Premack Principle, one would insist, by contingency management, that the patient engage in a given unit of work behavior before providing him/her with a cup of coffee or access to television. Coffee, then, is the reinforcer for performing work.*

Of course, in the hospital environment as in the outside environment, it is not at all practical to directly and immediately reinforce targeted behaviors (e.g., work) with a multitude of such varied reinforcers (e.g., candy, coffee, cigarettes, movies, television, etc.). Therefore, a medium of exchange involving some kind of currency (e.g., actual money, tokens, poker chips) is used.

Tokens

Tokens, presented in a wide array of colors, shapes, forms, and materials in different programs (see Carlson, Hersen, & Eisler, 1972), as well as points, are used to bridge the delay between the emission of the low frequency behavior and access to the high frequency behavior. In that sense tokens or points function as generalized secondary reinforcers. As reinforcers, they are symbolic of what can later be purchased when these tokens or points are redeemed for commodities or privileges (e.g., a grounds pass or a weekend pass). Again, tokens serve a parallel function to that which currency serves in the economic structure of the outside environment. Further discussion of economic theory as applied to the token economy will appear in a subsequent section.

Back-up Reinforcers

Just as in the real economy where currency can purchase a large variety of commodities (both necessities and luxuries), in the token economy a menu of reinforcers is usually available to patients redeeming their tokens. It is important to have different types of reinforcers in order to avoid the pitfall of stimulus satiation, thus leading to decreased productivity in patients. A typical list of commodities and privileges available to chronic psychiatric patients under token economic management appears in Table 8.3. Examination of the table indicates that within each category of reinforcer there were many choices available.

Rate of Exchange

Rate of exchange obviously involves some basic economic principles. However, in practice the rate of exchange should be such that the patient will maintain his "rate of productivity" in order to earn a sufficient number of tokens to purchase both necessities and luxuries. If prices for commodities are too low, a given patient will accumulate

---

* More socially relevant behaviors such as conversation between patients have been targeted for modification in withdrawn residents of the chronic wards.

TABLE 8.3

List of Reinforcers Available for Tokens[a]

	No. of Tokens Daily
I. Privacy	
Selection of Room 1	0
Selection of Room 2	4
Selection of Room 3	8
Selection of Room 4	15
Selection of Room 5	30
Personal Chair	1
Choice of Eating Group	1
Screen (Room Divider)	1
Choice of Bedspreads	1
Coat Rack	1
Personal Cabinet	2
Placebo	1-2
	Tokens
II. Leave from the Ward	
20-min walk on hospital grounds (with escort)	2
30-min grounds pass (3 tokens for each additional 30 min)	10
Trip to town (with escort)	100
III. Social Interaction with Staff	
Private audience with chaplain, nurse	5 min free
Private audience with ward staff, ward physician (for additional time – 1 token per min)	5 min free
Private audience with ward psychologist	20
Private audience with social worker	100
IV. Devotional Opportunities	
Extra religious services on ward	1
Extra religious services off ward	10
V. Recreational Opportunities	
Movie on ward	1
Opportunity to listen to a live band	1
Exclusive use of radio	1
Television (choice of program)	3
VI. Commissary Items	
Consumable items such as candy, milk, cigarettes, coffee, and sandwich	1-5
Toilet articles such as Kleenex, toothpaste, comb, lipstick, and talcum powder	1-10
Clothing and accessories such as gloves, headscarf, house slippers, handbag, and skirt	12-400
Reading and writing materials such as stationary, pen, greeting card, newspaper, and magazine	2-5
Miscellaneous items such as ashtray, throw rug, potted plant, picture holder, and stuffed animal	1-50

[a] From: Ayllon and Azrin, 1965 (Table 1).

savings (i.e., hoarding of tokens), may subsequently take a "vacation from work," and then targeted behaviors in the token economy will show a decrease. Hersen, Eisler, Smith, and Agras (1972) artificially resolved this potential problem by arbitrarily preventing patients from carrying over more than 10 points (tokens) from week to week. Other solutions involve: (1) "inflating" prices of back-up reinforcers, (2) decreasing the value of tokens, (3) decreasing amounts of tokens earned for specified target behaviors (i.e., a reduced rate of pay), and (4) increasing the range of back-up reinforcers available (therefore stimulating expenditures in the economy). It is of interest that these solutions stem from economic theory rather than from operant psychology (see Kazdin, 1975).

Banking Hours

Banking hours simply refer to the specific time or times when patients redeem their tokens for chosen commodities and privileges. In the Hersen et al. (1972) study banking hours served an additional therapeutic function. Specifically, patients who had difficulties planning ahead (even for a few hours at a time) were expected to "map out" their entire day at morning banking hours. In addition, they also learned how to plan their weekends at Friday morning banking hours.

Response Cost

Although the token economic system of management relies primarily on the use of positive reinforcement (i.e., tokens given contingently on performance of specified behaviors), punishment procedures have been used alone and in combination with positive reinforcement (see Kazdin, 1975, for a thorough discussion of the issues). Thus, in some token economies (e.g., Kazdin, 1971; Reisinger, 1972; Upper, 1973; Winkler, 1970) fines (i.e., loss of tokens) have been administered contingent on infractions of the rules governing the token economy. For example, Upper (1973) developed a "ticket" system whereby a ticket was given to the patient who "broke the rules." At the end of the day the patient receiving such a ticket lost tokens (i.e., the response cost) consistent with the infraction incurred. Although the role of response cost in token economic research is not fully clear at this time, there are some encouraging data reported. Winkler (1970) demonstrated that fines were able to reduce incidence of noise and violence on his psychiatric ward. Again, the analogue to the "real world" is apparent. However, as in the case of the "real world," the permanence of the effects of punishment have yet to be established.

Pinpointing of Behaviors

Although pinpointing of behaviors, precision, and definition are a sine qua non of behavior modification in general, this is especially highlighted on the token economy ward. In the well-planned and well-conducted token economy, each of the targeted behaviors (for which tokens are awarded contingently) is precisely defined. This is particularly important so that nurses and nursing assistants who administer tokens will do so reliably, and conflict over whether or not a token was earned is avoided. Thus, the vagueness usually associated with large scale psychiatric treatment is counteracted. Let us illustrate the point by examining the detailed description of two patient jobs available in Ayllon and Azrin's (1968) token economy. One of the jobs was a "Meal Server." Duration of this job was 60 min., with 10 tokens administered contingent on the required performance. "Patient puts food into proper compartments on steam table. Assembles paper napkins and silver on counter placed at beginning of serving line, puts tablecloths, napkins, salt and sugar shakers on tables. Prepares proper beverage for each meal putting ice in glasses for cold beverages and drawing coffee from urn. Prepares proper utensils for dirty dishes and garbage. Dips food, places food and beverage on trays. Gives patients their trays. After the meal is over Dietary workers empty all leftover food and garbage, place all trays, glasses and silver used on cabinets ready for the dishwasher" (Ayllon & Azrin, 1968, p. 245). A different type of job was labeled Secretarial Assistant for Commissary. This job required 30 min., with five tokens paid for good performance. The patient, "Assists sales clerk assistant. Writes names of patients at commissary, records number of tokens patients spent. Totals all tokens spent" (Ayllon & Azrin, 1968, p. 247).

Token Programs for Acute Patients

Most of the token economy programs established in psychiatric hospitals have been for the older and more chronic patients (e.g., Atthowe & Krasner, 1968; Ayllon & Azrin, 1965; Maley, Feldman, & Ruskin, 1973; Schaeffer & Martin, 1966; Winkler, 1970). For example, in the Atthowe and Krasner (1968) study the median age of their patients was 57. More than one-third of them were 65 years and older. Their median length of psychiatric hospitalization was 22 years (range = 3–48 years). Consistent with the aforementioned, Atthowe (1966) had argued, "that the token system is not as effective in modifying the behavior of noninstitutionalized and more active patients." However, there are two recent studies that contradict this point, suggesting that not only can the token economy be adapted for this younger and more active population, but that such patients do benefit from exposure to token economic ward management and treatment (Crowley, 1975; Hersen, Eisler, Smith, & Agras, 1972).

Hersen et al. (1972) developed a token economy for young psychiatric patients (18–35 years) in a Veterans Administration Hospital. Twenty-seven patients participated in the experimental program over a 24-week period. Forty-nine percent of these patients were first psychiatric admissions. Mean length of stay on this token economy unit was 28.70 days. In many ways the operation of this program was standard, with blue index cards serving as tokens. Tokens could be earned for targeted behaviors listed under four classifications: (1) work, (2), occupational therapy, (3) responsibility, and (4) personal hygiene. Tokens earned could then be exchanged for a variety of on and off ward privileges as well as material goods in the hospital commissary (using "canteen books").

There were several experimental conditions in this study: (1) *Baseline*-tokens earned for targeted behaviors but they had no exchange value (i.e., privileges were non-contingent), (2) *Contingent Reinforcement*-privileges contingent on earning requisite number of tokens, (3) *Inflation*-price of privileges doubled, (4) *Inflation plus $5 bonus*-in addition to price of privileges being doubled a $5 bonus (in canteen books) was added for working 2 hours a day for 5 days, (5) *Inflation plus $10 bonus*-same as previous condition but the bonus was doubled to $10.

The results of this study are plotted in Fig. 8.2 and show the efficacy of the various experimental manipulations. Inasmuch as patient stay on this unit was relatively brief, admissions and discharges took place during the different experimental conditions. Thus, the reader's attention is first directed to presentation of individual data (i.e., the *triangles*). These *triangles* represent data for patients entering the token economy system during different conditions. Evaluation of these data suggests that for most patients, adaptation to the token economy condition in force at the time of admission was quite rapid. That is, mean daily token earnings of these individual patients generally paralleled those earned by the entire group of six during each phase in question.

The reader's attention is next directed to examination of data for time blocks 1–12 and time blocks 45–48. Inspection of these two time blocks reveal that behavioral output (i.e., tokens earned) doubled from Baseline to the Inflation plus $10 bonus condition. Hersen et al. (1972) conclude that: "Baseline data in this study clearly indicate that even younger and more acute patients, when issued privileges on a totally noncontingent basis, quickly assume an inactive role that parallels the institutionalization characteristic of older populations prior to their treatment via token economy methods. . . . At the least, it appears that the application of token reinforcement methods in the management and treatment of younger psychiatric patients might retard or counteract some of the possible deleterious effects of hospitalization . . ." (p. 232).

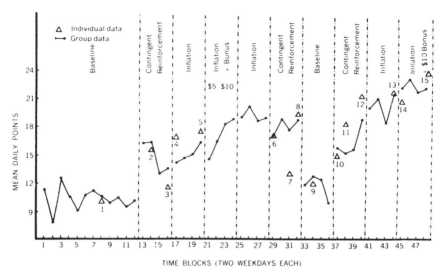

TIME BLOCKS (TWO WEEKDAYS EACH)

Fig. 8.2 Mean daily number of points plotted in blocks of two weekdays. (Reprinted with permission from: M. Hersen, R. M. Eisler, B. S. Smith, and W. S. Agras: *American Journal of Psychiatry*, 129: 228, 1972.)

Ward Management versus Treatment

The preceding sections certainly corroborate the efficacy of the token economy as a ward management strategy. With its emphasis on precision and the simultaneous reinforcement of positive behaviors and punishment and/or ignoring of negative behaviors, a standard for inpatient psychiatric management has been established. Thus, the usual vagueness and subjectivity with which the majority of inpatient services are conducted is avoided.

In most of the token economies, however, the major targets for modification have been work behavior and personal hygiene. Few token systems have focused primarily on "symptomatic" behaviors (e.g., hallucinations, odd gestures or language). Indeed, Ayllon and Azrin (1968) argued that the performance of positive behaviors on a work-oriented token economy was generally incompatible with symptomatic behaviors. (This contention was challenged by Wincze, Leitenberg, & Agras, 1972.) An examination of the research literature indicates that Ayllon and Azrin's original contention has received only partial support. For example, in a single-case analysis (involving three replications), Hersen, Eisler, Alford, and Agras (1973) found that behavioral ratings of depression improved during token reinforcement as opposed to baseline conditions in neurotically depressed male veterans. The authors concluded that, "These data lend support to Ayllon and Azrin's (1968) argument that functional behaviors are essentially incompatible with symptomatic manifestation under token economic management" (Hersen et al., 1973, p. 396).

In a comparison of a token economy ward with a standard psychiatric treatment unit, Shean and Zeidberg (1971) found that token economy patients required significantly less medication than matched patients on the control unit. This, then, provides indirect evidence that institution of the token economy may, at times, reduce symptomatic behavior.

However, in most studies (see Carlson, Hersen, & Eisler, 1972) group contingencies applied to all patients on the token ward have not been effective in diminishing such symptomatic behaviors as delusions, hallucinations, depression, excessive use of medications, etc. To the contrary, these behaviors have been observed both prior to and after instigation of a given token economy program (on and off the ward). Thus, individualized programs superimposed over the existing token economy have been implemented to deal more directly with resistive symptomatic manifestations. Along these lines, Shean and Zeidberg (1971) pointed out that, "While group administered reinforcement programs can effectively elicit higher frequencies of adaptive behavior, in many instances, they should be supplemented by individualized reinforcement programs. Individual programs are particularly necessary to reduce the frequency of systematized delusional speech and impulsive behavior" (p. 104).

Let us briefly review a few examples of individualized treatment applications. Upper and Newton (1971) developed a weight reduction program for two overweight chronic paranoid schizophrenics who were residents of a token economy in a Veterans Administration Hospital. Tokens, off-ward privileges, and social approval were administered contingently when each patient met his weekly criterion of a 3-lb. weight loss. The first patient began at 263 lbs. and over a 28-week period reached his target of 200 lbs. The second patient began at 201 lbs. and over a 26-week period reached his target of 170 lbs.

Parrino, George, and Daniels (1971) instituted a response cost procedure to reduce the excessive use of PRN (as required) medication exhibited by patients on their token economy ward. As noted by the authors, "Many patients enter the hospital with an established habit of taking sleeping pills, minor tranquilizers, aspirins, and other pills throughout the day on a self-scheduled or unscheduled basis. Sometimes, this kind of pill-taking is instituted during the hospital treatment to treat certain complaints or symptoms on a temporary basis. It is often learned from other patients and is a common part of the hospital subculture" (Parrino, George, & Daniels, 1971, p. 182). Thus, elimination of such PRN medication is important inasmuch as its continued use could very well lead to a permanent addiction (particularly the minor tranquilizers). Various experimental manipulations consisting of charging patients (i.e., the response cost procedure) 2–4 tokens per PRN request (in a 16-token per day economy) resulted in a marked decrease in unnecessary pill-taking. PRN requests for males decreased from a mean of 60 per week to a mean of 2 per week; such requests for females decreased from a mean of 170 per week to a mean of 20 per week.

In an interesting application of token economic procedures, Wincze, Leitenberg, and Agras (1972) examined the effects of feedback and token reinforcement on the longstanding delusional behavior of chronic paranoid schizophrenics who had not responded to medication (massive doses of phenothiazines). Tokens could be earned by these patients in individual sessions by "talking correctly" (i.e., responding non-delusionally to a standard series of questions designed to elicit each patient's particular delusional system). Tokens earned could then be exchanged for necessities (e.g., meals) as well as luxuries (e.g., extra dessert, time off the ward, books and magazines).* Simple feedback (e.g., "Your answer is incorrect, Jesus Christ lived almost two thousand years ago. Your name is Mr. M. and you are forty years old" [Wincze, Leitenberg, & Agras, 1972, p. 251]) resulted in improvement about 50% of the time. However, in three cases the effects of feedback were negative. On the other hand, token reinforcement led to a decrease in delusional talk for seven of nine patients. Unfortunately, decrease in delusional talk was specific to the individual sessions and *did not* generalize to the ward setting. An additional program (a token economic system applied to expression of delusional talk on the ward) was needed to insure generalization to that setting. Thus, the authors were cautious in interpreting their results, but did point out that, "longstanding symptomatic behavior of schizophrenics can be modified with token economy procedures" (p. 262).

Evaluation of the Token Economy

Clinical researchers interested in applications of the token economy to the psychiatric setting have conducted a variety of studies to assess its efficacy. A recent review of the literature (Kazdin, 1975) indicates that there is a growing body of research in this area. For purposes of classification, we will arbitrarily divide the studies into five distinct categories: (1) *Demonstrational Studies* — these reports (e.g., Gericke, 1965; Miller, Stanford, & Hemphill, 1974; Narrol, 1967) involve descriptions of procedures, populations, and general results, but do not involve experimental manipulations or comparative evaluations of any kind. (2) *Within-Subject Designs* — these reports (e.g., Atthowe & Krasner, 1968; Ayllon & Azrin, 1965, 1968; Hersen, Eisler, Smith, & Agras, 1972) consist of descriptions of within-subject changes (i.e., experimental analysis of behavior designs) in which adjoining baseline and token economy phases are compared for individual patients or an entire group of patients. Here the treated patient serves as his own control, with the

---

* Using food as a back-up reinforcer in a token economy presents some ethical dilemmas. See Begelman (1975) and Wexler (1973) for a comprehensive discussion of the legal and ethical issues involved.

relationship between contingency management and behavioral change demonstrated. However, token economic treatment is not contrasted with a control condition or another active treatment regime. The Ayllon and Azrin (1965) study, described earlier (see Fig. 8.1), is an example of this kind of research. More recently, studies using this type of experimental design have been conducted with inpatient drug addicts (Eriksson, Götestam, Melin, & Öst, 1975; Melin, Andersson, & Götestam, 1976). In these studies the controlling relationship of the treatment (the token economy) over the target behavior (tokens earned) was demonstrated. (3) *Controlled Group Comparisons with No Outcome Data* — these reports describe comparisons of token economy wards with control wards in which standard hospital treatment is accorded (e.g., Schwartz & Bellack, 1975). Follow-up data are not provided. (4) *Controlled Group Comparisons with Outcome Data* — these reports describe comparisons of token economy wards in which standard hospital treatment is accorded. However, follow-up data are provided here (e.g., Shean & Zeidberg, 1971). (5) *Token Economy versus Milieu* — these reports involve descriptions of more elegantly designed studies in which the token economy is compared with an active form of inpatient psychiatric treatment, usually the milieu approach (Curran, Lentz, & Paul, 1973; Greenberg, Scott, Pisa, & Friesen, 1975).

In our succeeding discussion we will focus on the last three types (3–5) of studies as we already have described studies falling into categories 1 and 2.

Controlled Group Comparisons with No Outcome Data

There are several studies (e.g., Gripp & Magaro, 1971; Maley, Feldman, & Ruskin, 1973; Schwartz & Bellack, 1975) that can be classified under this heading. The most recent investigation involved a direct comparison of a token economy ward and a ward in which standard inpatient treatment was administered (Schwartz & Bellack, 1975). Initially, 27 patients from each of the two wards were matched on a number of demographic variables (diagnosis, total length of hospitalization, age, and education). The dependent measure was the Nurses Observation Scale for Inpatient Evaluation (NOSIE-30) (Honigfeld & Klett, 1965), a rating scale filled out by nursing staff familiar with the patient's recent behavior. Ratings were obtained on a pre-post basis for both wards using a 15-week treatment interval. Due to a variety of factors (transfer, discharges, illness) the final sample included 15 patients on each ward. There were no pre-treatment differences between groups on any of the NOSIE-30 scales. The results indicated that the token economy group evidenced significantly greater improvement than the controls on the following sub-scales: Social Competence, Neatness, Total Positive Factors, Total Patient Assets. In addition, the token economy group demonstrated significantly greater decreases on a number of subscales: Manifest Psychosis, Retardation, Total Negative Factors. Schwartz and Bellack conclude that, "The token economy procedure thus appears to have been considerably more effective in generating a broad range of behavior changes including both an increase in positive and a decrease in negative behaviors" (p. 107). This study is of some additional importance in that the NOSIE-30 scale which was used is an appropriate measure to assess *both* behavioral and non-behavioral treatments.

In an earlier study, Maley, Feldman, and Ruskin (1973) had compared 20 female residents of a token economy in a large state psychiatric hospital with 20 control patients who remained on other units and "received typical custodial treatment." All patients were chronic schizophrenics matched on relevant demographic variables for the two groups. The token economy was modeled after Ayllon and Azrin (1968). At the time of the comparative evaluation, token economy patients had been in the program from 22–31 weeks (mean = 25.4 weeks).

Two kinds of measurement situations served as the dependent variables. The first, a standardized interview, consisted of five specific tasks on the patient's part: orientation, spending, discrimination, command, timed walk. The second involved a 7-min. videotape of the same standardized interview. These tapes were then rated on a 5-point scale using a 20-item questionnaire resulting in five scale scores (mood, cooperation, communication, psychoticism, desirability). Results of this study presented in Tables 8.4 and 8.5 clearly indicate the superiority of the token economy patients. Maley, Feldman, and Ruskin (1973) noted that, "All of these findings demonstrate that token-economy treated patients were more sociable, less withdrawn and afraid of people, and more likely to be able to interact with others in a 'normal manner' " (p. 143).

To summarize, the studies reviewed herein and others that have been conducted (e.g., Gripp & Magaro, 1971) point toward the superiority of

TABLE 8.4

Group Means, Standard Deviations, and t Values for Five Experimental Tasks[a]

Task	Token economy		Control		t Value
	X̄	SD	X̄	SD	
Orientation	13.90	2.77	9.65	3.24	4.35[b]
Spending	7.05	1.16	5.25	2.19	3.17[b]
Discrimination	4.95	0.22	4.14	1.42	2.43[c]
Commands	7.50	0.87	6.20	6.20	4.28[c]
Walk	139.35	37.27	133.95	42.67	0.42

[a] From: Maley, Feldman, and Ruskin, 1973 (Table 1).
[b] $p < 0.01$.
[c] $p < 0.05$.

TABLE 8.5

Group Means, Standard Deviations, and t Values for Videotape Ratings on Five Scales[a]

Scale	Token economy		Control		*t* Value
	X̄	SD	X̄	SD	
Mood	41.95	6.61	35.70	5.38	3.20[b]
Cooperation	43.25	9.45	36.15	7.95	2.51[b]
Communication	41.60	9.39	36.50	7.63	1.84[c]
Psychoticism	50.99	10.37	42.35	8.86	2.76[b]
Desirability	28.70	8.79	21.90	6.58	2.70[b]

[a] From: Maley, Feldman, and Ruskin, 1973 (Table 2).
[b] $p < 0.01$.
[c] $p < 0.05$.

the token economy system of ward management and treatment when contrasted to standard psychiatric treatment administered on the control wards. Such superiority is evidenced by decreased symptomatology, improved self-care skills, improved motor performance, and indications of greater social competence. These improvements are based on ratings of patient performance on the ward and on the basis of specially designed structured tasks.

Controlled Group Comparisons with Outcome Data

There are a few controlled group studies in which follow-up data were obtained (e.g., Birky, Chambliss, & Wasden, 1971; Heap, Boblitt, Moore, & Hord, 1970; Shean & Zeidberg, 1971). Heap et al. (1970) compared a token-milieu ward (reinforcement for self-care, ward government, attitude therapy) with a control ward where the orientation was "custodial." Patients on the two wards were matched on relevant demographic variables. After 6 months there appeared to be a greater discharge rate from the token-milieu ward but no differences in the recidivism or rehospitalization rate between the two wards. A 35-month follow-up indicated that 68% of the token-milieu patients had been given discharges or leaves, with only 14% returning to the hospital. Comparable data for the hospital as a whole yielded a 50% rate of recidivism. Although these data are promising, the study has been criticized on methodological grounds by Hersen and Eisler (1971). Criticisms leveled at this research were as follows: (1) there was a confounding of several treatment modalities (token economy, milieu therapy, and attitude therapy), (2) there were uncomparable living arrangements for patients on the experimental and control wards, (3) the control ward seemed to be entirely "custodial" in orientation, thus not providing an optimal comparison for the token-milieu condition.

Birky, Chambliss, and Wasden (1971) compared the rate of discharge from a token economy ward and two "traditional" psychiatric units in a state hospital. Patients from the three units were matched on demographic variables such as length of continuous hospitalization, age, diagnosis, marital status, and education. Although a comparison among the three units with respect to discharge or recidivism rates did yield significant differences, patients discharged from the token economy unit had been hospitalized for significantly longer periods of time than those from the two control wards (15.81 years versus 2.11 and 0.66 years). The authors argue that by virtue of the token economy focusing on elimination of pathological behaviors, the long-term residents of this unit became "more acceptable to relatives and proprietors of community facilities," thus facilitating their discharge into the community.

The best controlled group comparison study conducted to date (in this particular category) is the one by Shean and Zeidberg (1971). Male chronic patients were carefully matched on demographic variables and were assigned to two physically identical wards (a token economy unit and a standard psychiatric inpatient ward). At the 1-year follow-up, a significantly greater number of patients from the token economy unit had been granted indefinite leaves from the hospital. The recidivism rate for the token economy unit was 33% during the 1-year period; the control unit had a return rate of 50%.

Although the studies reviewed above provide useful demonstrations of the superiority of the token economy over traditional psychiatric inpatient units, when one considers that the control wards are essentially custodial (where positive patient behaviors tend to be ignored and negative patient behaviors tend to be reinforced), the results are less impressive. Indeed, any "therapeutic" endeavor superimposed over the "custodial" orientation is likely to result in patient improvement (Hersen & Eisler, 1971). Similarly, Kazdin (1975) points out that, "Although token programs in psychiatric hospitals seem to result in greater therapeutic effects relative to other procedures, they are sometimes confounded with a change in the setting . . ., selection of special staff for the token ward . . ., initial differences in patients . . ., and expectations for behavior change . . ." (p. 242). Despite the fact that such methodological limitations in the studies reviewed should be acknowledged, the reader also *should* be made aware that the "custodial" ward unfortunately tends to be the norm rather than the exception.

Given the aforementioned arguments, a real test of the efficacy of the token economy would be a *direct* comparison with some other form of active and concentrated therapeutic approach. As noted previously, this usually involves a comparison with the milieu approach. Indeed, Paul (1969), in his classic article on the status of the chronic psychiatric patient, noted that the two most promising therapeutic modalities for that category of patient were the token economy and the milieu approach (see below). In the next section we will survey studies that contrast token economic treatment with some other active treatment such as milieu or "relationship therapy."

Token Economy versus Milieu

Before going on to our examination of the comparative studies (token versus milieu, token versus "relationship" therapy), we will very briefly contrast the therapies offered on the token economy and milieu units. Whereas in the token economy the individual patient, by his own behavior, determines whether he has access to privileges (i.e., if he earns a sufficient number of tokens or points), in the milieu unit much greater emphasis is placed on the group as a whole. Patient activities, award of passes, discharges, and other issues all become subjects for group discussion and group decision (see Cumming & Cumming, 1962). Of course, administrative staff (psychologists, psychiatrists, social workers, nurses) *do* have "veto power" over unwise patient decisions. However, we should underscore that the group process and how the individual patient functions within the system of group deciding are prepotent factors. In the milieu unit individual patient behavior is considered within the group context, and consequences for positive and negative behavior do take place. Contrary to the token economy, implementation of such consequences may be delayed. Moreover, response-reinforcement and response-punishment relationships are usually not as precisely defined as in the token economy. On the other hand, some milieu programs incorporate a levels system through which patients progress during their hospital stay.

The most extensive comparative evaluation of token economy and milieu therapy has now been under investigation for the last several years by Gordon Paul and his colleagues at the University of Illinois (Curran, Lentz, & Paul, 1973; Lentz, 1975; Lentz, Paul, & Calhoun, 1971; Paul, McInnis, & Mariotto, 1973; Paul, Tobias, & Holly, 1972). Despite the fact that some of the preliminary results of this investigation have been published in the aforementioned articles, final outcome data for this study are still being analyzed and prepared for publication (Paul & Lentz, in preparation).

Let us, however, briefly look at preliminary data from two of these studies. Curran, Lentz, and Paul (1973) compared the use of off-ward facilities (passes for evening activities) by residents of the token and milieu units. Such passes were "free" for milieu residents but cost token economy patients a specified number of tokens. However, patients from both units made little initial use of passes (frequency was somewhat greater for milieu patients). Following baseline assessment, "reinforcer sampling" and "reinforcer exposure" procedures were applied to both units. This simply involved staff taking patients on passes and having them observe other patients on pass (token economy residents were *not charged tokens* during this phase). The experimental manipulation resulted in subsequent increased utilization of passes by the milieu group. By contrast, token economy patients *did not* change their behavior (i.e., frequency of taking passes). The investigators concluded that token economy patients were spending their token earnings on necessities (i.e., primary reinforcers), thus leaving little to spend on luxuries (i.e., special evening activities). However, it is important to note that two behavioral techniques ("reinforcer sampling" and "reinforcer exposure") were able to change the behavior of chronic patients residing on a milieu unit.

In a separate study, Lentz (1975) examined chronic patients' interview behavior as a function of differential treatment and management (2 years on the token economy versus 2 years on the milieu unit). However, statistical analysis failed to show the effects of differential treatment. The implications of this study are of some importance inasmuch as neither of the two approaches appeared successful in altering level of interview behavior of chronic psychiatric patients (mean of 19 years hospitalization). Moreover, an additional instructional set designed to help patients impress the interviewer also did not show differential effects between the groups. Thus, with respect to the token economy, even 2 years of being in an environment where positive behavior was systematically reinforced appeared insufficient to raise the social skill level (i.e., interview behavior) of these patients.

The most direct comparison between token economy and milieu therapy yielding outcome data was recently reported by Greenberg, Scott, Pisa, and Friesen (1975). Programs for 37 patients each (matched on demographic variables) on two state hospital wards were compared. One ward followed standard token economic treatment. The second ward combined token economic treatment with milieu principles of group participation and group decision making. However, the milieu program employed was atypical in that "good" participation in groups was systematically reinforced with the contingent administration of tokens. Thus, if a patient presented sensible proposals to the group at weekly patient-staff meetings the patient was given tokens. Also, patients on this ward were given tokens for activities very similar to those expected on the token economy ward. In brief, both the token and milieu aspects of the ward involved formal contingencies of reinforcement.

The results of the investigation showed that token-milieu patients spent more time out of the hospital during the 1-year study period than the token economy patients (219 days versus 130 days). Token-milieu patients had a mean of 60 days working off hospital grounds prior to discharge, 19 days on home visits before final discharge, and 140 days in the community following discharge. Comparable data for token economy patients were 21 days work, 9 days on home visits, and 100 days in the community. The authors conclude that, "the group incentive program was more effective than the token economy in promoting generalization of adaptive inhospital behavior to community settings" (Greenberg et al., 1975, p. 501).

We will examine one more study before formulating conclusions of the relative merits of the token economy and "active" therapy that is non-behavioral in orientation. In an earlier study, Marks, Sonoda, and Schalock (1968) compared token economic treatment with "relationship therapy," a treatment which consists of five 1-hour sessions per week with a therapist and in which focus is placed on the patient "expressing feelings." The study involved a counterbalanced design in which 11 pairs of chronic schizophrenics (matched on demographic variables) received 10–13 weeks of each treatment. That is, one-half of the patients first received token economy and then "relationship therapy," while the second half of the patients received the two treatments in reversed order. Measures of intellectual, social, and work productivity resulted in equal improvements for both types of therapy. The only advantage in favor of the token economy was that this treatment required less staff time.

On balance, then, the studies reviewed in this section *do not* indicate a clear cut superiority of either of the two approaches to inpatient management and treatment. However, the Greenberg et al. (1975) study suggests that when the better features of both approaches are combined in such a fashion that formal contingencies are in effect, the results are more powerful. It is apparent that further research in this area needs to be done to clarify the comparative and additive effects of the two major inpatient therapies that can be described as "active."

Generalization

A critical question for any therapeutic endeavor is whether the changes brought about in one setting (i.e., the consulting room, the inpatient ward in the psychiatric hospital) generalize (transfer) to the patient's natural environment. In the case of our chronic psychiatric patient who is a resident of the state hospital ward, are changes effected by token reinforcement procedures on the ward maintained when he is finally returned to the community? Although there are some data indicating that patients who were on token economy wards do better than those who were not when they return to the community (e.g., Heap et al., 1970; Shean & Zeidberg, 1971), there also is evidence that when tokens are removed generalization does not automatically occur (see Krasner & Krasner, 1972). As noted by Levine and Fasnacht (1974), "Removal of tokens constitutes an extinction paradigm, not a generalization paradigm" (p. 819). Therefore, researchers, bemoaning the fact that generalization effects are weak or have failed to occur altogether, should not register surprise.

To the contrary, there are many suggestions in the literature that generalization should be specifically programmed (Baer, Wolf, & Risley, 1968; Carlson, Hersen, & Eisler, 1972; Hersen, 1976; Hersen & Eisler, 1971; Kazdin, 1975). In this connection, Hersen and Eisler (1971) first point out that evaluation of generalization (post-hospital adjustment) should be done such that behaviors measured in the community are comparable to the ones shaped up on the token economy ward. "Since money in the real world economy serves similar reinforcement functions for responsible and productive behaviors that tokens do in the token economy, income earned and number of days worked subsequent to discharge would appear to be examples of easily obtainable, quantifiable measures of the maintenance of these relevant work behaviors, particularly for patients capable of being employed" (p. 585). To some extent, these guidelines were followed by Greenberg et al. (1975), who assessed days worked in the community for residents discharged from a token economy and a token-milieu unit.

More specifically with respect to programming of generalization, the reader might be reminded that when the patient is discharged from the hospital and then returned to the community (where the same stimulus conditions that led to his hospitalization in the first place still remain), absence of community adjustment should not be surprising. Carlson, Hersen, and Eisler (1972) recommended the use of behavioral contracting in the natural environment with family and friends of the patient to insure a smooth transition and to maintain gain observed in-hospital. "In each case relevant target behaviors of the patient should be identified. Lists of patient behaviors expected by family members and lists of family members' behaviors expected by the patient are to be drawn up. Reciprocal agreements between the patient and relevant family members can be negotiated in the form of an 'official' appearing contract signed by the patient, family, and therapist" (p. 201).

Behavioral training programs for relatives of patients have also been recommended and carried out (Cheek, Laucius, Mahncke, & Beck, 1971). In addition, the use of halfway houses run under operant lines (i.e., token economic management) have appeared, and may very well serve as the needed intermediary step between hospital living and full community adjustment (e.g., Henderson & Scoles, 1970). Kazdin (1975), in his incisive analysis, listed nine technical operations to promote the likelihood of generalization: (1) systematically substituting social reinforcers, (2) gradually fading tokens, (3) training individuals in the client's environment, (4) scheduling intermittent reinforcement, (5) varying the stimulus conditions of training, (6) self-reinforcement, (7) self-instruction training, (8) manipulating reinforcement delay, and (9) simultaneously manipulating several reinforcement parameters.

All of the above recommendations make practical sense and follow from the operant tradition. However, few of these procedures have been formally carried out or studied with psychiatric patients being transferred from the token economy ward into the community.

Side Effects

Reviews of the literature (e.g., Carlson, Hersen, & Eisler, 1972; Kazdin, 1975) indicate that target behaviors can be modified using a variety of token reinforcement techniques. Moreover, these reviews also reveal that there are additional benefits of instituting token economy wards in psychiatric hospitals. These added benefits may be subsumed under two headings: (1) changes in nontarget behaviors, and (2) staff changes in attitude.

Changes in Nontarget Behaviors

Not only are there changes seen in specific behaviors targeted for modification, but concurrent effects in nontargeted behaviors have been recorded in many studies. Winkler (1970) found that noise and violence decreased on his token ward when a combination of token reinforcement and response cost procedures were applied with respect to self-help skills, participation in exercises, and meal attendance. Shean and Zeidberg (1971) reported that token economy led to improved social interaction, increased communication, and decreased intake of medication. Gripp and Magaro (1971) noted that their token economy resulted in symptomatic improvement (e.g., decreased withdrawal and depression). Hersen et al. (1972, 1973) found that token economy effected improvement in patients' planning ability and depression. Maley, Feldman, and Ruskin (1973) showed that their token economy resulted in patients' improved mood, communication, orientation, etc.

Kazdin (1975) points out that, "response generalization is frequently invoked to provide an explanation of broad program effects. This notion is usually misused and at best only describes rather than explains current research findings. Concurrent changes following reinforcement for a response target do not necessarily entail response generalization. In some cases the occurrence of one response is inadvertently associated with the presence or absence of another response. Although the investigator has not designed the consequences to follow this other response, the contingency is present nevertheless" (p. 240). In short, it is quite likely that nontarget behaviors are being reinforced directly and consistently by ward staff. Only controlled research, however, can identify the specific contingencies maintaining nontarget behaviors.

Staff Changes in Attitude

The study reported by Trudel et al. (1974) demonstrated convincingly that nursing assistants from the token economy ward administered more correct contingencies (i.e., they proved to be better behavioral engineers) than those from the control ward. In a separate study (Mc-Reynolds & Coleman, 1972), evaluation of staff attitudes pre- and post-institution of the token economy were most revealing. Prior to the introduction of the token economy, ward staff (three nursing assistants, one registered nurse, one social worker) responsible for 48 chronic psychiatric patients believed that only 20% of their patients were responsive to either the ward staff or other patients. After the token economy was established this same staff now thought that 100% of their patients were responsive. Also, ward staff were of the opinion that 30% of the patients might make an adjustment to extra-hospital living. This contrasts with their opinion, held before introduction of token economy, that none of the patients was capable of such community adjustment. Attitudes held by token economy staff were also contrasted to those held by staff on control wards. Without going into great detail, token economy staff had much greater and more positive attitudes about their patients' futures than control ward staff.

Economic Aspects

Although the token economy had its genesis in the laboratories of operant psychology, there can be no doubt that it *is* an *economic system* albeit a small and relatively simple one. In the last few years the role of economics in the token economy has received increasing attention (Ruskin & Maley, 1972; Winkler, 1971a, 1971b, 1972, 1973). Winkler (1971b) shows how economic principles may be used to understand spending patterns exhibited by patients living under token economic systems of ward management and treatment. There are three key economic concepts that are needed to have a fuller understanding of the role of economics in token reinforcement programs: (1) consumption schedules, (2) Engel's law, and (3) elasticity of a demand curve.

Consumption Schedules

The consumption schedule describes the relationship between income (tokens earned) and expenditures (payment for privileges) within the token economic system. As in the real world economy, individuals who earn more tend to spend more, but expenditures in the token economy are usually within 10% of income. As the high earner in the token economy accrues greater token savings, he tends to spend less proportionally. Thus, further earning of tokens assumes less value for this individual and productivity may cease (this goal obviously is counter to that of the token economy ward administrator). As previously noted in the section on Characteristics of All Token Economies, there are several strategies to stimulate spending and increasing productivity, one of which involves the inflation of prices for back-up reinforcers.

Engel's Law

Engel's law simply states that as income increases, a proportionately smaller amount of income is expended on necessities (e.g., meals or rooms in the token economy). Consequently, there should be a wide variety of luxury items in order to stimulate spending and maintain a high level of productivity.

Elasticity of a Demand Curve

Elasticity of a demand curve relates to a percentage change in demand for goods as a result of a change in price. For items having "elastic" demands (necessities), a decrease in price will lead to an increase in demand above and beyond the percentage decrease. For example, if the price of coffee were decreased by 10% the increase in demand might reach 20%. Conversely, for items having "inelastic" demands (luxuries), a decrease in price will lead to an increase in demand that is smaller than the percentage decrease in price. For example, if the price of extra desserts were decreased by 10% perhaps the increase in demand might only reach 5%. The notion of elasticity is of some importance in determining the prices of both necessities and luxuries for maintaining optimal productivity in the token economy.

Ethical and Legal Issues

Of the currently practiced therapeutic orientations, there is little doubt that behavior modification has, of late, come under the most rigorous scrutiny from the courts, the media, and even the lay public. Furthermore, of the behavioral approaches, the token economy has recently received the greatest attention by those concerned with legal and ethical issues as they apply to psychiatric patients (cf. Begelman, 1975; Hersen, 1976; Wexler, 1973). Before our examination of the legal-ethical issues insofar as the token economy is concerned, we must point out that probably because of the behaviorists' penchant for measuring, evaluating the effects of their treatment strategies, and then reporting their results in an open manner, more "public" attention has been directed to the legal-ethical issues pursuant thereof. Indeed, Begelman (1975) has cogently argued that, "there may be many traditionally employed techniques that have not been subjected to the ethical scrutiny that they undoubtedly deserve" (p. 161).

Be that as it may, several aspects of token economy programs lead to major legal and ethical questions. In a recent paper, Hersen (1976) has outlined very specifically how *positive reinforcement* control over the patients' ward environment can be achieved by instituting an "artificial" state of deprivation. He notes that, "as most institutional settings do not have an abundance of additional reinforcers that might be used as incentives for patients . . . , the naturally occurring contingencies in the environment are restructured such that an 'artificial' state of deprivation is engineered. That is, privileges formerly granted noncontingently, or even capriciously, such as ward passes, day, night, and weekend passes, and better sleeping arrangements, are now automatically removed and are subsequently distributed strictly on a contingent basis in accordance with a predetermined schedule. Now the patient must earn his/her way by displaying 'good' behavior as so identified in the protocol for a given token economy. Depending on the particular institution or the particular state in which the institution is located, in some token economies patients are even required to earn their meals by displaying a specified set of appropriate behaviors" (p. 208). In short, Hersen is describing the systematic application of the Premack Principle, defined in an earlier section. (This principle is fundamental to the entire token economic system.) However, the very foundation of token economic ward management and treatment is in direct confrontation with some recent court decisions supporting patients' rights (most notably *Wyatt* v. *Stickney*).* This landmark decision has taken cognizance of the human rights of the institutionalized mental patient (especially those who are involuntarily committed to the institution). Thus, the patient is guaranteed adequate treatment, meals, appropriate sleeping quarters, right of privacy, visits from friends and relatives, access to mail and communications, personal possessions, and a minimum wage when performing work that is primarily of benefit to the institution as opposed to being solely "therapeutic."

The reader will quickly realize that many of the aforementioned "rights" pertain to activities and objects that were only presented *contingently* in the token economy. *Wyatt* v. *Stickney,* if applied religiously and consistently, clearly states that these are not "privileges" and are to be supplied *noncontingently*. What then is the fate of the token economy? Can it be administered effectively in the absence of these characteristic reinforcers? Certainly if institutions provided adequate funds, ample supplies of new, expensive reinforcers could be provided (e.g., private rooms, stereos, luxury meals). However, this is not likely to

---

* *Wyatt* v. *Stickney*, 344 F. Supp. 373 (M.D. Ala. 1972) (Bryce and Searcy Hospitals).

happen and cannot be used as an excuse for renewed non-treatment (e.g., the historical hospitalization pattern).

Wexler (1973), an eminent jurist, presents a concrete solution to the ethical dilemma that is being faced at this time. "By exploring creatively for reinforcers, it is likely that therapists could construct a list of idiosyncratic objects and activities – mail order catalogue items, . . . soft-boiled rather than standard hard-boiled eggs, . . . and feeding kittens . . . are actual clinical examples – that could be made available contingently in order to strengthen appropriate target responses. Moreover, to the extent that effective reinforcers are in fact idiosyncratic, it follows almost by definition that their contingent availability could not conflict with the legally emerging absolute general rights of patients" (p. 103).

Wexler's position, outlined above, is consistent with that espoused by some behaviorists who have conducted token economy programs in hospital settings (see Carlson, Hersen, & Eisler, 1972; Hersen, 1976; Shean & Zeidberg, 1971). However, Hersen (1976) has pointed out that one of the major reasons that deprivation tactics were utilized in the first place is due to the paucity of the environment (i.e., natural reinforcers) typically to be found in the large state psychiatric institution. It should also be noted that Wexler (1973) argues that if such deprivation (resulting in privileges being contingent on performance) were the only way to lead to improvements in the condition of the chronic psychiatric patient, then perhaps some of the implications of the *Wyatt* v. *Stickney* decision might have to be challenged, reviewed, and perhaps even revised. It should be noted that neither jurists nor mental health personnel are all good or all knowing. Some legal controls over treatment are necessary to avoid abuses resulting from well-intentioned treatment. However, the form and degree of control best suited to this problem has not yet been determined. The initial legal interest has resulted in what will probably be viewed as an overreaction to isolated cases of *real* violations of human rights (which, incidentally, reflect bad behavioral practice as well as being unethical).

In the meantime, Hersen (1976) contends that, "Patients' rights and right to treatment, both of which are critical issues today, find themselves intertwined with the token economic system of ward management. Of all therapists, behavior modifiers should not shrink from the task of unraveling these problems" (p. 210). As the legal-ethical issues in this domain have only begun to emerge and their implementation has been neither rapid nor absolute, the future of token economies is uncertain. We must be more creative in identifying effective procedures (reinforcers) that meet two criteria: (1) have maximal demonstrated generalizability to the extra-hospital environment, and (2) impose the lowest degree of aversiveness or deprivation necessary to achieve that end.

Summary

The impetus for the development of the token economy has been examined, with emphasis on the specific conditions present in the large psychiatric institutions where negative reinforcement contingencies are in operation. Historically the token economy was traced from animal analogues to present day applications. Characteristics common to all token economies were identified and defined. Descriptions of Ayllon's early work leading to institution of the first token economy were provided.

The various kinds of research designs used to assess the absolute and comparative efficacy of the token economy were surveyed. In addition, the important issues of generalization, side effects, and economics related to token economy were examined in some detail. Finally, the more controversial aspects of the token economy vis-à-vis ethical-legal concerns were considered.

References

Atthowe, J. M. *The token economy: Its utility and limitations*. Paper read at the Western Psychological Association meeting, Long Beach, Calif.: April 1966.

Atthowe, J. M., & Krasner, L. A preliminary report on the application of contingent reinforcement procedures (token economy) on a "chronic" psychiatric ward. *Journal of Abnormal Psychology*, 1968, *73*, 37–43.

Ayllon, T. Intensive treatment of psychotic behavior by stimulus satiation and food reinforcement. *Behaviour Research and Therapy*, 1963, *1*, 53–61.

Ayllon, T., & Azrin, N. H. Reinforcement and instructions with mental patients. *Journal of the Experimental Analysis of Behavior*, 1964, *7*, 327–331.

Ayllon, T., & Azrin, N. H. The measurement of reinforcement of behavior of psychotics. *Journal of the Experimental Analysis of Behavior*, 1965, *8*, 357–383.

Ayllon, T., & Azrin, N. H. *The token economy: A motivational system for therapy and rehabilitation*. New York: Appleton, 1968.

Ayllon, T., & Haughton, E. Control of the behavior of schizophrenic patients by food. *Journal of the Experimental Analysis of Behavior*, 1962, *5*, 343–352.

Ayllon, T., & Haughton, E. Modification of symptomatic verbal behavior of mental patients. *Behaviour Research and Therapy*, 1964, *2*, 87–97.

Ayllon, T., & Michael, J. The psychiatric nurse as a behavioral engineer. *Journal of the Experimental Analysis of Behavior*, 1959, *2*, 323–334.

Baer, D. M., Wolf, M. M., & Risley, T. R. Some current dimensions of applied behavior analysis. *Journal of Applied Behavior Analysis*, 1968, *1*, 91–97.

Bassett, J. E., Blanchard, E. B., & Koshland, E. Applied behavior analysis in a penal setting: Targeting "free world" behaviors. *Behavior Therapy*, 1975, *6*, 639–648.

Begelman, D. A. Ethical and legal issues in behavior modification. In M. Hersen, R. M. Eisler, & P. M. Miller (Eds.), *Progress in behavior modification: Vol. 1*. New York: Academic Press, 1975.

Birky, H. J., Chambliss, J. E., & Wasden, R. A comparison of residents discharged from a token economy and two traditional psychiatric programs. *Behavior Therapy*, 1971, *2*, 46–51.

Carlson, C. G., Hersen, M., & Eisler, R. M. Token economy programs in the treatment of hospitalized adult psychiatric patients: Current status and recent trends. *Journal of Nervous and Mental Disease*, 1972, *155*, 192–204.

Cheek, F. E., Laucius, J., Mahncke, M., & Beck, R. A behavior modification training program for parents of convalescent schizophrenics. In R. D. Rubin, H. Fensterheim, A. A. Lazarus, & C. M. Franks (Eds.), *Advances in behavior therapy*. New York: Academic Press, 1971.

Cohen, H. L., & Filipczak, J. *A new learning environment.* San Francisco: Josey-Bass, 1971.

Colman, A. D., & Baker, S. L. Utilization of an operant conditioning model for treatment of character and behavior disorders in a military setting. *American Journal of Psychiatry,* 1969, *125,* 1395–1403.

Cowles, J. T. Food-tokens as incentives for learning by chimpanzees. *Comparative Psychology Monographs,* 1937, *14* (Whole No. 71).

Crowley, T. J. Token programs in an acute psychiatric hospital. *American Journal of Psychiatry,* 1975, *132,* 523–528.

Cumming, J., & Cumming, E. *Ego and milieu.* New York: Atherton, 1962.

Curran, J. P., Lentz, R. J., & Paul, G. L. Effectiveness of sampling – Exposure procedures on facilities utilization by hard-core chronic mental patients in two treatment programs. *Journal of Behavior Therapy and Experimental Psychiatry,* 1973, *4,* 201–207.

Eriksson, J. H., Götestam, K. G., Melin, L., & Öst, L. G. A token economy treatment of drug addiction. *Behaviour Research and Therapy,* 1975, *13,* 113–125.

Gelfand, D. M., Gelfand, S., & Dobson, N. R. Unprogrammed reinforcement of patients' behavior in a mental hospital. *Behaviour Research and Therapy,* 1967, *5,* 201–207.

Gericke, O. L. Practical use of operant conditioning procedures in a mental hospital. *Psychiatric Studies and Projects,* 1965, *3,* 2–10.

Girardeau, F., & Spradlin, J. Token rewards in a cottage program. *Mental Retardation,* 1964, *2,* 275–279.

Goffman, E. *Asylums.* New York: Anchor, 1961.

Greenberg, D. J., Scott, S. B., Pisa, A., & Friesen, D. D. Beyond the token economy: A comparison of two contingency programs. *Journal of Consulting and Clinical Psychology,* 1975, *43,* 498–503.

Gripp, R. F., & Magaro, P. A. A token economy program evaluation with untreated control ward comparisons. *Behaviour Research and Therapy,* 1971, *9,* 137–149.

Heap, R. F., Boblitt, W. E., Moore, C. H., & Hord, J. E. Behaviour-milieu therapy with chronic neuropsychiatric patients. *Journal of Abnormal Psychology,* 1970, *76,* 349–354.

Henderson, J. D., & Scoles, P. E. A community-based behavioral operant environment for psychotic men. *Behavior Therapy,* 1970, *1,* 245–251.

Hersen, M. Token economies in institutional settings: Historical, political, deprivation, ethical, and generalization issues. *Journal of Nervous and Mental Disease,* 1976, *162,* 206–211.

Hersen, M., & Eisler, R. M. Comments on Heap, Boblitt, Moore, and Hord's "Behavior-milieu therapy with chronic neuropsychiatric patients." *Psychological Reports,* 1971, *29,* 583–586.

Hersen, M., Eisler, R. M., Alford, G. S., & Agras, W. S. Effects of token economy on neurotic depression: An experimental analysis. *Behavior Therapy,* 1973, *4,* 392–397.

Hersen, M., Eisler, R. M., Smith, B. S., & Agras, W. S. A token reinforcement ward for young psychiatric patients. *American Journal of Psychiatry,* 1972, *129,* 228–233.

Honigfeld, G., & Klett, C. J. The Nurses' Observation Scale for Inpatient Evaluation: A new scale for measuring improvement in chronic schizophrenics. *Journal of Clinical Psychology,* 1965, *21,* 65–71.

Katz, R. C., Johnson, C. A., & Gelfand, S. Modifying the dispensing of reinforcers: Some implications for behavior modification with hospitalized patients. *Behavior Therapy,* 1972, *3,* 579–588.

Kazdin, A. E. The effect of response cost in suppressing behavior in a prepsychotic retardate. *Journal of Behavior Therapy and Experimental Psychiatry,* 1971, *2,* 137–140.

Kazdin, A. E. Recent advances in token economy research. In M. Hersen, R. M. Eisler, & P. M. Miller (Eds.), *Progress in behavior modification: Vol. 1.* New York: Academic Press, 1975.

Krasner, L., & Krasner, M. Token economies and other planned environments. In C. E. Thoresen (Ed.), *Behavior modification in education: I.* Chicago: National Society for the Study of Education, 1972.

Lentz, R. J. Changes in chronic mental patients' interview behavior: Effects of differential treatment and management. *Journal of Behavior Therapy and Experimental Psychiatry,* 1975, *6,* 192–199.

Lentz, R. J., Paul, G. L., & Calhoun, J. F. Reliability and validity of three measures of functioning in a sample of "hard-core" chronic mental patients. *Journal of Abnormal Psychology*, 1971, *78*, 69–76.

Levine, F. M., & Fasnacht, G. Token rewards may lead to token learning. *American Psychologist*, 1974, *29*, 816–820.

Lindsley, O. R. Operant conditioning methods applied to research in chronic schizophrenia. *Psychiatric Research Reports*, 1956, *5*, 118–153.

Lindsley, O. R. Characteristics of the behavior of chronic psychotics as revealed by free-operant conditioned methods. *Diseases of the Nervous System*, 1960, *21*, 66–78.

Lindsley, O. R., & Skinner, B. F. A method for the experimental analysis of psychotic patients. *American Psychologist*, 1954, *9*, 419–420.

Maley, R. F., Feldman, G. L., & Ruskin, R. S. Evaluation of patient improvement in a token economy treatment program. *Journal of Abnormal Psychology*, 1973, *82*, 141–144.

Marks, J., Sonoda, B., & Schalock, R. Reinforcement vs. relationship therapy for schizophrenics. *Journal of Abnormal Psychology*, 1968, *73*, 379–402.

McReynolds, W. T., & Coleman, J. Token economy: Patient and staff changes. *Behaviour Research and Therapy*, 1972, *10*, 29–34.

Melin, L., Andersson, B. E., & Götestam, K. G. Contingency management in a methadone maintenance treatment program. *Addictive Behaviors*, 1976, *1*, 151–158.

Miller, P. M., Stanford, A. G., & Hemphill, D. P. A social-learning approach to alcoholism treatment. *Social Casework*, 1974, *55*, 279–284.

Narrol, H. G. Experimental application of reinforcement principles to the analysis and treatment of hospitalized alcoholics. *Quarterly Journal of Studies on Alcohol*, 1967, *28*, 105–115.

Panyan, M., Boozer, II., & Morris, N. Feedback to attendants as a reinforcer for applying operant techniques. *Journal of Applied Behavior Analysis*, 1970, *3*, 1–4.

Parrino, J. J., George, L., & Daniels, A. C. Token control of pill-taking behavior in a psychiatric ward. *Journal of Behavior Therapy and Experimental Psychiatry*, 1971, *2*, 181–185.

Paul, G. L. Chronic mental patient: Current status-future directions. *Psychological Bulletin*, 1969, *71*, 81–94.

Paul, G. L., & Lentz, R. J. *Psychosocial treatment of chronically institutionalized patients: A comparative study of milieu vs. social learning.* In preparation.

Paul, G. L., McInnis, T., & Mariotto, M. Objective performance outcomes associated with two approaches to training mental health technicians in milieu and social-learning programs. *Journal of Abnormal Psychology*, 1973, *82*, 523–532.

Paul, G. L., Tobias, L. T., & Holly, B. L. Maintenance psychotropic drugs with chronic mental patients in the presence of active treatment programs: A "triple-blind" withdrawal study. *Archives of General Psychiatry*, 1972, *27*, 106–115.

Reisinger, J. J. The treatment of "anxiety-depression" via positive reinforcement and response cost. *Journal of Applied Behavior Analysis*, 1972, *5*, 125–130.

Ruskin, R. S., & Maley, R. F. Item preference in a token economy ward store. *Journal of Applied Behavior Analysis*, 1972, *5*, 373–378.

Schaeffer, H. H., & Martin, P. L. Behavioral therapy for "apathy" of hospitalized schizophrenics. *Psychological Reports*, 1966, *19*, 1147–1158.

Schwartz, J. A., & Bellack, A. S. A comparison of a token economy with standard inpatient treatment. *Journal of Consulting and Clinical Psychology*, 1975, *43*, 107–108.

Shean, G. D., & Zeidberg, Z. Token reinforcement therapy: A comparison of matched groups. *Journal of Behavior Therapy and Experimental Psychiatry*, 1971, *2*, 95–105.

Skinner, B. F. *The behavior of organisms.* New York: Appleton-Century-Crofts, 1938.

Stenger, C. A., & Peck, C. P. Token-economy programs in the Veterans Administration. *Hospital and Community Psychiatry*, 1970, *21*, 371–375.

Szasz, T. S. *Law, liberty and psychiatry.* New York: Macmillan, 1963.

Trudel, G., Boisvert, J. M., Maruca, F., & Leroux, P. A. Unprogrammed reinforcement of patients' behavior in wards with and without token economy. *Journal of Behavior Therapy and Experimental Psychiatry*, 1974, *5*, 147–149.

Ullmann, L. P. *Institution and outcome: A comparative study of psychiatric hospitals.* New York: Pergamon Press, 1967.

Upper, D. A "ticket" system for reducing ward rules violations on a token economy program. *Journal of Behavior Therapy and Experimental Psychiatry.* 1973, *4*, 137–140.

Upper, D., & Newton, J. G. A weight-reduction program for schizophrenic patients on a token economy unit: Two case studies. *Journal of Behavior Therapy and Experimental Psychiatry*, 1971, *2*, 113–115.

Walker, H. M., & Buckley, N. K. *Token reinforcement techniques*. Eugene, Oreg.: E-B Press, 1974.

Wexler, D. B. Token and taboo: Behavior modification, token economies, and the law. *California Law Review*, 1973, *61*, 81–109.

Wincze, J. P., Leitenberg, H., & Agras, W. S. The effects of token reinforcement and feedback on the delusional verbal behavior of chronic paranoid schizophrenics. *Journal of Applied Behavior Analysis*, 1972, *5*, 247–262.

Winkler, R. C. Management of chronic psychiatric patients by a token reinforcement system. *Journal of Applied Behavior Analysis*, 1970, *3*, 47–55.

Winkler, R. C. Reinforcement schedules for individual patients in a token economy. *Behavior Therapy*, 1971, *2*, 534–537. (a)

Winkler, R. C. The relevance of economic theory and technology to token reinforcement systems. *Behaviour Research and Therapy*, 1971, *9*, 81–88. (b)

Winkler, R. C. A theory of equilibrium in token economies. *Journal of Abnormal Psychology*, 1972, *79*, 169–173.

Winkler, R. C. A reply to Fethke's comment on "The relevance of economic theory and technology to token reinforcement systems." *Behaviour Research and Therapy*, 1973, *11*, 223–224.

Wolfe, J. B. Effectiveness of token-rewards for chimpanzees. *Comparative Psychology Monographs*, 1936, *12* (Whole No. 60).

9

Other operant techniques

Introduction

In this chapter we will examine in some detail the use of additional behavioral techniques derived from the operant framework. As we have already evaluated the use of punishment techniques in Chapter 7, the focus here will be on the implementation of "positive" procedures to bring about behavioral change. We will further restrict our focus to adult psychiatric disorders, illustrating with material taken from single-case experimental analyses. Among the techniques to be described and assessed are: instructions, feedback, reinforcement (social, differential attention), shaping, extinction, fading, and contingency contracting.* Where the literature permits we will present the use of a given technique with several different types of disorders. In other instances we will show how a particular approach has been successfully applied to the same type of disorder but in several replications across different patients.

Some of the techniques (e.g., instructions) may appear to be woefully simple to the reader, leading him/her to question why they are subsumed as a behavioral technique in the first place. Others (e.g., behav-

---

* We will not discuss the innovative use of token economy here as this has already been examined in Chapters 6, 7, and 9. Similarly,we will not cover the modeling techniques as they have been described in Chapters 3 and 5. Extinction is sometimes considered to be a negative procedure as it involves the withholding of positive reinforcement which can be aversive. We include it here as it is substantively different from the active administration of punishment or aversive stimuli.

ioral contracting), on the other hand, are more complex and actually involve the compound use of several individual techniques. (In the case of behavioral contracting, elements of instructions, feedback, reinforcement, and extinction may all be incorporated into the total "treatment package.") Regardless of the simplicity or complexity of a given technical approach, in each section we will first define the technique and then present its theoretical basis or rationale. This will be followed with examples from the clinical literature.

Our objective in this chapter is not to present a fully comprehensive survey of all of the operant techniques that have been used with adult psychiatric patients. Rather, we would like the reader to become acquainted with those approaches that currently seem to offer the greatest promise. Moreover, we are interested in presenting applications of such techniques to difficult applied problems where at least some empirical support is beginning to emerge. In so doing, it will become readily apparent to the reader that often the separate application of techniques (e.g., feedback alone and reinforcement alone) may not lead to optimal behavioral change. On the other hand, the compound application of two such techniques (e.g., feedback and reinforcement combined) may result in further enhancement of behavioral change (see Kazdin, 1975, Chapter 5).

Instructions

The use of instructions (i.e., instructional control) in psychotherapy is much more commonplace than one might suspect at first blush. Indeed, a careful examination of a variety of psychotherapeutic approaches indicates that instructional control cuts across diverse theoretical persuasions. For example, in the so-called "supportive therapies" frequently conducted with chronic psychiatric patients, the therapist will direct his patient to carry out various tasks related to community adjustment. In "logotherapy," where paradoxical intention is used as a technique, the patient is asked to perform the very behavior (e.g., stuttering or a nervous habit) that is the target for change in the first place.* Even psychoanalysts instruct their patients to perform certain tasks during treatment. Consider, for example, the instruction that the patient *must* free associate by saying everything that "comes into his mind" during the course of the therapeutic hour. Consider also the analyst's instruction to his patient that he should make no major changes or decisions until the analysis is completed.

What, then, are the functions and unique differences of instructions in the behavioral model? The answer here is rather straightforward. *First,* as in the case of the administration of other behavioral tech-

---

* This is similar to the technique of massed practice (see Hersen & Eisler, 1973).

niques, instructions are applied to targeted responses that can be and
are measured. *Second,* instructions are presented precisely and systematically. *Third,* the controlling relationship of those instructions over
the target response (yielding an increase or decrease in frequency,
duration, etc.) is typically demonstrated. Therefore, in the behavioral
paradigm, instructions issued repeatedly by the therapist serve as discriminative stimuli. That is, a given instruction sets the stage for the
occurrence of a particular target behavior. With repeated presentation,
the instructional set should result in an increased or decreased rate of
the targeted behavior. Of course, in the clinical situation the use of
instructions is invariably confounded with such variables as social
reinforcement. Thus, it is difficult to ascertain how effective a given
instructional set may be in the absence of social reinforcement or some
other therapeutic variable (e.g., feedback) when the patient emits the
targeted behavior. On the other hand, in controlled experimentation the
unique contribution of each variable (instructions, feedback, reinforcement) to behavioral change can be assessed alone and in combination.

Experimental Support

The potent effects of instructional control in bringing about behavioral change for targeted responses (e.g., eye contact, loudness of voice)
in unassertive patients was clearly shown by Hersen, Eisler, Miller,
Johnson, and Pinkston (1973). In that study a simple instructional set
directed toward increasing eye contact and voice loudness was more
effective than no treatment, practice alone, modeling alone, or modeling
combined with instructions. However, with the exceptions to be described below, instructions, by themselves, generally are not used in
isolation nor are they as effective as when combined with feedback
(Bernhardt, Hersen, & Barlow, 1972), reinforcement (Agras, Leitenberg, Barlow, & Thomson, 1969; Hersen, Gullick, Matherne, & Harbert,
1972; Kazdin & Erickson, 1975; Turner & Hersen, 1975), or modeling
(Foy, Miller, Eisler, & O'Toole, 1976).

Miller, Becker, Foy, and Wooten (1976) demonstrated the effects of
instructional control over components of drinking behavior in three
hospitalized chronic alcoholics. Four components of alcoholic drinking
behavior (potency of the drink, mean amount in each sip, mean time
between sips, and amount of alcohol) were assessed in a multiple baseline design across behaviors. One of the patients was a 49-year-old male
who had a 24-year history of alcohol abuse following an initial period of
moderate drinking. Inasmuch as the treatment goal for this patient was
controlled or social drinking rather than complete abstinence, the patient was instructed to *decrease* the potency of drinks, the mean sip
amount, and amount of alcohol consumed and to increase mean intersip
interval.

During baseline assessment, this patient was permitted access to the following items placed on a small table: a glass, a bottle containing 150 cc of bourbon, a pitcher containing 300 cc of bourbon, a spoon, and a napkin. Each assessment and treatment period lasted about 30 min. and was videotaped. Behaviors targeted for modification were rated retrospectively from videotapes by trained judges.

In the assessment phase, the patient was first told to fix his drink the way he normally did before he was admitted to the hospital. During the treatment phase, he was instructed sequentially and cumulatively to decrease the potency of the drink (i.e., straight bourbon to bourbon mixed with water), decrease the amount consumed per sip, increase the interval between sips, and decrease the total amount of alcohol consumed per 30-min. session.

The results of this single case experiment are presented in Fig. 9.1. Examination of the data indicate that following baseline assessment application of instructions to each of the components of drinking behavior led to change in the therapeutic direction. It should be noted that such change occurred *only* after instructions were applied directly to each of the four components, thus demonstrating the controlling relationship of the instructional set on the targeted response. Similar results were obtained in two additional alcoholic patients, thereby generally confirming the positive effects of instructions in reducing drinking behaviors that contribute to the alcoholic's continued inebriation.*

Instructional control over a nonverbal target behavior (eye contact) in dysfunctional married couples was demonstrated by Eisler, Hersen, and Agras (1973) in an analogue study. In that study, the individual and combined effects of instructions and videotape feedback were evaluated. Each of the couples participating in the experiment evidenced a low rate of eye contact when engaged in conversation. For one group of subjects, segments of each couple's videotaped marital interaction were replayed to them six times (each videotaped segment was 2 min. long) during the course of a 45-min. session. In a second group of couples an instructional set ("We would like you to pay attention as to how much you are looking at each other") was administered six times during the session. In a third group of couples, videotape feedback and instructions were combined and also administered six times in the session. In a fourth group (the control condition), married couples, instead of being given videotape feedback, were shown six 2-min. segments of prevailing local television during the session. The results of the study indicated that focused instructions alone were more effective than videotape feedback alone in changing rate of eye contact. The irrelevant television feedback condition did not lead to any changes in rate of eye contact. Rate changes for

---

* However, in these two patients, when sip amount was first modified in the direction of controlled drinking, two other components (number of sips taken and potency of the drink) increased in the direction of "alcoholic" drinking.

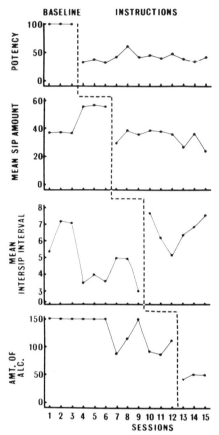

Fig. 9.1 Ratings of sequential effects of instructions on components of drinking behavior for Subject 3. (Reprinted with permission from: P. M. Miller, J. V. Becker, D. W. Foy, and L. S. Wooten: *Behavior Therapy*, 4: 472, 1976.)

the videotape feedback and instructions group combined were not greater than in the instructions group alone. However, in the combined group, rate of a concurrent behavior (smiling) showed an increase.

Once again, the controlling effects of instructions over a simple motor behavior such as eye contact (see Hersen et al., 1973) were documented. Generalizing from their study to some extent, Eisler, Hersen, and Agras (1973) concluded that videotape feedback in the absence of focused instructions (presented to the patient in the clinical situation) would not be likely to effect much behavioral change. Thus, the importance of instructional control in the videotape feedback paradigm would appear to be underscored.

Feedback

Feedback, as a therapeutic technique, has been applied alone and in combination with instructions and reinforcement (social or material) in a wide variety of disorders. Included are: anorexia nervosa (Agras, Barlow, Chapin, Abel, & Leitenberg, 1974), encopresis (Kohlenberg, 1973), unassertiveness (Eisler, Hersen, & Miller, 1974; Hersen & Bellack, 1976), speech dysfunction (Pineda, Barlow, & Turner, 1971), phobia (Leitenberg, Agras, Thomson, & Wright, 1968), spasmodic torticollis (Bernhardt, Hersen, & Barlow, 1972), psychogenic tics (Barrett, 1962), tension headache (Epstein, Hersen, & Hemphill, 1974), and defective posture (Azrin, Rubin, O'Brien, Ayllon, & Roll, 1968; O'Brien & Azrin, 1970). It should also be noted that feedback of autonomic nervous system functioning (i.e., biofeedback) has also shown considerable promise in recent years both at the analogue and clinical levels (Blanchard & Epstein, in press). (Issues related to biofeedback, however, have already been discussed in Chapter 4 on Self-Control.)

Feedback, as defined in most of the aforementioned studies, generally refers to an informational stimulus (about performance) provided to a given individual following performance of a well-defined and measurable target behavior. The effects of such feedback tend to be most effective when delivered *immediately* following (i.e., contingent upon) the targeted behavior. We should note at this point that there are two types of feedback: *positive* and *negative.* For example, in the knife and claustrophobic patients treated in the Leitenberg, Agras, Thomson, and Wright (1968) study (see Chapter 3), feedback simply involved providing each patient with a timer that indicated time spent in the presence of the phobic object. This type of feedback is generally conceptualized as positive feedback inasmuch as it is given in relation to behavior of a positive nature (i.e., the goal here was to increase amount of time spent in the phobic situation). On the other hand, an example of negative feedback was presented by Bernhardt, Hersen, and Barlow (1972). In this investigation, a light was illuminated each time the patient displayed his tic (i.e., a torticollis movement). This is considered to be negative feedback as feedback here (the light) appeared contingent on the emission of a negative behavior (i.e., the torticollis movement). If the light had been illuminated when the tic movement was absent, this would have been considered positive feedback.

Although the research findings indicate that precise feedback applied contingently will lead to behavioral change, the reasons for its effectiveness are not fully understood. Leitenberg et al. (1968) offer a number of possible interpretations. In one they suggest that feedback may serve a "reminder" of the specific goals of the therapy. In a second suggested that feedback may result in a patient's awareness of sm positive changes in his behavior. "Presumably this knowledg success increases the patient's expectations of a favorable outcome" (Leitenberg et al., 1968, p. 137).

A final issue needs to be addressed before we cr description of experimental studies. It should be not*r*   *s* is difficult to make the proper distinction between .

forcement. Consider the fact that when reinforcement is applied contingently its application definitely contains elements of feedback. As noted by Barlow, Agras, Abel, Blanchard, and Young (1975), "the delivery or non-delivery of a reinforcer provides the S with information about the rightness or wrongness of his response and hence, binary feedback about it. Likewise, if feedback or knowledge of whether the response has reached a criterion level or not is effective in leading to a change in the response, then feedback functions as a reinforcer" (p. 45). Barlow et al. further distinguish feedback and reinforcement by pointing out that the latter technique not only provides information but also provides the needed incentive to change it in the positive direction. In any event, it is apparent that there is some confounding between the two technical operations but that differentiating functions can be identified.

Experimental Support

In an early study, Barrett (1962) used both positive and negative feedback to reduce tics in a 30-year-old male patient whose disorder (contractions of the shoulder, neck, chest, and abdominal muscles; bilateral eye blinking) had a 14-year history. Using an ingenious measurement device, the patient's tics were recorded and amplified by an electroencephalogram (EEG) recorder while he was seated in a chair. This was arranged such that spasmodic movements activated the sensitive relay system. A recording device was also arranged so that the patient's favorite music played continuously when he *was not* evidencing spasmodic movement. Any spasmodic movement, however, resulted in interruption of the music. Thus, continuous music served as positive feedback. Negative feedback in this study consisted of white noise presented contingently on spasmodic movement.

Base rate level of tics was 64 to 166 per min. White noise feedback led to a reduced rate (40 per min.). Music feedback resulted in a further reduction to 15–30 tics per min. By contrast, non-contingent music and instructional control led to decreases of only 40 and 50–60 tics per min., respectively.

In a similar study, Rafi (1962) used negative feedback in the treatment of a female patient who suffered from a severe foot-tapping tic. Negative feedback in this study consisted of the activation of a buzzer whenever there was spasmodic movement in her foot, which was placed in a specially constructed treadle. During the course of 70 1-hour treatment sessions, sufficient progress was noted such that rate of tic frequency was neither disturbing to the patient nor her environment.

In a more recent study, Bernhardt, Hersen, and Barlow (1972) evaluated the effects of instructions and feedback in a case of severe spasmodic torticollis. The patient was a 50-year-old male who displayed spasmodic movements characterized by an upward positioning of the head along with a slight tilt to the left. During *baseline* the rate of spasmodic movement was recorded for two to three daily 10-min. videotaped sessions. The patient, videotaped while seated, was instructed to relax and maintain a comfortable position. The *instructions* phase involved asking him to keep his head level and forward during treatment sessions. *Negative feedback* consisted of providing the patient with a white light stimulus whenever he evidenced torticollis movement.

The results of this single case experiment appear in Fig. 9.2. During baseline, percentage of torticollis per 10-min. session ranged from 74 to 79%. Application of the instructional set in the second phase led to greater variability (70–90%). Negative feedback in the next phase led to a marked reduction of torticollis (21–30%), while removal of negative feedback and a return to baseline in the next phase resulted in an increase of torticollis (50–60%). In the last phase, the reinstatement of negative feedback and instructions led to a low of about 30% torticollis per 10-min. session. Thus, the controlling effects of negative feedback over spasmodic movements were demonstrated in this study. However,

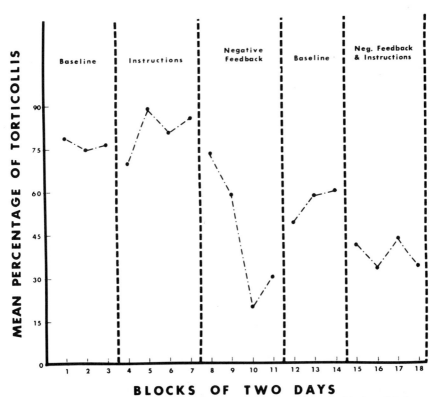

BLOCKS OF TWO DAYS

Fig. 9.2 Mean percentage of torticollis per 10-min. sessions in blocks of 2 days. (Reprinted with permission from: A. J. Bernhardt, M. Hersen, and D. H. Barlow: *Behavior Therapy*, 3: 294, 1972.)

instructions alone did not seem to be effective in changing rate of the targeted behavior.

Epstein, Hersen, and Hemphill (1974) used positive feedback (music played continuously contingent on low levels of frontalis muscle tension) as treatment for a patient who had suffered from tension headaches for a period of 14 years. Electromyogram (EMG) recordings of frontalis muscle activity were used to evaluate level of tension. Following baseline assessment of EMG activity, a criterion was selected such that whenever the patient's frontalis muscle activity was below that level, music played continuously. Thus, the patient's task was to "keep the music on." Conversely, if tension level exceeded the criterion music was interrupted. (This paradigm is analogous to the one used by Barrett [1962] with her ticquer.)

The results for this study are presented in Fig. 9.3. Examination of the data indicate that the baseline level was high (mean = 39.18). Introduction of feedback led to a decrease (mean = 23.18). With the return to baseline in the third phase EMG activity rose (mean = 30.25). When feedback was reintroduced in the final phase EMG activity declined once again (mean = 14.98). Concurrently during baseline and feedback periods, the patient was asked to record the intensity of his headaches (outside of the experimental situation) using a 5-point scale (0 = no headache to 5 = very severe headache). Mean intensity of headaches during alternating baseline and feedback phases was 5.00, 3.50, 5.80, and 2.50. Thus, it would appear that the effects of positive feedback in experimental sessions generalized into the natural environment, as indicated by decreased headache activity during feedback phases.

Pineda, Barlow, and Turner (1971) treated a severe speech disorder of longstanding duration in an 18-year-old college male using both positive

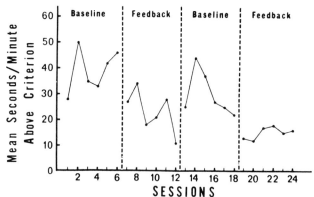

Fig. 9.3 Mean seconds per minute that contained integrated responses above criterion microvolt level during baseline and feedback phases. (Reprinted from: L. H. Epstein, M. Hersen, and D. P. Hemphill: *Journal of Behavior Therapy and Experimental Psychiatry*, 5: 159, 1974.)

and negative feedback procedures. The patient's disorder was characterized by a high rate of speech (200 words per min.) and an interdental lisp associated with reverse swallowing. Speech difficulties tended to be intensified when the patient was in new social situations. Because of his difficulty he avoided many types of interactions with others including those requiring assertive responding. The first goal of treatment involved gradually reducing the rate of speech. This was accomplished by using a voice-operated-relay in treatment sessions consisting of five 5-min. reading trials. In these sessions a white light was flashed whenever the patient exceeded the speech rate criterion (i.e., negative feedback). Conversely, a blue light was flashed when speech rate was at or below the criterion (i.e., positive feedback). Gradually over the course of 22 treatment days, speech rate was decreased to 130 words per min. To insure generalization of results into the patient's natural environment, two additional procedures were carried out. *First,* strangers were introduced during treatment sessions 19–27 in place of the familiar volunteer who had been working with the patient. *Second,* supervised practice in the natural environment (e.g., talking to a car salesman) was also incorporated into the treatment. Nine- and 18-month follow-ups indicated maintenance of treatment gains. Although several elements obviously contributed to success in this case, it would appear that the initial use of positive and negative feedback was instrumental in setting the stage for added procedures to ensure generalization and permanence.

In an interesting application of negative feedback, O'Brien and Azrin (1970) were able to improve posture (i.e., decrease slouching or "round shoulders") in state hospital employees volunteering for treatment. Negative feedback in this study was a vibrotactile stimulus activated by an electrical circuit contingent on "slouching" behavior (i.e., negative feedback). A shoulder harness worn by employees during training contained apparatus that activated the vibrotactile stimulus. The vibrotactile stimulus was arranged so as to provide conduction to the clavicle (shoulder blade) when activated by slouching. The entire apparatus was worn under normal outer clothing and could be calibrated with respect to individual levels of slouching.

Using within-subject experimental analyses, the efficacy of the feedback procedure in reducing percentage of slouching was demonstrated. O'Brien and Azrin (1970) point out that, "This finding shows that simple informational feedback will reduce an undesired behavior and suggests that feedback procedures could be used more generally as a behavior modification procedure for patients who are known to be motivated toward eliminating their undesired behavior" (p. 239).

In one final experimental analysis, we will document the additive effects of feedback to reinforcement in a case of anorexia nervosa (Agras et al., 1974). Anorexia nervosa can be a life-threatening disorder in which extensive weight loss (20% or more of total body weight) occurs in the absence of organic causes. Most anorexics are female, refuse to eat or do so and self-induce vomiting, were moderately overweight at one time, and have a fear of becoming obese.

The patient was a 41-year-old women who was admitted to a psychiatric service in a state of emaciation (36.2 kg.). Previous history indicated numerous hospitalizations for anorexia nervosa episodes. During *baseline* assessment the patient was restricted to her room with the exception of three daily visits to the ward dayroom. No privileges were given to the patient nor was she given information as to her weight or caloric intake. During all phases of treatment the patient was presented with four large meals at given intervals, each meal consisting of 1500 calories. Meals were served in the patient's room. After 30 min. the tray was removed but no comments were offered as to amount eaten. During *reinforcement* privileges (e.g., smoking) were made contingent on a 0.1 kg. weight increase per day over the previous weight.* *Reinforcement and feedback* included the previously stated contingency. In addition, after each meal the patient was informed about the number of calories consumed. She also counted mouthfuls eaten per meal and plotted this and daily weight on a graph.

The results of this experimental analysis are plotted in Fig. 9.4. Following baseline assessment, introduction of reinforcement did not lead to either increased weight or caloric intake. In the next phase, the addition of feedback resulted in increased caloric intake and weight gain. Removal of feedback in the following phase (reinforcement phase 2) led to stabilization of weight and caloric intake. Finally, reintroduction of feedback in the last phase effected renewed increases in both caloric intake and weight.

These results were replicated in another anorexia nervosa patient. In accounting for the additive effects of feedback in their study, Agras et al. (1974) argue "that knowledge of results (caloric intake, mouthfuls eaten, and weight gained) is required for reinforcement to be maximally effective" (p. 285).

Social Reinforcement

In this section we will focus on the contingent application of social reinforcement to increase targeted behaviors in a number of clinical problems. Social reinforcement, as conceptualized here, represents one facet of the more general term of positive reinforcement. Other technical applications subsumed under positive reinforcement could include primary or food reinforcement (Ayllon & Haughton, 1962), token reinforce-

---

* Reinforcement here may be conceptualized as a modified token economy program carried out on an individualized basis.

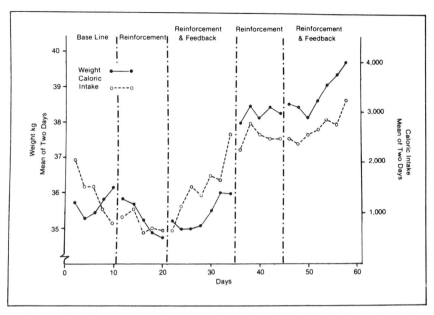

Fig. 9.4 Data from an experiment examining the effect of feedback on the eating behavior of a patient with anorexia nervosa (Patient 5). (Reprinted with permission from: W. S. Agras, D. H. Barlow, H. N. Chapin, G. G. Abel, and H. Leitenberg: *Archives of General Psychiatry*, 30: 279, 1974.)

ment (already discussed in Chapter 8), and material or monetary reinforcement (e.g., Epstein & Hersen, 1974). Before defining what we mean by social reinforcement a more global definition of positive reinforcement would seem to be in order. As recently noted by Kazdin (1975), the definition of positive reinforcement tends to be circular inasmuch as a reinforcer is identified on the basis of how it effects behavior. Thus, a positive reinforcer is an event which, when applied contingently on a targeted behavior, increases its rate of occurrence. It is clear, then, that the determination of whether the event is termed positive reinforcement is purely an empirical question.

Social reinforcement, as the term obviously implies, refers to the explicit use of an interpersonal interaction to increase the rate of a given behavior. Social reinforcers include attention (e.g., maintaining eye contact, a head nod, "mmm-hmmm," etc.), approval, smiles, praise, and even physical contact on some occasions (e.g., a pat on the back, a warm handshake, etc.). Kazdin (1975), contrasting the various types of reinforcers used during the course of applied behavior modification, has underscored the advantages of social reinforcement, namely, its portability:

> "Social consequences have a variety of advantages, as reinforcers. First, they are easily administered by attendants, parents, and teachers. A verbal statement or smile can be given quickly. The

complications of delivering food reinforcement are not present with praise and attention. Obviously, little preparation is involved before delivering praise. Providing praise takes little time so there is no delay in reinforcing a number of individuals almost immediately. Indeed, praise can be delivered to a group as a whole as in a classroom.

A second consideration is that praise need not disrupt the behavior which is reinforced. A person can be praised or receive a pat on the back while engaging in appropriate behavior. Performance of the target behavior can continue. Third, praise is a generalized conditioned reinforcer because it has been paired with many reinforcing events. As mentioned earlier, conditioned reinforcers are less subject to satiation than are food and consumable items. Fourth, attention and praise are naturally occurring reinforcers employed in everyday life. Some reinforcers (such as food and consumables) do not normally follow desirable behavior such as paying attention in a classroom, interacting socially with others, talking rationally with peers, or working on a job. In contrast, social reinforcers such as attention from others follow socially adaptive behaviors. Behaviors developed with social reinforcement in a treatment or training program may be more readily maintained outside of the setting than behaviors developed with other reinforcers. Social reinforcers in everyday life may continue to provide consequences for newly acquired behavior. In short, a desirable feature of using social reinforcement is that there is an increased likelihood that behaviors will be maintained outside of the specific training setting" pp. 119–120).

Historical Antecedents

Although the systematic use of social reinforcement in dealing with difficult clinical problems is of relatively recent origin, scientific psychology has a long history using social (verbal) reinforcement techniques both in the laboratory (e.g., Thorndike & Rock, 1934) and in the clinic (e.g., Matarazzo, 1962). Beginning with Greenspoon's (1951) classic dissertation, in which he found that the verbal stimulus "mmm-hmm" could serve as a positive reinforcer for certain classes of verbal behavior, a whole host of experimental and semi-clinical studies appeared in which the verbal reinforcement paradigm was employed (see Hersen, 1970, for a review). Despite the fact that the verbal reinforcement paradigm was initially seen as the bridge between the experimental laboratory and the clinic (see Hersen, 1968), the emergence of applied behavior modification (e.g., Franks, 1969) relegated the earlier verbal operant conditioning experiments to their historical role.

As was similarly noted in the section on instructions, it is obvious that therapists from other theoretical persuasions use social reinforcement in their practices. (Consider, for example, the psychoanalyst who fosters

the so-called "positive transference relationship" in his patient.) However, here too, as was the case with instructions, behavior modifiers
apply social reinforcement in a planned and methodical manner. That
is, they are specifically aware as to when, why, how often, and under
what circumstances a given social reinforcement is applied contingently
to a particular targeted behavior. This is not at all the case for the non-
behaviorists, who may not be aware that they are socially attending to
and reinforcing particular behaviors in their patients and clients. Indeed, Truax (1966), analyzing therapist-client transactions in a tape
recording made by Carl Rogers (the eminent client-centered psychother-
apist), surprisingly found "the presence of significant differential reinforcement effects embedded in the transactions of client-centered psychotherapy" (p. 7). That is, the tape revealed that Rogers selectively
attended to and provided verbal reinforcement for specific classes of his
patient's utterances. By so doing he provided social reinforcement which
increased the rate of those classes of verbal behavior.

Experimental Support

We will now examine the programmed administration of social reinforcement contingencies for a wide array of clinical disorders. Again, the
primary emphasis will be on evidence derived from single-case experimental analyses.

Agras and his colleagues have used social reinforcement techniques in
the treatment of many neurotic disorders such as anorexia nervosa
(Leitenberg, Agras, & Thomson, 1968), agoraphobia (Agras, Leitenberg, & Barlow, 1968), and astasia-abasia and claustrophobia (Agras,
Leitenberg, Barlow, & Thomson, 1969).

In an early study in their series, Leitenberg, Agras, and Thomson
(1968) combined social reinforcement and the contingent administration
of privileges (e.g., television, family visits, passes off the ward) in the
treatment of two anorexia nervosa patients (a 14-year-old girl and a 17-
year-old girl). The first patient weighed 76 lbs. and was 25 lbs. below her
normal weight; the second patient weighed 69 lbs. and was 22 lbs. below
her normal weight. Similar to the Agras et al. (1974) study, described in
the preceding section, each patient was presented with four daily meals
totalling 4,000 calories. Each meal lasted 30 min., and during non-
reinforcement phases of the study no comments were offered with regard
to quantity of food consumed. For both patients, during reinforcement
conditions, much verbal praise was given contingent on increased
mouthfuls of food eaten over the previous high number of mouthfuls for
any meal. The results of the study indicate that reinforcement procedures led to increased caloric intake and concurrent weight gains to a
normal level in each case. Moreover, follow-up data for the two cases at
4 and 9 months, respectively, indicated maintenance of gains. (It should

be noted that the efficacy of the contingent use of social attention in anorexia nervosa was also documented by Stumphauzer [1969].)

As already pointed out in Chapter 3, Agras, Leitenberg, and Barlow (1968) used contingent social reinforcement (e.g., "good," "you're doing well," "excellent") in the treatment of severe cases of agoraphobia. Such verbal reinforcement was systematically administered contingent on the patient's walking farther and for spending longer periods of time away from the hospital. Using single-case experimental designs, the investigators demonstrated the controlling relationship of the therapeutic variable (social reinforcement) over both dependent measures (time spent away, distance walked from the hospital).

In yet a third type of neurotic disorder, claustrophobia, Agras et al. (1969) compared the therapeutic efficacy of socially reinforcing and non-reinforcing therapists. In order to evaluate the patient's particular phobia, the patient (a 50-year-old widow who was claustrophobic from childhood) was instructed to enter a 4 foot by 6 foot windowless room and remain there until any "discomfort" was felt. In the baseline period, 'neither of the two therapists provided any reinforcement. In the next phase, one of the therapists administered social reinforcement (e.g., "you're doing well") contingent on her achieving increasingly difficult time criteria. In separate sessions the second therapist *did not* provide social reinforcement. In the next treatment phase the two therapists reversed their roles. The "reinforcing" therapist became "non-reinforcing" and vice versa. Finally, in the last phase, the two therapists once again reversed their roles. Visual inspection of graphed data, confirmed by statistical analysis, indicate the superiority of the "reinforcing" therapist (in all three phases) with respect to increased time spent by the patient in the phobic test situation.

Following an initial study reported by Agras et al., (1969), Hersen and his colleagues (Hersen, Gullick, Matherne, and Harbert, 1972; Kallman, Hersen & O'Toole, 1975; Turner & Hersen, 1975) have systematically examined the use of social reinforcement (i.e., differential attention for the treatment of conversion reaction ["leg paralysis"]). In each of the three cases reported, neurological and orthopedic evaluations had failed to reveal contributory causes. Therefore, the patients were admitted to the inpatient psychiatry service of a Veterans Administration Hospital. In two of the three cases, family members reinforced initial presentation of symptomatology, thus leading to worsening and maintenance of the disorder. Given a behavioral assessment of such deviant reinforcing contingencies, treatment in the hospital was directed toward the simultaneous extinction of somatic complaints and the contingent social reinforcement of attempts at standing and walking (i.e., differential attention).

A standard treatment strategy was applied in each of the three cases. During all phases of treatment a young and attractive female research technician visited the patient in his room thrice daily for 10-min. sessions. In these 10-min. sessions she engaged the patient in "small talk." At the end of the 10-min. period she would say: "I want you to walk as far as you can." During baseline no commentary was offered with respect to attempts at standing and/or walking. By contrast, during reinforcement phases, the research technician heavily praised such attempts (e.g., "good," "that's great," "you're doing fine").

The results of the experimental analysis for the first patient (a 19-year-old, unmarried, black male) appear in Fig. 9.5 (Hersen et al., 1972). Instructions (in the first phase) to attempt walking did not appear to be effective. However, the addition of contingent social reinforcement in the next phase led to initial success. Even when such reinforcement was removed in the third phase, continuation of improvement was noted. Finally, in the last phase, reinforcement was reinstated, leading to the most dramatic improvement in walking. At the conclusion of the

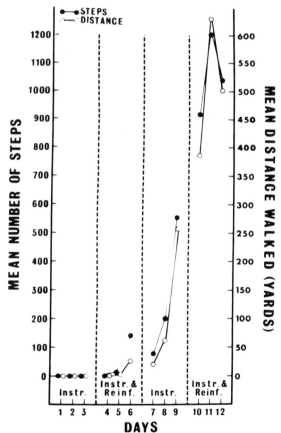

Fig. 9.5 Mean number of steps taken and mean distance walked as a function of instructions and reinforcement. (Reprinted with permission from: M. Hersen, E. L. Gullick, P. M. Matherne, and T. L. Harbert: *Psychological Reports*, 31: 719, 1972.)

fourth phase, the patient was walking normally and was discharged from the hospital.

In the second study (Turner & Hersen, 1975), the patient was a 54-year-old, white, divorced, male tugboat pilot who entered the hospital with complaints of numbness in his left side. He was unable to use his left arm or leg. In this case, the investigators were interested in determining whether sex of the research technician or contingent social reinforcement was the critical therapeutic ingredient. Therefore, following baseline assessment, alternating phases were conducted in which a female, a male, and then again a female research technician carried out social reinforcement procedures. Results of this experimental analysis suggested that the sex of the reinforcing agent was immaterial. Important, however, was the use of social reinforcement applied contingently on attempts at walking. A 5-month follow-up in this case indicated that satisfactory progress had been maintained following hospital discharge.

In the last case in this series (a 40-year-old, white, married male), social reinforcement was first applied to attempts at standing, then walking while using the assistance of a walker, and finally walking without the assistance of a walker. After 18 treatment sessions, the patient was walking normally and was discharged. A 4-week follow-up indicated maintenance of gains. However, shortly thereafter the patient presented with symptoms and family members began to reinforce symptomatic behavior (e.g., attending to "sick-role" behavior). The patient was subsequently readmitted and social reinforcement treatment for standing and walking was reinstated. This time within five sessions the patient was walking normally and was discharged. In addition, to ensure generalization of effects into the natural environment, family members were instructed in differential attention procedures (i.e., how to ignore symptoms while concomitantly paying attention to the patient's positive initiatives). Follow-up conducted at 2, 6, 10, and 12 weeks post-discharge indicated successful application of the treatment.

In summary, the three aforementioned cases illustrate the potent effects of social reinforcement contingencies applied within the hospital setting. The last case, in particular, underscores the need for programming the patient's natural environment (i.e., the family) to continue application of such differential reinforcement when he returns to the home setting. Continuation of such differential attention at home will insure the maintenance of positive behavior.

The important role of social reinforcement contingencies in the etiology and maintenance of depressive behavior has been carefully reviewed and examined by Lewinsohn (1975).* Lewinsohn and Atwood (1969) specifically point out that in depression: "(a) a reduced rate of positive reinforcement is a critical antecedent condition for the occurrence of depressed behavior; (b) social interactions provide contingencies

---

* The role of social reinforcement contingencies in maintaining depressive behavior has also been demonstrated by Liberman and Raskin (1971).

which strengthen and maintain depressive behavior" (p. 166). From this theoretical framework, it naturally follows that by restoring a schedule of positive reinforcement to the depressed patient, his depressive episode will lift. This kind of approach was used by Lewinsohn and Atwood (1969). The patient, Mrs. G., was a 38-year-old, married woman with several children. She had been depressed for about 6 years, beginning after the death of her mother. Over the course of the 6 years, Mrs. G. had received psychotherapy from several practitioners. Evaluation of family interaction patterns indicated that upon presentation of depressive symptoms, Mr. G. reduced the number of interactions with his wife. This was clearly documented in an initial behavioral assessment of family interaction patterns at home and around the dinner table. An analysis of interaction patterns is presented in Table 9.1. A careful examination of this table shows that on November 9, 1967, Mrs. G. initiated 29 interactions, whereas Mr. G. initiated only three comments directed toward the patient, two of which involved food. Similarly, the children only initiated one comment toward their mother. In the ensuing time period between November 9, 1967 and December 12, 1967 (a subsequent home observation visit), behavioral treatment was directed toward improving marital communication (increasing number of communications directed toward the patient) and encouraging the patient to develop interests outside of the family context. Examination of communication patterns for the December 12, 1967 home visit reflect considerable change. Indeed, communications between the patient and her husband and children seemed to be more balanced. That is, Mrs. G. initiated 11 comments, Mr. G. directed 13 comments to his wife, and the children directed four comments to their mother. In addition, content of the conversations was more varied and less concerned with concrete family concerns. Continuation of this treatment approach resulted in further improvements and decreased depression as assessed with self-report inventories.

In an interesting application of reinforcement principles, Milby (1970) evaluated the effects of contingent social attention on social interaction behavior of two hospitalized chronic schizophrenics. In this study social interaction referred to the following: (1) talking to another patient or staff member, (2) walking with another patient or staff member, or (3) playing with another patient or staff member. Behavior of these two patients was observed 12 times a day for 2-min. intervals. Percentage of interaction was scored by dividing the 12 intervals by number of 2-min. intervals during which social interaction was observed. Baseline assessment for the two patients was 13 days and 17 days, respectively (16% social interaction for patient 1; 18% social interaction for patient 2). During the treatment phase, approval and attention of nursing assistants and other staff members was administered contingent on the patients' social interactions. Staff approval and attention consisted of being close to the patient, talking to the patient in a positive manner, or

TABLE 9.1

*Interactions during Home Observations on November 9, 1967 (6:00–6:40 P.M.)
and December 12, 1967 (5:30–6:00 P.M.)* [a, b]

	Content of Communications					
Initiated	November 9			December 12		
	Mrs. G.	Mr. G	Children	Mrs. G.	Mr. G.	Children
Food	8	2	0	8	2	3
School	1	0	0	0	0	0
Finances	0	0	0	0	0	0
Children	2	0	0	0	1	0
In-laws	1	0	0	0	0	0
Other people	1	0	0	0	1	1
Somatic complaints	2	1	0	1	1	0
Psychological complaints	1	0	0	0	0	0
Mutual outside activities	4	0	0	0	2	0
His work	0	0	0	0	3	0
Other	9	0	1	2	3	0
Total	29	3	1	11	13	4
Verbal behavior						
Continues topic	13	13	13	26	15	6
Listens	4	0	0	1	0	0
Approval	0	0	0	0	0	0
Command	3	0	0	2	0	0
Affection	0	0	0	0	0	0
Sympathy	0	0	0	0	0	0
Ignore	0	2	1	0	0	0
Criticism	0	0	1	0	0	1
Disapproval	1	0	1	0	0	0
Changes topic	0	0	0	0	0	0
Non-verbal behaviors						
Social activity	12	0	0	2	0	0
Help	1	0	0	0	0	0
Compliance	0	0	1	0	0	1
Affection	0	0	0	0	0	0
Laugh, smile	0	1	0	1	1	0
Non-compliance	0	0	2	0	0	1
Aggression	0	0	0	0	0	0
Self-stimulation [c]	17	0	0	7	0	0

[a] From: Lewinsohn and Atwood (1969) (Table 1).

[b] Note: The numbers in this table reflect the number of 30-sec. intervals during which the behavior was observed.

[c] Periods during which the subject is not interacting with another member of the family. Only interactions involving Mrs. G. were counted. Interaction between the children, or between Mr. G. and the children are not included.

looking at or nodding to the patient. When social reinforcement contingencies were put into effect, percentage of social interaction rose from 16% to 39% for the first patient and 18% to 30% for the second patient.

Milby (1970) points out that this study was carried out in a setting where limited control was possible (i.e., no token economy was in force). He further notes that, "The effect of social reinforcement . . . demonstrated in this study . . . would seem to be extremely important because it is social reinforcement that probably maintains much interpersonal behavior in the community. Thus, utilization of social reinforcement in treatment could increase the probability of generalization of adaptive behavior to the community where similar reinforcers and contingencies exist" (p. 152).

In a most unusual application of social reinforcement contingencies, Liberman (1970a, 1970b, 1971a, 1971b) evaluated the systemic interventions of a therapist during the course of long-term group psychotherapy. In their landmark investigation, conducted over a 9-month period, the effects of "dynamic" (psychoanalytic) and "behavioral" group therapy were compared. Not only were the two groups of patients matched on relevant demographic variables, but the two therapists were matched on the following variables as well: (1) amount of prior group experience, (2) level of interest in group psychotherapy, (3) personality variables as assessed by their supervisors. Many complicated findings emerged from the comprehensive analyses of data undertaken. However, in general, the behavioral therapist (who administered social reinforcement contingent on particular classes of patient behavior) was more effective in prompting and reinforcing cohesiveness (i.e., intimacy, solidarity, and affection among members) in his group than the "dynamic" therapist. The "dynamic" therapist had conducted group sessions "using a more conventional, intuitive, group-centered approach." Patients in the behavioral group evidenced earlier symptomatic improvement than those in the "dynamic" group. Also, the behavioral therapist, through the planned use of social reinforcement contingencies, was able to increase or decrease expression of hostility from group members to the therapist. Liberman (1970a) concluded that, "The findings support the utility of a reinforcement or learning approach to the understanding and practice of group therapy" (p. 141).

Shaping

Shaping is an operant technique that has been used by behavior therapists to develop new behavioral repertoires. The terminal behavior is often complex and composed of several elements. Technically, during the course of shaping, successive approximations to the terminal behavior will be systematically reinforced. Catania (1968) notes that, "Shaping takes advantage of the fact that the variability of responses after one

response has been reinforced usually provides an opportunity for reinforcement of a response that still more closely approximates the criteria
of the to-be-established operant class" (p. 346). Animal trainers have
systematically used shaping techniques for thousands of years, astound-
ing their audience with the unusual "tricks" their animals perform
(e.g., a seal balancing a basketball, an elephant dancing a waltz, a lion
jumping through a burning hoop). What the unsuspecting audience does
not know (and probably does not care to know) is that literally thousands of approximations to the terminal behavior were systematically
reinforced (usually with choice tidbits of food) over extensive periods of
time until the terminal behavior was achieved and then overlearned.

At the human level, many complicated motor behaviors (e.g., riding a
bicycle, playing a musical instrument, etc.) are learned through a
shaping process. Similarly, many of the social skills needed to function
effectively in society are gradually learned in such a fashion. At the
applied clinical level, shaping has usually been included as one of a
group of operant techniques used in sequence or in conjunction with
other operant strategies (e.g., Sherman, 1965). In Sherman's (1965)
study, shaping, fading, modeling, and social reinforcement were used
during various stages of the treatment. However, for purposes of illustration, we will focus here on the part of the study involving shaping
alone.

Sherman's (1965) subjects were three chronic psychotic patients, each
hospitalized continuously in the state psychiatric facility for more than
20 years. Each of the patients had been mute (electively) for many
years. (Mutism unassociated with organic or physiological causes is
frequently seen in the "back wards" of state hospitals.) For two of the
three patients, shaping and fading techniques proved effective in restoring speech. Let us illustrate the process of shaping with Sherman's first
patient (a 63-year-old male with a diagnosis of dementia praecox [i.e.,
schizophrenia] hebephrenic type dating back to 1916). This patient had
been mute for 45 of the 47 years he had been hospitalized. Treatment
sessions were held three times a week for about 45 min. a session. Candy
and cigarettes were used as primary reinforcers; "good" and "very good"
served as social reinforcers. In the first two sessions, the experimenter
began reinforcing *eye contact* lasting at least 1 sec. in duration. In
sessions 3–8, any type of *vocalization* (e.g., a grunt, moan, burp, cough,
etc.) was reinforced. Of course, the experimenter notes that if words had
been uttered, these too would have been reinforced. Unfortunately, this
was not the case. By session 6 there were five to eight vocalizations per
session. In sessions 9–11 portions of the patient's lunch were made
contingent on his *vocalization* (for obvious medical-ethical reasons,
weight checks were maintained throughout this phase). Concurrent
with administration of primary reinforcement, the therapist said,
"good," (thus pairing social reinforcement with primary reinforcement).

In sessions 12–25, the experimenter began instructing the patient to say "food" whenever a bit of food was held up. At first, any vocalization following the instruction was reinforced. Then only vocalizations *approximating the word food* were reinforced. By session 22 the patient was saying "food" upon instruction and began repeating other words (e.g., water, pie, Jell-o). By the 25th session the patient was able to repeat 25 words but experimental control over verbalizations was weak. In sessions 26–43 the reinforcement contingency was made more difficult for the patient. That is, his meals for three consecutive days were made contingent on appropriate responding. Thus, by the 43rd session the therapist had good control over the patient's responses, but the patient would not respond wth a non-imitative word.

In sessions 44–122, fading, differential reinforcement of other behaviors, modeling, etc. were used to further restore this patient's speaking ability. However, it should be noted that it is the shaping procedure that first led to reinstatement of speech. The reader will note the italicized words in the previous paragraph, underscoring the gradual nature (i.e., successive approximations) of the shaping strategy.

Extinction

Extinction essentially refers to a zero rate of reinforcement. That is, the reinforcing stimulus is no longer administered for a targeted behavior previously reinforced. In practice, extinction paradigms in applied behavior modification typically involve the withdrawal of contingent attention. The reader will recall our discussion in Chapter 7 of Ayllon and Michael's (1959) simple extinction program for the patient who had the annoying habit of entering the nurses' station without invitation, and Ayllon and Haughton's (1964) extinction program for decreasing delusional talk. Extinction programs have also been used successfully to eliminate symptomatic presentation in hysterical neurotics (Blanchard & Hersen, 1976).

A good clinical example of the use of extinction procedures in an hysterical disorder was presented by Alford, Blanchard, and Buckley (1972). Their patient was a 17-year-old female who had a 10-year history of vomiting after every meal. The patient was admitted to a university psychiatry service following a suicidal gesture. An analysis of her behavior on the ward indicated that she persistently sought the attention of all personnel and patients. In light of her sensitivity to social attention, a treatment strategy consisting of removal of attention contingent on vomiting was carried out.

During each phase of the study the patient was presented six small meals per day. Two staff members stayed with the patient at meal time, assessing latency and frequency of vomiting. During baseline these staff members remained with the patient until she finished her meal irrespective of vomiting. In the treatment (extinction) phase staff left her room when she vomited and did not return. The third phase involved a return to baseline conditions, while the fourth phase consisted of a reinstatement of extinction procedures. The final phase involved generalization training in order to insure permanence of treatment gains into the natural environment. Results of this single-case analysis confirmed the efficacy of extinction procedures. During baseline the patient vomited a mean of 4.1 times per meal period. Extinction led to a marked improvement (few episodes of vomiting). In the third phase a return to baseline conditions did not lead to a worsening of the disorder. In fact, improvement surprisingly had been maintained. In phases four and five further improvement was observed. A 7-month follow-up indicated that the patient had vomited only once since her hospital discharge.

Many other reports attesting to the efficacy of extinction procedures for dealing with surplus disorders (i.e., undesirable behavior) have appeared. For example, Hallam (1974) showed how obsessive questioning in a 15-year-old girl was controlled when she was placed on a 24-hour extinction schedule (with no reassurance provided to the patient) for a 3–4 week period. In a more recent single-case evaluation, Singh (1975) showed how an attention withdrawal condition used in combination with positive reinforcement strategies served to control "hysterical fits."

Fading

Fading as a behavioral treatment technique consists of the transfer of control of responding from one stimulus to a totally distinct stimulus. To carry out such transfer without disrupting performance requires a very graduated approach. This is precisely what Barlow and Agras (1973) accomplished when transferring sexual responsivity in three homosexuals from a homosexual stimulus (slide of a nude male) to a heterosexual stimulus (slide of a nude female). In this study, sexual arousal was measured as mean penile circumference expressed as a percentage of maximum erection. Penile circumference was recorded with a mechanical strain gauge (a ring placed over the shaft of the penis that expands with increased erection) that was connected electronically to a polygraph.

One of the three study patients was a 29-year-old male who had a 14-year history of homosexual behavior. Although he occasionally dated women "for important occasions," he was exclusively homosexual. He had sought psychotherapeutic treatment for homosexuality on three previous occasions but without apparent benefit.

During baseline assessment penile responsivity to slides of male and female nudes was measured. In the fading procedure phase the patient was asked to choose a male slide (one that elicited a penile response of at least 80%) and a female slide that was considered "least unattractive."

These two slides were projected on a screen by two separate projectors. The projector arrangement was such that the two slides appeared on the screen superimposed over one another, with focus on the genital area. The projector arrangement also permitted an increase in brightness in one slide (e.g., the female) which then led to a decrease in brightness in the other (i.e., the male slide). During fading the patient was first shown a 0% female image and 100% male image. If he evidenced at least 75% of full erection during the 2-min. presentation, he advanced to the next step (6% female and 94% male). Throughout, the 75% criterion of full erection at each step was required for advancement to the next step. If at any given step the 75% criterion was not met, the same image was repeated until criterion responding was attained. A maximum of six trials were held per session. Fading for this patient continued until a 50% female brightness level was achieved. In the next six sessions fading procedures were temporarily discontinued. In the last phase fading was reinstated, and the patient slowly progressed until penile responding was achieved in relation to 100% female illumination (i.e., the female slide alone) for four sessions. Total treatment had required 105 trials.

Generalization data are presented in Fig. 9.6. The generalization task (conducted the morning following treatment) involved penile responding to slides of three different female nudes and three different male

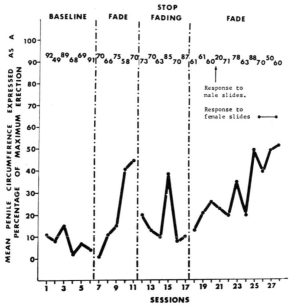

Fig. 9.6 Mean penile circumference as a percentage of full erection for Subject 3. Percentage of homosexual arousal as presented numerically. Lower scores indicate less sexual arousal. (Reprinted with permission from: D. H. Barlow and W. S. Agras: *Journal of Applied Behavior Analysis*, 6: 355, 1973.)

nudes. Examination of the data indicate low level responding to females during baseline, marked improvement during fading, a return to near baseline levels when fading was suspended, and a further improvement during reinstitution of fading. However, response to male slides continued to be relatively elevated during the first three phases of treatment but decreased in the last phase. During the course of treatment homosexual urges decreased concomitant with the patient's first report of heterosexual intercourse. A 9-month follow-up indicated continuation of a heterosexual orientation as confirmed by the patient's girlfriend.

Contingency Contracting

A contingency (or behavioral) contract is a negotiated agreement (usually put into writing) identifying the conditions under which two individuals are to behave in regard to one another (see Eisler & Hersen, 1973; Stuart, 1969). That is, the contract explicitly defines the relationship between each individual's behavior and the consequences (positive or negative) for that behavior. Built into the contract is the notion of reciprocity (i.e., mutually reinforcing consequences) in order to improve the quality of the relationship between two people (e.g., a dysfunctional marital pair). Indeed, contingency contracting has often been used as a treatment strategy to remediate dysfunctional marriages and to improve interpersonal functioning in discordant families (Azrin, Naster, & Jones, 1973; Miller, 1972; Miller & Hersen, in press; Patterson, 1971; Stuart, 1969, 1971; Wieman, Shoulders, & Farr, 1974; Weathers & Liberman, 1975). However, contracting has also been used with success for ameliorating problems of overweight (Mann, 1972) and alcoholism (Miller, Hersen, & Eisler, 1974).

It should be noted that a critical ingredient in behavioral contracting is reciprocal reinforcement. That is, if person X does something for person Y, then person Y must do something in return for person X. For example, Eisler and Hersen (1973) provide an illustration of a dysfunctional couple who agreed to the following. The husband agreed to spend $1/2$ hour after work in conversation with his wife on a topic of her own choosing. In return, she agreed to prepare his breakfast each morning. The importance of such reinforcement in contingency contracting was clearly documented by Miller, Hersen, and Eisler (1974). In this analogue study the results indicated that while instructions and signed agreements effected some changes in the target behavior (drinking), reinforcement (with instructions or written agreement) provided the needed ingredient for effecting *significant* behavioral change (decrease in drinking).

Stuart (1971) has listed four assumptions that underlie the use of contingency contracting. The *first* is that the receiving of positive reinforcement in interpersonal interactions is a privilege to be earned rather than a mere given (i.e., a right). The *second* is that reciprocity (i.e., reciprocal reinforcement) is the cornerstone of an effective interpersonal agreement. The *third* is that an effective interpersonal agreement is determined by the strength, rate, and diversity of reinforcements (reciprocal) established in such exchange. The *fourth* states that although rules in the contract delimit certain behaviors, they also foster "freedom" in the interpersonal exchange by clearly specifying "privileges" to be granted to each party.

Although the individual steps for carrying out successful behavioral contracts have been articulated in several publications (e.g., Stuart, 1969, 1971), considerable skill and sensitivity is needed on the part of the therapist. Indeed, the first step in negotiating a behavioral contract between two "warring" parties (e.g., the dysfunctional married couple) is to inform and convince them of the logic of the procedure. Following Stuart's (1969) recommendations, the couple must be convinced "that the impressions which each spouse forms of the other is (sic) based on the behavior of the other" (p. 677). It then follows that each partner must make changes in his/her behavior before reciprocal changes can be effected in the other partner's behavior. Stuart (1969) subsequently asks each partner to list three behaviors that he/she would like to see accelerated in the other (e.g., sexual activity, casual chats after work, household chores, etc.). Frequently much help is needed here to clarify and operationalize the behavior. If, for example, the husband states: "I want her to be more feminine," upon extended questioning this may really mean: "When I come home from work I would like Mary to have on a nice dress and for her to be wearing make-up." In contingency contracting, as much specification as possible is encouraged. It is *not at all assumed* that each partner automatically understands, knows, or appreciates the requests and needs of the other partner. A third step in the treatment requires that the three behaviors needing acceleration be written down and posted in the couple's home (i.e., a Behavior Checklist placed in an accessible area). The fourth step in the treatment involves the negotiation of a rate of exchange with respect to the two sets of three targeted behaviors. Sometimes a very explicit token or point economy may facilitate initial improvement in the relationship. For example, husbands were charged 3 tokens for kissing or light petting, 5 for heavy petting, and 15 for sexual intercourse. Of course, these tokens were earned for behaviors that wives were particularly interested in accelerating (Stuart, 1969).

Despite the fact that there are some obvious mechanical features to the process of contingency contracting, a primary object is to defuse (i.e., decrease) the reciprocal hostility that is characteristic of disordered interpersonal relationships. This is done with couples and families by stressing positive objectives and by teaching married partners and family members how to negotiate. In fact, once they learn how to negotiate for positive objectives in the consulting room, they often will renegotiate contracts at home at their own initiative as new situations arise.

Case Illustrations

An example of a negotiated contingency appears in Fig. 9.7. The case here (Miller & Hersen, in press) involved a 49-year-old married male alcoholic (Frank) and his wife of 29 years (Wilma). Frank had an extensive record of alcohol abuse over a period of 10 years that had resulted in numerous arrests, automobile accidents, and severe marital dysfunction. At the time of his hospitalization in a Veterans Administration psychiatry service, Frank was consuming 1 pint to 1 fifth of vodka per day. Wilma had threatened Frank with divorce if he did not seek treatment, and he was most intent on saving the marriage.

A behavioral assessment, consisting of interviews and ad libitum (naturalistic) videotaped interactions of the couple, revealed an absence of reciprocal positive reinforcement (e.g., Frank's inattention of Wilma)

Weekly Marital Contract

The undersigned, Frank and Wilma B., enter into the following agreement with each other. The terms of this agreement include the following:

1. During this weekend Wilma agrees not to mention any of Frank's past drinking episodes or possible drinking in the future.
2. Wilma will be allowed one infringement of this agreement per day provided that she immediately terminates her alcohol-related conversation contingent upon Frank's reminding her of this agreement.
3. On Friday, Saturday and Sunday afternoons or evenings Frank agrees to take Wilma out of the house for the purpose of a shopping trip, dinner, movie, or a drive depending on her choice.
4. Wilma's agreement to refrain from alcohol-related conversation is binding only if Frank fulfills his agreement stated under term number 3.
5. Frank's agreement to take Wilma out each day of the weekend is binding only if Wilma fulfills her agreement stated under term number 1.
6. The terms of the contract are renewable at the beginning of each day so that failure of one partner to fulfill his or her part of the agreement on any one day breaks the contract for that day only.

_____

Frank B.

_____

Wilma B.

_____

Witness

Fig. 9.7 Weekly Marital Contract. From: Miller and Hersen (1977) (Fig. 1).

and an excess of negative verbal interchanges (e.g., Wilma's nagging). Over the course of several treatment sessions the contract presented in Fig. 9.7 was successfully negotiated between Frank and Wilma while Frank was still hospitalized. Subsequently, outpatient counseling sessions were carried out biweekly for 3 months and then monthly for another 3 months. Both parties began to implement the clauses stated in the contract despite some initial difficulties. In fact, because of the negotiating skills Frank and Wilma had learned in treatment sessions, they were able to resolve contractual difficulties at their own initiative. In short they were able to renegotiate. A 9-month follow-up revealed improved marital satisfaction as indicated by self-report and corroborated by the couple's children and additional videotaping of ad libitum marital interaction.

Miller (1972) reports the case of a couple referred by a physician for marital difficulties. A major source of friction appeared to be the husband's increased consumption of alcohol over the past 2 years to about 4–6 pints of alcohol per week. Such drinking resulted in critical commentary from the wife and led to severe marital discord and further increases in drinking. Following a careful behavioral analysis, a contract relating to alcohol consumption and marital interaction was negotiated:

> "By mutual agreement the couple decided that between one and three drinks per day was an acceptable limit for the husband's drinking. Neither partner considered complete abstinence a necessary or desirable goal. Via the written contract the husband agreed to limit his drinking to this level. Unless the couple were invited for the evening or entertaining friends, these drinks were to be consumed in the presence of the wife before the evening meal. Drinking in any other situation (as determined by actual observation, liquor on his breath, or 'drunken' behavior) was forbidden and resulted in a monetary fine ($20.00) payable to his wife (to be spent as frivolously as possible on a nonessential item) and withdrawal of attention by the wife (she would immediately leave his presence). Both partners were working independently, and the dispensation of money in this manner was reported to be highly aversive to the partner paying the fine. The behavioral contract also required the wife to refrain from negative verbal or nonverbal responses to her husband's drinking. A monetary fine ($20.00) payable to her husband in addition to withdrawal of attention by the husband were the consequences of this behavior. In addition, the husband agreed to increase his attentive behavior towards his wife when she engaged in noncritical nonalcohol related conversation. The wife also agreed to provide the husband with attention and affection whenever he voluntarily limited his drinking (i.e., stopped after one or two drinks) or when he refrained from drinking. The conditions of this agreement were written into a contract form and signed by both partners. Separate copies were kept by the husband and wife" (Miller, 1972, pp. 594–595).

Drinking records were maintained during baseline, treatment, and follow-up, and were corroborated by the wife and friends. The results of treatment are presented in Fig. 9.8. During baseline, drinking (defined as 1¹/₂ oz. of alcohol straight or mixed) ranged from five to nine drinks a day. When the contract was first instituted little progress was noted. However, after a few monetary fines were levied by the wife the husband quickly began to decrease his consumption to zero to three drinks per day. A 6-month follow-up conducted for a 10-day period indicated maintenance of improvement. In this case, not only was marital satisfaction increased as a function of the behavioral contract, but the husband was still able to drink albeit in a controlled fashion.

Experimental Support

Although most of the experimental support for the efficacy of contingency contracting comes from case reports and within-subject analyses (e.g., Azrin, Naster, & Jones, 1973; Miller, 1972; Stuart, 1969; Wieman, Shoulders, & Farr, 1974), a few controlled group comparisons have appeared in the literature (e.g., Alexander & Parsons, 1973; Stuart & Tripodi, 1973). In general, the use of contingency contracting has worked relatively well with dysfunctional married couples, but results with families of delinquents have been mixed. For example, Wieman, Shoulders, and Farr (1974) used reciprocal reinforcement strategies in a case of marital discord in addition to communication and sexual skill training. Evaluating the effects of treatment in a multiple baseline

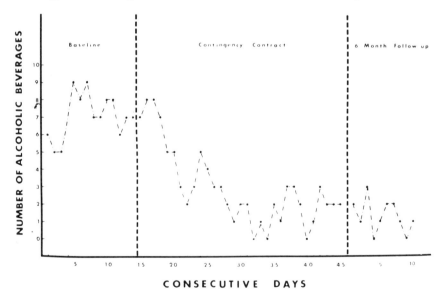

CONSECUTIVE   DAYS

Fig. 9.8 Number of alcoholic beverages consumed daily. (Reprinted with permission from: P. M. Miller: *Behavior Therapy*, 3: 593, 1972.)

design across behaviors, the investigators found that sequential application of contractual agreements led to good improvement in two behaviors but less improvement in a third (sexual responsivenes). In a more comprehensive within-subject analysis, Azrin, Naster, and Jones (1973) first applied a "catharsis-type" counseling approach for 3 weeks and then a behavioral approach (reciprocity counseling) that included many elements of contingency contracting. Results of this study indicated the superiority of the behavioral procedure with respect to "marital happiness," as assessed by the couples.

Weathers and Liberman (1975) recently conducted a within-subject evaluation of contingency contracting with families of delinquent adolescents. Target behaviors selected for modification were school attendance, compliance with curfew and chores, and verbal abusiveness to parents. The systematic application of contracting to each of the three target behaviors in sequence resulted in no change with the exception of verbal abusiveness to parents. Acknowledging the short-term nature of their treatment (only three interventions), Weathers and Liberman nonetheless are skeptical as to the efficacy of this type of behavioral strategy with delinquents and their families (see also Stuart & Lott, 1972). It should also be pointed out that in an earlier controlled group trial with over 100 families of delinquents, Stuart and Tripodi (1973) had found no differential effects in the following: (1) using three types of treatment duration, (2) contracts as compared with activity group interventions, (3) standard versus negotiated contracts, (4) fading versus precipitous termination of contracts.

There is one study, however, showing the superiority of contingency contracting over client-centered or "psychodynamic" therapy with families of delinquents (Alexander & Parsons, 1973). Unfortunately, there are some methodological difficulties with this investigation (e.g., unclear criteria for recidivism, variable follow-ups, unequal treatment time expenditures with the different treatment groups) that prohibit clear-cut interpretation of the data.

In brief, contingency contracting seems to be very useful in the case of marital discord. The efficacy of contingency contracting with families of delinquents has not yet been satisfactorily documented.

Comprehensive Treatments

In the foregoing sections we have defined and provided illustrations of a number of treatment strategies emanating from the operant framework. The examples we have selected have usually focused on the application of one or, at best, two specific techniques at a time (e.g., instructions and feedback). Although such focused application of treatments strategies exists in the behavioral literature, the behavior therapist is for the most part faced with compound clinical problems that may require a multitude of concurrent and sequential treatments in order to effect relevant behavioral changes (e.g., Blanchard & Hersen, 1976; Cautela & Baron, 1973; Lazarus, 1973). Not only may several behavioral treatments be required, but additional interventions such as pharmacotherapy may be a prerequisite in the hospitalized patient (see Hersen & Bellack, 1976; Hersen, Turner, Edelstein & Pinkston, 1975; Liberman & Davis, 1975).

Let us illustrate some of the above points. For example, Agras et al. (1974) concluded that the effective variables in the comprehensive behavioral treatment of anorexia nervosa were: (1) the negative reinforcing properties of the hospital environment, (2) the use of informational feedback as to caloric consumption and weight gained, (3) the systematic application of reinforcement (social and token), and (4) presentation of large, frequent, and attractively served meals.

Commenting on the comprehensive behavioral treatment of hysterical neurosis (conversion type), Blanchard and Hersen (1976) recommended a three-part program to insure permanence of effects. *First,* it was recommended that extinction procedures be systematically applied during the patient's hospitalization upon symptomatic presentation. *Second,* it was suggested that the patient's family (i.e., natural environment) be taught how to reinforce his/her positive behaviors while ignoring presentation of symptoms (i.e., differential attention). *Third,* the importance of teaching the patient new social skills in order to obtain gratification from the environment was stressed.

As the reader will undoubtedly understand, comprehensive behavioral treatment requires attention to all aspects of a patient's presenting problem(s). And, such treatment can only follow from the carefully conducted behavioral assessment. We will present a more detailed discussion of comprehensive interventions in the next chapter.

Summary

We have examined several types of treatment techniques that are derived from the operant conditioning framework. Included were: instructions, feedback, social reinforcement, shaping, extinction, fading, and contingency contracting. Applications of these techniques (alone and in combination with one another) have been presented for adult clinical disorders. In addition to a description of each treatment technique, illustrations of research, primarily from single-case experimental analyses, have been provided as empirical support. Finally, the importance of combining relevant techniques in a broad spectrum behavioral approach to effect maximum change in a variety of targeted behaviors has been underscored.

References

Agras, W. S., Barlow, D. H., Chapin, H. N., Abel, G. G., & Leitenberg, H. Behavior modification of anorexia nervosa. *Archives of General Psychiatry,* 1974, *30,* 279–286.

Agras, S., Leitenberg, H., & Barlow, D. H. Social reinforcement in the modification of agoraphobia. *Archives of General Psychiatry,* 1968, *19,* 423–427.

Agras, S., Leitenberg, H., Barlow, D. H., & Thomson, L. E. Instructions and reinforcement in the modification of neurotic behavior. *American Journal of Psychiatry,* 1969, *125,* 1435–1439.

Alexander, J. F., & Parsons, B. V. Short-term behavioral intervention with delinquent families: Impact on family process and recidivism. *Journal of Abnormal Psychology,* 1973, *81,* 219–225.

Alford, G. S., Blanchard, E. B.,& Buckley, T. M. Treatment of hysterical vomiting by modification of social contingencies: A case study. *Journal of Behavior Therapy and Experimental Psychiatry,* 1972, *3,* 209–212.

Ayllon, T., & Haughton, E. Control of the behavior of schizophrenic patients by food. *Journal of the Experimental Analysis of Behavior,* 1962, *5,* 343–352.

Ayllon, T., & Haughton, E. Modification of symptomatic verbal behaviour of mental patients. *Behaviour Research and Therapy,* 1964, *2,* 87–97.

Ayllon, T., & Michael, J. The psychiatric nurse a a behavioral engineer. *Journal of the Experimental Analysis of Behavior,* 1959, *3,* 324–334.

Azrin, N. H., Naster, B. J., & Jones, R. Reciprocity counseling: A rapid learning-based procedure for marital counseling. *Behaviour Research and Therapy,* 1973, *11,* 365–382.

Azrin, N., Rubin, H., O'Brien, F., Ayllon, T., & Roll, D. Behavioral engineering: Postural control by a portable operant apparatus. *Journal of Applied Behavior Analysis,* 1968, *1,* 99–108.

Barlow, D. H., & Agras, W. S. Fading to increase heterosexual responsiveness in homosexuals. *Journal of Applied Behavior Analysis,* 1973, *6,* 355–366.

Barlow, D. H., Agras, W. S., Abel, G. G., Blanchard, E. B., & Young, L. D. Biofeedback and reinforcement to increase heterosexual arousal in homosexuals. *Behaviour Research and Therapy,* 1975, *13,* 45–50.

Barrett, B. H. Reduction in rate of multiple tics by free operant conditioning methods. *Journal of Nervous and Mental Disease,* 1962, *135,* 187–195.

Bernhardt, A. J., Hersen, M., & Barlow, D. H. Measurement and modification of spasmodic torticollis: An experimental analysis. *Behavior Therapy,* 1972, *3,* 294–297.

Blanchard, E. B., & Epstein, L. H. The clinical utility of biofeedback. In M. Hersen, R. M. Eisler, & P. M. Miller (Eds.), *Progress in behavior modification: Volume 4.* New York: Academic Press, in press.

Blanchard, E. B., & Hersen, M. Behavioral treatment of hysterical neurosis: Symptom substitution and symptom return reconsidered. *Psychiatry,* 1976, *39,* 118–129.

Catania, A. C. (Ed.). *Contemporary research in operant behavior.* Glenview, Ill.: Scott, Foresman and Company, 1968.

Cautela, J. R., & Baron, M. G. Multifaceted behavior therapy of self-injurious behavior. *Journal of Behavior Therapy and Experimental Psychiatry,* 1973, *4,* 125–131.

Eisler, R. M., & Hersen, M. Behavioral techniques in family-oriented crisis intervention. *Archives of General Psychiatry,* 1973, *28,* 111–116.

Eisler, R. M., Hersen, M., & Agras, W. S. Effects of videotape and instructional feedback on nonverbal marital interaction: An analog study. *Behavior Therapy,* 1973, *4,* 551–558.

Eisler, R. M., Hersen, M., & Miller, P. M. Shaping components of assertive behavior with instructions and feedback. *American Journal of Psychiatry,* 1974, *131,* 1344–1347.

Epstein, L. H., & Hersen, M. Behavioral control of hysterical gagging. *Journal of Clinical Psychology,* 1974, *30,* 102–104.

Epstein, L. H., Hersen, M., & Hemphill, D. P. Music feedback in the treatment of tension headache: An experimental case study. *Journal of Behavior Therapy and Experimental Psychiatry,* 1974, *5,* 59–63.

Foy, D. W., Miller, P. M., Eisler, R. M., & O'Toole, D. H. Social skills training to teach alcoholics to refuse drinks effectively. *Journal of Studies on Alcohol,* 1976, *37,* 1340–1345.

Franks, C. M. (Ed.), *Behavior therapy: Appraisal and status.* New York: McGraw-Hill Book Co., 1969.

Greenspoon, J. *The effect of verbal and nonverbal stimuli on the frequency of members of two verbal response classes.* Unpublished doctoral dissertation, Indiana University, 1951.

Hallam, R. S. Extinction of ruminations: A case study. *Behavior Therapy,* 1974, *5,* 565–568.

Hersen, M. Awareness in verbal operant conditioning: Some comments. *Journal of General Psychology,* 1968, *78,* 107–111.

Hersen, M. Controlling verbal behavior via classical and operant conditioning. *Journal of General Psychology,* 1970, *83,* 3–22.

Hersen, M., & Bellack, A. S. A multiple-baseline analysis of social-skills training in chronic schizophrenics. *Journal of Applied Behavior Analysis,* 1976, *9,* 239–245.

Hersen, M., & Eisler, R. M. Behavioral approaches to study and treatment of psychogenic tics. *Genetic Psychology Monographs.* 1973, *87,* 289–312.

Hersen, M., Eisler, R. M., Miller, P. M., Johnson, M. B. & Pinkston, S. G. Effects of practice, instructions, and modeling on components of assertive behavior. *Behaviour Research and Therapy,* 1973, 11, 443–451.

Hersen, M., Gullick, E. L., Matherne, P. M., & Harbert, T. L. Instructions and reinforcement in the modification of a conversion reaction. *Psychological Reports,* 1972, *31,* 719–722.

Hersen, M., Turner, S. M., Edelstein, B. A., & Pinkston, S. G. Effects of phenothiazines and social skills training in a withdrawn schizophrenic. *Journal of Clinical Psychology,* 1975, *31,* 588–594.

Kallman, W. M., Hersen, M., & O'Toole, D. H. The use of social reinforcement in a case of conversion reaction. *Behavior Therapy,* 1975, *6,* 411–413.

Kazdin, A. E. *Behavior modification in applied settings.* Homewood, Ill.: Dorsey Press, 1975.

Kazdin, A. E., & Erickson, L. M. Developing responsiveness to instructions in severely and profoundly retarded residents. *Journal of Behavior Therapy and Experimental Psychiatry,* 1975, *6,* 17–21.

Kohlenberg, R. J. Operant conditioning of human anal sphincter pressure. *Journal of Applied Behavior Analysis,* 1973, *6,* 201–208.

Lazarus, A. A. Multimodal behavior therapy: Treating the "BASIC ID." *Journal of Nervous and Mental Disease,* 1973, *156,* 404–411.

Leitenberg, H., Agras, W. S., & Thomson, L. E. A sequential analysis of the effect of selective positive reinforcement in modifying anorexia nervosa. *Behaviour Research and Therapy,* 1968, *6,* 211–18.

Leitenberg, H., Agras, W. S., Thomson, L., & Wright, D. E. Feedback in behavior modification: An experimental analysis in two phobic cases. *Journal of Applied Behavioral Analysis,* 1968, *1,* 131–137.

Lewinsohn, P. M. The behavioral study and treatment of depression. In M. Hersen, R. M. Eisler, & P. M. Miller (Eds.), *Progress in behavior modification: Volume 1.* New York: Academic Press, 1975.

Lewinsohn, P. M., & Atwood, G. E. Depression: A clinical-research approach. *Psychotherapy: Theory, Research and Practice,* 1969, *6,* 166–171.

Liberman, R. P. A behavioral approach to group dynamics. I. Reinforcement and prompting of cohesiveness in group therapy. *Behavior Therapy,* 1970, *1,* 141–175. (a)

Liberman, R. P. A behavioral approach to group dynamics. II. Reinforcing and prompting hostility-to-the-therapist in group therapy. *Behavior Therapy,* 1970, *1,* 312–327. (b)

Liberman, R. P. Reinforcement of cohesiveness in group therapy. *Archives of General Psychiatry,* 1971, *25,* 168–177. (a)

Liberman, R. P. Behavioural group therapy: A controlled clinical study. *British Journal of Psychiatry,* 1971, *119,* 535–544. (b)

Liberman, R. P., & Davis, J. Drugs and behavior analysis. In M. Hersen, R. M. Eisler, & P. M. Miller (Eds.), *Progress in behavior modification: Volume 1.* New York: Academic Press, 1975.

Liberman, R. P., & Raskin, D. E. Depression: A behavioral formulation. *Archives of General Psychiatry,* 1971, *24,* 515–523.

Mann, R. A. The behavior-therapeutic use of contingency contracting to control an adult behavior problem: Weight control. *Journal of Applied Behavior Analysis*, 1972, *5*, 99–109.

Matarazzo, J. D. Prescribed behavior therapy: Suggestions from interview research. In A. J. Bachrach (Ed.), *Experimental foundations of clinical psychology*. New York: Basic Books, Inc., 1962.

Milby, J. B. Modification of extreme social isolation by contingent social reinforcement. *Journal of Applied Behavior Analysis*, 1970, *3*, 149–152.

Miller, P. M. The use of behavioral contracting in the treatment of alcoholism: A case report. *Behavior Therapy*, 1972, *3*, 593–596.

Miller, P. M., Becker, J. V., Foy, D. W., & Wooten, L. S. Instructional control of the components of alcoholic drinking behavior. *Behavior Therapy*, 1976, *4*, 472–480.

Miller, P. M., & Hersen, M. Modification of marital interaction patterns between an alcoholic and his wife. Unpublished manuscript, 1977.

Miller, P. M., Hersen, M., & Eisler, R. M. Relative effectiveness of instructions, agreements, and reinforcement in behavioral contracts with alcoholics. *Journal of Abnormal Psychology*, 1974, *83*, 548–553.

O'Brien, F., & Azrin, N. H. Behavioral engineering: Control of posture by informational feedback. *Journal of Applied Behavior Analysis*, 1970, *3*, 235–240.

Patterson, G. R. *Families: Applications of social learning to family life*. Champaign, Ill.: Research Press, 1971.

Pineda, M. R., Barlow, D. H., & Turner, B. B. Treatment of a severe speech disorder by behavior modification: A case study. *Journal of Behavior Therapy and Experimental Psychiatry*, 1971, *2*, 203–207.

Rafi, A. A. Learning theory and the treatment of tics. *Journal of Psychosomatic Research*, 1962, *6*, 71–76.

Sherman, J. A. Use of reinforcement and imitation to reinstate verbal behavior in mute psychotics. *Journal of Abnormal Psychology*, 1965, *70*, 155–164.

Singh, R. Experiments in two cases of hysterical fits. *Journal of Behavior Therapy and Experimental Psychiatry*, 1975, *6*, 351–353.

Stuart, R. B. Operant-interpersonal treatment for marital discord. *Journal of Consulting and Clinical Psychology*, 1969, *6*, 675–682.

Stuart, R. B. Behavioral contracting within the families of delinquents. *Journal of Behavior Therapy and Experimental Psychiatry*, 1971, *2*, 1–11.

Stuart, R. B., & Lott, L. A. Behavioral contracting with delinquents: A cautionary note. *Journal of Behavior Therapy and Experimental Psychiatry*, 1972, *3*, 161–169.

Stuart, R. B., & Tripodi, T. Experimental evaluation of three time-constrained behavioral treatments for predelinquents and delinquents. In R. D. Rubin, J. P. Brady, & J. D. Henderson (Eds.), *Advances in behavior therapy: Volume 4*. New York: Academic Press, 1973.

Stumphauzer, J. S. Application of reinforcement contingencies with a 23-year-old anorexic patient. *Psychological Reports*, 1969, *24*, 109–110.

Thorndike, E. L., & Rock, R. T. Learning without awareness of what is being learned or the intent to learn it. *Journal of Experimental Psychology*, 1934, *17*, 1–19.

Truax, C. B. Reinforcement and nonreinforcement in Rogerian psychotherapy. *Journal of Abnormal Psychology*, 1966, *71*, 1–9.

Turner, S. M., & Hersen, M. Instructions and reinforcement in modification of a case of astasia-abasia. *Psychological Reports*, 1975, *36*, 607–612.

Weathers, L., & Liberman, R. P. Contingency contracting with families of delinquent adolescents. *Behavior Therapy*, 1975, *6*, 356–366.

Wieman, R. J., Shoulders, D. I., & Farr, J. H. Reciprocal reinforcement in marital therapy. *Journal of Behavior Therapy and Experimental Psychiatry*, 1974, *5*, 291–295.

10

Comprehensive approaches

Introduction

In this final chapter, we will identify some of the factors that contribute to the successful implementation of a comprehensive behavioral approach in a number of applied settings. In so doing, we will attempt to distinguish between sophisticated and unsophisticated behavior therapy. As noted throughout this book, there is a vast difference between isolating variables for purposes of laboratory demonstrations and conducting behavior therapy in the "real world," where careful control over environmental events and staff cooperation may not be ideal. Thus, in the applied clinical setting or applied educational setting, irrespective of how well the staff is trained, the precision of laboratory conditions is rarely if ever approximated. Moreover, uni-dimensional problems tend to be the exception rather than the rule. For example, the monophobia dealt with in the laboratory setting is rarely seen in day-to-day clinical practice. To the contrary, patients and clients present with a variety of phobic symptoms that are often associated with other disorders (e.g., depression, interpersonal difficulties). (The same applies to the non-phobic disorders.)

In addition to the above, behavior modifiers frequently work in settings where other professionals (peers, supervisors, subordinates) do not share their theoretical leanings. In the case of subordinates, staff training programs in behavior modification need to be carried out. Therefore, we will discuss issues pertaining to the effective training of paraprofessional staff. However, with supervisors and peers, persuasion and "political expertise" are necessary if successful behavioral programs are to be conducted. This is obviously critical if the behavior modifier is dependent on the cooperation of such individuals to help implement his program. Certainly, for psychologists working in psychiatric settings, a happy marriage between the pharmacological and behavioral approaches is not only desirable but mandatory at times (see Liberman & Davis, 1975). That is, the comprehensive treatment of some disorders (e.g., schizophrenia) may first require adjusting levels of medication to control psychotic symptomatology. This will be followed by attention to particular skill deficits (cf. Hersen, Turner, Edelstein, & Pinkston, 1975).

Finally, as suggested in the aforementioned reference, multi-dimensional problems will undoubtedly involve more complicated approaches to treatment. Not only will some problems require the assistance of drugs, but others may require either concurrent or sequential application of several behavioral techniques. The earlier behavioral reports probably contributed to the notion that behavior therapy was simplistic and could only be used with precisely-defined disorders (e.g., the phobias). However, our examination of several comprehensive treatment approaches that have been developed for a variety of more complex disorders (e.g., alcoholism, schizophrenia, hysterical neurosis) should help to dispel such inaccurate perceptions.

Training Paraprofessionals and Staff

Perhaps more than any other therapeutic approach, behavior modification has made extensive use of the paraprofessional. Individuals with high school degrees (e.g., nursing assistants) and B.A. and B.S. level degrees have carried out many behavioral programs in clinical and educational settings.* That is not to say that behavior modification is so simple that a terminal degree (e.g., Ph.D., M.D., M.S.W., D.S.W.) is not required in order to successfully implement treatment. However, it does underscore the fact that behavioral principles and techniques derived therefrom are sufficiently explicit in order to permit relatively routine application by individuals with less education. On the other hand, the conceptualization and planning of specific behavioral interventions does ordinarily require advanced training. It is likely that this aspect of treatment will remain the province of the degreed professional.

The range of programs and settings in which paraprofessionals have implemented behavioral strategies is extensive. Treatment of psychiatric inpatients and children in both school and residential settings has

---

* Training of such staff and maintaining their continued cooperation are often the most difficult aspects of conducting behavioral programs.

been almost exclusively carried out by non-professional staff. The token economy, for example, is a program that typifies the application of group reinforcement contingencies by paraprofessionals (namely nursing assistants) (Ayllon & Azrin, 1968). The day-to-day administration of tokens requires a tremendous amount of staff cooperation and effort. Similarly, paraprofessionals have helped to conduct behavioral programs in classroom settings (see Walker & Buckley, 1974). Social skill training procedures with chronic schizophrenics (e.g., Bellack, Hersen, & Turner, 1976; Hersen & Bellack, 1976a) have been carried out entirely by bachelor's level research technicians.

In light of the heavy reliance on the paraprofessional as a behavioral change agent, it is of utmost importance to teach him behavioral principles and techniques in an efficacious manner. Moreover, it is equally, if not more, important to ensure that the paraprofessional continue to apply behavioral strategies reliably long after in-service training has been completed. Given their penchant for "hard" data, behaviorists have carefully examined those strategies that are most successful in bringing about behavioral change in behavior change agents (i.e., the paraprofessional). Over the years, behavior modifiers have learned that the time-honored method of conducting in-service training in the traditional fashion (e.g., lectures, some reading material, classroom discussion) may not lead to the greatest payoff (i.e., the paraprofessional religiously implementing the specifics of the behavioral program). Furthermore, there is increased evidence (e.g., Hollander & Plutchik, 1972; Panyan, Boozer, & Morris, 1970) that even if the paraprofessional does learn new techniques in the classroom situation, there is little assurance that he will apply them in the clinical setting in the absence of systematic reinforcement and feedback.

Research Studies

Let us now examine several studies in which behavioral techniques were used to improve the training and post-training behavior of paraprofessionals and other staff members in institutional settings. Mc-Keown, Adams, and Forehand (1975) conducted a study in which they evaluated several types of training methods for instructing grade school teachers in behavior modification principles. There was a total of four experimental and control conditions, with five teachers assigned to each. One group received a manual on behavior modification and participated in laboratory sessions (six 1½-hour meetings) in which techniques were presented and role played. A second group participated only in laboratory sessions. A third group read the manual, while a fourth group received neither "source of information." Pre-post scores were obtained on two dependent measures: (1) a multiple choice examination containing 20 questions about behavior modification, and (2) observation of each teacher's classroom for disruptive behavior of children.

The results indicated that teachers who participated in the laboratory sessions not only showed significant increases in knowledge about behavior modification, but also were able to obtain significant decreases in disruptive behaviors in their classrooms by using operant techniques. Such improvements were not evidenced by teachers who did not receive laboratory training. McKeown et al. (1975) suggest that, "Success in decreasing disruptive behaviors in the teachers' classrooms is believed to have been the result of having trained behavioral technicians who could effectively apply behavioral principles as opposed to having trained teachers who have only a cognitive understanding of behavioral principles" (p. 91). Put in other words, it would appear that when the teacher actually practices in the laboratory those behaviors that may lead to successful classroom management, then there is a higher probability that such behavior will generalize to the classroom situation itself.

In an interesting study, Hollander and Plutchik (1972) examined the effects of a reinforcement program for psychiatric attendants (10 females and 3 males who had an average of 3 years of high school education) following a 6-week course on the application of behavioral techniques. Reinforcement consisted of 150 trading stamps given contingently for each research task that was completed. In a within-subject ABA design, the investigators found that the "stamp contingency" led to substantial increases and improvements in attendants' behavior on a psychiatric ward run under operant lines. During reinforcement conditions, not only did the attendants show an increase of assigned tasks completed* (Fig. 10.1), but substantial increases were also noted with respect to number of attendants who completed volunteer research tasks (see Fig. 10.2). That is, volunteering increased from 38% in baseline to 74% in the contingency phase.

An important concurrent effect of the reinforcement contingency was that the psychiatric attendants increased their amount of contact with the patients. This is in direct contrast to baseline conditions, during which time attendants avoided such contact with the exception of their "custodial" duties (when patients required feeding, washing, clothing, or acted out). In addition, Hollander and Plutchik point out that the entire program was relatively inexpensive, that it did not contradict union or institutional policies, and that it allowed for the implementation of their operant research program. A similar reinforcement program for improving the performance of staff who work with adolescent retardates has been described by Martin (1972). Here too, institution of

---

* Tasks included observation and recording of patient behaviors on the ward, at lunch, and at work, as well as graphing each patient's performance.

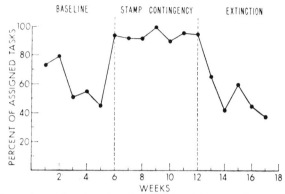

Fig. 10.1 Percentage of assigned tasks completed by attendants during baseline, stamp contingency, and extinction conditions. (Reprinted with permission from: M. A. Hollander and R. Plutchik: *Journal of Behavior Therapy and Experimental Psychiatry*, 3: 297, 1972).

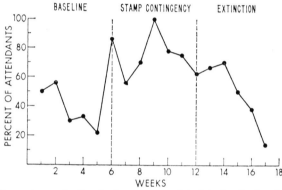

Fig. 10.2 Percentage of attendants who completed tasks during baseline, stamp contingency, and extinction conditions. (Reprinted with permission from: M. A. Hollander and R. Plutchik: *Journal of Behavior Therapy Experimental Psychiatry*, 3: 297, 1972.)

a financial contingency resulted in marked improvement in carrying out the dictates of the operant program.

In yet another study, Panyan et al. (1970) provided feedback (visual) to attendants in a state institution for the retarded and found that their daily use of operant training methods increased as a result. The study is illustrative of the fact that in the absence of external feedback and reinforcement, in spite of adequate training and preparation, attendants' use of operant techniques will decrease. Indeed, attendants in this program had previously completed a formal 4-week training course in operant methodology. Following operant training, attendants from each of four halls were asked to conduct training sessions directed toward teaching the retarded residents specific self-help skills. A number of such self-help skills had been listed by the investigators. Also, attendants were asked to maintain performance records for each of the residents. In baseline, data were collected with respect to number of self-help training sessions conducted by the attendants. However, no feed-back was provided here. In the feedback phase, these data (number of sessions completed) were tabulated but also "written on a feedback sheet" and presented to each attendant.

As can be seen in Fig. 10.3, the effects of feedback were evaluated in a

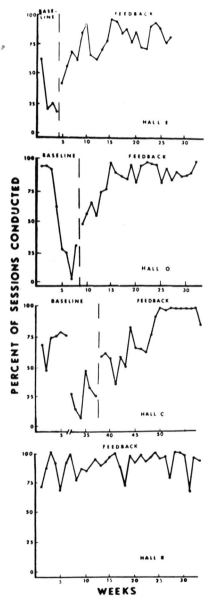

Fig. 10.3 Percentage of requested training sessions conducted by the staff on *Halls E, O, C, and R.* (Reprinted with permission from: M. Panyan, H. Boozer, and N. Morris: *Journal of Applied Behavior Analysis,* 3: 1, 1970.)

multiple baseline design across halls. That is, feedback was introduced in Halls E, O, and C under time-lagged conditions. Feedback, however, was presented throughout the study in Hall R, which served as a control. Examination of these data clearly indicate a decrease in performance during baseline conditions where no feedback was provided (Halls E, O, C). By contrast, when feedback was introduced, substantial linear increases in performance were noted in Halls E, O, and C. Performance in Hall R remained at a steady rate throughout while feedback was repeatedly administered.

A difficulty frequently encountered by professionals working in institutional settings is the apparent unwillingness of paraprofessional staff (i.e., psychiatric attendants) to interact with their patients. As noted by Hollander and Plutchik (1972), there seems to be a general unwillingness to interact unless custodial duties are warranted. Recognizing this problem, Wallace, Davis, Liberman, and Baker (1973) were concerned with evaluating methods to increase staff interaction with patients in a psychiatric unit in a state hospital. Although the investigators were well aware of the previous studies (reviewed in this chapter), they were concerned with the limitations inherent in each of the techniques used. Monetary reinforcement, although effective, is obviously costly and limited in supply. Feedback and social reinforcement techniques, also successful, require consistent and systematic programming. Thus, Wallace et al. set out to assess the effects of simple instructions, the removal of possible competing activities interfering with staff-patient interactions, and the relative effectiveness of various professionals (e.g., psychologist, nursing supervisor) modeling the targeted behaviors. In general, the results of this study show the ineffectiveness of both instructions and the removal of competing activities in increasing staff-patient interactions. However, modeling by professional staff seemed to increase such interactions, with the most substantial increases observed when the model was a nursing supervisor. Wallace et al. conclude the following on the basis of their study: "The results of the study point to several variables that should be considered in maintaining treatment programs in institutional settings. Simply scheduling the time and instructing staff what to do is not effective. Some other intervention is necessary. This study suggests that the necessary intervention can be modeling of appropriate behavior by various authority figures. Although direct interventions such as the dispensing of bonuses can be used, modeling can be considerably more economical since only the model's behavior need be directly reinforced. By implication, if a nursing authority figure models the incorrect behavior, then staff members will similarly emit the incorrect behavior" (p. 425).

To summarize the findings of the aforementioned studies, it is safe to say that behavior modifiers have found that to effect maximum staff performance, behavioral strategies, such as those used with patients and clients, are most effective. *First,* with respect to initial instruction, classroom work that includes practical application and an opportunity to practice and role play in the laboratory will yield better results than mere discussion or reading. *Second,* in terms of maintaining appropriate behavior in the actual applied setting, additional techniques are needed such as feedback, social reinforcement, monetary reinforcement, or modeling by authority figures. The latter represents the most cost-effective of the procedures that can be used and should be relatively easy to implement.

Role of Drugs in Behavior Modification

In a truly comprehensive treatment approach to behavioral disorders, the important role of drugs in behavior modification cannot be ignored (cf. Lazarus, 1973; Liberman & Davis, 1975; Silverstone, 1970). Although comparatively little attention has been accorded to this subject in the behavioral journals, the interactive role of drugs and behavioral analysis and modification is extensive in clinical practice. Indeed, we are able to identify six separate categories in which drugs and behavior modification interact: (1) Drugs have been used to make severely disturbed psychiatric patients (e.g., psychotics) more receptive to behavioral intervention (e.g., Hersen & Bellack, 1976a). (2) Drugs have been used to facilitate application of behavioral treatments (e.g., Pecknold, Raeburn, & Poser, 1972; Turner, Hersen, & Alford, 1974). (3) The complementary application of drugs and behavior modification in disorders such as non-psychotic unipolar depression has been suggested (cf. Lewinsohn, 1975; Pacoe, Himmelhoch, Hersen, & Guyett, 1976). (4) The use of behavioral strategies to motivate compliance with drug regimes has been outlined (e.g., Duncan, Hilton, Kraeger, & Lumsdaine, 1973). (5) The effects of drugs have been evaluated in behavioral research strategies such as the single case design (see Hersen & Barlow, 1976; Liberman, Davis, Moon, & Moore, 1973). (6) Drugs have been used as punishing agents as in the case of Antabuse and apomorphine treatments of alcoholics (see Chapter 7).

There are several reasons that the above mentioned interactions between drugs and behavior modification have not received the attention they deserve in the behavioral literature. *First,* most behavior therapists are psychologists, who are not legally permitted to administer drugs. Therefore, their efforts have been directed toward non-medical treatments. *Second,* as stated in Chapters 1 and 4, behavior therapists are committed to developing self-control in their patients. This goal often is in contradiction to the external control associated with drugs and drug administration. However, Liberman and Davis (1975) are quick to point out that there is a long and well-established relationship between behavior analysis and psychopharmacology at the infrahuman level of study (cf. Laties & Weiss, 1969; Lindsley, 1961). Therefore, it would seem natural that such intimate collaboration would be extended to the study at the applied clinical level with humans. Liberman and Davis argue that, "A collaboration between researchers in behavior analysis and clinical psychopharmacology also promises to lead to a more reliable, valid, and comprehensive classification of behavior disorders based on differential response to environmental and chemical interventions. The identification of various subgroups within the large, clinical populations referred to as schizophrenic, hyperkinetic, and depressed would promote behavioral-biological research and contribute to the state of the art when we will be closer to predicting what treatment in which setting is most effective for a specific individual" (pp. 326–327). In addition, the behavioral commitment to pragmatic and meaningful change implies that drugs should be employed when they produce the most effective or rapid changes.

In the succeeding sections we will examine some of these collaborative efforts that have proved successful in dealing with behavioral disorders that represent difficult treatment challenges.

Preparatory Role of Drugs

For hospitalized psychiatric patients, drugs are generally used to control their more florid symptomatology; this is particularly the case with those who are diagnosed psychotic. For example, in the case of schizophrenics, major tranquilizers such as the phenothiazines (e.g., thioridazine, chlorpromazine, trifluoperazine, fluphenazine) are effective in suppressing hallucinations, delusions, thinking disturbances, and general agitated behavior. Without the tranquilizing and suppressing effects of anti-psychotic medication like the phenothiazines, most schizophrenics would not be in a state sufficiently receptive to benefit from behavioral interventions such as the token economy (Agras, 1976) or social skills training (Bellack et al., 1976; Hersen & Bellack, 1976a; Hersen et al., 1975). That is, during the course of acute psychotic episodes, patients are generally *unable to learn new material* due to the interference of internal processes (e.g., hallucinations, delusions). Let us illustrate this point with some examples taken from the clinical research literature.

Agras (1976) showed how a young brain-damaged patient benefited from a token economy program *only* when he was administered a sufficient dose of chlorpromazine. Similarly, Bellack and Hersen (Bellack et al., 1976; Hersen & Bellack, 1976a) have not attempted social skills training (see Chapter 5) with chronic schizophrenics until medication level has been properly titrated (i.e., adjusted). To the contrary, when levels of anti-psychotic medication are inappropriately adjusted, schizophrenic patients fail to show improvement in specific social skill behaviors that are targeted for change despite intense and prolonged training.

Thus, in the aforementioned examples, it is clear that there is an interactive function between drugs and behavior modification. As previously noted by Hersen and Bellack (1976b), drugs can control psychotic symptomatology but cannot improve the patient's behavioral deficits. On the other hand, it is equally clear that it is only by using behavioral techniques that schizophrenic patients can learn new skills to enable them to cope better with their natural environments. But then again, this can only be accomplished when psychotic symptomatology is under control and this control is most easily achieved pharmacologically.

Facilitative Role of Drugs

Not only have drugs been used in a preparatory role in behavior modification, but they have been employed to facilitate behavioral strategies such as desensitization (Brady, 1966), flooding (Marks, Viswanathan, Lipsedge, & Gardiner, 1972), and massed practice (Turner et al., 1974). For example, diazepam (Valium — a commonly prescribed minor tranquilizer) was given intravenously by Pecknold et al. (1972) to two severely neurotic patients who were unable to relax sufficiently using standard relaxation instructions (i.e., deep muscle relaxation). Fifteen relaxation sessions had been conducted during the course of systematic desensitization therapy. In the 16th session the patient was administered a 5-mg. dose of Valium (intravenously) concurrently with verbal instructions to relax. In about 15 min. he was sufficiently relaxed to continue movement up the hierarchy (i.e., systematic desensitization was resumed). In the four succeeding sessions Valium was reduced by 1 mg. per day, with the same degree of relaxation still being achieved. Shortly thereafter diazepam was discontinued, and in the remaining 14 sessions of systematic desensitization therapy, relaxation was obtained strictly via verbal instruction. Similar results were reported for a second patient.

In a comparable procedure, Brady (1966) has used intravenous methohexital sodium (Brevital — "an ultrashort acting barbiturate") to induce deep muscle relaxation during the course of the systematic desensitization treatment of sexually dysfunctional women (i.e., they were unable to achieve orgasm). While seated in a comfortable reclining chair, the patient is given an injection of 1% solution of Brevital. During the next 2–4 min., while the drug is beginning to take effect, verbal instructions to relax are administered. Then the patient is taught how to visualize scenes from the hierarchy (involving progressively more intimate sexual interactions with her husband) in a standard desensitization format. In a 20-min. Brevital-relaxation session two to three scenes may be presented (each visualized for 3 min. followed by a 2-min. rest period). Inasmuch as the relaxing effects of the drug wane within 4–5 min., additional amounts of Brevital are usually administered (as indicated by the patient's subjective reports of relaxation and tension). In a typical 20-min. session, 50–75 mg. of Brevital may be given. Brady recommends that treatment be conducted one to three times weekly until all items of the hierarchy have been completed. In this initial report, four of five patients appeared to benefit from Brevital-induced relaxation.

Marks et al. (1972) conducted an interesting crossover study in which the effects of diazepam (Valium) and placebo were paired with an in vivo flooding procedure for 18 patients suffering from chronic specific phobias. The three experimental conditions were as follows: (1) flooding of 2 hours duration begun 4 hours after ingestion of Valium 0.1 mg. per kg. (the "waning" phase and effect of Valium); (2) flooding of 2 hours duration begun 1 hour after ingestion of Valium 0.1 mg. per kg. (the "peak" phase and effect of Valium); and (3) flooding of 2 hours duration begun 1 hour or 4 hours after ingestion of a placebo.

Although flooding in each of the above-mentioned treatment combinations led to significant improvements in the patients' phobic conditions, the "waning" group was superior to both the "peak" and placebo groups. These differences were noted with respect to *clinical, attitudinal,* and *physiological* measures of change. As might be expected, the placebo group showed the least amount of improvement. Marks et al. point out that, "Under diazepam patients touched the phobic object for the first time earlier in the session than they did under placebo. It may be that patients can only tolerate a particular maximum of anxiety during exposure before they escape, and that the same maximum is reached higher up the hierarchy under influence of a sedative than with placebo. In other words, mild sedation may increase the amount of confrontation that is possible" (p. 503).

Turner et al. (1974) describe the use of massed practice and meprobamate (a minor tranquilizer) in the treatment of spasmodic torticollis, a tic-like disorder. The patient's particular form of torticollis "was characterized by a slightly downward positioning of the head, with jerky movements directed towards the right shoulder." Torticollis movements were rated from 10-min. videotaped sessions held three times a day. During the baseline phase there were about 17–26 tics per minute, with an upward (increasing) trend in the data (see Fig. 10.4). In the next phase massed practice was instituted. This involved having the patient *voluntarily duplicating* and practicing the tic as rapidly and as accurately as possible. Four hundred such trials were held thrice daily. Although massed practice reversed the trend in the data (i.e., a decreasing trend), at the conclusion of this phase tic rate was still about 19 per min. Thus, in the next phase meprobamate 400 mg., q.i.d. (four times a day) was added to massed practice. Examination of these data indicate a

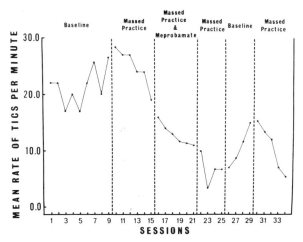

Fig. 10.4 Mean rate of tics (involuntary torticollis movements per 10-min. probe sessions during baseline and treatment phases.) (Reprinted with permission from S. M. Turner, M. Hersen, and H. Alford: *Behaviour Research and Therapy,* 12: 259, 1974.)

further decrease in tic rate, which was continued in the following phase when massed practice was the only treatment being applied. The rest of the experimental analysis (the last two phases) confirms the controlling effects of massed practice over tic rate.

With respect to the effects of meprobamate in this study, Turner et al. note that, "the role of meprobamate in reducing rate of involuntary torticollis movements is unclear, especially since discontinuation of the drug in the fourth phase did not result in deterioration. To the contrary, improvement continued when massed practice was the only treatment variable in force. It is possible that the addition of meprobamate in Phase 3 helped relax the subject, thus enhancing the effects of massed practice" (p. 260). In this regard, it might be noted that Feldman and Werry (1966) had pointed out that in the anxious patient massed practice may worsen the disorder rather than leading to its amelioration.

Finally, Wolpe (1973) describes a biological technique he uses to facilitate relaxation in patients suffering from "free-floating" anxiety. In these cases the patient is asked to inhale through a gas mask a mixture containing 65% carbon dioxide and 35% oxygen. Wolpe indicates that, "by far the most satisfactory measure is to administer to the patient one to four single, full-capacity inhalations . . . " (pp. 182–183) of the mixture. Throughout the treatment the patient is required to estimate the amount of subjective distress he experiences on a 100-point scale. As the level of subjective distress decreases to manageable proportions, then a return to verbally induced relaxation may be attempted with greater success. Wolpe notes that at the psychophysiological level, inhalation of the mixture results in a slower pulse and decreased skin conductance (responses associated with increased levels of relaxation).

Complementary Use of Drugs and Behavior Modification

Although interest in combining drugs and behavior modification is relatively new, there definitely is precedent for combining psychotherapeutic and pharmacological approaches, particularly in the area of depression (Ulenhuth, Lipman, & Covi, 1969; Weissman, Klerman, Paykel, Prusoff, & Hanson, 1974). However, in these studies the psychotherapeutic techniques used have been "traditional," and are characterized by their vagueness and absence of precision. In any case, let us examine one of the studies to see how behavioral approaches might be substituted more efficaciously. Weissman et al. (1974) conducted a long-term maintenance study of neurotically depressed female outpatients who previously had responded well to amitriptyline (an anti-depressant). One hundred fifty such patients were divided into high and low contact conditions. High contact involved weekly 1-hour "psychotherapy" sessions from an experienced social worker. Low contact involved monthly 15-min. sessions with a psychiatrist. Furthermore, high and low contact groups were subdivided into amitriptyline, placebo, and no pill conditions, thus yielding a 2 × 3 factorial design.

Of the 150 patients who began the study, there were 106 who completed it after 8 months. The specific effects of drugs and psychotherapy were as follows: (1) Amitriptyline prevented relapse whereas psychotherapy did not. (2) Weekly psychotherapy led to improved social functioning (seen only 6–8 months after treatment began), whereas amitriptyline had no effect on social functioning. (3) There were no drug × psychotherapy interactions.

Thus, one of the primary findings was that psychotherapy resulted in improvement in patients' *social skills*. This finding is consistent with Jerome Franks's (1961) position that psychotherapy is more effective in ameliorating social functioning than in reducing manifestation of particular symptoms (e.g., those associated with depression such as dysphoric mood). Given the results of the Weissman et al. (1974) investigation, Pacoe et al. (1976) have suggested that social skills training might provide a superior alternative to the relatively imprecise and difficult-to-replicate psychotherapy used therein. Pacoe et al. argue that social skills training (see Chapter 5) is more likely to have impact on patients' social adjustment, especially as the treatment *is* directed toward that end. In that sense, specific social skill deficits might be identified in the behavioral analysis that can be dealt with behaviorally. Consequently, social skills training may prove to be a successful complement to amitriptyline in the comprehensive treatment of "neurotic" depression. However, such a study as outlined herein has not yet been carried out (cf. Lewinsohn, 1975) and obviously is warranted. (It is, of course, also possible that a behavioral intervention would make the drug superfluous.)

Single-Case Evaluation of Drugs

Another example of the interaction of pharmacology and behavior modification is represented by the evaluation of drug effects in single-case experimental designs. The single-case research design is particularly well suited for the assessment of drugs for a number of reasons. *First,* repeated measures of actual motoric behavior permit a clear description of the specific effects of given drugs and placebos on given individuals. *Second,* inasmuch as data are plotted daily, the treating physician receives relatively quick and accurate feedback as to the success of the treatment. *Third,* instances of failure are easily recorded and, because of the flexibility inherent in this research strategy, changes in experimental drug treatment can readily occur as dictated by the patient's condition. Thus, drugs can be added or removed or dosages can be changed at will, without interfering with the research process as would be the case in a group comparison design.

We will illustrate the use of the single-case evaluation of drug effects by presenting a case taken from the clinical research efforts of Liberman et al. (1973). The purpose of this case study was to determine the effects of trifluoperazine (Stelazine)* on the social behavior of a 21-year-old, hospitalized, withdrawn male schizophrenic. To assess social behavior, the patient was approached by a member of the ward staff 18 times a day and asked on each occasion to partake in a 30-sec. informal chat. The staff member simply recorded whether the patient complied and carried through with the conversation.

During the first 14 days of the study (No Drug) the patient was removed from all medication. In the next phase he was given a placebo which had all of the physical characteristics of the Stelazine but was pharmacologically an inert substance. In the third phase he was given a daily dose of 60 mg. of Stelazine. The fourth phase involved a return to Placebo and the final phase a reinstatement of Stelazine.

The results of this experimental analysis appear in Fig. 10.5. During the No Drug condition mean number of asocial responses (refusals to chat) showed a marked linear increase. Institution of Placebo in the next phase resulted in some initial improvement which disappeared over the following 3 days. Institution of Stelazine in the 12th through the 17th session led to a marked improvement in social responsivity. This improvement, however, was reversed in the next phase when Placebo conditions were restored. Finally, in the last phase the positive effects of Stelazine were once again evidenced.

In summary, the controlling effects of Stelazine over social responding were documented in this single-case analysis. Concurrently, the pa-

---

* Stelazine is a major tranquilizer, is of the phenothiazine family, and functions as an anti-psychotic agent.

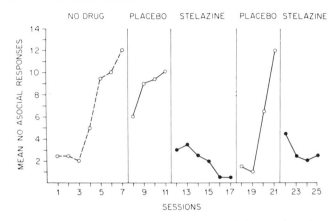

Fig. 10.5 Average number of refusals to engage in brief conversation. (Reprinted with permission from: R. P. Liberman, J. Davis, W. Moon, and J. Moore: *Journal of Nervous and Mental Diseases,* 156: 432, 1973.)

tient's rate of rational talk increased substantially during Stelazine phases (56–72%) and showed a large decrease (to 17%) during the second Placebo phase.

Comprehensive Behavioral Programs

Throughout most of this book we have presented examples of clinical research that illustrate the application and experimental confirmation of very specific behavioral techniques for circumscribed behavioral disorders. However, as has already been noted in Chapters 7 and 9 and in the Introduction to this chapter, such extreme specificity of application where variables are carefully controlled is primarily characteristic of the scientific research enterprise. Of course, in daily practice in applied settings more comprehensive approaches to a particular problem (but with less experimental rigor and finesse) are typical. In the following sections we will examine some of the more comprehensive behavioral approaches that have been applied to problems such as alcoholism, hysterical neurosis, schizophrenia, and delinquency. It will become apparent that there are two types of comprehensive approaches that have been used. The first includes a combination of techniques (e.g., operant conditioning, classical conditioning, pharmacological) for a specific disorder (e.g., schizophrenia). The second involves a unified approach (e.g., operant) to the problem, but one that encompasses numerous facets of the patient's existence (cf. Cohen & Filipczak, 1971). The reader will note that some of the comprehensive approaches to be described have confirmatory data; others have been employed clinically; and still others, at present, represent theoretical proposals.

Alcoholism

A comprehensive community reinforcement approach to alcoholism conducted under operant lines has been described in detail by Hunt and Azrin (1973). Patients in this program were male chronic alcoholics who were admitted to a state hospital facility and were suffering from withdrawal symptoms. As noted by the investigators, "The Community-Reinforcement program was designed to rearrange the vocational, family and social reinforcers of the alcoholic such that time-out from these reinforcers would occur if he began to drink" (p. 93). There were several components to the program. Included were vocational counseling, marital and family counseling, social counseling, reinforcer-access counseling, the existing hospital treatment program for alcoholics, and community maintenance. We will examine these individual components in turn.

Marital and family counseling consisted of reciprocal reinforcement agreements between the patient and his spouse as well as information relating to areas of marital life such as money management, sexual adjustment, and social activities. Reinforcers granted the patient (e.g., sexual interaction with his spouse) were totally contingent on absolute sobriety. Hunt and Azrin point out that many of the couples were in a state of near-divorce at the beginning of treatment, but they were persuaded to carry out some of the agreements on a "reinforcer sampling" basis (i.e., trying out each suggestion for a week at a time).

Social counseling was directed toward helping the patient to develop a "circle" of friends whose interaction was not dependent on alcohol as a *social lubricant*. As part of this phase of the program, a former tavern was renovated and made into a social club that provided a variety of activities for the patient and his wife (e.g., picnics, games, movies). Of course, alcohol was strictly forbidden on these premises.

Reinforcer-access counseling essentially consisted of helping the alcoholic and his family to obtain facilities previously unavailable to them (e.g., newspaper, telephone, television). "The rationale for priming these activities was to increase the ease with which the alcoholic could engage in the areas of vocational, marital, and social activities, these three activities already being incompatible with drinking" (p. 96).

The existing hospital program for alcoholics was didactic and involved 25, 1-hour lectures on alcoholism. Topics covered were the role of Alcoholics Anonymous, physical illnesses associated with abusive drinking, sexual difficulties resulting from alcoholism, etc.

Finally, community maintenance consisted of extensive follow-up care immediately after hospital discharge. During the 1st month post-discharge each patient was visited by the counselor in his community once to twice weekly. Subsequently, such visits were decreased to twice and then once a month. The primary objectives of these visits were to evaluate post-hospital functioning and to assist the patients with social, family, and vocational problems.

Hunt and Azrin (1973) present comparative data for eight male alcoholics who received the entire community reinforcement program with eight male alcoholics (matched on relevant demographic variables) who received detoxification and the didactic hospital program. The results indicated the superiority (at statistically significant levels) of the community reinforcement approach with respect to sobriety, work performance, social and marital adjustment, and ability to remain out of the hospital.

Another comprehensive approach to alcoholism involving several behavioral modalities has been described by Miller, Stanford, and Hemphill (1974). This program, conducted on a psychiatric unit in a Veterans Administration Hospital, is predicated on the following theoretical position: "alcoholism is viewed as a socially acquired, habitual behavior pattern which enables the alcoholic to avoid or escape from unpleasant anxiety-producing situations, to exhibit spontaneous social behavior, to gain increased attention (either positive or negative) from friends and relatives, and to avoid withdrawal symptoms associated with termination of drinking" (p. 279).

Thus, a three-pronged approach was devised. The *first* was concerned with strategies to make the ingestion of alcohol more aversive to the patient. Therefore, techniques such as covert sensitization, apomorphine aversion, and electrical escape conditioning were routinely applied on an individual basis. The *second* was specifically directed toward improving the patient's self-discipline (i.e., the ability to complete requisite tasks) and social interactions. Each patient was a member of the ward token economy program, which fostered a work and responsibility orientation. Also included in the ward program were thrice-weekly group psychotherapy sessions emphasizing methods of dealing with the vicissitudes of life (i.e., frustration, anger, disappointment, boredom, etc.). Role playing of strategies for dealing with such a variety of life stresses was carried out in group sessions. Assertion training techniques were widely used to promote the patients' expression of both positive and negative feelings. That is, the patients were taught to discriminate the appropriate context in which assertive responding might "pay off."

The *third* part of the program involved specific attention to the patient's family and vocational needs and deficiencies. Family therapy was directed to teaching the patient and his spouse methods to bring about reciprocal reinforcement. Behavioral contracting was used as a treatment vehicle to enhance the likelihood of new interactional patterns being maintained outside of the therapy session. Wives were specifically taught to reinforce the patient when sober and to ignore him when drinking (see Hersen, Miller, and Eisler, 1973). Equal care and attention were given with respect to the patient's post-hospital vocational adjustment. As in the Hunt and Azrin (1973) program, the vocational counselor helped patients to prepare resumés and coached them with respect to suitable vocational goals. In addition, help was provided in scheduling interviews with prospective employers.

Many of the patients in the Miller et al. (1974) program were maintained on Antabuse (see Chapter 7, for a description of the drug) following hospital discharge. Moreover, for the first 2 months postdischarge, weekly follow-up visits were scheduled. Over a 1-year followup period these visits were continued with decreasing frequency. Behavioral techniques applied during the inpatient phase of treatment were carried out during the outpatient phase when needed. Once again, the focus of treatment was on the "here-and-now."

Still another comprehensive approach for the treatment of alcoholism has been developed by Sobell and Sobell (1973). This program has emphasized four distinct components: (1) Avoidance conditioning procedures (i.e., the use of electric shock) have been applied in order to counteract the pleasurable aspects of excessive drinking. Avoidance conditioning was used with patients who chose both controlled drinking (i.e., social drinking) and abstinence as their treatment goals. (2) Alcoholics were trained to discriminate those stimulus situations directly associated with abusive drinking. (3) Alcoholics were taught behaviors associated with social drinking (e.g., smaller sips, longer inter-sip intervals, fewer drinks altogether, smaller proportion of alcohol in the mixed drink). (4) Videotape feedback of inebriated behavior was used to point out behavioral deficits as well as a method to increase the patient's motivation for change.

An important feature of the Sobell and Sobell approach is their meticulous and intensive effort at obtaining follow-up data on their initial 70 patients treated at Patton State Hospital in California. In that study, chronic alcoholics either chose a treatment goal of abstinence (N = 30) or controlled drinking (N = 40). Half of the patients in each of the groups were given 17 behavioral treatments consistent with the goal chosen. The remaining half received conventional hospital treatment usually afforded alcoholics. The most recent follow-up report of these patients (Sobell & Sobell, 1976) indicates that *only* the patients who received behavior therapy with the controlled drinking goal "engaged in a substantial amount of limited non-problem drinking during the second year interval, and those subjects also had more abstinent days than subjects in any other group" (p. 195).

Hysterical Neurosis (Conversion Reactions)

Hysterical neurosis (conversion type) is characterized by loss of function in the voluntary (i.e., peripheral) nervous system, leading to symptoms such as leg paralysis, writer's cramp, "hysterical blindness." These symptoms *do not* have any physiological basis and often do not make any anatomical sense. With respect to behavior therapy, there is evidence that simple differential attention (reinforcement of positive behaviors, extinction or inattention of negative behaviors) can result in substantial improvements in some cases of hysterical neurosis (e.g., Hersen, Gullick, Matherne, & Harbert, 1972; Turner & Hersen, 1975). More recent work (e.g., Kallman, Hersen, & O'Toole, 1975) indicates that therapeutic concern directed solely toward symptomatic manifestation may not be enough to prevent either the return of symptoms or the development of yet new symptoms. However, psychodynamic interpretations for the aforementioned symptoms are not considered to be appropriate here. To the contrary, a careful examination suggests that an incomplete behavioral analysis may have been carried out, thus leading to an incomplete treatment approach. Based on clinical-research findings and clinical observation, Blanchard and Hersen (1976) present the rationale for a behavioral approach for the patient hospitalized with a diagnosis of hysterical neurosis (conversion reaction). Indeed, a three-part approach is recommended. The first part of the approach focuses on reinforcing (usually with social approval and praise) all of the patient's positive initiatives (e.g., the patient suffering from hysterical leg paralysis who begins to make efforts at standing and walking) while concurrently ignoring symptomatic manifestations (i.e., aches and pains that do not have a physiological basis). Of course, a thorough medical evaluation is necessary to rule out possible organic causes. The objective in this phase of the treatment is to reverse the contingencies that have been in operation in the patient's natural environment. For example, frequently this type of patient *is* able to obtain much attention (i.e., reinforcement) for "sick-role" behaviors. It is obvious, then, that this is contrary to the patient's best interests in that he will not regain full functioning of the affected area (e.g., his leg) if such reinforcement is maintained.

Once success has been achieved during the patient's hospitalization, it is critical that differential attention procedures be transferred to the natural environment (usually the family). This was amply demonstrated in the Kallman et al. (1975) study. Only when the patient's family was specifically instructed to carry out differential attention procedures at home were gains seen in the hospital actually transferred into the home situation. In that sense, it is clear that generalization needs to be carefully programmed and not left to chance (see Baer, Wolf, & Risley, 1968).

The third phase of treatment is conducted concurrently with the other two phases, and involves an attempt to teach the patient how to obtain gratification from his environment through *positive means*. In so doing, techniques derived from the assertion training (Hersen, Eisler, & Miller, 1973) and social skills literatures (Hersen & Bellack, 1976b) are recommended. If successful, the patient does not need to resort to a pathological life style in order to receive environmental attention. Blanchard and Hersen (1976) document their theoretical position by presenting four clinical cases successfully treated using the above outlined procedures.

Schizophrenia

Schizophrenia accounts for a majority of patients requiring complete psychiatric hospitalization and is probably one of the most extensively studied of the psychiatric disorders. However, in spite of the literally thousands of studies that have been conducted with schizophrenics, major treatment problems still remain. Treatment difficulty is underscored by the fact that the disorder is of the chronic variety and that repeated hospitalizations typically ensue throughout its course.

A major break-through in the treatment of schizophrenia was the development of the phenothiazines in the 1960s. These anti-psychotic medications not only proved to be effective in reducing psychotic symptomatology (hallucinations, delusions, thinking disturbances, agitation), but seemed to be effective in their maintenance roles, particularly in preventing relapse. Although the phenothiazines (or any other family of drugs for that matter) result in symptomatic improvement, there is no drug that is able to remediate basic skill deficiencies in patients. Such skill deficits are frequently extensive in the case of schizophrenics, especially when there have been repeated hospitalizations. (In these cases the debilitating effects of repeated institutionalizations and being out of contact with the "real world" are most apparent.) As recently articulated by Hersen and Bellack (1976b), basic social and life management skill deficits in schizophrenia may be a function of disuse over the course of numerous hospitalizations or may simply represent an inadequate learning history. In any event, it is obvious that many schizophrenics, although asymptomatic (due to drug therapy) are ill-equipped to deal with life stresses to be faced in their natural environments.

In light of the above, Hersen and Bellack (1976b) and Hersen and Luber (in press) have outlined comprehensive behavioral methods for dealing with chronic patients (primarily the schizophrenics). Hersen and Bellack's (1976b) presentation is essentially theoretical whereas Hersen and Luber (in press) describe their multi-faceted approach as practiced in an applied clinical setting (a Partial Hospitalization Service). Patients in this service, although chronically disabled, are not hospitalized on a full-time basis, but do live in the community (e.g., some with their families, others in boarding homes, and still others in half-way houses).

Hersen and Luber make it quite clear that their patients need to be under good pharmacological control with respect to psychotic symptomatology. Once this is achieved, the major function of the Partial Hospitalization Service is educational. That is, the various group activities and psychotherapies that comprise the service are geared toward teaching the patient basic life management and social skills. There are several groups which represent different levels of patient functioning. Thus, a given patient is assigned to groups consistent with his particular needs and skill levels. For example, there are some patients who are unaware of the specifics involved in grooming, doing laundry, sewing, cooking, and nutrition and physical fitness. Consequently, each of these topics is covered in a group specifically tailored to the needs of the participants. In addition to group discussion and participation, actual demonstration by the group leader and practice by the patient (frequently in the community setting, e.g., shopping at the supermarket) are carried out.

Groups subsumed under Activities of Daily Living include community orientation, recreation counseling, community readjustment, and bureaucratic systems. As the titles imply, the topic matter of the groups is directed toward facilitating the patient's reintegration into the community. Skills that most of us take for granted (e.g., dealing effectively with utility companies, getting information and help from governmental and social agencies such as Social Security) represent enormous challenges for the socially unskilled patient. Thus, in the bureaucratic systems group, a patient might learn how to contact the telephone company in order to have a phone installed in an apartment. In the community orientation group, the patient may learn for the first time about the services and recreational opportunities available in his particular community.

A different classification of groups is represented by those focusing on discussion, such as the current issues group. The objective in this group is to enable the patient to become more aware of local, national, and world events. The chronic schizophrenic, again largely as a function of numerous hospitalizations, often has lost the ability and/or interest in events beyond his immediate needs. It is clear that if the patient is to become more integrated in his community that greater awareness of such issues is needed. Not only are newsworthy items discussed in the group, but the possible sources of information are listed for the patient.

There are two primary behavioral therapy groups conducted in Hersen and Luber's (in press) program. One involves teaching the patient deep muscle relaxation and other relaxation techniques to enable him to withstand environmental stresses with greater success. The second is specifically concerned with teaching the patient requisite social skills (see Chapter 5) such as appropriate eye contact, gestures, and speech patterns in addition to helping the patient express both positive and negative feelings in a constructive manner. Research studies emanating from this phase of the program have already been described in detail in Chapter 5 (e.g., Hersen & Bellack, 1976a). These studies, however, are representative of social skills training for individuals rather than groups.

In addition to the above, other behavioral strategies are applied to specific symptomatic manifestation on an individual basis. Also, an integral part of the entire program involves attention to family difficulties via behavioral contracting.

There are two components to the Partial Hospitalization Service. The Day Hospital (9:00 A.M.–3:00 P.M.) best serves the schizophrenic who needs much support and whose life management and social skills are at a relatively low level. When first admitted to the program such patients are required to participate on a 5-day a week basis. As behavioral improvements are evidenced, frequency of contact with the program is gradually decreased (faded out). Finally, as the patient improves to the point where he is possibly gainfully employed, attending school, or in a work-rehabilitation program, transfer (i.e., graduation) to the Night Hospital (5 days a week – 6:00 P.M.–9:00 P.M.) will take place. Here too, contact is gradually decreased as the patient shows decreased dependence on the institution for support. Thus, when the Partial Hospitalization Service is considered in toto, there is a gradual shaping process that occurs within and between the two groups and within and between the two components of the program. Also, when the reverse occurs and a patient deteriorates, return to a lower level group or program (including rehospitalization) is effected.

Delinquency

The traditional approach to the treatment of juvenile delinquency has been marked by poor results and high rates of recidivism. When apprehended by the authorities for their misdeeds and subsequently adjudicated, delinquents and pre-delinquents are frequently placed in institutional and correctional settings where numerous other delinquents are currently residing. Given this kind of milieu, the "new" delinquent (i.e., pre-delinquent), instead of learning behaviors considered appropriate in society, tends to model after the more "senior" delinquents already there, thus learning behaviors that are likely to extend his "criminal" career. A behavioral analysis of such settings clearly indicates that negative contingencies are in operation. That is, the "payoff" for the "new" delinquent, largely as a function of peer pressure, is not in the direction of positive and acceptable behavior, but in the direction of socially unacceptable behavior (e.g., aggressiveness, flaunting of rules and regulations, a disdain of education, poor grammar, a dislike of authority).

In light of the above, a group of operant psychologists at the University of Kansas (Phillips, 1968; Phillips, Phillips, Fixsen, & Wolf, 1971; Phillips, Phillips, Wolf, & Fixsen, 1973) set out to evaluate the use of token reinforcement procedures with delinquents "in a home-style residential treatment program," now known as *Achievement Place*. In the initial study (Phillips, 1968) three boys (labeled "pre-delinquent") with histories of theft, fighting, disruptive behavior, truancy, and academic failure participated in this token economy program that encompassed all aspects of their lives. These boys ranged in age from 12–14 years.

Positive behaviors resulted in points being awarded by the two "house-parents." As in a typical token economy, privileges were contingent on earning tokens (or points), and specific privileges had a differential cost (see Table 10.1, for the price list). Table 10.2 lists those behaviors that led to point earnings as well as those resulting in a response cost procedure (i.e., loss of points).

In a series of carefully designed within-subject analyses, Phillips (1968) showed that the point economy was able to reduce aggressive statements, increase bathroom cleanliness, improve punctuality at activities, and decrease the use of the word "ain't." Phillips notes that, "The points seemed almost as convenient to administer as verbal consequences . . . the house-parents removed or presented points by requesting the youth's point card and recording the consequence. Subsequent to these studies, the youths themselves have performed the recording tasks equally well. The house-parents have simply instructed the boys to 'take off' or 'give yourself' points. Cheating has not appeared to be a problem, possibly because of the heavy fine if caught" (p. 222).

In subsequent studies, Phillips et al. (1971) showed that point economy procedures were effective in increasing promptness at meals and the saving of money (when points were given contingently for these behaviors). Similarly, point consequences for responding correctly to a "news quiz" increased attendance during the course of a televised news program. In addition, room-cleaning behavior was again reinforced, but with apparent success using a fading condition (point consequences delivered on 8% of the days). In still another series of studies, Phillips et

TABLE 10.1

Privileges That Could Be Earned Each Week with Points[a]

Privileges for the Week	Price in Points
Allowance	1000
Bicycle	1000
TV	1000
Games	500
Tools	500
Snacks	1000
Permission to go downtown	1000
Permission to stay up past bedtime	1000
Permission to come home late after school	1000

[a] From: Phillips (1968) (Table 1).

TABLE 10.2

Behaviors and the Number of Points That They Earned or Lost[a]

Behaviors That Earned Points	Points
1. Watching news on TV or reading the newspaper	300 per day
2. Cleaning and maintaining neatness in one's room	500 per day
3. Keeping one's person neat and clean	500 per day
4. Reading books	5 to 10 per page
5. Aiding house-parents in various household tasks	20 to 1000 per task
6. Doing dishes	500 to 1000 per meal
7. Being well dressed for an evening meal	100 to 500 per meal
8. Performing homework	500 per day
9. Obtaining desirable grades on school report cards	500 to 1000 per grade
10. Turning out lights when not in use	25 per light
Behaviors That Lost Points	Points
1. Failing grades on the report card	500 to 1000 per grade
2. Speaking aggressively	20 to 50 per response
3. Forgetting to wash hands before meals	100 to 300 per meal
4. Arguing	300 per response
5. Disobeying	100 to 1000 per response
6. Being late	10 per min
7. Displaying poor manners	50 to 100 per response
8. Engaging in poor posture	50 to 100 per response
9. Using poor grammar	20 to 50 per response
10. Stealing, lying, or cheating	10,000 per response

[a] From: Phillips (1968) (Table 2).

al. (1973) evaluated the effects of employing a "manager" selected from the peer group of "pre-delinquents" to supervise tasks and administer points and fines. Managers were able to earn a considerable number of points if they performed well and were successful in getting peers to complete their assigned tasks. A comparison of a "manager" selected at *auction* by bidding the highest number of points for the position and one *elected* by peers indicates that the elected one proved to be the most effective. This was most apparent when he had the power both to give points and to impose fines contingently on peer behavior.

Taken together, the studies conducted by Phillips and his colleagues illustrate the comprehensive use of operant techniques with regard to most aspects of predelinquents' lives in a home-style residential setting. These studies are particularly important inasmuch as they show the efficacy of operant techniques in reversing the usual negative reinforcing contingencies operating in institutional settings for the delinquent. The data clearly indicate that comprehensive behavioral programs for delinquents can be directed toward shaping and reinforcing behaviors that are considered to be appropriate for extra-institutional living in the community.

Probably one of the most comprehensive and innovative of the operant programs developed for male juvenile offenders was instituted by Cohen and Filipczak (1971) on the grounds of the National Training School for Boys (NTS) in Washington, D. C. (1966–1967). This program is referred to as the CASE-II MODEL (Contingencies Applicable to Special Education-Motivationally Oriented Design for an Ecology of Learning). The participants in this project were 41 convicted male juvenile offenders (mean age = 16.9 years). They had been convicted of such offenses as: postal violations, auto theft, petty larceny, homicide, robbery, assault, etc. Common to all participants was their history of school failure.

A continuous, and all-encompassing, 24-hour per day operant environment was created in which privileges were given on a strictly contingent basis (necessary services were provided non-contingently). However, in contrast to most point or token economies, most points *were not* earned by completing jobs. Indeed, the greatest number of points could be earned through academic achievement (i.e., by passing tests related to material learned via "teaching machines," i.e., programmed learning texts). Cohen and Filipczak underscore, "that educational behavior is functionally related to its consequences and that—by setting up a situation in which appropriate consequences are made contingent upon changing behavioral requirements—these behaviors can be established, altered, maintained, and transferred" (pp. 5–6).

In order to earn points, the youths were required to pass academic tests at a 90% level or better on such topics as reading, language usage, mathematics, science, and social studies. The results of this program showed that not only were there substantial increases in grade level achievement on standardized tests, but overall improvements in IQ scores (e.g., 16.2 points for those who spent more than 90 days in the program) were also observed. When compared with the usual changes in academic level found for boys in other programs at the NTS, these results are all the more remarkable, especially if one considers the non-voluntary status of the boys participating.

It also should be noted that despite the fact that the program was primarily educational in nature, recidivism level (with respect to legal offenses) was considerably lower for CASE II students than others at the NTS (e.g., two-thirds less for the 1st year post-program). However, these differences were not apparent 3 years post-program in the absence of further treatment.

Summary

In this final chapter we have examined those factors that contribute to the successful implementation of a comprehensive behavioral approach.

One of these involves the training of paraprofessional and professional staff in behavioral methodology. Research data indicate that those behavioral strategies that have proven to be effective in bringing about change in patients' behaviors (e.g., feedback, reinforcement, modeling) are equally effective in changing and maintaining staff behavior (i.e., with respect to implementing given features of behavioral programs). A second feature of comprehensive approaches to treatment has greatest relevance to behavioral programs conducted in psychiatric settings—the use of drugs. The potentially important interface between drugs and behavioral analysis and modification was carefully outlined, with examples drawn from the clinical research literature. Finally, examples of truly comprehensive behavioral treatment paradigms for alcoholism, hysterical neurosis, schizophrenia, and delinquency were presented.

References

Agras, W. S. Behavior modification in the general hospital psychiatric unit. In H. Leitenberg (Ed.), *Handbook of behavior modification and behavior therapy.* Engle-wood Cliffs, N. J.: Prentice-Hall, 1976.

Ayllon, T., & Azrin, N. H. *The token economy: A motivational system for therapy and rehabilitation.* New York: Appleton-Century-Crofts, 1968.

Baer, D. M., Wolf, M. M., & Risley, T. R. Some current dimensions of applied behavior analysis. *Journal of Applied Behavior Analysis,* 1968, *1,* 91-97.

Bellack, A. S., Hersen, M., & Turner, S. M. Generalization effects of social skills training in chronic schizophrenics: An experimental analysis. *Behaviour Research and Therapy,* 1976, *14,* 391-398.

Blanchard, E. B., & Hersen, M. Behavioral treatment of hysterical neurosis: Symptom substitution and symptom return reconsidered. *Psychiatry,* 1976, *39,* 118-129.

Brady, J. P. Brevital-relaxation treatment of frigidity. *Behaviour Research and Therapy,* 1966, *4,* 71-77.

Cohen, H. L., & Filipczak, J. A. *A new learning environment.* San Francisco: Jossey-Bass, 1971.

Duncan, D., Hilton, L., Kraeger, P., & Lumsdaine, J. *Fertility control methods: Strategies for introduction.* New York: Academic Press, 1973.

Feldman, R. B., & Werry, J. S. An unsuccessful attempt to treat a ticqueur by massed practice. *Behaviour Research and Therapy,* 1966, *4,* 111-117.

Frank, J. D. *Persuasion and healing.* Baltimore: Johns Hopkins University Press, 1961.

Hersen, M., & Barlow, D. H. *Single-case experimental designs: Strategies for studying behavior change.* New York, Pergamon Press, 1976.

Hersen, M., & Bellack, A. S. A multiple baseline analysis of social skills training in chronic schizophrenics. *Journal of Applied Behavior Analysis,* 1976, *9,* 239-246.

Hersen, M., & Bellack, A. S. Social skills training for chronic psychiatric patients: Rationale, research findings, and future directions. *Comprehensive Psychiatry,* 1976, *17,* 559-580 (b).

Hersen, M., Eisler, R. M. & Miller, P. M. Development of assertive responses: Clinical, measurement, and research considerations. *Behaviour Research and Therapy,* 1973, *11,* 505-521.

Hersen, M., Gullick, E. L., Matherne, P. M., & Harbert, T. L. Instructions and reinforcement in the modification of a conversion reaction. *Psychological Reports,* 1972, *31,* 719-722.

Hersen, M., & Luber, R. F. Use of group psychotherapy in a partial hospitalization service: The remediation of basic skill deficits. *International Journal of Group Psychotherapy,* in press.

Hersen, M., Miller, P. M., & Eisler, R. M. Interactions between alcoholics and their wives: A descriptive analysis of verbal and nonverbal behavior. *Quarterly Journal of*

Studies on Alcohol, 1973, *34,* 516–520.

Hersen, M., Turner, S. M., Edelstein, B., A., & Pinkston, S. G. Effects of phenothiazines and social skills training in a withdrawn schizophrenic. *Journal of Clinical Psychology,* 1975, *31,* 588–594.

Hollander, M. A., & Plutchik, R. A reinforcement program for psychiatric attendants. *Journal of Behavior Therapy and Experimental Psychiatry,* 1972, *3,* 297–300.

Hunt, G. M., & Azrin, N. H. A community-reinforcement approach to alcoholism. *Behaviour Research and Therapy,* 1973, *11,* 91–104.

Kallman, W. M., Hersen, M., & O'Toole, D. H. The use of social reinforcement in a case of conversion reaction. *Behavior Therapy,* 1975, *6,* 411–413.

Laties, V. G., & Weiss, B. Behavioral mechanisms of drug action. In P. Black (Ed.), *Drugs and the brain.* Baltimore: John Hopkins Press, 1969.

Lazarus, A. A. Multimodal behavior therapy: Treating the "Basic ID." *Journal of Nervous and Mental Disease,* 1973, *156,* 404–411.

Lewinsohn, P. M. The behavioral study and treatment of depression. In M. Hersen, R. M. Eisler, & P. M. Miller (Eds.), *Progress in behavior modification: Volume 1.* New York: Academic Press, 1975.

Liberman, R. P., & Davis, J. Drugs and behavior analysis. In M. Hersen, R. M. Eisler, & P. M. Miller (Eds.), *Progress in behavior modification: Volume 1.* New York: Academic Press, 1975.

Liberman, R. P., Davis, J., Moon, W., & Moore, J. Research designs for analyzing drug-environment behavior interactions. *Journal of Nervous and Mental Disease,* 1973, *156,* 432–439.

Lindsley, O. R. Operant behavior during anesthesia recovery: A continuous and objective method. *Anesthesiology,* 1961, *22,* 937–946.

Marks, I. M., Viswanathan, R., Lipsedge, M. S., & Gardiner, R. Enhanced relief of phobias by flooding during waning diazepam effect. *British Journal of Psychiatry,* 1972, *121,* 493–505.

Martin, G. L. Teaching operant conditioning to psychiatric nurses, aides, and attendants. In F. W. Clark, D. R. Evans, & L. A. Hamerlynck (Eds.), *Implementing behavioral programs for schools and clinics.* Champaign, Ill.: Research Press, 1972.

McKeown, D., Adams, H. E., & Forehand, R. Generalization to the classroom of principles of behavior modification taught to teachers. *Behaviour Research and Therapy,* 1975, *13,* 85–92.

Miller, P. M., Stanford, A. G., & Hemphill, D. P. A social-learning approach to alcoholism treatment. *Social Casework,* 1974, *55,* 279–284.

Pacoe, L. V., Himmelhoch, J. M., Hersen, M., & Guyett, I. Pharmacologic and behavioral approaches to the treatment of "neurotic" depression: A needed integration. Unpublished manuscript, 1976.

Panyan, M., Boozer, H., & Morris, N. Feedback to attendants as a reinforcer for applying operant techniques. *Journal of Applied Behavior Analysis,* 1970, *3,* 1–4.

Pecknold, J. C., Raeburn, J., & Poser, E. G. Intravenous diazepam for facilitating relaxation for desensitization. *Journal of Behavior Therapy and Experimental Psychiatry,* 1972, *3,* 39–41.

Phillips, E. L. Achievement place: Token reinforcement procedures in a home-style rehabilitation center for "pre-delinquent" boys. *Journal of Applied Behavior Analysis,* 1968, *1,* 213–223.

Phillips, E. L., Phillips, E. A., Fixsen, D. L., & Wolf, M. M. Achievement place: Modification of the behaviors of pre-delinquent boys within a token economy. *Journal of Applied Behavior Analysis,* 1971, *4,* 45–59.

Phillips, E. L., Phillips, E. A., Wolf, M. M., & Fixsen, D. L. Achievement place: Development of the elected manager system. *Journal of Applied Behavior Analysis,* 1973, *6,* 541–561.

Silverstone, J. T. The use of drugs in behavior therapy. *Behavior Therapy,* 1970, *1,* 485–497.

Sobell, M. B., & Sobell, L. C. Individualized behavior therapy for alcoholics. *Behavior Therapy,* 1973, *4,* 49–72.

Sobell, M. B., & Sobell, L. C. Second year treatment outcome of alcoholics, treated by individualized behaviour therapy: Results. *Behaviour Research and Therapy,* 1976, *14,* 195–215.

Turner, S. M., & Hersen, M. Instructions and reinforcement in modification of a case of astasia-abasia. *Psychological Reports,* 1975, *36,* 607–612.

Turner, S. M., Hersen, M., & Alford, H. Effects of massed practice and meprobamate on spasmodic torticollis: An experimental analysis. *Behaviour Research and Therapy,* 1974, *12,* 259–260.

Ulenhuth, E. H., Lipman, R. S., & Covi, L. Combined pharmacotherapy and psychotherapy. *Journal of Nervous and Mental Disease,* 1969, *8,* 52–64.

Walker, H. M., & Buckley, N. K. *Token reinforcement techniques.* Eugene, Oreg.: E-B Press, 1974.

Wallace, C. J., Davis, J. R., Liberman, R. P., & Baker, V. Modeling and staff behavior. *Journal of Consulting and Clinical Psychology,* 1973, *41,* 422–425.

Weissman, M. M., Klerman, G. L., Paykel, E. S., Prusoff, B., & Hanson, B. Treatment effects on the social adjustment of depressed patients. *Archives of General Psychiatry,* 1974, *40,* 771–778.

Wolpe, J. *The practice of behavior therapy* (2nd ed.). New York: Pergamon Press, 1973.

Author index

Abel, G. G. 305, 306, 309, 310, 311, 313, 330, 331
Abelson, R. 9, 10, 12, 36
Adams, H. E. 70, 72, 94, 336, 337, 360
Agras, W. S. 21, 36, 58, 61, 63, 64, 66, 69, 72, 73, 74, 75, 76, 77, 92, 93, 94, 221, 235, 236, 237, 252, 257, 259, 262, 277, 279, 280, 282, 291, 297, 299, 302, 303, 304, 305, 306, 309, 310, 311, 313, 314, 322, 323, 330, 331, 332, 342, 359
Alexander, J. F. 207, 211, 328, 329, 331
Alford, G. S. 252, 259, 280, 291, 297, 321, 331
Alford, H. 164, 170, 341, 343, 344, 345, 361
Allen, K. E. 27, 28, 35, 185, 212
Allen, R. 66, 74, 75, 76, 94
Anant, S. 241, 259
Anderson, B. E. 283, 298
Argyle, M. 168, 169
Argyris, C. 145, 169
Arkowitz, H. 15, 35, 130, 138, 150, 151, 169
Armel, S. 130, 140
Armstrong, E. 230, 262
Armstrong, M. 184, 189, 214
Arnold, J. E. 207, 211
Ashem, B. 235, 236, 241, 259
Atthowe, J. M. 278, 282, 296
Atwood, G. E. 164, 171, 316, 317, 318, 332
Austin, J. B. 235, 236, 237, 238, 239, 242, 260
Ax, A. F. 41, 62
Axelrod, S. 183, 190, 191, 211, 212
Ayllon, T. 97, 138, 200, 201, 211, 264, 269, 270, 271, 272, 273, 274, 276, 278, 280, 282, 283, 284, 296, 305, 311, 321, 331, 336, 359
Azrin, N. H. 110, 115, 139, 188, 193, 194, 195, 203, 211, 212, 219, 222, 223, 224, 234, 242, 243, 244, 259, 260, 262, 264, 269, 272, 273, 274, 276, 278, 280, 282, 283, 284, 296, 305, 309, 324, 328, 329, 331, 333, 336, 349, 350, 351, 359, 360

Bachman, J. A. 187, 188, 211
Baekeland, F. 252, 261
Baer, D. M. 6, 20, 21, 24, 35, 177, 178, 179, 192, 211, 212, 290, 296, 352, 359
Baker, S. B. 122, 138
Baker, S. L. 263, 297
Baker, V. 340, 361
Bancroft, J. H. J. 71, 94
Bandura, A. 6, 11, 18, 22, 35, 40, 41, 62, 66, 77, 78, 79. 80, 82, 83, 84, 85, 86, 87, 92, 93, 96, 98, 101, 103, 104, 105, 106, 107, 115, 136, 137
Barab, P. 80, 82, 93
Barlow, D. H. 24, 25, 32, 35, 66, 73, 74, 77, 92, 93, 94, 154, 169, 215, 217, 219, 234, 235, 236, 237, 238, 239, 242, 252, 259, 260, 302, 305, 306, 307, 308, 309, 310, 311, 313, 315, 322, 323, 330, 331, 333, 341, 359
Barocas, V. S. 250, 261
Baroff, G. S. 193, 214
Baron, M. G. 330, 331
Barrera, F. 253, 254, 260
Barrett, B. H. 305, 306, 308, 331
Barrett, C. L. 69, 93
Barrish, H. H. 181, 183, 185, 212
Barton, E. S. 192, 212
Bassett, J. E. 263, 296
Baumeister, A. A. 242, 245, 262
Beck, R. A. 290, 296
Becker, H. G. 61, 62, 72, 73, 93
Becker, J. V. 302, 304, 333
Becker, W. C. 176, 184, 185, 186, 189, 197, 198, 199, 200, 202, 212, 213, 214
Begelman, D. A. 23, 35, 215, 255, 259, 282, 293, 296
Beigel, A. 168, 171
Bellack, A. S. 15, 35, 40, 48, 52, 59, 61, 62, 104, 109, 110, 112, 114, 118, 119, 120, 126, 137, 142, 144, 145, 149, 150, 153, 155, 159, 162, 164, 165, 166, 167, 169, 203, 214, 240, 241, 252, 258, 259, 260, 262, 283, 298, 305, 330, 332, 336, 341, 342, 343, 352, 353, 354, 359
Benson, C. 203, 213
Berger, S. M. 78, 93
Bergin, A. E. 47, 55, 62, 63
Bergin, A. E. 154, 169, 302, 305, 306, 307, 331
Bernstein, D. A. 38, 59, 60, 63
Berwick, P. T. 168, 171
Bieber, I. 258, 259
Bigelow, G. 247, 248, 259, 260
Bijou, S. W. 27, 28, 35
Birky, H. J. 285, 286, 296
Birnbrauer, J. S. 193, 212, 224, 234, 259
Black, A. H. 72, 93
Black, J. L. 112, 139
Blake, B. G. 220, 232, 233, 259
Blanchard, E. B. 9, 35, 41, 62, 66, 83, 84, 85, 93, 134, 135, 137, 148, 170, 252, 253,

363